Handbook of Management Accounting

Handbook of Management Accounting

Second edition

Edited by Roger Cowe

in association with
The Chartered Institute of Management Accountants

A Gower Handbook

~~176002~~

0540800

© Gower Publishing Company Limited 1988
Chapter 2 © Kenneth Simmonds

All rights reserved. No part of this publication may be reproduced, stored in a retrieval system, or transmitted in any form or by any means, electronic, mechanical, photocopying, recording, or otherwise without the prior permission of Gower Publishing Company Limited.

Published by
Gower Publishing Company Limited,
Gower House,
Croft Road,
Aldershot,
Hants GU11 3HR,
England

Gower Publishing Company,
Old Post Road,
Brookfield,
Vermont 05036,
U.S.A.

Reprinted 1991

British Library Cataloguing in Publication Data

Handbook of management accounting. – 2nd ed.
  1. Managerial accounting
  I. Cowe, Roger   II. Chartered Institute of
  Management Accountants
  658.1'511   HF5635

Library of Congress Cataloging-in-Publication Data

Handbook of management accounting.
  Published in association with the Chartered Institute
  of Management Accountants.
  Includes bibliographies and index.
  1. Managerial accounting. I. Cowe, Roger
  HF5635.H228   1988   658.1'511   86-29616

ISBN 0 566 02615 5

Contents

PART ONE: PLANNING AND BUDGETING

176002
0540800

Contents

PART TWO: MEASUREMENT AND CONTROL

Contents

List of illustrations

List of illustrations

TABLES

Notes on contributors

David Allen, ACMA, MCIT *(Relevance in controls)* is Director, Sector Evaluation with British Rail. As such he has been responsible for the design, development and implementation of comprehensive, new management information packages to serve the 5 Rail Businesses (Sectors). He has been with BR since 1969 in a number of key financial posts. He has contributed to Railway Gazette International and featured in 'International Railway Economics' (Gower, 1985).

Duncan Bennett, FCMA, FCCA, RAPC *(Not-for-profit organisations)* is a Colonel in the Army and Head of the Management Accounting and Costing Services unit. He has been a regular army officer since 1948 and has had considerable experience in the 'not-for-profit' field, dealing with state finance, charitable trusts and cash administration. A founder member of the CIMA's Defence sub-branch, he is a member of the Institute's Public Sector and Education & Training Committees.

Michael Bromwich, BSc (Econ), FCMA *(Costing for planning)* is CIMA Professor of Accounting and Financial Management at The London School of Economics. Author of *The Economics of Capital Budgeting* (Penguin, 1976; Pitman, 1980), *The Economics of Accounting Standard Setting* (Prentice-Hall, 1985), co-editor of *Essays in British Accounting Research* (Pitman, 1981) and *Auditing Research: Issues and Opportunities* (Pitman, 1982). He is a member of the Accounting Standards Committee and is Vice President of the CIMA. An experienced writer and researcher, he has been a member of the Industry and Employment Committee of the Social Science Research Council.

J. Lewis Brown, MSc, FCMA, FBIM *(Absorption costing* and *Marginal costing)* is Lecturer in Management Accounting at the City

University Business School, having spent earlier parts of his career in industry and in further and higher education institutions in Britain and Iran. He has special interests in corporate planning and inventory control and has jointly written *Cost Accounting and Costing Methods* (Macdonald and Evans, 1978) and *Managerial Accounting and Finance* (Macdonald and Evans, 1982). He has lectured extensively in the Middle East and in the Far East.

Bernard Cox, M Phil, FCMA, FCCA *(Value added)* is Technical Director Research of the Chartered Institute of Management Accountants, having previously held accountancy appointments with Marconi, EMI and Westland Helicopters. He is the author of *Value Added* (Heinemann, 1979), *A Study of Value Added Incentive Schemes in the UK* (ICMA, 1983), and joint author of *Management Accounting in Inflationary Conditions* (ICMA, 1976).

Roger Cowe, MBA, ACMA *(Introduction* and *Relevance in controls)* is now a financial journalist with the *Guardian* newspaper, and was until recently a self-employed writer, lecturer and consultant in business, finance and technology. He worked as a management accountant in the textile industry before becoming a financial journalist with *Accountancy Age* and then editor of *DataBusiness*. He is the author of *Computers for Accountants*.

Jeffrey Davies, BA, MA, ACMA *(Transfer pricing)* is a principal lecturer and Head of the Division of Accounting and Finance at the Polytechnic of Wales, Pontypridd. Joint author of *Pricing in Practice* (Heinemann, 1975), *Managerial Economics* (Macdonald and Evans, 1977) and *Investment in the British Economy* (Heinemann, 1980), his earlier career included periods with Rolls-Royce and at the North Staffordshire Polytechnic. Among his research and teaching interests are the initiation and development of small firms and the design and implementation of computerised accounting systems.

Richard Dobbins, PhD, MSc, FCCA *(Capital budgeting)* is Senior Lecturer in Financial Management at the University of Bradford Management Centre. He qualified as a certified accountant in 1968 after several years' experience in professional offices, industry and public service. He studied for his MSc and PhD in Management and Administration, at the University of Bradford, where he was appointed Esmee Fairbairn research assistant in 1972, Lecturer in Finance in 1973 and Senior Lecturer in Financial Management in 1979. He is an active consultant, editor of *Managerial Finance*, has contributed to several academic journals, and has lectured on management programmes in Europe, the Far East, Africa, Australia and North America. He is the co-author of *The Growth and Impact of Institutional Investors* (Institute of Chartered Accountants in England and Wales, 1978), *Portfolio Theory and Investment Management* (Martin Robertson, 1983; Basil Blackwell, 1986) and *Investment Decisions and Financial Strategy* (Philip Allan, 1986).

David Fanning, BSc, MPhil, FCollp *Divisional performance measurement)* is Lecturer in Finance and Accounting at the Cardiff Business School, University of Wales Institute of Science and Technology, Cardiff, and he has written a considerable number of newspaper and journal articles on business finance. The author of *Marketing Company Shares* (Gower, 1982), joint author of *Company Accounts – a Guide* (Allen & Unwin, 1984), and editor of *Pension Funds: Issues in Accounting and Finance* (MCB, 1981), his main teaching and research interests are in the areas of business finance and managerial accounting.

Douglas Garbutt *(Budgeting and cash forecasting)* is an independent management consultant in finance, business policy and management information systems. He has undertaken consultancy and research assignments in a wide range of industries and professional services in the UK, USA, Australia, the Far East and the Middle East. He has held visiting professorships at Southern Illinois, Georgia State and Indiana Universities in the USA, and in Australia and Iraq. In the UK, he was Professor at Dundee College of Technology until 1982 and previously at Cranfield and the Polytechnic of Central London. He has written many articles in a wide range of management and accounting journals and is the author of several books, the latest of which is *How to Budget and Control Cash*, published by Gower in 1985.

Roger Groves, BCom, MSc, PhD, FCA *(Organisational and behavioural issues* and *Mathematical techniques)* is Sir Julian Hodge Professor of Accountancy at the University of Wales Institute of Science and Technology, having spent earlier parts of his career in a professional accountancy practice and in university teaching positions in Britain and America. Joint author of *Company Finance in Europe* (ICAEW, 1975), he has written numerous articles in professional and academic journals on various aspects of accountancy and finance. He is a consultant to a number of manufacturing and service companies.

Gordon V. Hill, BSc, DIC, ACMA, CEng, MIChemE, MInstE, FIPDM, MIMC *(Physical distribution)* is Vice president and Director of A.T. Kearney Ltd, management consultants, and the author of a number of publications on management subjects. Formerly a research scientist with the National Coal Board and experimental engineering manager with Johnson Wax International, he now specialises as a management consultant in materials management and physical distribution. He is a member of the board of the Centre for Physical Distribution Management and of the Council of the Institute of Physical Distribution Management.

Anthony Hollis, MBE, ACMA, RAPC *(Cost reduction)* is a Major in the Army and Chief Technical Officer in the Management Accounting and Costing Services unit. He was awarded the MBE in the 1982 New Year Honours List on the bais of his work on cost reduction schemes while Transport Management Accountant in London. An army officer for 27 years, Major Hollis has a strong interest in government and public sector accounting, and he has served with all three logistics corps in the Army.

C. Stuart Jones, MSc, FCMA, ACIS, JDipMA, PhD *(Variance accounting)* is Senior Lecturer in Accountancy and Finance at the University of East Anglia, having previously lectured in accounting at the University of Hull, following appointments in financial management and planning with Massey Ferguson and Chloride. He is the author of *Successful Management of Acquisitions* (Beattie, 1982), and of several articles in the professional press. His special interest is in the post-acquisition control of merged firms and the role of management accounting in that control task.

John MacArthur, MA, PhD, FCCA *(Alternative budgeting methods)* is Assistant Professor in Accounting in the School of Business of the University of Northern Iowa. Previously a lecturer at the University of Wales Institute of Science and Technology, his research interests include management accounting practices and the economic consequences of accounting choice.

Richard Pike, MA, PhD, FCA *(Capital budgeting)* is Senior Lecturer in Finance and Accounting at the Management Centre at the University of Bradford. His earlier career included teaching appointments and he was group planning controller with the Burton group, responsible for the capital planning process. His main teaching and research interests are in the field of capital investment, but he has published extensively on a variety of accounting and finance topics.

Janusz Santocki, BCom, MPhil, FCA *(Management auditing)* is Senior Lecturer in Auditing at the City of Birmingham Polytechnic, following earlier appointments in further education and ten years in professional chartered accountancy. He is the author of *Case Studies in Auditing* (Macdonald and Evans, 1978) and *Auditing: A Conceptual and Systems Approach* (Polytech, 1982). With special research and teaching interests in auditing, he has written a number of articles in professional and academic journals.

Kenneth Simmonds, BCom, MCom, DBA, PhD, FCA (NZ), FCMA, FCIS, JDipMA, FInstM *(Strategic management accounting)* is Professor of Marketing and International Business at the London Graduate School of Business Studies, having spent earlier parts of his career in industry and in teaching positions in the United States and in Britian. The author of *Strategy and Marketing* (Allan, 1986) and joint author of *International Business and Multinational Enterprises* (Irwin, 1982), he has written a considerable number of articles in professional and academic journals on topics in management and strategy. He is a director of a number of public companies.

John Sizer, BA, FCMA, FBIM, FRSA *(Pricing)* is Professor of Financial Management at Loughborough University of Technology and Chairman of its Business and Management Studies Sub-Committee. He is also a member of the Council and Executive Committee of CIMA and Chairman of its Finance Committee. His previous appointments include Head of the Department of Management Studies at Loughborough, Chairman of the Directing Group of the OECD/CERI Programme on Institutional Management in Higher Education, Financial Adviser to GKN Ltd. He is the author or editor of numerous books on management accounting.

Richard M.S. Wilson, MSc, BPhil, BA, BCom, FCMA, FCCA, DipM, MInstM, MCAM *(Marketing and the management accountant)* holds a joint appointment in marketing and accounting at the University of Sheffield where he is currently Head of Accounting & Financial Management. He has been active as a consultant in both fields for a number of organisations (including Harbridge House and the Egyptian Ministry of Industry). Prior to his appointment at Sheffield he worked for various commercial organisations (covering industrial and consumer goods as well as services), and he has also held non-executive directorships.

Foreword

by Professor M. Bromwich, BSc (Econ.), FCMA, IPFA, President of
the CIMA

I am particularly pleased to write this introduction. A carefully
revised edition of what is already an established work deserves
success, especially since it is made up of contributions from such a
large group of distinguished and popular authors. Two thirds of these
work in the academic world; one third are practitioners of management accounting day by day in the real world.

Here then is an amalgam of many different views of today's
management accounting scene. One of the book's virtues is that it
does not try to be as consistent as if a single author had written every
word. One of the merits of the book is that the various authors have
in no way felt constrained by their understanding of what is today's
orthodoxy in accounting. They have tried to get back to fundamentals,
and thus to describe what *ought* to be done by professional management accountants rather than what *is* done by them, limited perhaps
by tradition and inertia.

This book should be of great value to those numerous members
and students who think deeply about the future of our profession:
where it is, how it got there, where it should go next and what
changes an ever more competitive world will require us to make.
This book places all these various strands in the context of many of
the age old topics of management accounting.

It is launched with my best wishes for its deserved success.

Preface to the second edition

Management accounting, both as a practice and as an academic subject, draws on a number of disciplines. In publishing a handbook such as this, which attempts to bring together the many strands, a number of different approaches are possible. Each inevitably stresses one aspect at the expense of another. Each way of segmenting the subject matter creates artificial dichotomies. In this second edition I have attempted to build on the foundations laid by the editor of the first edition by retaining but reorganising much of the original material. I have perhaps created new dichotomies in the process of removing others.

My aim has been to make the handbook even more useful to the practical reader, concerned primarily with applying concepts to live problems in industry, commerce or the public sector. I have been particularly concerned to cater fully for readers working outside management accounting's traditional base in manufacturing. Also, I have tried to ensure that the handbook conveys something of the impact of information technology on this information-based discipline, although in a text of this kind it is impossible to keep fully up-to-date with the advance of computing and telecommunications.

In keeping with these objectives the four parts of the handbook are now concerned with rather different subject matter than in the first edition.

The bulk of the basic concepts are dealt with in the first two Parts, as before. But these have been re-arranged to focus more closely on planning and control respectively, while less central and more specialised aspects such as mathematical techniques have been included instead in the final part of the book concerned explicitly with such special techniques and issues. Part Three is a new section concerned solely with management accounting in a non-manufacturing environment.

Within that framework a number of chapters have been replaced with subject matter which now seems to be more central to the concerns of managers and management accountants. A chapter on the basics of budgeting and cash forecasting has been included in Part One, and Part Three opens with a contribution on marketing and the management accountant. Some other chapters have been completely re-written, and others updated where appropriate.

It is to be hoped that the resulting handbook performs an even more useful service to managers and management accountants than the first edition did.

This second edition is published in association with the Chartered Institute of Management Accountants (formerly the Institute of Cost and Management Accountants). Thanks are due to them, and in particular to their representative John Ambler, MA, FCMA, JDipMA, CIMA Editorial Board Member, for his constructive comments on the various stages of this book. While this edition is published 'in association' with the CIMA, the contributions contained herein are the authors' own, and do not necessarily reflect the policy of the Institute.

Roger Cowe

1

Introduction

Roger Cowe

As a discipline, management accounting is relatively young. For example, the term was only incorporated in the title of the Institute of Cost and Management Accountants in 1972, although recognised some time before that. But it is clear that management accounting, in one form or another, has been practised by astute managers for centuries. In analyses of farm economics and in early industrialisation financial information was used to help business people make decisions.

However widespread such practices were, though, they were not formalised as part of business accounting until well into this century. Accounting remained primarily concerned with external reporting. Even the development of cost accounting, generally seen as the forerunner of modern management accounting, did not alter the predominantly backward-looking stance of business accountants. Cost accounting grew initially from engineers' concern with cost-finding and was given a considerable impetus by the need to validate government contract costs during the First World War. During the early part of this century much effort was put into developing sophisticated methods of calculating product costs, and these techniques are valuable in many circumstances. But as a management tool cost accounting can now be seen as excessively concerned with determining actual production costs after the event, and many fundamental assumptions can be seriously challenged, as described, for example, in Chapter 7.

Such criticisms are not new. Towards the end of the nineteenth century economists were pointing out that cost finding was perhaps less important than asking which costs were relevant to business decisions. But the influence of economists on cost and management accounting was minimal until much more recently. Even in the inter-war years of this century academics who argued that different costs

1

were relevant for different purposes were generally ignored by practitioners.

But the inter-war years saw the growth in the United States of larger, more complex organisations which required greater control and co-ordination than previously. The development of budgetary control methods, partly as an aid to resource allocation, control and co-ordination in such companies, marks an important point in the emergence of management accounting from its costing roots. These methods began to be adopted widely in the UK during the 1950s and 1960s, building on standard costing systems which had previously been the main contribution to business accounting of the non-financial accountacy profession.

The influence of cost accounting on modern management accounting, however, can still be seen by the co-existence of the two terms in the former title of the CIMA until 1987. The distinction between the two terms is by no means precise, although generally speaking it can be said that management accounting is more forward-looking, more concerned with aiding management decisions about future plans than with merely controlling operations. The concern of cost accounting and cost accountants with historical production costs is mainly of interest to management accountants only in so far as historical information provides a guide to the future.

Definitions are of course available. The CIMA, being Britain's professional body in this field, can be taken as having the most authoritative version, which is:

> The application of professional knowledge and skill in the preparation and presentation of accounting information in such a way as to assist management in the formulation of policies and in the planning and control of the operations of the undertaking.

Like all such definitions, this can be criticised as being too all-embracing and too vague, but it is as good an attempt as any to capture the essence of management accounting in a formal statement. It encapsulates the three formal aspects of management accounting – recording, reporting, and decision making – and the two major management functions with which they are concerned – planning and control.

Two specific omissions are worth mentioning. First, the definition is too limiting in restricting the subject to 'accounting information'. Management accountants are increasingly aware that accounting numbers are necessary but not sufficient management information. Performance measures concerned with issues such as quality, customer satisfaction, headcount and market share are also essential constituents of management information.

The second omission concerns the less formal purposes of management accounting. Behavioural research has made clear in recent years that management information systems in large companies do not merely have the formal purposes quoted above, but also have an important role to play in the informal 'games' and managerial politics of large organisations. Much management accounting in these circumstances has an excuse-generating purpose at least as important as its formal purposes defined above.

The four purposes now identified, and the kind of questions which management accounting attempts to answer, are summarised in Table 1.1.

Table 1.1
The role of management accounting

Purpose	Questions addressed
Recording	How are we doing?
Reporting	What problems are there?
Decision making	Which is the best alternative?
Excuse-generating	What can we tell the boss?

This definition of management accounting identifies clearly what the subject is concerned with, but further consideration might usefully be given to the distinction and differences between management accounting/internal reporting and financial accounting/external reporting.

The division is not in any way clear-cut. Frequently the same departments within organisations and even the same people produce both internal and external information. It is certainly rare to find completely separate systems for the production of each type of information. The recording purpose of management accounting is often unified with recording for financial accounting purposes. Internal reporting, too, is often little more than detailed analysis of reports prepared for external purposes, or to put it the other way round, external reports are often summaries of internal reports. Thus management accounting might produce profit statements for each division and product group, and with greater detail and analysis of sales and expenses, but still in the general format adopted for external profit reporting, and which allows straightforward consolidation of subunit figures to produce the group results.

Escaping from the limiting requirements of financial accounting is one of the main practical challenges which face management accountants. Financial accounting numbers will inevitably remain of significant importance in managerial information, but that need not preclude management accountants from presenting that and other information in forms which are not merely analysed versions of external financial reports.

It may well make sense to present segment or division reports in ways which do not reflect those units' financial performance in strict accounting terms, but which have a much closer bearing on their contribution to the group. For example, the profitability of a vertical market division could be assessed in terms of the total profits earned by the group in that vertical market. This might include profits earned by other, non-vertical market operations within the group but could be more useful information than the accounting profit of the operation on its own. Figures prepared in such a way for each vertical market operation would not neatly consolidate to produce accounts for the group as a whole, but management accountants need not be too concerned by such arithmetical niceties. Financial accountants can still be prepared from the same basic data in accordance with external reporting requirements. Especially with cheap and powerful computing resources it is relatively easy to manipulate one set of accounting numbers to produce such information in various forms, each suiting the needs of different users.

So even in reporting, management and financial accounting can diverge. But it is in planning and decision making that management accounting departs most clearly from financial accounting, and where the forward-looking emphasis can be seen more clearly. It is also in these areas that management accounting fulfils its main purpose – to aid management in taking business decisions.

Table 1.2 summarises the differences between internal and external reporting.

It has already been noted that management accounting serves managers rather than shareholders, is forward looking rather than backward looking, is concerned primarily with planning and control rather than reporting, and focuses on sub-units of the organisation rather than the legal entity as a whole. A brief comment on the other factors in this table is now required.

External reporting exists in a fairly tightly regulated environment, with reporting principles and practices defined in law, accounting principles and standards and quasi-legal regulations such as those published by the stock exchanges. Its primary purpose is to satisfy government requirements as laid down in company and tax law. There can be no question of a public company not publishing its ex-

Table 1.2
Differences between internal and external reporting

	Internal reporting	*External reporting*
Users	Managers	Investors, competitors, suppliers etc.
Orientation	Future	Past
Purpose	Planning and control	Reporting
Context	Organisational control	Statutory and quasi-statutory requirements
Regulation	Few rules, situation-specific	Generally-accepted accounting principles, accounting standards, stock exchange requirements etc.
Time periods	Flexible	Fixed
Focus	Managerial units	The entity

ternal reports, and little scope for the company accountant to deviate from the required format and content.

None of this applies to internal reporting. No external bodies require companies to prepare management information, although auditors would clearly be concerned at the lack of internal control that would suggest. No external authority regulates how management information should be prepared, its scope and content, its frequency or target audience. These matters are entirely at the discretion of the organisation's management.

This freedom emphasises the organisational control context of internal reporting, its diversity and the breadth of disciplines which have a bearing on an understanding of the subject.

While firmly rooted in accounting, management accounting has been increasingly influenced in recent years by mathematical, economics, behavioural and organisational inputs. Mathematical and economic approaches have helped to expand and refine management accounting techniques, while behavioural and organisational theorists have emphasised that management accounting is more than merely a collection of techniques applied objectively in an organisational vaccuum.

All these influences are reflected in this handbook, which attempts to provide a round introduction to all aspects of the subject, primarily for managers and accountants working in industry, commerce and the public sector. The contributions, from academics and practitioners, combine explanations of basic techniques such as budgeting and variance analysis with commentaries on the role of management accounting and how it might better aid managements.

It is hoped that these latter contributions, such as Professor Simmonds' argument for strategic management accounting and Professor Bromwich's call for a more creative approach to costing, might stimulate financial and other managers to develop management information which is of greater use to management in improving business performance.

The book is divided into four parts, the first two covering the central subject matter of planning and control, while the last two sections deal with special issues of particular importance. A division between planning and budgeting on the one hand, and measurement and control on the other, is bound to be somewhat arbitrary. In reality, planning and control are inseparable. Neither can sensibly be carried out in isolation. But for purposes of conciseness and clear organisation it is appropriate to deal with planning and budgeting in one section of the book and measurement and control in another. Each of these sections contains both explanations of the basic techniques and more adventurous and thoughtful comments on possible directions for the future.

As has already been pointed out, management account has its roots in cost accounting, whose early proponents were engineers and which is primarily oriented to manufacturing businesses. But management accounting is clearly important for all types of organisation, including those which are not profit-seeking enterprises. This is not always recognised in the literature and the third section of this handbook seeks to redress the undue emphasis often placed on management accounting in a manufacturing environment. It achieves this by considering the place of management accounting in relation to other functions, i.e. marketing and distribution, and in non-manufacturing organisations.

The final section of the handbook considers a number of special issues of importance to managers in many different kinds of organisation. These include organisational and behavioural considerations. A separate chapter on such a subject might suggest this is something which can be considered in isolation but this is clearly not the case. In fact these issues are covered in many other chapters as well, emphasising that they are implicit in many aspects of the subject.

The opposite approach has been taken with a very different topic – information technology. In a book such as this it is difficult to deal practically with such a fast-changing subject without quickly becoming outdated. But it is of particular importance to management accounting and reference to it has been made, where appropriate, in individual subject chapters.

To aid the busy reader and to place each chapter and each section in context each of the four parts and each chapter begins with an editorial introduction. These provide links between the separate contributions and outline the place of each separate topic in the cohesive subject of management accounting.

This handbook is intended to be helpful to managers in their work rather than as a textbook or reference manual. It offers a combination of practical, theoretical and innovative contributions on this important subject and it is hoped that it will aid and stimulate readers to improve management accounting practice.

FURTHER READING

Belkaoui, A., *Conceptual Foundations of Management Accounting.* Reading, Mass.: Addison-Wesley, 1980.

Parker, R.H., *Management Accounting: an Historical Perspective.* London: Macmillan, 1969.

Sizer, J., *An Insight into Management Accounting.* Harmondsworth: Pelican, 1979.

Solomons, D., *Studies in Cost Analysis.* London: Sweet & Maxwell, 1968.

Part One
Planning and Budgeting

OVERVIEW

One of the greatest criticism of financial accounting is that it is of little use to managements because of its preoccupation with the past. Management accounting does not always overcome that objection, since it is sometimes little more than detailed financial reporting, but it does aim to be forward looking even if that aim is not always achieved.

This first part of the handbook deals with the one area of management accounting which is predominantly forward looking – planning and budgeting.

All organisations engage in some form of planning, however informal that might be, and major companies have complex formal systems for developing plans. But as the contributors to this part point out, going through the motions of planning, will not necessarily produce the benefits which should accrue from an intelligent attempt to contemplate the future and develop ways of moving towards long term objectives.

In the first chapter of this section Professor Kenneth Simmonds argues forcefully that management accountants generally adopt too 'tactical' a stance, even when it comes to planning. He stresses the need for strategic thinking and shows that major components of strategy are almost always missing from the management accountant's sphere of interest. But he suggests that a company's success or failure is determined by its competitive position. Management accountants should therefore be concerned with reporting changes in and returns on competitive positions, rather than variances from last year's results and return on investment. Investment itself does not produce returns, Professor Simmonds points out. It is the company's competitive position which produces returns from the investments, and investment decisions should therefore focus on the effect on the company's position in the market.

Professor Simmonds argues that 'investment' should not merely be considered as spending on physical assets. But regardless of the nature of the spending the investment decision will involve difficult choices and require sophisticated analysis.

In Chapter 3 Richard Dobbins and Richard Pike describe the problems inherent in the capital investment process. They explain the main methods used for evaluating capital projects and test each of these methods against three main criteria:

1   the need to measure cash flows rather than accounting profit,
2   the need to recognise the timing of returns,
3   the need to take account of risk.

They conclude that common methods of capital investment fail to satisfy these fundamental objectives.

Strategic thinking and long-term planning must eventually trickle down into short-term budgeting, and Chapters 4 and 5 are concerned with this aspect of planning.

In Chapter 4 Douglas Garbutt outlines the key aspects of a short-term budgeting system, concentrating on the design of such a system. He emphasises the dangers of the short-term budgeting process becoming merely accounting exercises, stressing that a budget should always be a management tool. Indeed he argues that management is the most important aspect of the budgetary process. Garbutt develops a budget framework and explains each of the elements in it, suggesting a number of stages in the design and implementation of a budgeting system. He highlights the main issues which must be considered in such a development, and shows how computer systems can help to make the budget more useful and less of a clerical exercise.

In the final chapter of this part, John MacArthur examines some alternative ways of developing budgets. He deals in particular with budgeting for non-manufacturing overheads and with handling risk.

Non-manufacturing overhead is commonly dealt with using an incremental approach, beginning with the current level of spending and considering only changes from that due to changes in service or activity levels. MacArthur argues that this completely ignores the major problems of determining an appropriate level of staffing and expenditure for a given level of activity or service. Zero-based budgeting is one approach which aims to tackle this fundamental problems in overhead budgeting. Conventional budgeting also tends to ignore risk, which is curious given that budgets are about the future and therefore inherently open to risk. The author describes some methods to cope with the fact that the future is uncertain.

The thrust of this first part of the book is that management must look forward, developing long-term plans in the light of corporate objectives, their perceptions of environmental changes and competitors' actions. Such plans are then distilled into shorter-term budgets which guide immediate action and form a basis for evaluating performance (although as Professor Simmonds points out, the plans should perhaps be in terms of competitive position rather than conventional accounting statements).

The second part of the book will consider the counterpart to this planning process – measurement and control.

2

Strategic management accounting

Kenneth Simmonds

In this chapter Professor Simmonds argues for a more strategic thrust to management accounting. He begins by suggesting that management accountants have historically been too concerned with the details of cost calculation and control, at the expense of a greater involvement in strategic decision making and measurement. They have concentrated on the technicalities of information preparation, he argues, not the purpose of the information, focusing on the accounting system rather than the decisions which it purports to help.

Having made a case for a strategic dimension to management accounting Professor Simmonds then proceeds to examine the nature of business strategy and to consider how management accounting can play a part in strategic thinking.

First he explores business strategy, identifying 11 aspects which seem to be common to many different definitions. In particular, he points out that strategy development is not a procedural matter. Broad prescriptions cannot readily be applied. Instead individual organisations must develop their own individual strategies in their own ways. In short, he suggests that 'thinking is required'. But there are common elements, notably corporate objectives, competitive position and market share.

Professor Simmonds argues that market share is of major importance in defining a company's strategic position, and appears to be of intrinsic value in itself, possibly as a determinant of relative cost. He casts some doubt on learning curve theory, however, but suggests that despite such doubts it is clear that relative costs are an important aspect of companies' competitive positions. Pricing policy is a third major ingredient.

Few, if any, management accountants would consider including such aspects in their corporate reporting systems, yet the author believes that these issues are much more fundamental to a business success or failure than internal measures such as cost and profit comparisons with previous years. He proposes that accountants should develop measures of return on competitive position rather than return on investment, since it is not the investment which produces the returns, but the company's competitive position. Competitor assessment ought therefore to be part of the management accountant's armoury.

Finally Professor Simmonds outlines some ways in which management accounting systems can routinely incorporate data which will help to track changes in competitive position.

Were information for strategy to be made the first and primary focus of management accounting, the profession would take its greatest change of direction since Garcke and Fells produced *Factory Accounts* in 1887. The change from cost analysis to value of information analysis is radical. This does not mean, however, that strategy has only recently been perceived as one of the purposes of management accounting. A clear case for the strategic role of cost accounting, as it was then, was put forward as long ago as 1932 at an international cost conference of the National Association of Cost Accountants. Since then, however, for every treatise that has proclaimed the accountant's role in strategy, a thousand papers have outlined some picayune aspect of a standard cost system. Even where there has been an attempt to look at strategic uses, the bias has been strongly towards the provision of data from the existing accounting system.

In recent years, American academic accountants, in particular, have given a lot of attention to the relationship between accounting and management information systems. The Committee on Foundations of Accounting Measurement of the American Accounting Association held the view in 1971 that, despite the two extreme schools of thought that put either accounting or management information systems as a subset of the other, the answer lay somewhere in between. In its report (American Accounting Association, 1971), the committee saw two distinct fields with some degree of overlap:

> Should accountants extend their effort to cover the entire area of management information systems? Essentially, this questions whether the intellectual skills required to be an 'expert' in accounting are easily transferred to the whole area of management information systems. At present, it must be concluded that they are not. This opinion is based on the fact that there is a certain advantage, at least initially, in limiting our efforts only to financial data, because processing and analysis of non-

15

financial data require technical knowledge unfamiliar to accountants. Besides, the processing and analysis of financial data alone offer challenges and opportunities that will not be exhausted in any forseeable future.

One can question whether the committee's diagnosis was correct. A strong case could be made that the lack of attention to management decision requirements lies at the core of the problem – not the lack of technical skills in recording non-financial data.

The same report went on to evaluate decision making and information needs, but instead of looking at real needs, hypothetical situations were tabulated. The conclusion was reached that the more users there were and the more decisions to be made from a data source, the greater the need for an accounting system consisting largely of primary measures with most aggregation occurring at the time of decision making. The orientation was back to the details of the accounting system not forward to the details of the decisions. It is this traditional data-recording orientation that has held back accounting (Simmonds, 1972).

Curiously, another American Accounting Association committee which reported at exactly the same time seemed to sense that the role of accounting was threatened by providing and analysing information. It seemed also, however, to see most hope for management accounting in the area of strategic planning.

Somewhere, over the years, the accounting profession appears to have lost its belief in its natural leadership in providing strategic management information. Gone is the clarion call of the 1930s. Perhaps the cause of the doubts is the concentration on the technicalities of information supply, rather than a deep concern for the purpose of the information supplied. A closer look at strategy formation, however, gives a picture of tremendous needs for appropriate accounting information.

THE ESSENCE OF BUSINESS STRATEGY

The word 'strategy' is derived from the Greek word *strategos*, meaning a general, and the Greek verb *stratego*, describing generalship. The concepts of military strategy were discussed by early writers like Homer and Euripides, and at one point Socrates likens the duties of a general and a businessman, both planning the use of resources to meet objectives in the face of competition.

Despite the long history of writing on strategy, however, the field of business strategy is predominantly a creation of the past two decades with its own set of subtle business terms and meanings that have become firmly embedded in the business terms and meanings that have become firmly embedded in the business policy and marketing literature. One attempt in the mid-1960s to relate the emerging field of business planning to modern principles of military strategy showed a very considerable distance between what the military saw as strategy and the business concept of strategic planning (Caplan, 1965).

There are generally agreed to be three distinct levels of business strategy: corporate strategy, business strategy and functional area strategy (Hofer and Schendel, 1978). At the corporate level, the allocation of resources among different businesses is the prime concern. At the level of the individual business, strategy is concerned with the thrust of competitive actions in that business alone. Functional level strategy is further limited to the configuration of business variables falling within the purview of the particular function. This hierarchy of strategy levels parallels organisational levels. At each subsequent lower level, the scope of the strategist is further constrained and subject to the strategy of the higher levels.

This chapter focuses predominantly on the second level of business strategy. In many ways, this level of strategy dominates the other two. Without well considered business strategies as a basis, it would be foolish to develop an elegant corporate strategy and even more foolish to build a detailed functional strategy.

The precise definition of strategy in business situations is less clear. Published definitions vary, with each text adding its own ideas and emphasis. To many, strategy refers to the plan, the end product of strategy formation, with no emphasis placed on the strategic nature of the configuration of actions included in the plan. Some include the objectives as part of the strategy, others see the objectives as what the strategy is to achieve, and some argue that the strategy defines the goals. Others distinguish between goals and objectives. In some cases, the strategy is depicted as a planned series of actions; in other cases, it is a series of decisions about actions; occasionally, it is a set of rules for making decisions. Many mention allocation of resources as the essence of strategy, and some refer to the time scale of achievement, seeing strategy as long term relative to tactics as short term. Emphasis is occasionally placed on determining strategy according to a particular situation and in other cases the environment is picked out for analysis to arrive at the strategy. Some specify a review of market scope and a few mention competitive position.

To some extent these differences in definition stem from identification with different levels in the business organisation, but in most cases the divergencies lie less in underlying concepts of strategy than in the attributes the writers chose to emphasis. Largely unmentioned in definitions, yet implicitly accepted by the way strategy is described, are a range of generally agreed elements of the business situation against which business strategy is designed. It is these elements which shape strategy to the contemporary business situation, and give business strategy quite a different meaning from the strategy of war. It is these elements, too, which condition the information needed. Both the strategy and the information are determined by the nature of the game or the conflict.

Of course, business does not conform to one standard pattern. But by reducing the confusion of reality to some basic elements, patterns of strategy have become examinable. Eleven such elements that apply to the majority of business strategy writing are proposed as follows:

1 Strategy is applicable to business within defined boundaries. While the boundaries may change, the strategy applies at any specified time to actions affecting a delimited area of demand and competition.

2 There are direct competitors. These competitors sell essentially the same products or services within the defined demand area. Indirect competitors operate outside the defined business and their products are not direct substitutes. Indirect competition is usually ignored or covered by the concept of price elasticity of demand.

3 There is zero-sum competition between the direct competitors for the market demand, subject to competitive action affecting the quantity demanded.

4 Demand within the defined market varies over time. This variation in demand is largely independent of supplier strategies and is often referred to as the product life cycle. At its simplest, it is depicted as a normal curve over time with regularly growing then declining demand.

5 Strategy unfolds over a sequence of time periods. Competition evolves through a series of skirmishes and battles during the product life cycle.

6 Single period profit is a function of (a) the price level ruling for the period, (b) the accumulated volume experience of the firm, and (c) the firm's achieved volume as a proportion of capacity.

7 Market share has intrinsic value. Past sales levels influence sub-

sequent customer buying, and costs reduce with greater single period volume and accumulated experience.

8 Competitors differ in market share, accumulated experience, production capacity, and resources. Competitors are unequal, identified and positioned.

9 Objectives differ. Firms composed of ownership, management and employee factions and operating a range of different businesses have different objectives. Strategic business thinking, however, will usually express these as different time and risk preferences for performance within an individual business, measured in monetary terms.

10 Within a given situation, a core of strategic actions will determine changes in competitive position. Non-strategic, or contingent, actions will support strategic actions and should be consistent with them, but will not change competitive position significantly.

11 Identification of an optimal core of strategic actions requires reasoning and diagnosis, is not attained through the application of a fixed set of procedures, and is situational. In short, thinking is required.

Together, these eleven elements build a picture of business strategy as the choice of a core of actions through which position in a market relative to competition is manipulated over time to maximise the firm's objectives. In a sense, business strategy presents a framework for modelling certain strategic elements of real situations so as to produce the most favourable result, much as a complex game – not at all unlike the game of Monopoly. A circuit of the board in Monopoly is like the single period of the business strategy. Just as period financial performance is not, on its own, a measure of a firm's strategic performance, so, too, in Monopoly. Performance over a circuit is not judged solely by the increase in cash and historic cost of property assets. An assessment of any change in the strategic position of one player relative to other players is also required. To the extent that a property enables a player to build up a limited monopoly position on a segment of the board and charge monopoly rents or to prevent a competitor doing so, then it has a strategic value.

Monopoly has other similarities to contemporary business strategy – for example, the concept of a changing core of strategic actions. At some stages in the game, strategic gain is seen as buying the maximum number of properties, at others it is forcing up the prices others pay, draining competitors' cash resources, forming coalitions or reinforcing a limited monopoly by building houses. This last is very similar to the proliferation in model development adopted by some market leaders.

THE DEFINITION OF A BUSINESS

What is a unit of business? The question was first raised in exactly this form by Clark (1923) in his classic *The Economics of Overhead Costs*. Nevertheless, the problem has recurred over the years in economics, accounting, marketing, and now strategy literature. Possibly marketing literature is now the most sophisticated in its measurements.

The difficulty is not so much with the concept of a unit of business in static terms, but rather with the concept applied to dynamic competition when every attribute on which a definition rests can change or disappear. It would be generally agreed that in its static definition a business provides products or services in the face of competition to meet market needs. Furthermore, it may be defined either by product, competition, or market attributes. The preference, however, is to lean towards definition based on market attributes which indicate a gap in the chain of product substitutes. It is when competition cuts across an accepted definition that the difficulties arise. Mathematical economists have tended to step around the problem by defining the product, and hence the business, in ever more precise terms until it becomes unique. Economists with an industrial bias, however, have inclined towards a variable unit economics in which the business is re-defined on a changing attribute base according to the strategic needs.

It is this latter approach that seems to match best the concepts of business strategy. Strategic definition of a business is prompted by the need to adjust actions to build or defend the unit of business. Just as a campaign for a military commander may cover a large or a small area, so may a strategic move for a businessman. For the true strategist there can be no fixed definition of a business. Units will need to be changed and reformed in step with perceptions of the need for defence or the opportunity for advance.

Strategy texts, not surprisingly, lay great emphasis on the definitions of strategic businesses and segments. For example, Abell and Hammond (1979) argued that:

> Knowing how to segment a market and knowing when and to what extent to differentiate the offering to each segment is often the most creative part of strategy formulation,

20

0540800

while Porter (1980) held that:

> Usually there are a small number of strategic groups which capture the essential differences among firms in the industry.

Management accounting clearly has a major role to play in enabling the identification and definition of the appropriate business units at any time. To do so, the management accounting system must be designed so that management can be both stimulated to consider what might be appropriate units for strategic action and also able to search further in a process of confirming or rejecting possible units of action. Classification and indexing thus become crucial issues. The problems of classification, coding and flexibility are not new to management accounting. These are the bases on which cost accounting was founded (Risk, 1956).

Thus, the requirement to design the management accounting system to enable diagnosis of the units of business requiring strategic attention, does not require a major reorientation of the technical aspects of classification. The missing ingredient is the acceptance of strategic competitive position as the determinant for identifying units. To achieve such acceptance, the findings of contemporary research into the patterns of competitive strategy will need to take their place at the beginning of management accounting. 'What should we cost?' should be confronted before 'How do we design a cost system?'.

COMPETITION AND RELATIVE COSTS

The need to defend a business unit against aggressive competition and the opportunity for initiating offence to build its performance can both exist at the same time, because each business stands in a different strategic position against different competitors. Other things being equal, competitors with a cost advantage are threatening and those without such an advantage are weaker.

The recent concern for strategy gained its initial impetus from an article by Hirschman (1964) showing how the learning curve phenomenon could affect relative costs and hence strategic positions. Measuring cost in constant money terms, he showed how a straight line relationship could be obtained between cost and cumulative units produced when plotted on a double logarithmic scale. On an arithmetic scale with linear coordinates, however, the relationship plots as a curve with a rapid initial decline that later tails off.

21

Hirschman showed the slope of the logarithmic curve was such that for each doubling of the accumulated production experience, the unit cost would fall to around 80 per cent of the previous level, depending on the mixture of man and machine work involved:

> The phenomenon has many names: 'manufacturing progress function', 'cost-quantity relationship', 'cost curve', 'experience curve', 'efficiency curve', 'production acceleration curve', 'improvement curve', and 'performance curve'.

Hirschman's formula for the curve was straightforward and he argued that the curve should be used as a basis for management planning and action to secure such cost reduction. He also argued that the concept applied to industries and to nations could be defensibly projected ahead because of the inevitable nature of the human drive for survival against competition – the cause of the dynamic nature of the environment.

Hirschman's ideas were picked up by The Boston Consulting Group, related to price experience, and, as the 'experience curve' approach, widely popularised as a basis for business strategy. A whole range of elegant strategy concepts was built upon this experience effect (Boston Consulting Group, 1968). If costs can be made to decline predictably with total accumulated production, then the competitor who has produced the most units should have the lowest cost per unit and the highest profits. Figure 2.1 shows a cross-section of an industry's performance at one point in time with Competitor A leading in production experience and profits and Competitor C only breaking even. Faster growth in sales than the competition would reflect in increased market share and either reduce cost disadvantage or increase advantage. Market share thus has an intrinsic value through its effect on relative costs. Early experience with a new product could confer an unbeatable lead over the competition and the leading manufacturer should be able either to reduce price or increase customer value, further increasing volume and eventually forcing some lagging competitor out of the industry.

Long before the experience curve was propagated, economists had argued from empirical evidence that long term instability in competition and decreasing costs were widespread (Wiles, 1956). So these ideas are not new, yet despite many careful attempts to measure long term cost functions, economists did not succeed in establishing a standard shape for the curve – and certainly not that of the experience curve. Against those efforts the evidence produced by experience curve proponents looks rather sparse. It is possible that the experience effect is merely a reflection of well spread gains in national productivity and would not hold its linear relationship in periods in which productivity decreased.

While management accounting should incorporate the experience curve into its body of knowledge, it should not do so at the expense of the tried and true concepts of short run cost curves. Short run cost variation is still here, and may be the clue to much strategic action. It is noticeable that in many mature industries such as steel, motor vehicles, consumer electrical goods, competition has come from behind to overtake firms with huge accumulated experience. Competitive breakthrough in some segment areas has forced the established leader back up a short term cost curve at a much steeper slope than the longer term experience curve. Defence becomes retrenchment and retrenchment rout as financial resources are drained. Figure 2.2 indicates what may have been happening. For a short time, the expanding competitor B may record rising marginal costs causing average costs to fall more slowly than when plant is optimally adjusted to the increased volume. Nevertheless, such an expanding competitor

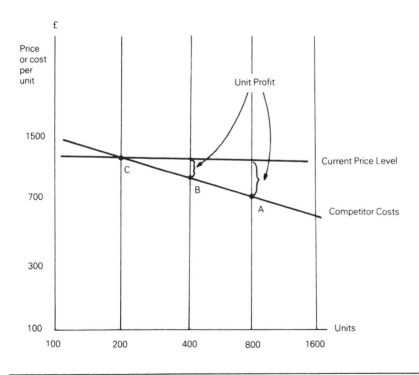

Figure 2.1   Accumulated production experience, relative cost and profitability for three competitors (log/log scale)

can very quickly reduce costs to the level of a much larger retrenching competitor. In this figure, the section of the short term cost curves for production below 'normal' capacity assumes the experience effect completely overriden by the under recovery of fixed overheads.

However questionable the factual basis for the experience curve, what is clear for management accounting is that relative costs are crucial to strategic action. An actual level of cost is of limited value for helping management's strategic thinking – even if honed to five decimal points. Without knowledge of relative competitor costs, the firm does not know whom to attack, nor how strong a defence should be. In those circumstances, management must take strategic decisions in the dark.

Despite the importance of relative cost, it is rare to find management accounting systems designed to collect comparative competitor costs, price and volume data. Accountants have even been known to argue that it cannot be done. It can. It is surprising how much pro-

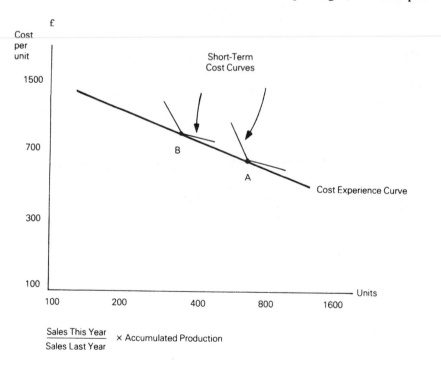

Figure 2.2 Short term reversal and the vanishing experience effect (log/log) scale

duction people know about competitors' plants. Management accounting skill that can construct internal budgets from minimal data can be just as readily turned towards external costing despite minimal competitor data. If little is known internally, it may be possible to question equipment suppliers about other installations they have made, or spend money on travel and observation. A new camera could be more valuable than another office calculator! Detailed value assessment of competitor products can also go a long way to showing cost differences.

Competitor cost assessment will probably involve more than national competitors. Today's competition is largely multinational. Even if international competition is not yet felt directly, a competitor may be building up accumulated experience and a cost advantage in a market with a higher price level unimpeded by leading competition. Again, where the international competition is more developed, competitive cost assessment may require quite complex investigation. For example, it might require reconstruction of a competitor's international production system. Economies stemming from component production on a scale far beyond that required for any individual market are not necessarily revealed by studies of performance in the end product markets.

Accounting skills may also be utilised to comparative financial advantage. It has become common to think of covering exchange risk to the revenue or capital accounts in terms of the home country currency; that is, the currency in which the accounts are kept. A foreign competitor, however, may cover in another currency, bringing a potential for relative gain or loss. Strategically, it may be appropriate to cover in the same currency as the competitor. There are occasions when to do otherwise would be to run the risk of relative loss in some market just when the competitor was most likely to attack.

Price experience

Variations in costs from those of competitors are not the only indicators of strategic advantage or vulnerability. A competitor may use price policy to gain market share or, potentially as dangerous, holding prices up to gain higher profits. Precision is needed to highlight the effects of price variations over time because significant changes in competitor fortune so often result from a chain of small variations mounting up over the years.

Under inflation, most real price reduction takes place through firms holding prices while costs escalate, or raising prices less than the cost inflation. Moreover, the timing of price setting and hence

176002

strategy review is forced upon management by the rate of inflation rather than chosen as part of the strategy. Frequent price changes caused by rapid inflation make it even more important for precision in measuring progress.

While external reconstruction of competitor costs requires skill and imagination, collection of competitor prices is much more straightforward. Of course, few competitors sell just one product at one price, but it should not be difficult for management accountants to build a weighted price index for a competitor. Where competitor revenues are also available, these may be used to check the accuracy of such an index, or as an alternative in the calculation.

There is a legal requirement in the United Kingdom for companies to disclose the turnover and profit of substantially different classes of business. Emmanuel and Gray (1977, 1978) have shown that, from published reports, it should not be difficult to segment data down to a three-digit Standard Industrial Classification code by industry, but segmentation by customer industry is rarely possible. While disclosure to competitors has not been foremost in financial accountants' minds, the failure to define what constitutes a separate segment highlights the scanty attention paid to strategy within accountancy. The general impression is that most accountants, and auditors, overlook segments identified and used by management for strategy formulation if they are not classified as products within the chart of accounts.

Volume and demand

Given price and cost data, the missing ingredient for strategic management accounting is volume. But current volume is not enough; for size and pattern of future demand is all important to strategy formulation. After all, strategy concerns performance over the entire conflict, not a summation of separate performance in a succession of periods.

Market share is one indicator of the link between cost and profit performance for a single period and long term, or product life cycle, profit. It is a proxy for the future earnings flows, enabling rudimentary assessment of the economists' concept of profit in place of the one-period accountants' profit. Movement in market share further indicates the extent to which a firm is gaining or losing position, while relative market share indicates the strength of the firm compared with important rivals.

The incorporation of market share assessment into management accounts seems one of the most obvious steps in moving towards strategic management accounting. The simple addition of market share change enables any set of accounts to be viewed much more intelligently. A high profit obtained through holding prices above competition may indicate a real loss of present value from reduced market share and relative cost position. Conversely, low profits may be more than justified by rising market share and relative cost advantage.

Probably it will not be many years before financial accounting also moves to publication of market share data. Definition of markets will require more attention, but is far less fraught with theoretical difficulty than, say, asset valuation. Weighted and consolidated market share data would be significant in interpreting consolidated accounts, even for a multinational conglomerate.

Though a valuable indicator of strategic position, market share discloses nothing about the size, pattern and duration of expected demand. Yet present value of a market share can be severely curtailed if, for example, demand fluctuates dramatically or is expected to drop rapidly. The management accountant assessing various strategic alternatives will want to employ the best forecast available rather than rely on market share as a proxy. To date, the strategy literature has not advanced far in its use of market forecasts or in the sensitivity testing of strategies to variations in demand. General statements like high and low growth, maturity, decline and decay are sprinkled throughout the strategy literature as bases for prescribing broad lines of strategy.

A great deal of effort has also been expended in trying to identify a standard product life cycle and relate strategy to it. Demand that followed a regular bell shaped pattern over time with predictable growth and decay would make strategy calculation so much simpler, and there is substantial evidence that product adoption does follow such a shape. Beyond the introductory adoption period, however, no such standard pattern has been found. Moreover, merchandising effort by competitors may condition the product life cycle, even though it is conventional to regard demand for generic products, as opposed to brands, as being little influenced by supplier activity.

While management accountants are unlikely to take over the task of forecasting from marketers and econometricians, its need for the best possible forecasts as input for strategic calculations gives management accounting a vested interest in monitoring the quality of the forecasts. There is certainly a role for monitoring the quality of the forecasts. There is certainly a role for monitoring this vital input into strategy and planning, and probably a case for the management accounting audit taking over from the marketing audit. Precision is needed when formulating a business strategy, particularly in interpreting the cost effects over time.

RETURN ON COMPETITIVE POSITION

The emphasis that accountancy and finance have placed on return on investment over the years has subtly transmuted into a widely and deeply held belief that return comes from the investments themselves. In a typical comment, Van Horne (1971) held that:

> The capital expenditure decisions of a firm are, perhaps, its most important decisions. The scarce resource of capital is allocated to investments from which benefits or returns are expected over varying future periods of time. Consequently, the future success and profitability of the firm are dependent upon investment decisions made previously.

Furthermore, investments are nearly always regarded as either physical assets that are valued and described in the accounting records or accumulated costs of creation – as for research and development of a new product. This whole belief pattern is further supported in many firms by the way in which investment forms are drawn up and administered. Sales and profitability are shown as coming from the physical asset with, frequently, no mention of competitive market position.

The truth is very different. Sustained profit comes from the competitive market position. New production investment to expand sales must imply a change in competitive position and this change should be the focus of the investment review forms. Without it, the calculations must be a nonsense.

Return from investment in competitive position will differ according to the future demand pattern. In a high growth market, for example, the doubling of accumulated experience is rapid and the opportunity for correspondingly high cost reduction is equally great. A firm that can increase its market share in a high growth market stands to gain considerably. It is also possible that the cost of doing so will be low because the gain is achieved from the market growth without taking business away from competitors. In many situations, competitors are only aware of competitive attack when their sales fall.

The competitor or competitors from whom the market share is taken can also affect the return on investment in competitive position. A fast growing competitor, aggressive in pricing and likely to continue until stopped, is a threat to an existing position. Sales taken away from such a competitor can have much greater value than the intrinsic worth in the sales themselves. Added to the cost reduction value and profitability of the sales gained would be the profit saved by retaining business the competitor would otherwise have taken.

If strategic thinking is allowed to filter through the entire breadth of conventional management accounting, it will inevitably change the way investment is regarded. Calculations of returns from changes in competitive position will replace the return on investment forms and be used for expenditures frequently classified now as revenue expenditures. Generally, there will be a comparison of returns between the existing position of 'no action' and a strategic proposal. It will also become common to calculate competitors' positions under the alternatives in order to provide a picture of the relative gain or loss and assess the stability of the competitive situation.

A simple worked example, will serve to illustrate the type of calculation that will be needed. Firm X is considering a proposal to invest an amount of £100,000 in product improvement and promotion to bring these up to the levels of its major competitor, Y, and expand its market share from 25 per cent to 35 per cent. Competitor Y, with 20 per cent of market share, has been gaining gradually on X and, if X takes no action, Y is expected to erode X's market share to the extent of 1 per cent of market each year. X calculates that the product improvement and promotion will switch 4 per cent of the market from Y and 6 per cent from smaller competitors. Currently, the price stands at £10.00 per unit, with X making profits of 5 per cent on sales and Y making 3 per cent. Costs decrease on an 80 per cent experience curve and X and Y have accumulated experience of 200,000 and 150,000 units, respectively. Cost of capital, used for discounting, has been set at 15 per cent, a year. Prices have tended to decline at about 3 per cent a year in real terms, held up by the smaller competitors and by the fact that both major competitors would expect the other to follow. Based on calculations of likely relative costs, X's management accountants can see no reason for this pattern not to continue, as it would be more or less in line with the cost experience of the second firm under either alternative.

Forecasts of the market for six years and calculations of volumes, costs and profits for both X and Y are presented in Tables 2.1 and 2.2, and it can be seen that the investment is more than justified. Note how much clearer the evaluation can be when the competitor data is included as a test of the validity of the calculations. Were data on the smallest firms included, confidence would be even stronger, eliminating the feeling that Y might gain by attacking them, with repercussions for X. On the other hand, the small firms could be protected in special market segments able to survive with lower spending on quality and promotion. Also omitted is any allowance for short term cost increase as a result of the actual volume decrease for Y and the smaller competitors in the first year. In this case, such an

Table 2.1
Base case: take no action

Year		1	2	3	4	5	6
Market size	(000 units)	100	100	120	150	180	180
Market price	(£)	9.70	9.41	9.13	8.86	8.59	8.33
FIRM X							
Market share	(%)	25	24	23	22	21	20
Sales	(000 units)	25.0	24.0	27.6	33.0	37.8	36.0
Accumulated sales	(000 units)	225.0	249.0	276.6	309.6	347.4	383.4
Increase in acc. sales	(%)	12.5	10.7	11.1	11.9	11.2	10.4
Experience effect – reduction in cost per unit	(£)	.34	.28	.30	.33	.30	.28
Cost per unit (current=£9.50)	(£)	9.16	8.88	8.58	8.25	7.95	7.67
Profit per unit	(£)	.54	.53	.55	.61	.64	.56
Total profit	(£000's)	*13.5*	*12.7*	*15.2*	*20.1*	*24.2*	*20.2*
Present value deflator 15%			1.0	.870	.756	.658	.572	.497
Present value of profit	(£000's)	13.5	11.0	11.5	13.2	13.8	10.0
COMPETITOR Y							
Market share	(%)	20	21	22	23	24	25
Sales	(000 units)	20.0	21.0	26.4	34.5	43.2	45.0
Accumulated sales	(000 units)	170.0	191.0	217.4	251.9	295.1	350.1
Increase in acc. sales	(%)	13.3	12.4	13.8	15.9	17.1	18.6
Experience effect – reduction in cost per unit	(£)	.36	.34	.37	.42	.45	.47
Cost per unit (current=£9.70)	(£)	9.34	9.00	8.63	8.21	7.76	7.29
Profit per unit	(£)	.36	.41	.50	.65	.83	1.04
Total profit	(£000's)	*7.2*	*8.6*	*13.2*	*22.4*	*35.9*	*46.8*

Table 2.2
Investment alternative: £100 000 in product improvement and promotion

Year		1	2	3	4	5	6
Market size	(000 units)	100	100	120	150	180	180
Market price	(£)	9.70	9.41	9.13	8.86	8.59	8.33
FIRM X							
Market share	(%)	35	35	35	35	35	35
Sales	(000 units)	35.0	35.0	42.0	52.5	63.0	63.0
Accumulated sales	(000 units)	235.0	270.0	312.0	364.5	427.5	490.5
Increase in acc. sales	(%)	17.5	14.9	15.6	16.8	17.3	14.8
Experience effect – reduction in cost per unit	(£)	.46	.40	.42	.44	.46	.40
Cost per unit (current=£9.50)	(£)	9.04	8.64	8.22	7.78	7.32	6.92
Profit per unit	(£)	.66	.77	.91	1.08	1.27	1.41
Total profit	(£000's)	*23.1*	*27.0*	*38.2*	*56.7*	*80.0*	*88.8*
Present value deflator 15%			1.0	.870	.756	.658	.572	.497
Present value of profit	(£000's)	23.1	23.5	28.9	37.3	45.8	44.1
COMPETITOR Y							
Market share	(%)	16	16	16	16	16	16
Sales	(000 units)	16.0	16.0	19.2	23.0	28.8	28.8
Accumulated sales	(000 units)	166.0	182.0	201.2	224.2	253.0	281.8
Increase in acc. sales	(%)	10.6	9.6	10.5	11.4	12.8	11.4
Experience effect – reduction in cost per unit	(£)	.28	.26	.28	.31	.34	.31
Cost per unit (current=£9.70)	(£)	9.42	9.16	8.88	8.57	8.23	7.92
Profit per unit	(£)	.28	.25	.25	.29	.34	.41
Total profit	(£000's)	*4.5*	*4.0*	*4.8*	*6.7*	*9.8*	*11.8*

allowance would strengthen the decision to spend, but it might lead to a higher price level.

Resources, cash flow and portfolios

The ebb and flow of competition against any one firm is normally of much longer duration than a few accounting periods. It can be very difficult to defeat even a small competitor outright. Threatened competitors will draw on reserves and reorganise to defend their position. Since 1959, successive generations of business school students have studied and discussed the appropriate reaction for Scripto Pens when attacked head on by Bic in the ball point pen market. Despite the resounding defeat suffered by Scripto, the firm limped on over the years and suddenly launched an aggressive and so far successful attack in late 1980. This time the attack appeared as an erasable ball pen directed at the 21 per cent of the American ball point market which had been captured by Gillette's Paper Mate division with its 'Eraser Mate'.

Given the ever present possibility of competitor reaction, it is not sufficient to base strategic actions on an assessment of their direct contribution to the firm's profits and market share. Ideally, any decision should reflect an assessment of the effect on competitors' profits and market shares extended to forecast the pattern of conflict over the longer term. This pattern of conflict will, in turn, depend on competitors' resources and liquidity as well as their profits. Sometimes, competitors will lack the resources to retaliate; at other times, some competitors will be protected within a profitable market segment and will remain unaffected by competitive attack.

More than any other business function, management accounting has the skill for such competitor assessments. The skill needed amounts to accounting for competitors, from outside, and projected ahead to a suitable strategic horizon. Such 'competitor accounting' is usually complicated by the fact that most firms operate more than one business. Thus, each competitor is sitting at several Monopoly boards, not just one. Resources may be switched from board to board as appropriate. The objectives and time preferences for profits from any one business will probably vary between competitors, owing to their differing requirements for other businesses. To handle this portfolio complication, the starting point would be an analysis of the competitor's actions and statements in order to identify his objectives for each business. An initial classification into three objectives of 'build', 'maintain', or 'harvest' can then lead to a projection of the cash flows from each and from the entire competitor

Table 2.3
Competitor business portfolio – five year cash flow projections

Business title	A	B	C	D	Total
Competitor classification	Grow	Maintain	Grow	Harvest	
Profits					
Depreciation					
Working capital reduction					
* * * *					
* * * *					
* * * *					
Total cash in					XXX
New investment					
Working capital expansion					
* * * *					
* * * *					
* * * *					
Total cash out					XXX

Net cash by business		XX
Research and development	XX	
Finance charges	XX	
Taxation	XX	
Dividends	X	XX
Surplus or deficit		X

portfolio. Underlying the assessment will be the concepts of balanced cash flow and balanced risk, for the competitor organisation. Again, these assessments fall within the skill of the management accountant more than other functional specialist. Some form similar to that reproduced in Table 2.3 would be helpful in assessing competitor cash flow portfolios. At a more advanced level, some firms have set up an entire competitive intelligence system (Porter, 1980), and some have developed interactive computer models.

STRATEGIC MANAGEMENT ACCOUNTING AS AN OPERATING SYSTEM

A fashionable claim in the strategy literature has been that strategy is a function of structure (Chandler, 1962, for example). It might be more accurate, however, to move the emphasis away from organisation structure and place it on accounting measurement. Managers have a tendency to do what is measured and not to do what is not measured. Few management accounting systems are adequately structured to measure strategy.

Budgeting is one area where management accounting has traditionally laid a claim to expertise and every business budget implies a strategy of some sort. Yet the format traditionally adopted for budget preparation negates strategic reasoning! There is a noticeable absence of any attempt to incorporate data which depict the situation with regard to customers or competitors or even to highlight strategic variables. Tabulations of spending under different accounts provide no indication of which is carrying the core of any strategic thrust or defence. Worse that this, it has become a tradition to measure spending against past levels for the same account heading. So ingrained has historical internal comparison become that the same six-column pattern appears in firm after firm:

Month			Year to Date		
Last year	Budget	Actual	Last year	Budget	Actual

Admittedly, broader planning data are available for some firms, although it is usually outside the management accounting system. In a few, zero base reviews (Pyhrr, 1970) have removed the 'historisis' effect. These developments do not change the underlying truth, however. Budgeting as widely used is anything but strategic.

If strategic management accounting is to become a reality, some fundamental changes must be made to the format of management accounting records, plans and reports. Amey (1979) has argued that planning budgets should be separated from control budgets because they serve different purposes and a good plan might not yield a good control. Such a move, however, runs the risk of failing to control strategy as the moves unfold. Why should not management accounting reports be routinely presented in a strategic format with, say, columns for 'Ourselves', 'Competitor A', 'Competitor B', and so on? It would make a welcome change from the usual six columns!

The more data that are formally incorporated into management accounting reports to indicate buyer response to spending on different variables, the easier it will be to identify actions which build competitive advantage. The more that can be incorporated about competitor spending and the cost-volume-profit conditions which they face, the more informed can be the estimate of their reactions.

Incorporation of strategic reasoning is even more important than data. Competition with numerous opponents and multiple reactions is complex; it is not solved by a simple set of decision rules. What will identify a good budget is sound reasoning that holds up well when tested against the market, competitor and cost facts. It may not be possible to provde that a strategy is optimal, but it is certainly possible to establish degrees of quality for strategies advanced to match a given situation. If forms are altered to include terse statements of strategic reasoning, the reasoning may be measured against the outcome. If it is so measured, it will become more dominant and perhaps less prone to unsubstantiated rules of thumb.

Changes in competitive position generally build gradually through the ebb and flow of many moves and counter-moves. Thus strategy is a field in which an ongoing precision can pay off handsomely. Management accounting has the concepts and the skills to provide that precision; it does have a strategic purpose. With formal acknowledgement of the legitimacy of a strategic focus and a firm step away from the search for information from internal cost analysis, strategic management accounting is ready to flower as a prime function of the management accountant.

(Editorial note: This chapter is an edited version of a paper presented to a technical symposium of the Institute of Cost and Management Accountants at Pembroke College, Oxford, in January 1981.)

REFERENCES AND FURTHER READING

Abell, D.F., and Hammond, J.S., *Strategic Market Planning: Problems and Analytical Approaches*, Englewood Cliffs, N.J.: Prentice-Hall, 1979.

American Accounting Association, *Report of the Committee on Foundations of Accounting Measurements*, New York: AAA, 1971.

Amey, L.R., 'Budget planning: a dynamic reformulation', *Accounting and Business Research*, Winter 1979.

Ansoff, H.I., *Corporate Strategy*, New York: McGraw-Hill, 1965.

Boston Consulting Group, *Perspectives on Experience*, Boston, Mass.: Boston Consulting Group, 1968.

Caplan, R.H., 'Relationships between principles of military strategy and principles of business planning', *in* Anthony, R.N., *Planning and Control Systems*, Cambridge, Mass.: Harvard University Graduate School of Business Administration, 1965.

Chandler, A., *Strategy and Structure*, Cambridge, Mass.: MIT Press, 1962.

Clark, J.M., *Studies in the Economics of Overhead Costs*, Chicago: University of Chicago Press, 1923.

Emmanuel, C.R., and Gray, S.J., 'Segmental disclosures and the segment identification problem', *Accounting and Business Research*, Winter 1977.

Emmanuel, C.R., and Gray, S.J., 'Segmental disclosures by multi-business multinational companies: a proposal', *Accounting and Business Research*, Summer 1978.

Hirschman, W.B., 'Profit from the learning curve', *Harvard Business Review*, January–February 1964.

Hofer, C.W., and Schendel, D., *Strategy Formulation*, St Paul, Minn.: West Publishing, 1978.

Porter, M.E., *Competitive Strategy*, New York: Free Press, 1980.

Pyhrr, P.A., 'Zero-based budgeting', *Harvard Business Review*, November–December 1970.

Risk, J.M.S., *The Classification and Coding of Accounts*, London: Institute of Cost & Works Accountants, 1956.

Simmonds, K., 'From data-oriented to information-oriented accounting', *Journal of Business Finance*, 1972.

Van Horne, J.C., *Fundamentals of Financial Management*, Englewood Cliffs, N.J.: Prentice-Hall, 1971.

Wiles, P.J.D., *Price, Cost and Output*, Oxford: Basil Blackwell & Mott, 1956.

3

Capital budgeting

Richard Dobbins and Richard Pike

Planning and controlling capital expenditure is a major aspect of planning in all organisations. This is particularly true for those companies in the manufacturing sector but also applies to other organisations, all of which must make decisions from time to time on acquiring equipment ranging from vehicles to computers.

The authors begin this chapter by placing the capital investment process in the context of strategic planning. They point out that investment proposals need to be related to the underlying corporate objectives and strategies. A key challenge for all organisations is to identify projects which fit these strategies and promise to be profitable in the broadest sense, i.e. to create wealth for the organisation.

Once a number of potential projects have been identified it is necessary to evaluate them and the main part of the chapter discusses the principal methods of project evaluation. Three financial aspects of a project must be considered – the returns it promises, the timing of those returns and the riskiness of the project. Dobbins and Pike examine the major commonly-used techniques for evaluating projects in the light of these three aspects. They show that simpler methods based on accounting profit (payback, return on capital and effect on earnings per share) are unsatisfactory. They produce distorted results because of accounting conventions used to calculate profit, they fail to take full account of the timing of returns, and they ignore risk.

Methods based on a discounting approach, on the other hand, can take into account risk and the timing of returns. If they are based on cash flows rather than profits they also avoid the distortions introduced by accounting conventions in calculating depreciation, for example.

Dobbins and Pike suggest that the net present value method is the simplest and most appropriate of the three discounting methods con-

sidered, although they recognise that the simple payback period calculation is still the most popular system in most companies.

The authors go on to examine in more detail the problem of risk and how to allow for it in capital appraisals. They explain the capital asset pricing model, which can help companies make the trade-off between risk and return, and show with an example how it can be applied in practice.

The final section of the chapter considers the further stages in the capital investment process – review and approval, project control and post-implementation review.

Capital budgeting has been described by Myers (1976) as the art of finding assets that are worth more than they cost. This may look deceptively simple in concept, but it is, arguably, the most difficult of all the tasks facing the manager. Those who have worked on large scale projects know well the frustrations and difficulties entailed in capital investment planning, decision making, budgeting and controlling. Primarily, this is because those activities demand the approval, co-operation, enthusiasm and co-ordination of a variety of people, corporations, financiers and, possibly, local authorities and governments.

STRATEGIC PLANNING

Investment planning is an integral part of the wider processes of strategic planning and budgetary control. Investment proposals should not be generated on an *ad hoc* basis but should be viewed in relation to the existing and possible future investment programmes based on underlying corporate objectives and strategies. The capital investment planning process and its relationship with the overall planning process is outlined in Figure 3.1 and discussed below.

Financial decision making involves purposeful behaviour, which implies the existence of a goal or, rather more likely, some combination of goals. In the absence of any objective, the firm would have no sound criterion for choosing among alternative investment strategies and projects. In recent years a wide variety of goals has been suggested for a firm – from the traditional goal of profit maximisation to the survival of the firm, maximisation of sales, achievement of satisfactory profits, or attainment of a target market share. Modern financial management asserts that directors should seek to maximise the market value of the firm. Empirical studies suggest that firms have at least a minimum profit target and seek long run profitability and stability, rather than maximising market value (see, for example, Lowes and Dobbins [1978]).

Following the formulation of basic objectives and policies, specific objectives should be established to ensure that a balanced investment programme, which achieves financial and other goals, is obtained. As part of the decision process, investment opportunities will be generated in line with the developed strategy adopted to achieve defined objectives. Action programmes specifying responsibilities for carrying out the investment programme turn hopes and forecasts into achievable plans. They break down the investment strategy into specific tasks, dates and, sometimes, costs, which if fulfilled, will ensure that investment objectives are achieved. The capital budget is then compiled as a financial model which describes the planned activities and goals. It provides a framework for management control by the comparison of actual and budget performance.

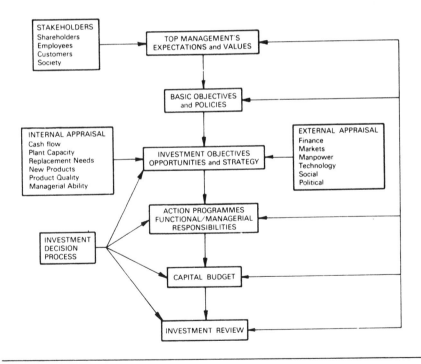

Figure 3.1   Capital investment planning process

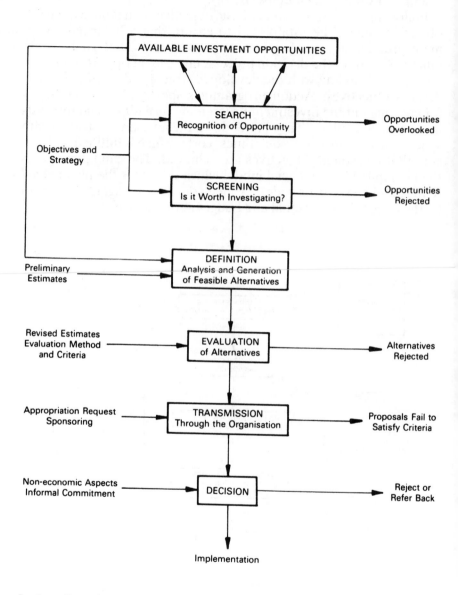

Based on a diagram by King (1975)

Figure 3.2   Investment decision process

INVESTMENT DECISION PROCESS

At the heart of any investment planning process is the decision process which commences at the perception of an investment opportunity or problem, concludes with the investment decision, and is represented in the implementation of the decision. The various stages between idea and attainment are many and complex, but a procedure along the lines of that shown in Figure 3.2, whether formalised or not, should exist in every organisation.

The first, and probably most crucial, stage in the process involves the recognition of opportunities. Economic theory regards investment as the interaction of the supply of capital and the flow of investment opportunities. Rarely, however, does a regular flow of investment opportunities present itself for evaluation. Some investments are recurrent, of course, such as the need to replace existing plant or equipment, but even here, recognition will often be too late. Typically, profitable opportunities do not throw themselves onto the manager's desk. They require imagination and diligence by management if they are to be detected at an early stage.

At any time, a number of potential investment opportunities which would satisfy the firm's basic objective(s) will be feasible. It is management's task to conduct a creative search for such opportunities and to generate proposals. The earlier an opportunity is identified, the greater should be the potential returns before competitors and imitators react. Many large companies are obviously aware of this and place heavy emphasis on innovation and research, but even the smaller firm can – at little additional expense – place a higher priority throughout its organisation on encouraging early identification of investment opportunities. Naturally enough, it is difficult to know quite how much attention should be given to this vital area. The costs of ignoring opportunities do not show up directly in the income statement; the costs of searching do.

In the second stage – that of screening proposals – it is neither feasible nor desirable to conduct a full scale evaluation of opportunities. All that is required is to determine whether such opportunities are worth further investigation. Readily available information must be used to ascertain whether the opportunity is compatible with the existing business and corporate strategy, whether the resources required are to hand, whether the idea is technically feasible, whether that type of investment is known to be profitable elsewhere or has been so previously, and whether the likely returns compensate for the risk involved. In the case of major projects, it is advisable at the outset to establish the total level of investigatory expenditure that the firm is prepared to put at risk in coming to a decision on acceptance or rejection. This could be a very costly exercise, sometimes as much as 5 per cent of total planning capital expenditure.

Project definition – stage three – involves specifying both the technical aspects of the proposal (project life, capacity and so on) and the generation of cash flow estimates. An investment proposal is vague and shapeless until it has been properly defined. Even at this early stage, proposals are gaining management commitment. As information is being gathered, a number of people are beginning to give backing and tacit promises, and minor decisions are being made – such as incurring expense on a feasibility study.

PROJECT EVALUATION

Financial management theorists generally assert that the objective of the firm is to create as much wealth as possible. Wealth is created when the market value of the outputs exceeds the market value of the inputs. In assessing all capital projects, managers should follow the net present value rule, which states that a project is acceptable if the present value of anticipated incremental cash inflows exceeds the present value of anticipated incremental cash outflows. We are aware that studies of managerial behaviour reveal that managers pursue objectives relating to sales, market share, employees, assets and personal satisfaction. However, the fundamental objective of industrial and commercial enterprises is the creation of consumable goods and services. Managers create wealth by ensuring that the market value of the firm's outputs is greater than the market value of its inputs. Cash flows in from customers and cash flows out to suppliers of goods, labour, services and capital items. Within that framework, all projects can be assessed by calculating the net cash flows accruing to the firm, using the net present value rule described below, after taking into account the risk and timing of cash flows associated with the project.

NET PRESENT VALUE

As already stated, the objective of the firm is to create wealth by using existing and future resources to produce goods and services now and in the future with greater value than the resources consumed. To create wealth now, the present value of all future cash inflows must exceed the present value of all anticipated cash outflows. The net present value (NPV) rule is illustrated as follows:

$$NPV = \sum_{t=1}^{n} \frac{R_t}{(1+k)^t} - C$$

where R_t = expected net cash inflows, k = the required rate of return on the project, C = the immediate capital outlay. In other words, the net present value (NPV) of a project is the sum (Σ) of all anticipated net cash inflows (R_t) from now (t=1) to the end of the project (n), discounted at the project's required rate of return (k), less the cost of buying into the project (C). A brief example will serve to make the matter clearer.

The initial capital outlay to finance an investment is £100. Anticipated net cash inflows are £60 receivable at the end of the Year 1 and £60 at the end of Year 2. The firm operates in a low risk industry and divides its various projects into three categories: class A where the risk is low and the required rate of return is 10 per cent; class B where the risk is average for the industry and the required rate of return is 13 per cent; Class C where the risk is higher and the required rate of return is 16 per cent. Evaluating the project from the NPV viewpoint and using the NPV formula given above will provide the estimates illustrated in Table 3.1, which shows the NPV of the project under each of the three risk classifications.

Table 3.1
Net present value of a project

Risk class	Discount rate	Present value of cash inflows Yr 1	Yr 2	Cost	NPV
A	10%	£54	£50	£100	£4
B	13%	£53	£47	£100	£0
C	16%	£52	£44	£100	−£4

If the project is classified as low risk, the cash flows are discounted at a rate of 10 per cent. The Year 1 cash flow has a present value of £54 and the Year 2 cash flow has a present value of £50. The present value of the inflows is therefore £104 and, after deducting the initial outlay which has a present value of £100, the project has a net present value of £4. The project should be accepted; it has a positive NPV. It creates wealth. Given the expected cash flows the value of the firm should rise by £4.

On the other hand, if the project is classified as high risk, the cash inflows are discounted at a rate of 16 per cent and the NPV is estimated at −£4. The project is unacceptable; it has a negative NPV. Its acceptance would have the effect of reducing the firm's value by £4. Clearly, it would not be wise to exchange £100 today for future cash flows having a present value today of only £96.

If the project is classified as average risk, the discount rate used is 13 per cent, yielding a NPV of £0. The project is just acceptable; it yields 13 per cent.

From this example, we can draw three important conclusions: (1) project acceptability depends upon cash flows and risk; (2) the present value of a given expected cash flow decreases with time; (3) the higher the risk of a given set of expected cash flows (and the higher the applied discount rate), the lower will be its present value. The present value of a given expected cash flow decreases as its risk increases.

The NPV rule is not difficult to apply in practice. The tedium of using formulae and power functions has been reduced by the creation of discount tables and the availability of computer programs. Extracts from a set of discount tables are presented in Table 3.2, which shows values of £1 receivable in the future and of £1 receivable annually for a number of years. The column headings in the table are discount rates which increase from left to right. The rows represent increases in time from Year 1 to Year 10. To find the value today of £1 expected to be received in one year's time assuming a required rate of return of 10 per cent, it is only necessary to find the value in row 1 (that is, Year 1) located in the column under 10 per cent. The value shown is 0.909, giving an answer of £0.909 or 90.9p. How much is the same £1 worth if the required rate of return (discount factor, cost of capital, percentage factor) is increased to 16 per cent? The value indicated is 0.862, giving a value of £0.862 or 86.2p. It will be seen that all the values in the table fall from left to right, in line with our earlier conclusion (3) that present values decline as the discount rate increases. Furthermore, all the values get smaller as the table progresses into the future (from top to bottom) in line with conclusion 2. As a further example, the present value of £1 000 receivable in Year 10 and discounted at 25 per cent is calculated at £107 (that is, £1 000 × 0.107).

The lower section of the table shows the present value of an annuity of £1 receivable annually for a number of years. An annuity is a sum of money paid or received each year. To find the present value

Table 3.2
Discount tables (extracts)

PRESENT VALUE OF £1 RECEIVABLE

Discount rate	10%	13%	14%	16%	22%	25%	34%
Year							
1	0.909	0.885	0.877	0.862	0.820	0.800	0.746
2	0.826	0.783	0.769	0.743	0.672	0.640	0.557
3	0.751	0.693	0.675	0.641	0.551	0.512	0.416
4	0.683	0.613	0.592	0.552	0.451	0.410	0.310
5	0.621	0.543	0.519	0.476	0.370	0.328	0.231
6	0.564	0.480	0.456	0.410	0.303	0.262	0.173
7	0.513	0.425	0.400	0.354	0.249	0.210	0.129
8	0.467	0.376	0.351	0.305	0.204	0.168	0.096
9	0.424	0.333	0.308	0.263	0.167	0.134	0.072
10	0.386	0.295	0.270	0.227	0.137	0.107	0.054

PRESENT VALUE OF AN ANNUITY OF £1 RECEIVABLE

Discount rate	10%	13%	14%	16%	22%	25%	34%
Year							
1	0.909	0.885	0.877	0.862	0.820	0.800	0.746
2	1.736	1.668	1.647	1.605	1.492	1.440	1.303
3	2.487	2.361	2.322	2.246	2.041	1.952	1.719
4	3.170	2.974	2.914	2.798	2.494	2.362	2.029
5	3.791	3.517	3.433	3.274	2.864	2.689	2.260
6	4.355	3.998	3.889	3.685	3.167	2.951	2.433
7	4.868	4.423	4.288	4.039	3.416	3.161	2.562
8	5.335	4.799	4.639	4.344	3.619	3.329	2.658
9	5.759	5.132	4.946	4.607	3.786	3.463	2.730
10	6.145	5.426	5.216	4.833	3.923	3.571	2.784

of £1 receivable for each of the next ten years assuming an interest rate of 10 per cent, it is necessary to find the value in row 10 located under the 10 per cent heading. The value shown is 6.145 which gives an answer of £6.145 (that is, £1 × 6.145). If the interest rate is increased to 16 per cent, the annuity is worth £4.833. Again, it is possible to demonstrate the power of discounting by way of a further example. The present value of an annuity of £1 000 payable for 10 years at a rate of 25 per cent is £3 571 (that is, £1 000 × 3.571).

INTERNAL RATE OF RETURN

The net present value rule offers the best available answer to the accept/reject problem. An alternative approach is to calculate an investment's internal rate of return, sometimes called the yield. The internal rate of return is the rate of return which equates the present value of anticipated net cash flows with the initial outlay. To calculate the internal rate of return (IRR), it is necessary to solve the following formula for r:

$$0 = \sum_{t=1}^{n} \frac{R_t}{(1+r)^t} - C$$

where r is the rate of return which gives a zero NPV. A project is acceptable if its yield or internal rate of return is greater than the required rate of return on the project (k). This method of project appraisal gives exactly the same accept/reject decision as NPV. Projects with positive NPVs will have values of r greater than k. In the case of the example above, the project's yield is 13 per cent:

$$\frac{60}{(1 + .13)} + \frac{60}{(1 + .13)^2} - 100 = 0$$

If the project is class A then it is acceptable as the yield of 13 per cent is greater than the required rate of return of 10 per cent. If the project is classified as B, it is just acceptable, but it would be rejected as a class C project. Managers are recommended to use the NPV method, if only because it is easier to handle. Without the use of a computer the IRR calculation can be a laborious business.

PROFITABILITY INDEX (COST–BENEFIT RATIO)

A third reasonable method of assessing capital expenditure opportunities is the profitability index, sometimes called the cost–benefit ratio. The profitability index (PI) is the present value of anticipated net future cash flows divided by the initial outlay. The only difference between the NPV and PI methods is that when using the NPV technique the initial outlay is deducted from the present value of anticipated cash flows, whereas with the PI approach the initial outlay is used as a divisor. In general terms, a project is acceptable if its PI value is greater than 1. Clearly a project offering a PI greater than 1 must also offer a net present value which is positive.

In the example used above, PI values can be calculated easily. As a class A project, it has a PI of 1.04; as a class B project, its PI is 1.00; as a class C project, its PI is 0.96.

PAYBACK, RETURN ON CAPITAL EMPLOYED, AND EARNINGS PER SHARE

The NPV rule helps managers to make wealth-creating decisions. There are, however, several other techniques for assessing capital projects which may give misleading indications as to whether or not an investment should be accepted. Three popular methods are the project payback period, the return on the capital employed in the project, and the effect on earnings per share.

The payback period is the length of time required to recover the initial investment. This method is unacceptable because it involves the subjective establishment of an acceptable payback period – 2½ years, for instance. Should managers ignore substantial payoffs in years 3 and 4?

Return on capital employed is 'accounting profit' expressed as a percentage of the capital employed. This must be dismissed as a rule of thumb approach. The technique does not use cash flow, ignores the timing of cash flows, and ignores risk.

Earnings per share is calculated by dividing 'accounting profit' by the number of shares in issue. Again, this calculation ignores cash flows, timing and risk. In consequence, the latter three methods must be rejected as inappropriate. As the following example demonstrates, they can give faulty indications as to acceptability.

The expected results of a project are shown in Table 3.3. An immediate cash outlay of £20 000 is required to finance the project. The firm's policy is to depreciate the initial outlay in equal instalments over the estimated project life, giving depreciation charges of £5 000 a year. For a project of this risk class, the firm's required rate of return is 14 per cent. The firm issues 20 000 ordinary shares of £1 each to finance this, its only project.

Using the various methods discussed earlier, we can make a number of calculations. The payback period is 2½ years, with £8 000 being received in year 1 and year 2 and £4 000 in the first half of year 3. Return on capital employed can be calculated as follows: accounting profit divided by average capital employed. Average capital

Table 3.3
Expected results of a project (£s)

Year		1	2	3	4
Incremental cash inflows		14 000	22 000	14 000	10 000
Incremental cash outflows		6 000	14 000	6 000	4 000
Net cash flows		8 000	8 000	8 000	6 000
Depreciation		5 000	5 000	5 000	5 000
Accounting profit		3 000	3 000	3 000	1 000
ROCE	%	17.1	24.0	40.0	40.0
EPS	p.	15	15	15	5

employed is the £20 000 initial investment less successive years' depreciation charges, averaged on the basis that depreciation charges properly accrue evenly throughout the year. For year 1, average capital employed is beginning capital employed (£20 000) plus ending capital employed (£15 000) divided by 2 – giving an average of £17 500. For year 2, average capital employed is £15 000 plus £10 000 divided by 2 = £12 500. Similar calculations can be carried out for years 3 and 4. Accounting profit for each year is given in Table 3.3. Rates of return on capital employed are: year 1, 17.1 per cent; year 2, 24.0 per cent; year 3, 40.0 per cent; year 4, 40.0 per cent. Are these returns on capital employed acceptable? The general assumption is that the greater the return on capital employed, the better. Rates of return clearly depend to some extent on the firm's depreciation policy. Arbitrary accounting procedures such as these do not enable managers to make rational wealth-creating decisions.

Turning to the earnings per share approach, it can be seen that earnings per share (EPS) for each of the first three years is 15 pence – £3 000 divided by the 20 000 ordinary shares in issue. For year 4, the EPS figure falls to 5 pence. Again, it is not clear whether these rates are acceptable. The assumption is that the greater the EPS the better, but no EPS decision criterion is established.

The NPV approach gives a theoretically correct decision, and results in the following calculation of NPV:

$$NPV = (£8\ 000 \times 2.322) + (£6\ 000 + 0.592) - £20\ 000 = £2128$$

The project is acceptable. It has a positive NPV.

The IRR approach reveals that the internal rate of return on the project is between 19 per cent and 20 per cent (actually, 19.3 per cent), rendering it acceptable on the basis that the yield on the project is greater than the 14 per cent required rate of return.

The PI method reveals an index of 1.1 (£22 128 divided by £20 000), giving an acceptable result with a PI greater than 1.

On balance, then, the NPV rule is a practical and rational approach to project evaluation. Notwithstanding its intrinsic faults, however, payback analysis is the most popular technique used by managers. This may stem from the ease of calculation. Perhaps, then, both techniques should be used: NPV because it gives a guide to the amount of wealth being created, and payback because it tests a manager's instinctive reaction to cash at risk and because it is very easy to calculate.

RISK ANALYSIS

It was stated earlier that the acceptability of projects depends upon cash flows and risk. Cash flow is operational cash receipts less operational cash expenditure and investment outlay. In the NPV formula, R_t is the difference between operational cash income and operational cash expenditure, and C is the amount of new investment. Where additional investment outflows are anticipated in future periods, they can either be deducted from the cash flows in those future periods or be discounted back to the present and added to C. Both approaches have an equal effect on NPV.

Most managers can readily appreciate cash flows but risk is a more difficult operational concept to grasp. Intuitively it is not liked. In attempting to maximise the value of the company, it can be assumed that neither shareholders nor lenders like risk. Providers of capital expect to be compensated for risk exposure. Risk must be taken into account when estimating the required rate of return on a project.

Risk relates to the volatility of the expected outcome, the dispersion or spread of likely returns around the expected return. In Figure 3.3, the expected return on a project is 16 per cent. Statistically 67 per cent of the actual returns will lie within one standard deviation of the expected return. (The standard deviation is a measure of dispersion or spread.) Accordingly, in Figure 3.3, four out of six outcomes should, on average, lie between 10 per cent and 22 per cent, with 6 per cent being the standard deviation in this example. On average, one time in six the outcome will be above 22 per cent (upside potential). Unfortunately, one time in six the actual return will be less than 10 per cent (downside risk). This is known as the 'one-in-six rule'.

Investors do not like risk and the greater the riskiness of returns on a project, the greater the return they will require. There is a trade-off between risk and return which must be reflected in the discount rates applied to investment opportunities.

Figure 3.4 shows the risk-return relationships of seven projects. The best available project is number 2. It is a high return and low risk project, and represents the most desirable combination of these characteristics. The least desirable project is number 1, which is a low return and high risk project. Investment number 3 will always be preferred to investment number 4, because it is a lower risk project for the same return. Investment number 5 will always be preferred to investment number 4, because it has a higher return for the same level of risk. The highest risk project is number 7, but it also has high expection return. Project 6 is a zero risk investment with a certain outcome. Such an investment might be a short dated government security, where the exact interest rate is known in advance.

If it is assumed that the line joining projects 6, 3 and 7 represents the trade-off between risk and return in the real world, these three projects can be examined further. Since these three projects are on the risk-return line, they have zero net present values. Their expec-

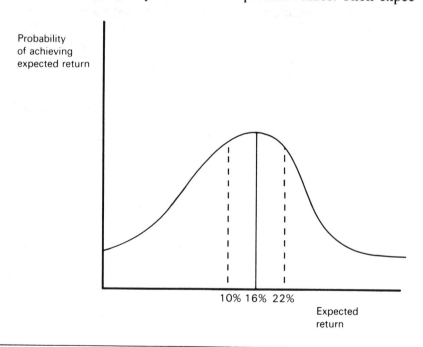

Figure 3.3 Distribution of returns on a project

ted returns are just enough to compensate for their riskiness. Investors can be logical in their choice patterns and yet select either 6 or 3 or 7. Equally, an investor could choose to invest anywhere along the risk-return line 6–3–7 by varying the proportions of his total portfolio.

Modern capital markets are very competitive and can therefore be considered to be efficient in the sense that the prices of securities generally reflect all available information relating to those securities' anticipated cash flows and risks. In such markets, it would be difficult, though not impossible, to earn returns greater than those generally expected for the level of accepted risk. Most securities and portfolios lie fairly close to the hypothetical line 6–3–7.

Managers, however, operate in product markets which are neither perfectly efficient nor perfectly competitive. It is a manger's job to

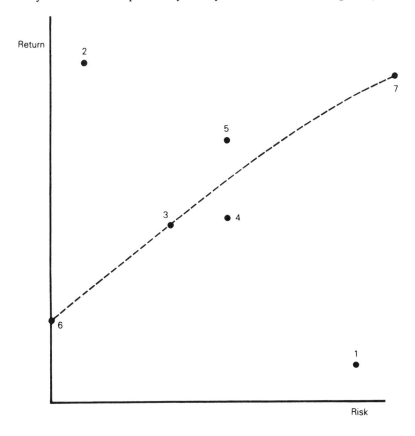

Figure 3.4   Risk-return relationships for alternative projects

locate projects, such as numbers 2 and 5, which have positive net present values and therefore offer wealth-creating opportunities. Not surprisingly, this is a fairly difficult task. It is easy to find projects, such as numbers 4 and 1, which have negative net present values.

Several rules of thumb have been devised for taking risk into account in the investment decision-making process.

Subjective discrimination

Managers can assess their intuitive or 'gut' reactions to risky projects and accept 'less risky' projects with similar net present values. Although it is 'unscientific', this method is fairly easy to use in practice.

Certainty equivalents

A more numerate approach is to reduce the estimated future cash flows to their certainty equivalents and then discount at the rate of interest. The NPV formula should be adjusted as follows:

$$NPV = \sum_{t=1}^{n} \frac{aR_t}{(1 + k)^t} - C$$

where aR_t represents the adjusted cash flows. An obvious problem with this method is that it is difficult to devise a rational approach to cash flow adjustment.

Simulation

The computer facilitates a probabilistic approach to forecasting cash flows along the lines pioneered by Hertz (1964, 1968). Probabilities can be assigned not only to the net cash flows but to all those factors affecting the wealth-creating properties of the project – including units sold, selling price, investment outlay, residual values of plant, fixed and variable costs, and project life. Once the risk variables are identified, and the probability distributions estimated for each variable, the computer program selects at random a large number of possible outcomes. A sufficient number of outcomes will result in a clear picture of the investment's risk-return profile. This approach provides a great deal of information about the risk-return characteristics of an investment, but it does not provide an accept/reject decision.

Risk-adjusted discount rate

A method which is fairly easy to handle and which is theoretically appealing is the risk-adjusted discount rate approach. Perhaps the easiest way to take risk into account is by classifying projects into risk categories. Having established risk classes the NPV formula can be adjusted as follows:

$$NPV = \sum_{t=1}^{n} \frac{R_t}{(1 + k_a)^t} - C$$

where k_a is the risk-adjusted required rate of return. Modern portfolio theory has provided many insights into the trade-off between risk and return in efficient capital markets and the 'new' methods for assessing capital projects are rather similar to the risk-adjusted discount rate method.

THE MODERN APPROACH

A refinement of the risk-adjusted discount rate method is derived from modern portfolio theory. So far, this chapter has discussed the total risk of an investment. The total risk (variability of outcomes) can be broken down into two parts, namely the specific risk and the market risk. The specific risk of a quoted company relates to the company itself, regardless of general movements in the economy. This specific risk can be removed by diversifying across a number of companies. Many studies show that investment in 15 to 20 companies can remove between 80 and 95 per cent of this specific risk. Since specific or unique risk can be avoided, stock markets offer no rewards for taking on specific risk. Investors are rewarded for taking on economic or market risk.

The theory is that the expected return on an investment is a function of the investment's market risk. Furthermore, this can be measured for a quoted company by plotting the periodic returns for a given company against the periodic returns on the All-Share Index, which is a reasonable surrogate for the UK economy. This is illustrated in Figure 3.5. If the return on a company rises 10 per cent when the return on the index rises 10 per cent, and if the return falls 10 per cent when the index falls 10 per cent, then those periodic returns could be plotted and the line of 'best fit' though all the points would be a 45 degree line as shown for Security B. So the slope of the line, its beta (ß) would be 1.0. The beta coefficient is therefore the measure of a security's market risk. Most companies have a beta fairly close to 1.0. A high risk investment such as Security A might have a beta of 2.0 (with periodic returns rising or falling by 20 per cent when the returns on the index rise or fall by only 10 per cent). A low risk investment such as Security C might have a beta of 0.5 (with periodic returns rising or falling by 5 per cent when the index returns rise or fall by 10 per cent). These beta values, measures of market risk, are now available from several sources – for example, in the quarterly Risk Measurement Service of the London Business School.

A company's beta, adjusted for corporate gearing (Pike and Roberts, 1980), offers a guide to the weighed average beta of all the company's projects. It does not give betas for individual projects, products or divisions. These would have to be estimated by relating individual project betas to the firm's average project or by relating changes in anticipated cash flows from individual projects to unanticipated changes in the economy. Estimating betas for individual

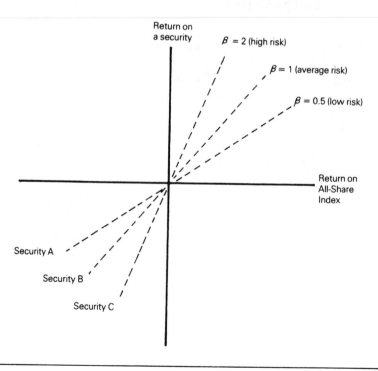

Figure 3.5 Returns on securities

projects is therefore not easy. Corporate betas change over time, are subject to a wide range of error, and historic betas are generally used as proxies for future betas. Nevertheless, this approach to adjusting required rates of return for market risk is probably the most theoretically acceptable method available.

The securities market line (SML) illustrates the trade-off between risk and return, as shown in Figure 3.6. As stated, the expected return on an investment or portfolio is determined by its market risk as measured by beta, rather than total risk because the specific risk can be removed by diversification. The risk free rate of interest, R_f, may be represented by the certain rate of return on a short dated government security. The return on the market, R_m, is the return on the all-share index, which clearly has a beta of 1.0 because it moves up and down in perfect lockstep with itself. A straight line through R_f and R_m is the securities market line, representing the trade-off between risk and return. The expected return on any project, investment or portfolio is dictated by its beta. An investor can invest all resources in R_f or in R_m. Furthermore, an investor can mix R_f and R_m and lie anywhere along the line $R_f - R_m$. For risk-lovers, it is possible to push further up the line by borrowing at R_f and investing in R_m.

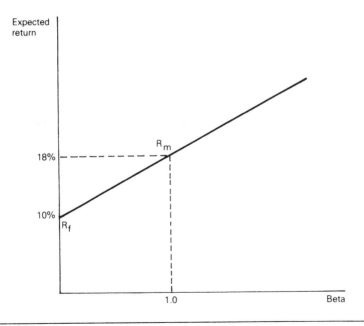

Figure 3.6   The securities market line

The SML represents the minimum rate of return acceptable on all investments, because it represents the opportunity cost, that is the foregone opportunity of equal market risk.

It is necessary to adjust the NPV formula for risk in accordance with the securities market line. The new formula is:

$$NPV = \sum_{t=1}^{n} \frac{R_t}{[1 + R_f + \beta (R_m - R_f)]^t} - C$$

We replace k, in the NPV formula, with $R_f + \beta (R_m - R_f)$. To be more theoretically correct, interest rates and risk premia should be forecast for future periods, but this is extremely difficult.

If it is assumed that the after tax risk-free rate of interest is 10 per cent and that the expected after tax return on the all-share index is 18 per cent, the market risk premium is 8 per cent. The average required rates of return for the three companies shown in Figure 3.5 can be calculated by using an equation known as the capital asset

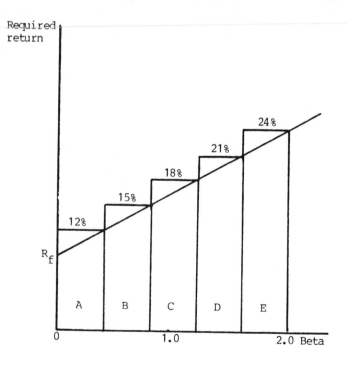

Figure 3.7   Company's project risk classes

pricing model where the expected return $R = R_f + \beta (R_m - R_f)$.
Company A has a beta of 0.5: $R = 10\% + 0.5 (18\% - 10\%) = 14\%$.
Company B has a beta of 1.0: $R = 10\% + 1.0 (18\% - 10\%) = 18\%$.
Company C has a beta of 2.0: $R = 10\% + 2.0 (18\% - 10\%) = 26\%$.
These expected returns are averages, of course, as discussed earlier.
For individual projects or products it is necessary to carry out the
kind of exercise described earlier (see, for example, Broyles and
Franks, 1975).

Perhaps the best that can be done is to establish the required rate
of return on a company's average project and then relate other projects to this average. It should be possible, for a company with an
average beta of 1.0, to classify all projects into perhaps five risk
classes as shown in Figure 3.7.

A worked example

As a practical example of risk analysis, the following case has been
used by the authors in many situations and offers some useful guidelines.

Delta Engineering Limited is an all-equity company, undertaking
high risk maintenance contracts in the UK oil industry. Its historic
beta coefficient has been estimated at 1.5.

At the beginning of 1983, the directors are considering tendering
for a maintenance contract worth about £600 000 gross for each of
the next five years. The directors believe that this contract will be
about twice as risky as the company's average project. The financial
director estimates that the constant after tax risk-free rate of interest
will be 10 per cent and that the overall after tax return on a weighted
average portfolio of industrial investments will be 18 per cent.
Having made several errors in the past when attempting to forecast
future interest rates and risk premia, he is now a firm believer in the
efficient market hypothesis which asserts that the best estimates of
future rates and premia are existing rates and premia.

Equipment costing £400 000 will be required immediately,
although the usual tax benefit (assuming for the sake of simplicity a
first year allowance of 100 per cent) will be received at the end of
1984. The equipment could be sold at the end of the contract for approximately £100 000, taxable at the end of 1988. The incremental
costs associated with the contract are £150 000 each year, excluding
depreciation charges, and the company expects to pay corporation
tax throughout the period at the rate of 52 per cent, payable approximately one year after the 31 December financial year end.

In assessing the project, the directors are advised to take a CAPM

Table 3.4
Delta Engineering – contract estimates (£000s)

Year	1983	1984	1985	1986	1987	1988
Incremental income	600	600	600	600	600	–
Incremental expenditure	(150)	(150)	(150)	(150)	(150)	–
Operational cash flow	450	450	450	450	450	–
Taxation @ + 52%	–	(234)	(234)	(234)	(234)	(234)
After tax cash flow	450	216	216	216	216	(234)
First year allowance (on £400 000)		208				
Balancing charge (on £100 000)						(52)
Sale of equipment					100	
Net cash flow	450	424	216	216	316	(286)

approach to risk analysis. The financial director calculates the figures reproduced in Table 3.4. The required rate of return, k, can be calculated as follows: k = 10% + 3.0 (18% − 10%) = 34%. The beta used is 3.0, twice the company's average beta of 1.5. Using the discounted cash flow factor for 34% (see the final column in Table 3.2), the NPV of the contract can be calculated as shown in Table 3.5. The contract has a net present value of £352 202. The contract is clearly acceptable, offering a wealth-creating opportunity even after taking its riskiness into account.

Table 3.5
Delta Engineering – discounted cash flows

Year	Net cash flows	34% Discount factors	Present value
1983	£450 000	0.746	£335 700
1984	£424 000	0.557	£236 168
1985	£216 000	0.416	£ 89 856
1986	£216 000	0.310	£ 66 960
1987	£316 000	0.231	£ 72 996
1988	(£286 000)	0.173	(£ 49 478)
		Total present value	£752 202
		Capital outlay	(£400 000)
		Net present value	£352 202

SUMMARY OF EVALUATION TECHNIQUES

The evaluation stage in the decision process involves the assembling of information in terms of inputs and outputs and the application of specified investment criteria to produce the optimum project mix. It is important that inputs and outputs are measured by cash flows rather than profit flows.

Only net present value is wholly compatible with the objective of maximising the value of the firm. The internal rate of return criterion is less likely to give correct solutions where mutually exclusive projects differ significantly with respect to the size of investment, pattern of cash flows, or length of project life.

Uncertainty surrounds the future returns from any capital investment. Over the past few decades a variety of techniques has been developed in an attempt to evaluate the risk dimension. These include sensitivity analysis, simulation techniques, decision-tree analysis, and certainty equivalent factors. Nonetheless, the evaluation of risk is not an optional extra. It is fundamental to the appraisal of any investment opportunity or proposal.

Companies vary widely in the extent to which evaluation systems are formalised and sophisticated. Simple models such as payback period are still popular today, and have the merit of being easy to understand and interpret. One reason given for the use of payback analysis is that its strong emphasis on the early years of a project's life is appropriate to recent economic conditions under which long run forecasting has been extremely difficult and hazardous.

Detailed evaluation of major projects is essential but it is only one stage of a complex investment process. The rest of this chapter considers the remaining stages.

PROJECT REVIEW AND APPROVAL

Once the evaluation stage has been completed, the investment proposal moves through the various levels of the organisational hierarchy until it is eventually approved or rejected. It is well to remember that this process, like the whole of the capital budgeting operation, is not an abstraction from reality, considered theoretically in an academic setting. It takes place in an active organisation with all the attendant problems of human relations, ambitions and motivations, and of political manoeuvring. The willingness of a manager to sponsor a project often depends not so much on the intrinsic merits of the project as on the possible enhancement of his own standing as a manager. It is for that reason that some economically viable projects ultimately founder and never reach the approval stage. Middle management may well be more risk-averse than senior management, in which case very few projects with high rewards and moderate or high risk will ever be sponsored. In most organisations a decision maker appraises the sponsor as much as the project.

For most firms, the approval stage is little more than a formal endorsement of commitments already given or pledged. However, this stage performs a vital quality control service. If the earlier stages have been executed correctly and if established criteria are met, there is little reason to reject proposals at this late stage. Senior management should review the proposal and ask the following questions. Are the estimates well based and reasonably accurate? What is the likelihood (and cost) of failure? Have all available alternatives been explored fully? Are there any unquantified aspects to be considered? No matter how sophisticated the evaluation techniques employed, the effectiveness of a capital budgeting process is dependent largely upon the accuracy of cash flow estimates. These estimates are, in their turn, dependent upon the validity and soundness of the assumptions concerning a number of economic variables, as depicted in Figure 3.8.

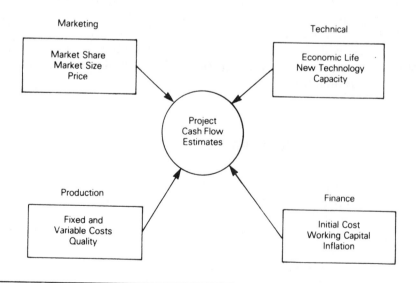

Figure 3.8   Economic assumptions influencing cash flow estimates

Over the past decade the problem of estimating rates of inflation has caused great concern. A recent survey revealed that, although firms have improved their approach to the inflation problem over the past five years, only 29 per cent of the largest organisations surveyed specify separate rates for costs and revenues. The most popular approach is to specify cash flows in constant prices and to apply a real rate of return (that is, excluding inflation) to these figures. While it is clear that some firms are very careful in their calculation of the real rate of return, many have given little thought to the full implications of excluding the impact of inflation in hurdle rates and cash flows.

The senior management review should examine also the likelihood of project failure and the associated costs. Although the main reason for failure is usually poor estimation of economic variables, failure could also result from such problems as delays in project construction and implementation. A formal assessment of those risks should be conducted, to explore ways of reducing the probability and cost of failure. Wherever possible, an abandonment option (that is, an opportunity at specified times to abandon the project and liquidate the investment) should be built into the project's programme. This can have the double effect of reducing the anticipated cash outflows and reducing the riskiness of the project.

PROJECT COST CONTROL

It may be many years before the success or failure of a long-term capital investment is fully appreciated. In the meantime, the decision maker will have judged many investment options with little informational feedback on the profitability of earlier projects. Learning by trial and error is a slow and costly business and some form of project control and review is necessary. Figure 3.9 outlines the stages and information requirements for such a control and review system. It includes the use of critical path analysis, which provides a systematic approach to the planning and control of project implementation, and regular capital expenditure progress forecasts of overspending and underspending against plan. Review information will include feedback on investment performance against plan and, where appropriate, a post-completion audit review.

The primary purpose of these reports is to furnish management with information on the success or otherwise of the investment so that the quality of future investment decisions will be improved. It may become apparent, for example, that sales estimates are consistently higher than actual results. This kind of information can be used to improve the quality of the marketing data input into the evaluation process.

Potential for cost control exists in the early stages of implementation – such as in the design, tendering and procurement stages. Figure 3.10 shows the relationship between project life and cost control potential. As projects move towards completion and become fully operational, the potential for cost control diminishes rapidly. Typically, cost reporting increases in inverse ratio to cost control potential. In summary, sound investment decisions require a comprehensive capital investment planning and control process. Investment control and review should, as far as possible, control the cost and timing of project implementation and improve the planning of future investments.

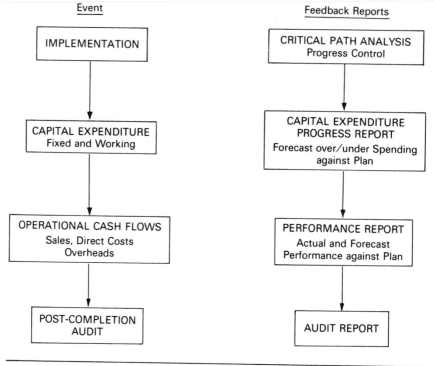

Figure 3.9   Implementation and control

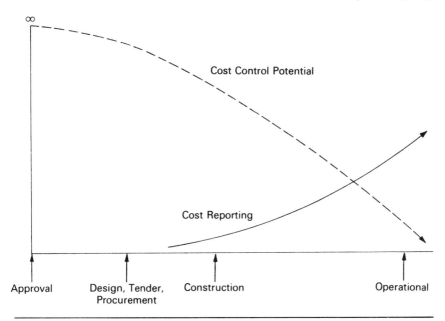

Figure 3.10   Cost control potential

REFERENCES AND FURTHER READING

Bierman, H., and Smidt, S., *The Capital Budgeting Decision*, 4th edn, New York: Macmillan, 1976.

Broyles, J., and Franks, J., 'Capital project appraisal: a modern approach', *Managerial Finance*, 1975.

Cyert, R.M., Dill, W.R., and March J.G., 'The role of expectations in business decision-making', *Administrative Science Quarterly*, 1958.

Hertz, D.B., 'Risk analysis in capital investment', *Harvard Business Review*, January–February 1964.

Hertz, D.B., 'Investment policies that pay off', *Harvard Business Review*, January–February 1968.

King, P., 'Is the emphasis of capital budgeting theory misplaced?' *Journal of Business Finance and Accounting*, Spring 1975.

Levy, H., and Sarnat, M., *Capital Investment and Financial Decisions*, 2nd edn, Englewood Cliffs, N.J.: Prentice-Hall, 1982.

Lowes, B., and Dobbins, R., 'Objective setting: a corporate planning approach', *Managerial Finance*, 1978.

Merrett, A.J., and Sykes, A., *The Finance and Analysis of Capital Projects*, 2nd edn, London: Longman, 1973.

Myers, S.C., *Modern Developments in Financial Management*, Hinsdale, Ill.: Dryden, 1976.

Pike, R., and Roberts, B., 'How to adjust investment hurdle rates for risk', *Management Accounting*, June 1980.

Sharpe, W.F., *Portfolio Theory and Capital Markets*, New York: McGraw-Hill, 1970.

Solomon, E., *The Theory of Financial Management*, New York: Columbia University Press, 1963.

Van Horne, J.C., 'Capital budgeting decisions involving combinations of risky investments', *Management Science*, October 1966.

Van Horne, J.C., *Financial Management and Policy*, 5th edn, Englewood Cliffs, N.J.: Prentice-Hall, 1980.

Weingartner, H.M., *Mathematical Programming and the Analysis of Capital Budgeting Problems*, Englewood Cliffs, N.J.: Prentice-Hall, 1963.

Weingartner, H.M., 'The excess present value index – a theoretical basis and critique', *Journal of Accounting Research*, Autumn, 1963.

4

Budgeting and cash forecasting

Douglas Garbutt

Every organisation makes plans. Some plans are more formal than others and some organisations plan more formally than others but all make some attempt to consider the risk and opportunities which lie ahead and how to confront them. In most businesses this process is formalised at least in the short term, with considerable effort put into preparing annual budgets and monitoring performance against those budgets.

In this chapter Douglas Garbutt explains how short-term planning is formalised in the budgetary process. A budget is merely a collation of plans and forecasts, expressed largely but not exclusively in financial terms. Even though many organisations do not plan formally for more than the year ahead, the annual budget must be set in the context of longer-term plans, which are likely to exist even if they have not been made explicit.

Garbutt emphasises that budgets should be a management tool rather than merely an accounting exercise, and stresses that the most important element in the budget process is management – the individuals and the managerial process. He outlines a budget framework in which management is a crucial ingredient, determining the organisation's goals, the design of the budgeting system, its implementation and operation and the monitoring routines, as well as the ultimate rewards and penalties for success or failure.

The author explores the issues in each of the three main stages he has identified, concentrating especially on the design of a budgeting system. He explains in detail how a budget cycle must be developed, and that managers must decide at what level budgets are to be developed. He also considers both top-down and bottom-up budgeting, and contrasts static and flexible budgets.

Computer systems can help to make the budgeting process both more meaningful and easier to handle, and Garbutt explains the basis of computer models. He shows that any budget is a model, and that if this model is computerised it will allow easier computation and greater flexibility. Management will be able to explore alternative scenarios much more easily, for example, and apply sensitivity analysis much more thoroughly.

In the final section the author considers how the budget can best be used to measure actual performance. He considers appropriate financial ratios and points out the need to match measures to the objectives included in the budget. He also explains that the monitoring process is an input into the next budget cycle, affecting future strategic and operational goals.

A budget is a plan of future activities for an organisation. It is expressed mainly in financial terms but usually incorporates many non-financial quantitative measures as well. As in other areas of management accounting, terms are often used interchangeably. To avoid confusion it is therefore worth clarifying the main ones.

Budgeting is the whole process of designing, implementing and operating short-term or operating budgets, sometimes called revenue budgets to distinguish them from capital budgets. The main emphasis in this short term budgeting process is the provision of resources to support plans which are being implemented.

Collectively, the budgets for an organisation are called a **master budget**. It is generally assumed they will be drawn up for a set period, often a year, and that the plans will cover all on-going operations and activities.

These plans are mainly a continuation of existing operations, modified to meet expected changes but also including new facilities coming on stream. Proposals for new activities should be evaluated under separate capital budgeting procedures (see Chapter 3) but once such proposals are approved and come on stream, they are incorporated into the master budget.

A **forecast** is a prediction of the future state of the world, not necessarily the whole world, but in this connection those aspects of the world which are relevant to and likely to affect or impinge on future activities.

A **plan** is a set of actions activities and target which are intended to modify the future state of the world, and therefore the forecast conditions, in favour of the planning entity.

STRATEGY AND LONG-RANGE PLANNING

As organisations grow in size and their activities become more international, they are forced to look further ahead in their planning, perhaps five, ten or twenty years. Managers seeking to forecast far ahead recognise that, of necessity, their plans become more general, more uncertain in their details, and more subject to change. Conversely, managers are able to give their plans greater precision as they come nearer to fruition. The annual budget is the crystallisation of strategic plans for the immediate period ahead and as such it is detailed and precise. Looking ahead for several years, the corporate planners may identify the basic strategy of the firm and the gaps which exist between future needs and present capacities.

A budget prepared in this context is not simply an extension of what has gone before, it is also a step towards closing the gap between the present and the future position to which the organisation is striving. Strategic management accounting requires a radically different stance from the management accountant and this has already been considered in depth in Chapter 2.

Budgets are a clear expression of what the organisation can realistically achieve in the coming period. Strategic plans state the directions which top management expects the organisation to take in the medium to long term. A long-range plan is a statement of the preliminary targets and actions to be taken by an organisation to achieve its strategic plans, together with broad estimates of the resources to be deployed and procured for each year in the period covered. As each period comes closer, the estimates become more detailed and precise until, finally, they become the basis for a forthcoming annual budget.

Figure 4.1 shows the relationship between annual and long-term budgets in a Local Authority.

BUDGETING AS A MANAGEMENT TOOL

A budget is of little use unless it is a management plan of action. Otherwise it is purely a device for improved accountancy services. Of course, the use of budgets shifts the focus of accountancy from reporting the past to influencing the future and requires a great deal of financial analysis in translating the plans into financial terms, but the ultimate effectiveness of budgets depends on their use by managers in making decisions.

67

Planning and budgeting

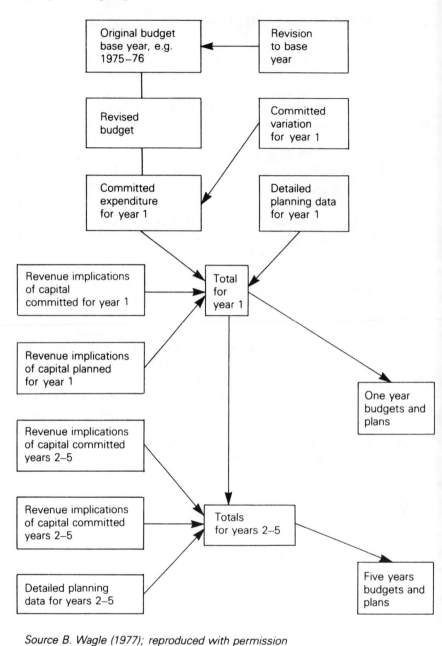

Source B. Wagle (1977); reproduced with permission

Figure 4.1   Annual and long-term budgets in a Local Authority

The initiative for setting up a budgeting system may come from the financial manager in the first place and budgeting may be a salutory exercise in compelling managers to make plans and forecasts but in the long run budgeting must be the servant of top management.

COMPUTER-BASED MODEL BUILDING

A model is a representation of a chosen reality, and an organisation which chooses to construct a budget is thereby building a model. To be useful, budgets must be realistic but at the same time budgets cannot include every detail of reality. The model must therefore concentrate on what is significant. In practice, the central model in budgeting is the accountancy model of the firm which is built up from a series of logical chains.

For instance, making a sale leads to an increase of debtors and, after a time delay, to an increase in cash. Making prediction of future sales means predicting previous production, which must be preceded by the purchase of materials, which gives rise to trade creditors and eventually to a fall in cash when payments are made. These relationships are expressed in a series of accounting equations which can all be related to the basic balance sheet relationship:

$$Assets = Liabilities + Owners\ equity$$

However, although the basic logical building blocks are simple enough, they have to be used to build a realistic model of all the major aspects of an organisation. Thus the final model may be very complex.

The model may also be used in several ways. At the prediction stage, it may be desirable to explore the effects of alternative policies over several years. At the control stage it will be desirable to compare actual to predicted results month by month or even day by day. Large volumes of data may be stored and processed and handled on various levels of aggregation.

Computer-based models allow greater range for changing assumptions, more flexibility in processing and reporting.

A computer requires the user to identify both logic and data and major computerised modelling systems deal with each of these separately. Logic is the set of rules or chain of reasoning which, in this context, underlines the budgets. Data are the raw facts or observations, in this case financial or quantitative, which are incorporated in the budgets or which represent the actual results.

Logic can be tested using trivial data but, once agreed, the computer can apply the logic quickly to large volumes of data. Budget Managers can then devote themselves to clarify what should and should not be done and leave the drudgery of the number crunching to the machine. The advantage of separating logic and data is that the same logic can then be applied to many different sets of data.

Circumstances can easily change the data used in budgeting. For instance, a run of bad weather, war or revolution, a change in tax rates, a new invention, can all affect a sales forecast on which many other budgets have been based. This may mean a complete recalculation of forecasted cash flows, balance sheets and so on. For the person using manual calculations, this may mean days of work. For the computer user, provided the logic of the system is unchanged, the problem is less serious. The new forecast can easily be used to calculate a new set of budgets. Indeed, the computer will be used systematically to answer 'What if . . . ?' questions such as: Suppose we sell 10% more in Patagonia? 'What happens if the Chancellor puts up VAT to 20%?' and so on.

Sensitivity analysis

The use of 'What if . . . ?' questions can be applied systematically to test how much outputs (i.e. results) depend on a change in various inputs. Taking one factor at a time and holding others constant, does a 10 per cent change in input produce a change in output? Is the change more or less than the input change? The results are sometimes surprising. Facts which an organisation tends to ignore may turn out to be very important. Others, which are considered of vital importance may turn out to be of little account. There are many useful practical case studies of financial budgeting models in J.W. Bryant (1982).

CONSTITUENTS OF A BUDGETING SYSTEM

There are a number of elements in a budgeting system, as shown in Figure 4.2.

It also shows how financial and computing services must underpin the whole budgeting process. Figure 4.2 also shows the separation of the logical structure of the budgets from the organisation's data base. This chapter is mostly concerned with the logical structure of budgets and how to build up a budgeting system. Finally, Figure 4.2 indicates

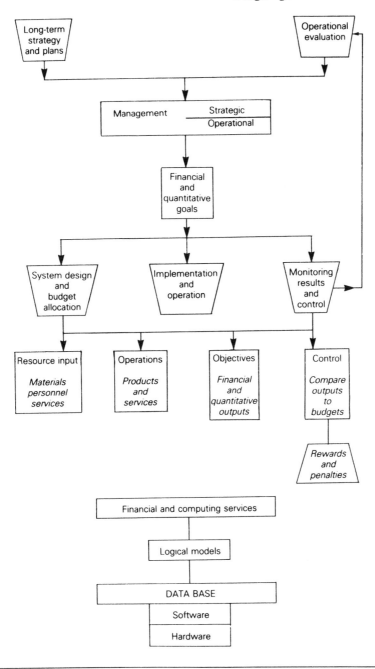

Figure 4.2   Constituents of a budgeting system

the need for software and hardware to support the financial and computing services.

Management

The most important element in the budgeting system is management. The style and system of management determine the organisational approach to problems, including the methods of budgeting, but experience of budgeting will also tend to influence management towards formalisation of practices. Budget practices should reflect management structures.

Organisations are composed of groups of people who work together towards the achievement of common objectives. Or, at least, they should! Organisations are based on the principle of division of labour between people. Greater efficiency can be achieved by specialisation and as organisations grow, so it becomes necessary to have formal mechanisms which co-ordinate activities and serve as vehicles for communication. 'If only production would supply us with what the customers want. . .' Sales complain, to be answered by Production 'If only you people would sell what we've been set up to make. . .'!

Participation in budget setting. Senior managers from all major activities *should* play a leading role in developing their own budgets. Some organisations insist that all levels of management should participate in setting budgets, since this can produce more realistic targets, lead to better understanding of corporate objectives and the constraints within which all organisations work. As a consequence, it is hoped that personnel will be better motivated to achieve budget levels of efficiency and activity. Certainly, all personnel can gain from clear targets and some organisations provide incentive payments based on budget achievement.

FINANCIAL AND QUANTITATIVE GOALS

From a budgeting point of view a primary purpose of management must be to set financial goals for the organisation. Most financial values can be analysed in terms of some quantitative element multiplied by a price, so setting financial goals also implies setting quantitative goals where applicable.

Notice that in Figure 4.2, management derives its goals from long-term strategy and plans and evaluation of operations. The diagram indicates the separation found in some organisations, between strategic and operational management. It has been said that if you want a person to run an operation, don't also ask them to worry about whether it should be done or not.

Most businesses have a variety of objectives, depending on the type of product or service which the organisation provides.

There are a wide range of business objectives which are difficult, if not impossible to quantify. For example, organisations often differ in the emphasis they place on objectives such as maintaining good customer and community relations; developing employee expertise; leading in research and innovation; providing market leadership; and so on. The fact that objectives may not be fully quantifiable does not mean they are unimportant, in fact, all organisations have their own styles and approaches which may well be the secrets of success.

Performance indicators may be of some value in monitoring variables which are hard to quantify.

Budgeting systems should be developed in relation to quantifiable objectives as far as possible but not neglecting the non-quantifiable factors.

Despite their diversity, all organisations do share many characteristics, especially in the financial dimension. If objectives are to be achieved, it is essential that sufficient finances should be available to procure and deploy the resources in material, human and physical terms. But resources have a cost which must be recovered from sales revenues, and sufficient profit must then remain to meet shareholders needs for dividends, lenders needs for interest and repayment and government needs for tax revenue. Businesses must generate sufficient profits to meet the expectations of those who provide capital and also to generate growth. In deciding prices, in controlling costs or levels of activity, businesses look for an optimum level of profit. Looking for a maximum might result in a short term bonanza but lead to long-term instability or collapse, and survival is usually a strong business objective. The optimum balances short-term against long-term gain.

Another way to look at business operations is to consider the increase in market value which results from organisational activities. Since the value of bought-in materials and services is excluded, value added includes both profit and employee remuneration (see Chapter 20).

Capital forecasts. An important aspect of budgeting is obtaining sufficient capital to provide the long and short-term assets – the fixed and circulating capital – to support the planned level of operations.

For businesses there are two main sources of new capital: owners equity and borrowing, to which might be added a third, Government grants. In different ways, each of these sources of capital looks to the organisation to produce a profit from operations. Lenders do so in the expectation of receiving interest payments and eventual repayment of their loan.

Shareholders expect some form of return by way of dividends and/or capital growth and presumably the Government makes grants in the hope that future economic growth will provide enough receipts from taxes to justify its interventions in the market place.

A business may have adequate capital and be making sufficient profits but still fail to survive if it runs out of cash. This can easily happen if the balance between fixed and current assets is wrong, or if, within working capital, the balance between cash and stocks or debtors or creditors is wrong. Inflation also can affect overall demands for cash. For these reasons, it is increasingly being recognised that liquidity or the ability to meet all financial demands as they arise must be identified as a key objective in the budgeting process (see Garbutt 1985).

The hierarchy of goals

Some organisations are able to arrange their goals in a hierarchy based on the end-means logical chains which underlie the accounting model. This means the organisation may, for instance, look for a Master Budget which produces a balance sheet and income statement which conform to requirements for ratios such as: debt to equity; return on total assets; return on shareholders funds; working capital ratios; rate of asset turnover; and so on.

Ratio analysis as such is outside the scope of this book but is dealt with in many accounting text books, such as Garbutt 1972. Some significant ratios are defined later in this chapter.

Referring again to Figure 4.2, it can be seen that setting financial and quantitative goals leads to three phases of budgeting:

1   System design and budget allocation.
2   Implementation and operation.
3   Monitoring results and control.

Each of these will now be considered in turn, but before doing so, consider the four stages which underlie these budgeting phases, and which profoundly influence the budget model which the organisation has to build.

These four stages lead logically from one to the other, from left to right in Figure 4.2. Resource inputs flow into the organisations operations – its production of products and/or services. Measurements of the outputs indicate whether the financial and quantitative objectives have been achieved. Finally, in the fourth stage, outputs are compared to budgets to aid judgement of results. Notice that at this stage, the organisation will have to consider the rewards and penalties which may follow from the results.

SYSTEM DESIGN AND BUDGET ALLOCATION

Setting up a Master set of budgets is a complicated process. Organisations exist in a changing environment with which the organisation interacts, and as it does so, the organisation itself changes and learns. Organisational skills are developed and adapted. New technology affects the style and design of products, the ways in which products are made, and services presented. The tastes of customers changes, new markets open up and old markets decline or are subject to new competition.

Drawing up a new set of budgets should never be seen as a routine process. If sales revenues are expected to rise by 10 per cent, this does not mean that costs will rise proportionally. Nor, if inflation is expected to be 5 per cent does this mean all budgeted costs should rise by 5 per cent. Some might well go down and others rise by more than 5 per cent.

Budget structure

The structure of the budgets will normally be based on the organisational structure and, again, changes may have occurred since the last budgets were prepared. Organisation structures reflect many factors in the activities undertaken. For instance, the sales and marketing organisation reflects area and regional coverage, products and product groups, and channels of marketing. Production organisational structure reflects these factors but is also influenced by technology and skills factors. Head office budgets are divided between line functions in selling and production and to the provision of central services such as R & D, computer and accounting services. In the process of preparing budgets, diverse quantitative and financial measures will be required.

Budget model level

The budgeting managers must establish the level at which they intend to establish their budget model. The budget does not have to encompass all possible detail. For example, in the 1970s when the engineering group Turner and Newall introduced monthly accounts throughout the group they had to decide whether to computerise their budgets:

1 At product level at which 10 000 standard costs were produced; or
2 At product family level at which there were 200 families; or
3 At product group level at which there were about 20 groups.

In fact, they chose the intermediate level (2) of 200 families, although this allowed them to incorporate aggregation procedures into their model, which meant they could also produce the reports required at the product group (3) level. This meant that data was collected and analysed normally at the product level for input to the computer model (see Crawford 1982).

The budgeting cycle

An important element in the design of the budgeting system is the establishment of the budgeting cycle, which lays down the time sequence over which preparation of the budgeting will be completed. This is not normally a straightforward, one-directional process.

The implications of change on budgets are not always intuitively obvious and because of this the budgeting process has to be one of trial and error – an iterative process. In an ideal world the following process might apply.

The budgeting cycle is best triggered off by top management issuing budget guidelines, perhaps six months or more before the commencing date of the new budget. These guidelines should lay down the broad parameters within which the organisation is expected to operate in the budget period if the organisational goals are to be achieved.

Among the questions answered by the guidelines are:

1 How will sales be made up in terms of products and market locations?
2 What level of sales and market shares for each product should be achieved?
3 What influences will operate on costs in terms of inflation, changes in exchange rates, and industrial relations?

4 What restraints will be placed on capital expenditures?
5 What new production facilities will be on stream?
6 What shut-downs and closures are envisaged?

Draft or preliminary budgets are now prepared for each division or section of the organisation as the guidelines percolate down the hierarchy and the implications are worked out.

A reverse process then starts, as the draft budgets are assembled together to constitute a preliminary master budget, based on the first guidelines. These may take several months.

At this stage, we can expect conflicts to have arisen within the organisation over the draft budgets and that these will necessitate a review of the guidelines. Top management will review both guidelines and the preliminary budgets, indicate the lines along which the conflicts are to be resolved and remit back the preliminary budgets for further revision. The new guidelines and policy decisions are used as the basis as final budgets are prepared.

When final budgets have been drawn up, they are considered by top management and copies are signed and authorised for implementation on the first day of the new budget period.

That is a rather idealised account. Since the process *is* interactive, the comings and goings on budget-setting are often continuous.

Types of budget

At the system design stage it will be necessary to consider the type of budgets which are to be applied in the light of the various aspects of management accounting which are considered in later chapters of this book, particularly Chapters 6 to 11.

However, a fully comprehensive budget which reflects all the complexities of the organisation is best built up gradually over a period of years. This can be done in several ways:

1 From the top downwards. This approach gives a set of budgets at the most senior level which are immediately useful and which secure the support of senior management for the development of more realistic budgets based on increasing depth and complexity of detail.

2 From the bottom up. This approach yields low-level budgets based on realistic detail which are immediately useful in day to day control. A series of budget models can be built up, section by section and gradually extended to cover the organisation as a whole. The difficulties with this approach are that a general benefit is not immediately obvious, top-level support is less likely

and there may be problems in linking modules into a comprehensive picture.

Static and flexible budgets. There are some activities for which a fixed or static budget may be allocated but such budgets are often unsatisfactory.

It is preferable to use flexible budgets but this is usually only possible when the level of spending can be clearly related to some underlying measure of activity. The clearest case is that of standard product costs for direct labour, direct materials and, to a lesser extent, variable overheads. Suppose a product has a standard material cost of 5 kilos at £2 per kilo = £10 per unit. If expected production in a year is 12 000 units, then the annual budget would be 12 000 × £10 = £120 000. However, if the production rises to 13 000 units, then material costs of £130 000 would be allowed in the budget. In profit the cash terms, the assumption behind flexible budgeting is that increased sales mean improved profits and cash flows although the timing of cash flows might not be so straight forward.

The structure of the master budget

The master budget is composed of two kinds of budget, operating and financial.

Operating budgets: The operating budgets must closely reflect two dimensions of the organisation:

1   *The organisational structure*: All revenues and expenditures *must* be attributed to the budget centre and managers responsible for them. At the control stage, later, a system of responsibility accounting reports *must* be built up to inform responsible managers of the progress of actual results against budgets.
2   *The products or programmes*: In this dimension, the budget information is organised to show the revenues, costs, contributions, profits and levels of production/sales activity for each product or programme produced by the organisation.

These two dimensions reflect in different ways the locational, procurement, stock-holding, production, and distribution factors which also affect the organisation. Organisations differ, also, in the type of structure they operate, for instance, divisional/departmental or holding company/subsidiaries.

Obviously, then, the detailed breakdown of the operating budgets will differ considerably between organisations, and Figure 4.3 shows a simple, general pattern only.

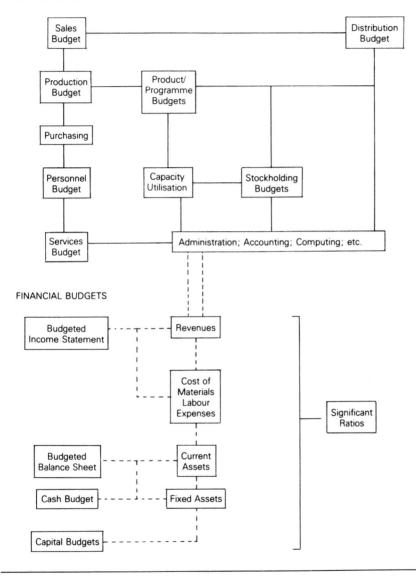

Figure 4.3   The master budget – a general structure

Financial budgets: The financial budgets are much more uniform, at least in the general pattern, because they reflect the accounting model. The main financial budgets are:

1 *Budgeted income statement or profit and loss account*: This follows generally accepted accounting principles in matching expected expenses against expected revenues to show the operation profit for the period. A budgeted statement showing interest, tax and dividend payments may also be produced.

2 *Budgeted balance sheet*: This shows the budgeted assets liabilities and owners equity and may also show additional financing requirements needed to support the planned budget.

3 *Cash forecasting*: The cash budget shows the cash flows arising from the operational budgets and the profit and asset structure. There are several ways in which it can be prepared.

   (a) The receipts and payments method: In this method the expected receipts and payment for budget sub-periods of, usually, a month or four weeks, are calculated from the planning sales, production and stock-holdings, taking into account expected time delays.

   (b) The adjusted income method: In this method the annual cash flows are calculated by adjusting the sales revenues and cost figures for delays in receipts and payments (changes in debtors and creditors) and eliminating non-cash items such as depreciation.

   (c) The sales percentage method: In this method, the budgeted balance sheet is predicted by expressing each type of asset, and short-term liabilities as percentage of the expected sales.

   The profit is also calculated as a percentage of sales, so that the increase in owners equity can be forecast.

Known adjustments may be made to long-term liabilities and the balance sheet will then show if additional finance is needed.

The most useful method in annual budgeting is the receipts and payments method but for a fuller treatment of cash budgeting see Bryant (1982). Figure 4.3 shows the general structure of the master budget.

Notice that the capital budget has been shown under the financial budgets because the annual budget may disclose a need for new capital investments and, also, the costs and revenues of any new projects coming on stream will need to be incorporated in the short-term budgets. However, as has already been pointed out, capital budgeting is normally a separate process (see Chapter 3).

A number of additional financial statements, such as a Sources and Application of funds statement, or schedules or loan service payments or capital raising schedules may be produced.

Significant ratios

It is important that the financial budgets conform to the expectations of top management, in respect of adequate capital, liquidity and profitability, factors which were discussed earlier. In addition, financial managers will use ratios to assess the financial efficiency.

There are no standard ratios and a wide range are used by individual firms, in inter-firm comparison schemes and by stockbrokers' analysts. For a comprehensive treatment of this subject, see Westwick (1973).

Some of the ratios commonly used are:

	Formula
Tests of liquidity	
Current ratio	Curret assets
	Current liabilities
Times interest earned	Earnings before interest and tax
	Interest charges
Debtors collection period	Debtors
	Sales per day
Creditors payment period	Creditors
	Purchase per day
Tests of profitability	
Margin on sales	Net profit after tax
	Sales revenues
Return on assets	Earnings before interest and tax
	Total assets
Return on net worth	Net profit after tax
	Owners equity
Tests of capital adequacy	
Asset turnover	Sales revenues
	Total assets
Stock turnover	Cost of goods sold
	Average stocks
Fixed asset turnover	Sales revenues
	Fixed assets
Gearing	Total Debt
	Total Assets

Budget management structure

An important aspect of designing the budget system and making the resource allocations is the management of the budget process itself. The arrangements made will reflect the management style of the organisation.

In some cases, budgets are seen as the product of financial experts and the responsibility lies in the finance and accounting function. This approach is often taken by highly centralised organisations, in which case the budgets are very much the creation, and creature, of top management.

In some systems a budget committee is formed with the managing director as chairman, and all divisional or departmental heads are members. The chief accountant or finance director then acts as secretary to the committee which assumes responsibility for issuing guidelines, discussing preliminary budgets, agreeing the final master budget and implementing budgetary control. This means that all budget revisions are to be agreed by this committee and they should also approve and monitor the arrangements for control reports.

The MD acting as chairman gives the committee authority and the other members in their turn chair a series of sub-committee which produce the draft budgets for each section or division of the organisation. A sub-committee is drawn from the section heads within each organisational segment budget and an accountant acts as secretary.

The accountancy/finance staff provide technical support for each committee but they also provide a useful channel for co-ordination, especially in avoiding misunderstanding of the guidelines or informing sub-committees of developments in other meetings which may be relevant to their deliberations. Over the years, a lot of informal rules and precedents are set and the accounting staff act as the guardians of these.

BUDGET IMPLEMENTATION AND OPERATION

The dividing line between this phase and the preceding (or the following) phase is not hard and fast, especially if all levels of managers are involved in the system design and the budget allocation process. The main value of a budget system is in the conduct of operations when the budget is implemented.

The master budget and its various sections constitute the formal authority for the responsible managers to expand resources on materials, labour and facilities within the limits laid down. So far as the accounting function is concerned at this stage, they will authorise payments which fall within the budget limit. Of course, the manager is also expected to exercise reasonable control over spending and to make economies, even on the budget if this can be done without impairing efficiency or quality or achievement of objectives. With static budgets, the accountants will apply fixed limits but if flexible budgets have been agreed, the budgets will be adjusted up or down, according to the activity levels actually achieved for any period.

On the revenue side, managers concerned with selling products and services will treat their budgets as minima and hope to over-fulfil their targets if this is possible at the prices set. A selling budget may be set in terms of the contribution expected from sales, irrespective of the product mix. But in the short term there are often constraints on the variation of mix which the production function can tolerate.

MONITORING, RESULTS AND CONTROL

At this phase of the budgeting process, the budgeting system must be designed to produce reports on the results of operations, the extent to which financial and quantitative objectives have been achieved. The reports must contain comparisons between actual performance and the budget. Variance accounting is dealt with in Chapter 8.

Relevant information

Budget reports must contain information which is relevant to management decisions. At the system design stage, it is important to ensure that the costs and activities for which the budget is drawn up coincide with the authority and responsibilities of the managers concerned. During implementation the data collected should then be recorded within the same framework as the budget. If responsibilities are shuffled about between design and control stages, then the budgets should be revised accordingly.

Data are raw facts. Information is data arranged in ways which are meaningful to a user. Comparisons of actual costs/revenues to budgets will not be meaningful unless the budgets are relevant and the actuals are measured on the same basis.

Timing and intervals

Comparisons of actuals to budgets must as far as possible be provided at intervals which coincide with the time spans over which managers exercise their discretion and the results can be measured and observed.

Reporting intervals should be neither too long nor too short. Senior and top management will require reports on incomes and profitability at least monthly. Departmental and section managers require weekly cost and sales reports. Foremen and supervisors may be provided with daily reports on material usage, labour efficiency, sales and orders received. The intervals should not be too short because managers may then cease to pay attention to them but they should not be too long, because information would be too late for managers to take action.

With an on-line real-time computer-based system, it is possible to provide instant access to control information. If a batch processing mode is followed, it is important to schedule the production of budget control reports as a by-product of data processing whenever a new batch is processed. Scheduling control reports as separate operations may lead to unacceptable delays. Relevant information is still no good if it comes too late.

Within a broad context, a company is subject to this kind of evaluation when the Stock Market compares declared profits to expectations. If profits do not meet expectations, the price of the company's shares will fall. Many a company chairman has had the experience of declaring record profit and sales, only to see the price of his company's shares fall because the brokers were expecting more!

Companies report to their shareholders at least annually, but budget reports must be made more frequently because their purpose is to inform managers whether their performance is up to scratch in good time so that corrective actions may be taken before a situation becomes irretrievable.

Flexibility and motivation

The budgetary process is necessarily a formal process and it tends to introduce or reinforce formalisation. Critics argue that rigid budgeting procedures can be costly, counter productive and demotivating. Certainly,the costs of any system and its development, should be carefully evaluated in terms of the likely benefits. In the case of budgets, a crucial question is: are the budgets actually used by managers and, if so, do they improve decisions?

From a top management view-point, the crucial payoff from budgeting is at the final stage when control indicates whether the organisation is achieving the results aimed for. Those responsible for the budgeting system must constantly check the end results and maintain sufficient flexibility to adapt the budgets to the needs and structure of management, not the other way round.

REWARDS AND PENALTIES

An effective system of budgetary reporting inevitably carries with it implications of rewards for good performance and penalties for bad but many organisations integrate incentives with budget performance.

For example, a newsagent firm pays branch managers a bonus based on the branch net profit. Head Office produces budgets and area managers receive weekly figures of sales by each branch, the result of stock checks and a quarterly profit and loss account for each branch. The results are discussed with each branch manager and corrective action taken. Branches are graded by weekly gross profit. Unprofitable branches may be closed or sold off. Managers who do not perform are given further training but if they still do not succeed, their services are dispensed with. Another firm offers its salesmen bonuses, prizes, merit ratings which enhance basic salaries and opportunities for promotion on their performance as a percentage of sales by value. Salesmen may complain that the man who sells most, in the metropolitan area, has also a bigger budget to meet and a country salesmen may win promotion by a relatively small increase on a small budget. As targets are updated in the light of performance, there are also complaints that no one wins twice in a row!

OPERATIONAL EVALUATION

Referring again in Figure 4.2, this shows that the function of monitoring, results and control in the budgeting process leads back up the diagram to operational evaluation, which then feeds into Management, alongside long-term strategy and plans. Here, the assumption is that whereas the monitoring process is more or less continuous throughout the budget period, operational evaluation takes place less frequently. Indeed, the normal time for operational evaluation is when top management is considering the guidelines to be set at the commencement of the budgeting cycle. Whereas monitoring requires managers to pay close attention to day by day results, operational evaluation asks them to take a step away from operations and look at them and the budgeting systems as a whole.

In evaluating operations and the budgetary control system, management should be considering whether the objectives set are realistically attainable. Is the organisation proceeding in the right direction? Is it going too fast or too slow? What things is it not doing and what is it not doing well? It may be that a different group of managers considers these long-term questions from those who operate short-term control, but in that case, both groups need access to the reports on operational and financial performance which the budgeting system produces.

Maybe there will also be a need for special reports and for special exercises in budget planning using the data and computer models to explore 'what if . . .' questions and to conduct sensitivity analyses. From time to time or if circumstances change radically, there may be a need for a major overhaul of the computing system.

REFERENCES AND FURTHER READING

Bryant, J.W. (ed.), *Financial Modelling in Corporate Management*, New York: Wiley, 1982.
A useful collection of case studies with a few background articles which gives a good insight into the problems of designing computer-based financial models, many of which are of a budgeting nature. Does not require extensive computer knowledge.

Crawford, Ian, 'Budget Modelling in the Construction Materials Industry', *in* Bryant, J.W. (ed.), *Financial Modelling in Corporate Management*, New York: Wiley, 1982.
A step by step account of the build-up of a budgeting model without the TAC Construction Materials Ltd., which is one of the largest companies in the Turner and Newall group, operating six factories and split into five divisions.

Garbutt, D., *Carter's Advanced Accounts*, 7th edn, London: Pitman 1972.
A standard accountancy textbook which gives an introduction to ratio analysis with some worked examples.

Garbutt, D., *How to Budget and Control Cash*, Aldershot: Gower, 1985.
A comprehensible manual for businessmen on all aspects of budgeting with an emphasis on cash forecasting. CBI News says 'with cash flow as their lifeblood, many businessmen will find How

to Budget and Control Cash a valuable guide to what might be their survival . . . a worthwhile job . . .'.

Wagle, Bal, 'Corporate Planning in Local Authorities', *European Journal of Operational Research*, Vol. 1, pp. 221–224 (1977) – also in Bryant 1982.

A useful article on the practice of corporate planning in Local Authorities.

Westwick, C.A., *How to Use Management Ratios*, 2nd edn, Aldershot: Gower, 1987.

An authoritative guide to all aspects of ratio analysis and thoroughly recommended for those who wish to design effective reporting systems.

5

Alternative budgeting methods

John MacArthur

The preceding chapter dealt with the basics of budgeting – the nature of the budgetary process and its constituent parts, and how to develop a budgeting system from scratch. In this chapter the author examines some of the major difficulties in applying such techniques to practical business problems while still making the budget a useful management tool rather than merely an accounting routine.

John MacArthur begins by drawing a distinction between planning and control. He shows that one budget can hardly be expected to satisfy both purposes, as it is normally expected to do in most organisations. He points out that planning is about choosing between alternatives, while control is concerned with monitoring progress against the selected option. A single budget cannot satisfy both these aims, MacArthur argues. But he stresses that this is not to denigrate the value of the common master budget exercise. The master budget can be seen as an intermediate step between a planning and a control budget.

The rest of the chapter is concerned with two problems – how to budget for non-manufacturing overhead, and how to deal with uncertainty.

For the former, he contrasts the usual incremental approach with zero-based budgeting. Incremental budgeting starts from the present position without querying whether that is a sensible starting point. Zero-based budgeting, on the other hand, assumes nothing, building up required expenditure levels from scratch on the basis of specified objectives. MacArthur describes with the aid of examples six stages in the zero-based budgeting process. He then goes on to suggest that this approach can be carried through into routine reporting, perhaps by presenting reports in the same form as the zero-based budget justification.

The final section of the chapter deals with uncertainty in budgeting.

Since budgets are about the future they are inevitably surrounded with uncertainty, but this is seldom reflected in the budgeting process. Mac-Arthur describes some ways of incorporating uncertainty into the budget process, and identifies some traps to avoid.

As a ready guide, budgets can be classified conveniently into three groups that respresent the different time spans or budget periods covered by the planning process.

Typically, the planning horizon for long-term budgeting stretches fives years or more into the future, and two main types of budget emerge from the long-run planning process: strategic budgets and capital budgets. The strategic budget details the desired or planned profits and resources of an enterprise over its long-term future. In broad terms, it puts money values on the enterprise's longer term objectives as perceived by senior management. Capital budgeting is concerned with the selection and financing of capital investment projects in the next budget period that are designed to lead the company towards the desired future states depicted in the strategic budget. Failure to identify suitable investment proposals for selection in those circumstances, of course, may lead to a revision of the long run objectives and the strategic budget.

As described in Chapter 3, the general consensus of the 'how to do it' sections of the extensive capital budgeting literature is that investment proposals should be prepared on a project by project cash flow basis and analysed using discounted cash flow models. This is appropriate if the boundaries of projects can be defined easily and where they are largely independent of each other, but is less satisfactory otherwise. More recent discussion has suggested dealing with the interdependence of projects by linking them together using the models of portfolio theory.

Budget items with planning horizons between one and five years away fall into the medium-term category. Such items will be constrained by the long-term capital budgeting decisions taken and by the objectives of the enterprise. Budgets falling within this time span will include those for advertising and promotion, research and development, and training. Such expense items will be directed towards influencing or determining behaviour in the medium term, whether of sales demand, product quality, or labour skill.

Many budget items have only short-run impact, typically less than twelve months, but nonetheless form an integral part of the enterprise's planning to achieve long-run objectives. The main focus of this chapter is on this essential area of budgeting. The concern is with budgeting for the day to day operational aspects of the business, and the budgeting process may be conducted in several alternative ways to help management plan and control the short-term future of the enterprise. As with medium-term budgeting, management's planning freedom is limited by the 'fixed' constraints – such as existing organisational structure or plant capacity. Figure 5.1 depicts some of the more traditional aspects of budgeting for the short-term future.

Master budget

By definition, a master budget is the agreed master plan in money terms for the coming budget period, typically one year. It is the summation of all the separate budgets of an organisation's functional units and it represents the short-run targets for a business. The master budget is considered to be the central short-run planning document as it embodies the financial aspects of all the expected decisions during the year.

Failure to achieve the master budget in any way will mean that the company has not realised its short-run objectives, but this will not measure how efficient the company has been in producing its actual output. As discussed in Chapter 8, this requires a flexible budget, which is the operating part of the master budget adjusted to the revenues and costs expected for the actual level of production during the budget period. This the control budget. The arrows to and from the master budget and the flexible budget in Figure 5.1 represent these direct links between the costs and revenues of the master (plan-

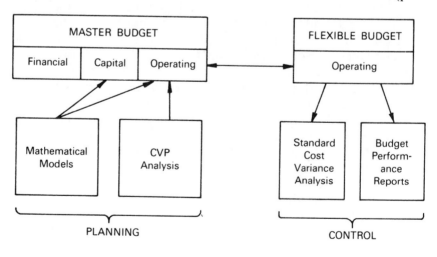

Figure 5.1 Traditional short run budgets

ning) budget and the flexible (control) budget in a traditional budget system. They are essentially different views of the same budget since they represent the output of the same budgeting process.

Recent research into budgeting from a behavioural theory and systems theory viewpoint has indicated that such a single budgeting process is unlikely to produce an effective multi-purpose budget – see, for example, Amey (1979) and Otley (1977). An interesting hypothesis is that a 'good' planning budget is not necessarily a 'good' control budget, because they serve different purposes. As Amey (1979) commented:

> Planning is . . . essentially an economic problem, which should be stated in economic terms. Control is concerned with quite different considerations, namely stabilization or regulation, which are not necessarily economic in character. The effectiveness of a control budget is measured solely by the results it produces, not by any relation the data it contains may have to economic reality.

As represented in Figure 5.1, traditional management accounting textbooks suggest that budgets based on the same principles can accomplish both purposes equally well.

PLANNING AND CONTROL BUDGETS

The essential features of both a planning budget and a control budget are outlined in Table 5.1, and a simplified worked example can be used to highlight those features and the differences between them. The traditional master and flexible budgets are examined in the light of that example. The example focuses attention on the production budget, ignoring budgeting for non-production overhead costs (which are considered separately later in this chapter).

A company is setting its production master budget for the coming trading period. The present output of products can be classified into three main groups – as suggested in Table 5.1 – and two new mutually exclusive alternative groups are being considered to replace the product lines in an existing group. The animal revenue and cost projections are given in Table 5.2.

Group C has been a stable product line for several years but is now experiencing a downward trend. The research and development department has proposed D and E as two equally profitable alternative product lines to replace C, either of which would involve minimal

91

Table 5.1
Essential features of planning budgets and control budgets

Planning budget	Control budget
Objective to facilitate choice between options, that is to aid decision making.	Objective to help keep the actual results within reasonable bounds, that is to help control the impact of decisions.
Problem of the allocation of, and claims on, resources.	Problem of stabilisation and regulation.
Consideration of costs and revenues in terms of programmes and outputs, that is to link inputs and outputs and indicate reasons for costs.	Consideration of items of expenditure and of functions, that is emphasising the inputs to the business.
Judged by its relation to reality.	Judged on its effectiveness in maintaining equilibrium.
Total business systems emphasis.	Individual partisan emphasis on responsibility and cost centres.

changes to the fixed production capacity charges since they could utilise plant and equipment currently used to produce Group C products. The production budget proposal, therefore, is to combine D or E with A and B. A more detailed analysis of the cost projections for the three groups under review, based on conventional absorption costing principles, is given in Table 5.3. That analysis is subject to the following constraints and practices.

Existing stocks of direct material type X are sufficient to produce three-quarters of the projected annual output of Product C. There is no alternative projected use for this material within the company; it cost £128 000 but would only realise £50 000 if sold. The remaining one-quarter of the annual requirement of this material would cost an

Table 5.2
Revenue and cost projections (£000s)

	Present product groups			Alternative product groups to replace C	
	A	B	C	D	E
Sales revenue	200	350	250	270	270
Production cost	160	320	289	215	216
Gross margin before non-production costs	40	30	(39)	55	54

estimated £32 000 – making a total cost of £160 000 for Type X material. Direct materials type Y and Z are in common use for product groups A and B, as well as for proposed groups D and E. The costs shown in the analysis are those of expected average replacement cost for the coming period.

Class I employees are paid a set annual wage, irrespective of output produced. If proposal E were accepted, half the present workforce would be idle, without any alternative work, for at least twelve months. The current union agreement precludes the company from making those employees redundant during the coming budget period. If either proposal D or proposal E were chosen, only a fifth of the present Class II workforce would be required. One month's paid notice would have to be given to the others at a cost of £4 000; total redundancy payments, wholly payable within the first nine months after leaving the company, are estimated at a further £30 000.

The foreman's salary is a fixed annual sum, irrespective of the product group selected. However, if none of the proposed alternatives were selected, the foreman would be transferred to product group A to replace a temporary employee earning £4 360 a year. The net saving, after one month's paid notice to the temporary foreman, would be £4 000.

The depreciation charge is for multi-purpose plant and machinery

Table 5.3
Detailed cost analysis (£000s)

		Product C	Product D	Product E
Direct materials:	Type X	160	–	–
	Type Y	–	130	130
	Type Z	–	10	20
Direct labour:	Class I	10	10	5
	Class II	60	12	12
Prime cost:		230	162	167
Variable overhead:		5	5	5
Variable cost:		235	167	172
Fixed overheads:	Foreman's salary	6	6	6
	Rent and rates	5	5	5
	Depreciation	20	20	15
	Re-tooling	–	1	1
	Factory overhead	23	16	17
Total cost:		289	215	216

93

purchased three years ago and suitable for either D or E, subject to relatively minor expenditure on re-tooling, estimated to cost £1 000 for either proposal. The net realisable value of the plant and machinery is currently £80 000 and is expected to have fallen to £50 000 by the end of the coming budget period. Proposal D would utilise existing equipment fully, but proposal E would require only three-quarters of it. It is considered that any machinery thereby left idle could be rented out for £2 000 a year.

An economic planning budget, based on the notion of opportunity

Table 5.4
Reconstructed economic cost analysis (£000s)

		Product C	Product D	Product E
Direct materials:	Type X (opportunity cost, 9 months)	50	–	–
	Type X (purchase cost, 3 months)	32	–	–
	Type Y (purchase cost, 12 months)	–	130	120
	Type Z (purchase cost, 12 months)	–	10	30
Direct labour:	Class I	–	–	–
	Class II (basic)	60	12	12
	Class II (paid notice)	–	4	4
	Class II (redundancy)	–	30	30
Variable overhead:		5	5	5
Fixed overheads:	Foreman's salary (opportunity cost)	4	4	4
	Rent and rates	–	–	–
	Economic depreciation	30	30	30
	Re-tooling	–	1	1
	Idle machinery rental	–	–	(5)
	Factory overhead	–	–	–
Total economic cost:		181	226	231
Sales revenue:		250	270	270
Net economic gain:		69	44	39

94

cost, can be reconstructed for the three groups C, D, and E as shown in Table 5.4, and a brief explanation of some of the calculations will serve to make the concept clearer.

If the Type X material in stock is used to make Product C, the best future alternative opportunity forgone (measured in money terms) is the possible sale of that material outside the company for £50 000. The original cost of that material is clearly 'water under the bridge' – a past sunk cost about which nothing can now be done – and is irrelevant for planning future alternatives to aid decision making.

There is a fixed commitment to pay Class I employees for the whole of the budget period, irrespective of the availability of work. Class I wages are not, therefore, an economic cost under any of the three alternatives. The desirability of having such an underemployed workforce is, of course, a qualitative input into the decision process and other, non-monetary considerations may influence the final choice.

In terms of ranking the three alternatives, any future costs that are the same for all three proposals – such as the variable overhead – can be left out without harm. This is the procedure commonly proposed for 'decision' budgets. For a 'planning' budget, however, it is advisable to include all future costs so that the total economic cost of each alternative proposal can be compared with the total revenue. The full short-term effect of each proposal can then be seen on the cash flows of the company. It is also the only sure way of determining that the best alternative is, in itself, acceptable by producing a positive net economic gain.

The foreman's salary is irrelevant as it will be paid whether any or none of the proposals is finally chosen. However, the company could save the salary of the temporary foreman if none of the proposals were accepted, and this salary represents, therefore, an opportunity cost for each of the three alternatives. This is an example of the 'total business systems emphasis' of the planning budget, as outlined in Table 5.1.

The rent, rates and factory overhead are future fixed commitments of the whole factory, irrespective of any choice between the three alternatives, and are not an economic cost to be included in the planning budget of any of the options. The allocation of such costs to product groups is decided by predetermined and arbitrary methods, which are always unnecessary for a planning budget.

The depreciation charge based on original cost does not involve any future expenditure and is clearly an irrelevant 'sunk cost'. The economic depreciation charge is the opportunity cost of deferring sale of the plant and machinery for one year, assuming that this is the best available alternative forgone if any of the three proposals is accepted. The initial re-tooling cost is an incremental cost, wholly included in the planning budget for the coming period.

The apparent decision to follow from the economic cost analysis in Table 5.4 would be to defer replacing Product C for at least one year, since C yields the highest net economic gain. This would be a mistake, stemming from the arbitrary choice of one year as the base period for the comparison of the three alternatives. In fact, the profitable first nine months projected for group C masks the final three months when the product group would make only a small gain, because of the need to buy new stocks of direct material X for this period. This is illustrated in Table 5.5 which examines the final three months of the year for Product C.

That analysis reveals that Product C would make a net economic gain of just £6 000 in that quarter of the period. By comparison, proposal D would generate a net gain of £11 000 (£44 000 × ¼) and proposal E would make a net gain of £9 750 (£39 000 × ¼). Product group C offers the worst alternative of the three.

The correct initial decision, then, is to retain product group C for nine months and thereafter to plan to adopt proposal D – if the current initial conditions still hold. This decision could not have been 'guessed' from the initial analysis of revenues and costs based on conventional absorption costing methods – which predicted a gross loss of £39 000 for Product C in the coming period. Yet this is the way in which a typical master budget is constructed. It fails to achieve the objective of a planning budget, which is to facilitate the chioce between alternatives (that is to aid decision making) primarily because it does not model the organisation in terms of the short run future decision-making opportunities available. Such a master budget is not designed to resolve 'what difference does it make' questions since it includes revenues and costs over which the organisation has no deci-

Table 5.5
Economic cost analysis – Product C (final three months) (£000s)

Direct materials:	Type X	32
Direct labour:	Class II (£60 000 × ¼)	15
Variable overhead:	(£5 000 × ¼)	1
Fixed overheads:	Foreman's salary (£4 000 × ¼)	1
	Economic depreciation (£30 000 × ¼)	8
Total economic cost:		57
Total revenue:	(£250 000 × ¼)	63
Net economic gain:		6

sion-making power during the budget period (sunk costs and committed costs) and ignores other revenues and costs which are within its control (opportunity costs). The master budget of that type fails, therefore, by not representing fully the economic reality of the budget period.

These comments should not be taken to suggest that a conventional master budget is useless. Its preparation promotes communication between, and coordination of, the subunits of an organisation. For example, the sales management team must be in touch with production managers to ensure internal consistency between the sales and production budgets. A master budget is also the only comprehensive summary of all the projected revenues and costs, irrespective of the organisation's discretionary decision-making power over those revenues and costs. That is essential for budgeting the financing requirements (the cash budget) for the forthcoming period. The master budget can, therefore, be considered as an intermediate step between the planning and control budgets.

Once a decision has been taken to adopt a particular alternative, the 'plan' becomes a 'decision'. A control budget is needed to monitor the effects of the decision, but this does not imply that the planning process ends as control of the actual output begins. There is also a need to monitor and control the planning budget.

Controlling the planning budget

Certain requirements must be met by a short-run planning budget which embodies, in greater or less detail, the totality of the 'correct decisions' to be made for a specified period.

The long-term and short-term objectives must be defined explicitly to that plans can be prepared with a clear end in mind. This is easier in theory than in practice. The objectives of the budget planning process may be a profit level and growth pattern deemed satisfactory to top management rather than optimal, however simplistic and undynamic such aims might appear.

The critical planning variables and parameters must be identified and specified accurately. Such components will include the following:

1 the projected rate of inflation;
2 the effect of technological progress on products and production processes;
3 the demand function for each of the enterprise's products or services;

4   the availability and/or quality of capital, labour, and material re-
    sources, and their cost;
5   the expected actions and reactions of competitors;
6   the interaction of the short run with the long run (a dynamic
    aspect) – the major concern being the long-run success of the
    enterprise;
7   legal and statutory controls and regulations;
8   the needs of suppliers and customers (credit terms, service
    levels, and so on);
9   the speed and effectiveness of advertising impact on future de-
    mand;
10 productivity levels of the workforce;
11 the prices and supply of the factors of production.

Significant shifts in the objectives, parameters, or variables will require changes in the short-term planning budget. If immediate and
previously unplanned decisions are called for, there will have to be
changes in the control budget as well. This is another dynamic aspect
of real life budgeting.

It will be clear from the list of typical parameters and budget variables that the planning boundaries should be wider than the internal
boundaries of the enterprise. Conventional budgeting tends to concentrate on identifying easily measurable endogenous (or internal)
variables and to ignore exogenous (external) variables that interact
with the endogenous variables. For instance, a company may require
a certain component for one of its products. During the most recent
peak production period, the quality of the components received from
the supplier was lower than normal. An investigation reveals that
this situation results from the supplier's recent difficulty in employing skilled labour of the required quality. On the surface such a
labour difficulty seems to be solely the supplier's problem and completely exogenous to the company's planning concerns. However,
further investigation reveals that part of the component supplier's
problem derives from the irregular ordering pattern of the company's buyer. That pattern forces the supplier to experience widely
fluctuating demand periods for the component. The supplier is not in
a position to stockpile during the periods of low demand. Accordingly, the scarcity of temporary skilled labour (required by the
supplier to meet high demand periods) is linked with the internal
ordering procedure of the company and is, therefore, within the con-
fines of its planning budget. Knowledge of that interaction may affect the company's operational behaviour. For example, the
company might decide to change to a different supplier for all or part

of its requirements, or it could change its ordering procedure and purchase stocks of the component on a regular basis; alternatively, it might do nothing at all, believing the supplier's labour problem to be temporary.

Control budgets

As mentioned, a control budget has a different purpose from a planning budget. A planning budget seeks to model the economic realities of alternative opportunities open to the enterprise, so as to help managers make the 'right' decisions, that is, choose the alternatives that best achieve the objectives of the enterprise. A control budget, in contrast, is designed to help make the selected decisions the 'correct' ones by providing warning signals so as to keep disturbances to a minimum. The intricacies of a control budget, outlined in Table 5.1, can be illustrated by examining the Class I and II direct labour budgets of the production discussed earlier (see Table 5.3 and 5.4).

For control purposes, the product (output) groupings of the planning budgets should be changed to more detailed and conventional input classifications, as outlined in Table 5.1. Suppose the Class II direct labour of the company described produce products A and C and are physically based in four separate departments – two machining departments, an assembly department, and a polishing department. The total wages projection will be separated into four control budgets, each for a different foreman, responsible for the effectiveness and efficiency of the workforce in his own department. Making certain assumptions, such a four-budget structure would be as shown in Table 5.6, which depicts the two different classifications.

Table 5.6
Class II direct labour budget classifications (£000s)

Control Budget Classification	Product A	Product C	Total
Machining Department 1	3	30	33
Machining Department 2	3	12	15
Assembly Department	9	6	15
Polishing Department	15	12	27
Total	30	60	90

For the reasons advanced earlier, the cost of Class I direct labour was excluded from the planning budgets for products C, D and E. This would, however, be inadvisable in a control budget for a number of fundamental reasons. Two such reasons are the need for internal consistency between the various parts of the total control budget, and behavioural considerations.

Internal consistency

Most management accounting textbooks give detailed illustrations of budgeting to show the underlying order of the budgeting process – sales budget, followed by production budget, and so on. This results from the view that a budget is primarily an aid towards coordination and implementation of the decisions taken by individuals within an organisation. From that standpoint, it is clearly necessary, for example, for the wages of Class I direct employees to be included in a cash budget as an outlay and in the production budget as a planned expense for an identical amount, subject to time lag adjustments.

Similarly, control budgets must be internally consistent to facilitate comparison with the actual results, which, in this term, should automatically be internally consistent. Deviations from the budget will then be meaningful as the control budget will be constructed along the same lines as the actual outcome is recorded and reported. It is interesting to note that the relationship of a control budget to reality differs from that of a planning budget – see Table 5.1. The equivalent criterion for a control budget is rather its effectiveness in giving 'signals' that indicate a need for action to maintain equilibrium.

Behavioural considerations

A planning budget including Class II direct labour at zero 'cost' may be a good thing from an economist's point of view for aiding decision making, but the inclusion of such a nil cost in a control budget may well have a marked demotivating effect. Class II employees may construe such a characteristic as reflecting a low value judgement of their 'worth' to the enterprise, especially when compared with the high positive 'value' included for Class I employees.

This is a simple example of the care needed when designing budgeting systems. It is dangerous to adopt a mechanistic view of budgeting – assuming that employees will automatically do their best to achieve a budget, irrespective of the way in which it has been prepared. Research into the behaviour aspects of budgeting (discussed further in Chapter 16 of this handbook) has revealed the fallacy of such a notion.

BUDGETING FOR NON-PRODUCTION OVERHEADS

The process of budgeting for non-manufacturing activities presents very different problems from budgeting for the direct costs of making a product or providing a service. The relationship between the input of resources and the final output of the organisation is much less clear cut. The number of employees and the quantity of direct material required to make a specified product can be measured physically, but the optimal size and composition of, for instance, a legal department may not be so easily or precisely determined. The tasks and output of a legal department cannot be linked directly with the organisation's physical output.

The traditional approach to budgeting for non-production costs is the incremental method. This deals very simply with the complexities involved in determining the total level of staff and support activities necessary to run an organisation effectively and efficiently; it ignores them. The focus of attention is limited to any proposed changes in the existing level of funding, rather than to the budget as a whole. Thus, inefficiencies in the existing arrangements may be carried forward year after year, unless management has other ways of identifying them. The incremental approach and an alternative, more comprehensive approach – the zero-based review or budget – are considered in this section, and they are represented diagrammatically in Figure 5.2.

Incremental and zero-base approaches

An incremental budget is presented by a manager to his superior in terms of total money required for the coming period. Except for any proposed increase, little explicit information is given about the activities covered by the total funds requested. By contrast, the starting point for developing a zero-base budget (ZBB) is, by definition, 'zero' activity – not taking existing levels of activity into account or for granted. ZBB describes in some detail the activities represented by both current funding and proposed increases. The focus of attention is, therefore, diverted from the required money input to a functional unit towards the activities and output of the unit in question. Accordingly, ZBB allows a far more critical and thorough analysis of

101

the unit's total activities in the light of the needs and objectives of the organisation and it facilitates the consideration of alternative ways of providing the required service for the coming budget period.

Zero-base budgeting is one member of a 'family' of output-oriented budgeting systems which emphasise a programmed or systematic approach to budget setting and resource allocation. Other related budgeting systems are the Planning – Programming – Budgeting Systems (PPBS) and Management by Objectives System (MBO). Much of the pioneer work has been carried out in the United States in the public sector – in which, of course, output and program achievement is of far greater concern – and there has only been a limited attempt to introduce these systems into private sector budgeting. Dean and Cowen (1979) and Stonich (1977) have, however, described significant applications of ZZB in the private sector; Pyhrr (1973) pioneered the formalisation of ZBB as a practical management procedure.

Phare (1979) described zero-base budgeting as:

> . . . comprehensive managerial planning and resourcing from the setting of specific goals for each project or activity through the setting of priorities on the basis of hard data – not emotion.

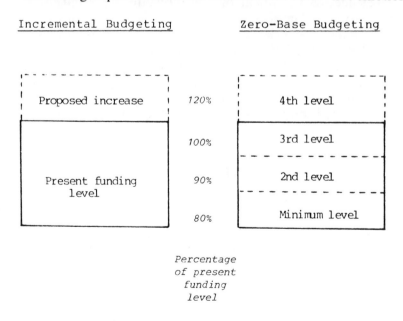

Figure 5.2   Incremental budgeting for non-production overheads

Six basic stages

In more practical detail, the ZBB process can be exemplified and described in six stages using the budgeting data of an hypothetical legal department of XY Limited. The legal department has three 'decision units': debtors' follow-up; litigation; estates.

Stage 1 is common to both ZBB and the traditional incremental approach. Senior management will decide the general assumptions regarding the state of the economy as a whole; within that framework, lower levels of management will determine the more detailed assumptions for each of the decision units (in Stage 2).

The planning assumptions for the XY legal department for 1983 are as follows:

1   proposed legislation will come into force by June 1983, giving customers wider statutory purchasing rights;
2   the average number of debtors and the repayment period allowed will remain unchanged from the current year;
3   planning permission for two additional factory buildings will be sought, requiring legal work in the Estates unit;
4   an outstanding claim against the company for damages will be settled by September 1983, entailing work in the Litigation unit.

Stage 2 identifies the 'decision units'. Decision units can comprise any groupings of activities which facilitates the analysis required later. The most convenient way to define the decision units is to make them synonymous with the traditional cost centre or budget unit, so that the responsible decision unit manager is easily identifiable. The legal department of the company can be considered as a single decision unit or, as is the case here, as a set of three decision units with distinctive functions – debtors' follow-up, estates work, and litigation work.

Decision units may be defined also by activity, such as travel or communication, or by special one-off projects or programmes. The choice of notional units should be based on the costs and benefits expected from the various alternatives.

Stage 3 calls for analysis of each decision unit. It is the stage at which incremental and zero-base budgeting part company. The ZBB of each decision unit can be considered in four convenient steps. First, the decision unit manager identifies the states the objectives of his unit, following discussions with his superiors and subordinates. Identifying the reasons for the activities of a unit is an obvious first step – if it can be done sensibly and meaningfully. Policy makers often agree as to the activities of a unit much more easily than they can agree its objectives.

For example, a manager may wish to expand his unit so as to gain recognition and subsequent promotion, but his immediate superior may wish to maintain the status quo because he does not want to take unnecessary risks so near his retirement. The eventual agreed objectives for the unit in question would probably represent some compromise between the manager and his superior and reflect the relative influences of the parties involved in the bargaining process. Further agreement would then be required on the means of achieving those objectives.

Owing to the potential conflict problem, stated objectives are often concluded in bland, general and somewhat obvious terms, with very little operational significance. Furthermore, any quantified targets tend to give agreed activity levels, without any indication of the reasons why those levels were chosen.

Secondly, the current activities and resources employed are described in sufficient detail for a higher level manager to understand.

Thirdly, alternative ways of achieving the purpose of the decision unit are considered by the decision unit manager and his superior; the best one is selected. Reasons for acceptance or rejection are stated in respect of each alternative. This third step is the 'creative' part of the process and calls for an estimate of the costs and benefits associated with each of the alternative 'decision packages'.

Traditional incremental budgeting concentrates on changes and improvements to existing activities and ignores completely any new, potentially better, ways of achieving purposes. In real life limited numbers of viable alternatives are available and marked degrees of resistance to change exist in any organisation, so the traditional incremental approach may be a more amenable and practicable line to follow.

Fourthly, having decided upon the most appropriate alternative, the decision unit manager determines different possible levels of activity and expenditure from the minimum level upwards which provide varying degrees of specified service. This permits 'fine tuning' in the allocation of resources to the activities of decision units in the order of priority.

These steps are illustrated below for the Debtors' Follow-Up Decision Unit in the legal department of the company.

Decision unit analysis

The objectives of the unit are agreed as: to expedite the receipt of money from debtors who have failed to pay their debts within the due period, and to advise the chief accountant on all legal aspects of deferred terms and invoice sales. The minimum performance target is set at the recovery of money from defaulting debtors which is at least double the operating costs of the unit.

Within the unit, a legally qualified unit head and deputy head, jointly responsible for general supervision, monitor the follow-up of outstanding debts which are more than six months overdue and/or greater than £5 000 in value, and advise the chief accountant. Other personnel include six debt follow-up clerks, one secretary/filing clerk and two mobile debt collectors. Other major resources comprise three company cars (one each for the unit head and the two debt collectors) and rented letter addressing and franking machines for legal action warning letters and other correspondence. It has been customary to send two warning letters before initiating legal action against defaulting debtors.

The decision unit manager has considered three principal alternative ways of achieving the unit's objectives. These are summarised in Table 5.7. Alternative 2, the use of an outside debt collection agency at a cost of £80 000, is rejected because it does not meet the minimum performance requirement. Alternative 3, the use of an outside debt collection agency at a cost of £75 000, is rejected because, while it meets the minimum performance requirement, it is not as cost effective as the unit's current activities. In addition, the big problem of re-deploying existing tenured staff would arise.

The decision unit manager proceeds, therefore, to assess the incremental levels of activity possible within the unit. That analysis is shown in Table 5.8, which examines five incremental levels – of which the first is the bare minimum service, including the fundamental tasks necessary to fulfil the top priority needs of management.

Table 5.7
XY debtors' follow-up decision unit – alternatives for 1983

	Cost	Money recovered	Margin	Money recovered as % of cost
Alternative 1: Current activities	£50 000	£150 000	£100 000	300.0%
Alternative 2: Use agency A	£80 000†	£150 000	£70 000	187.5%
Alternative 3: Use agency B	£75 000	£150 000	£75 000	200.0%

† includes consultancy fee for advising chief accountant on legal matters

Table 5.8
XY debtors' follow-up decision unit – incremental levels of activity for 1983

Description	% of current service level	Incremental cost	Cumulative projections 1983			
			Cost	Money recovered	Margin	Money recovered as % of cost
Increment 1 1 supervisor, 2 debt clerks, 1 secretary	24%	£18 000	£18 000	£36 000	£18 000	200.0%
Increment 2 Add 2 debt clerks, 1 mobile debt collector, 1 car	47%	£12 000	£30 000	£70 000	£40 000	233.3%
Increment 3 Add 1 deputy supervisor, 2 debt clerks, 1 mobile debt collector, 1 car	87%	£15 000	£45 000	£130 000	£85 000	288.9%
Increment 4 Add 1 rented franking machine, 1 letter addressing machine	100%	£5 000	£50 000	£150 000	£100 000	300.0%
Increment 5 Add 1 mobile debt collector, 1 car	120%	£10 000	£60 000	£180 000	£120 000	300.0%

106

The identification of those needs is a difficult but useful exercise in its own right, and should include any services needed to fulfil legal requirements imposed on the company.

For simplicity, the column in the table labelled '% of current service level' is based on money recovered – but consequently does not measure the quality of the advisory service provided to senior management. The fourth level is the current level of operating.

The legal department manager and the decision unit managers will formulate a consolidated set of decision packages for submission to senior management, ranking each increment of service in order of importance. Table 5.9 presents such a ranked submission.

Such a ranking will have been determined between the department manager and the decision unit managers, who will have agreed

Table 5.9
XY legal department's ranking of decision units and funds request for 1983

Ranking	Decision unit	Incremental cost	Cumulative cost	Current year projection
1	Litigation	£25 000	£25 000	£20 000
2	Debtors' Follow-Up	£18 000	£43 000	£48 000
3	Estates	£10 000	£53 000	£19 000
4	Debtors' Follow-Up	£12 000	£65 000	
5	Estates	£6 000	£71 000	
6	Debtors' Follow-Up	£15 000	£86 000	
7	Litigation	£5 000	£91 000	
8	Debtors' Follow-Up	£5 000	£96 000	
		£96 000		£87 000

Summary of proposed expenditure

	Proposed	Current	Change
Litigation Decision Unit	£30 000	£20 000	+50.0%
Debtors' Follow-Up Decision Unit	£50 000	£48 000	+ 4.2%
Estates Decision Unit	£16 000	£19 000	−15.8%
	£96 000	£87 000	+10.3%

between themselves on the level of service that will be funded during the coming period of each of the decision units.

In respect of the estates unit, incidentally, a cost reduction is proposed by cutting the present staffing level and using external legal services for some occasional legal estate work outside the scope of the reorganised unit. This cheaper alternative was identified through use of the zero-base approach.

As a final stage, after senior management has agreed the final selection of decision packages for the whole company, the conventional 'line-by-line' annual budget can be prepared. If the decision units are largely synonymous with the budget or cost centres of the organisation this will be a relatively straightforward conversion process.

Implementation of ZBB

At least one major international company has implemented a system that reports actual results in the same format and detail as the agreed decision unit budgets. As Phare (1979) has reported:

> This has converted the zero-based process from a static, once-a-year budget-negotiating exercise into a dynamic vehicle for on-going management planning, control and performance improvements.

The successes and failures of the implementation of zero-base budgeting in the 1970s have been well documented – see, for example, Thomas (1979). The main area of application has been in the staff and support functions, although it has been used in budgeting manufacturing overheads (for example, quality control, plant maintenance, and so on). It may be advisable to introduce ZBB into an organisation's budgeting system over a period of years, gaining experience and confidence in it as a management tool. In any case, ZBB is only beneficial in departments when managers have discretionary decision making power over significant costs. Otherwise, the potential cost savings and resources optimisations are minimal and would probably not justify the increased expenses of more detailed zero-based analysis.

One of the principal advantages of the ZBB approach is the large amount of analysis provided to decision makers, enabling them to consider alternative ways of providing a particular service. As with any management technique, however, a zero-based system must be designed and adapted to suit the organisation and not vice versa.

UNCERTAINTY

An underlying problem common to all forms of budgeting is future uncertainty. A manager is unlikely to be sure of the precise outcome of any decision. He may be faced with a range of possible outcomes that can be predicted with varying degrees of accuracy.

There are a number of ways of dealing with uncertainty in budgeting. Some of the more common ways can be illustrated by using the hypothetical vehicle running costs budget for a sales branch of a manufacturing company. The costs for the period 1970–1980 are shown in Table 5.10.

The variable running costs are to be budgeted at £1 a mile for 1981. It is expected that vehicle mileage will follow the historical ten or eleven year pattern during 1981. The management accountant preparing the budget might choose one of the three commonly used methods: single value budget estimate; high, low and most likely value budget estimates; probability analysis budget estimate.

Single value estimate

A manager may explicitly or implicitly ignore uncertainty by preparing only a single budget estimate that is representative of the whole range. The budget value chosen would probably be either the average value (that is, the mean or expected value) or the most likely value (that is, the mode value). As shown in Table 5.10, the mean value is near enough 9 182 miles a year; the most frequent or modal value is clearly 10 000 miles. It is higher than the mean because of the unsymmetrical frequency distribution of annual miles travelled, which is biased towards the higher mileage numbers, as shown in Figure 5.3.

Which is the better number to choose? Viewed from an individual branch level, the mode has distinct advantages over the mean value. For one thing it is an actual value that has been experienced. The mode is also, by definition, the most likely outcome in any one year. However, a problem arises in aggregating all the 'lower level' branch budgets into a 'higher level' total budget when the budget estimates are based on modal values.

Budgets based upon mean values can be added together quite safely. A mode is not a truly representative number for all the values in the frequency distribution – it is simply one of the values, the most likely one. It has been demonstrated that unit budgets which show a relatively small deviation from the mean value can lead to such pronounced distortions when the budgets are aggregated that the total budget is wholly unrealistic (Otley and Berry, 1979).

For example, if there are eight other sales branches virtually identical to Sales Branch A and if the standard deviation for each branch is approximately 1 170 miles, the total budget based upon mean values would be 81 800 miles (9 200 × 9), with a standard deviation of 3 510 miles; the distribution would be more symmetrical than each individual branch's frequency distribution.

The total budget based on modal values would be 90 000 miles (10 000 × 9). The individual branch modal budgets are less than one standard deviation away from the mean; (10 000 – 9 200)/1 170 = 0.68 standard deviation. The total modal budget is over two standard deviations away from the mean; (90 000 – 81 000)/5 510 = 2.336 standard deviations. It is a highly unrepresentative and slack budget for the nine branches considered together, with a very small probability of proving anywhere near the actual outcome.

The aggregation problem can arise whenever the unit budgets are not set equal to the mean value, whether or not the frequency distribution happens to be symmetrical. Budgets can be biased for a number of reasons other than inbuilt statistical skewness. For instance, an experienced and established manager may bias his cost budget upwards and/or revenue budget downwards to make attainment easier. A manager facing problems may do the opposite in order to create a favourable impression with his superiors.

Table 5.10
AB Sales Branch A – vehicle running costs 1970–1980

Mileage recorded:

1970	9 000	1974	10 000	1978	10 000
1971	10 000	1975	9 000	1979	7 000
1972	9 000	1976	11 000	1980	8 000
1973	8 000	1977	10 000		

Grouped frequency distribution

Mileage (x_i)	Frequency (f_i)	$x_i f_i$
7 000	1	7 000
8 000	2	16 000
9 000	3	27 000
10 000	4	40 000
11 000	1	11 000
	11	101 000

Mean = 9 182 (101 000/11)

Whatever the reasons for biasing lower level budgets, the aggregated budget has a much smaller chance of achievement than the individual lower level budgets. Obviously, there is as much need to control the budget setting process as the actual outcome of the period being budgeted. Otherwise comparisons between aggregated budgets and actual results are unlikely to be meaningful.

One way of monitoring the budget setting process for bias would be to prepare total budget estimates using alternative methods, as a rough check on the aggregation of lower level budgets. Using the earlier example, the total mileage expected by sales branch managers could be estimated by relating mileage to some other budgeted independent variable, such as budgeted sales volume, which might be expected to influence mileage, and this could be compared with the aggregated budget.

High, low and most likely value estimates

A relatively simple and straightforward way of indicating the uncertainty surrounding a budget estimate is to give the highest and lowest

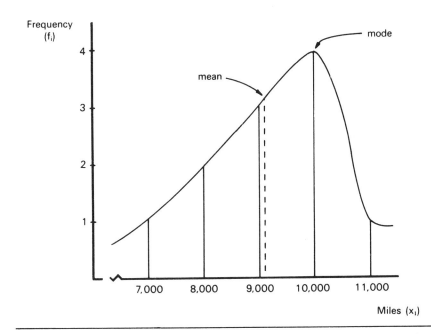

Figure 5.3 AB Sales Branch A – histogram of frequency distribution (with an approximate continuous probability density function superimposed)

perceived values, in addition to a representative central value such as the mode or the mean.

Using the data in Table 5.10, the high budget value is £11 000 (at the running cost rate of £1 a mile) and the low value is £7 000; the most likely value is £10 000. These values give a feel for the skewness of the expectations, while also indicating the range of possible outcomes. Although this method has the disadvantage that it does not use all the available data, it may represent the most sensible compromise between a simple method, such as described earlier, and a more complicated method, such as described below, when the likely frequency of possible values is very uncertain.

Probability analysis estimate

The frequencies in Table 5.10 can be translated into probability form by dividing each one by the frequency total (that is, 11); for example, the probability of 7 000 miles occurring in any one year is near enough 0.09 (1/11). The frequencies or probabilities can be used to calculate an average measure of deviation around the mean, known commonly as a standard deviation (o). The standard deviation for

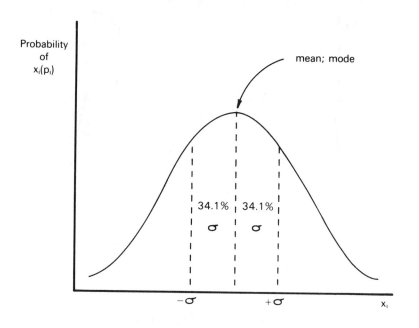

Figure 5.4   Normal probability density function

the sample values given in Table 5.10 is 1 168 miles (or £1 168) around a mean (μ) of 9 182 miles (or £9 182).

The standard deviation is a useful measure when it can be assumed that budget data are continuously and normally distributed, as depicted in Figure 5.4. In such cases, all that really needs to be known about the data are the average value (the mean) and the average dispersion (the standard deviation) in order to have a complete mathematical picture of the data. For example, it can then be confidently stated that just over 68 per cent of all possible budget values will lie within one standard deviation either side of the mean value, as is also depicted in Figure 5.4.

The data in Table 5.10 are in discrete rather than continuous form, as represented by the vertical histogram lines in Figure 5.3, which also illustrates an approximate continuous probability function superimposed on the histogram – clearly showing the non-normal or skewed nature of the distribution of data. There is no justification for the use of a continuous approximation in this case, given the very few data points and the relatively large interval between them.

The calculation of the standard deviation involved the use of all the available numerical data, but it is important to make two significant reservations. First, the number actually obtained cannot be observed from the data themselves; the deviation between each possible value is constant at 1 000 and not the standard deviation of 1 168. This is perhaps intuitively strange and unsatisfactory. Secondly, the standard deviation gives no indication of the skewness inherent in the data.

In these circumstances, the standard deviation may not be a useful measure of uncertainty, and it might be better to adopt the second method – high, low and most likely value estimates. At least the 'high-low' measure of uncertainty points up actual numbers in the distribution and partially indicates the presence of skewness.

Alternatively, consider the coefficient of variation, which expresses the percentage relationship between the standard deviation and the mean. In the sales branch example, the coefficient of variation is 12.7 per cent (1 168/9 182). The higher the coefficient, the larger are the expected relative variations of likely outcomes around the mean – in other words, the greater is the perceived uncertainty. This is a relative measure rather than an absolute difference and can be usefully compared, for example, with the actual percentage variation from budget to gauge the latter's significance.

Whichever uncertainty measure is chosen, an important general point to bear in mind is that actual results can usually be expected to deviate from budget, simply due to 'random' fluctuations. Such deviations are not necessarily the 'fault' of any particular manager or controller. One of the main purposes for considering uncertainty during the budget setting process should be to establish the acceptable limits for deviations which are to be considered random and, as such, will not require investigation.

REFERENCES AND FURTHER READING

Amey, L.R., *Budget Planning and Control Systems*, London: Pitman, 1979.

Dean, B.V., and Cowen, S.S., 'Zero-base budgeting in the private sector', *Business Horizons*, August 1979.

Otley, D.T., *Behavioural Aspects of Budgeting*, London: Institute of Chartered Accountants in England and Wales, 1977.

Otley, D.T., and Berry, A., 'Risk distribution in the budgetary process', *Accounting and Business Research*, Autumn 1979.

Phare, G.R., 'Beyond zero-base budgeting', *Managerial Planning*, July–August 1979.

Pyhrr, P.A., *Zero Base Budgeting: a Practical Management Tool for Evaluating Expenses*, New York: Wiley, 1973.

Stedry, A.C., *Budget Control and Cost Behaviour*, Englewood Cliffs, N.J.: Prentice-Hall, 1970.

Stonich, P.J., *Zero Base Planning and Budgeting*, Homewood, Ill.: Dow Jones-Irwin, 1977.

Thomas, M.T., 'Another look at zero base budgeting', *The CPA Journal*, August 1979.

Part Two
Measurement and Control

OVERVIEW

In many respects it is easier to plan than to measure performance. But measurement is inevitably a central part of the planning and control process. It is the vital feedback activity through which progress towards the achievement of plans can be assessed, and provides the impetus for the development of new plans.

A central difficulty in the measurement of business performance is the impossibility of providing simple answers even to simple questions such as 'how much did it cost to make product X?'. The currency of business may be common, but when accounting techniques are used in an attempt to analyse transactions to provide a detailed picture of business activity there immediately opens up a variety of possible interpretations.

This second part of the handbook explores some of the different ways in which accounting information can be manipulated to provide appropriate management information on the performance of the business. The first two chapters are concerned with the basic issue of how to develop product costs – the continuing debate between the traditional approach of including all manufacturing costs in product costs and the alternative of writing off all fixed costs in the period in which they were incurred. These alternatives have important implications for performance measurement and both contain dangers if used rigidly. The author explains the advantages and disadvantages of each method, especially in the context of pricing.

The following chapter in this section continues the discussion of basic costing techniques with an explanation of variance analysis and flexible budgeting. The author emphasises that the correct interpretation of variances is important if they are to be used as a tool for management control. It is important, therefore, for management to understand the significance of variances, but causes of over or under spending are not always obvious. Fixed cost variances are particularly problematic, and the author proposes an opportunity cost approach as a way of focusing on decision alternatives.

This theme is continued in the chapter by Professor Bromwich, who attacks conventional costing practice as being inadequate for decision-making purposes. He argues that traditional variance analysis is concerned with control, whereas a switch to a planning orientation would be more useful to management. He shows how variance calculations can be amended to achieve this re-orientation and provide a more flexible and more useful management tool.

Chapters 10 and 11 are concerned with the difficulties encountered in groups of companies where it is considered necessary to measure the performance of parts of the total group.

In Chapter 10 the authors consider the concept of responsibility accounting and its limitations in the context of complex organisation structures. They argue that it will be most productive to treat different types of cost in different ways, suggesting a continuum of cost types from those which can be assigned directly to profit centres to general costs which can only be arbitrarily allocated.

The final chapter in this section lifts the focus from detailed measurement and control to a more comprehensive view of business performance. It is concerned with the concept of management auditing as a way of analysing the performance and prospects of business units. The author explains the concept and argues that it can be used profitably by many organisations.

6

Absorption costing

J. Lewis Brown

Absorption costing, or as it is sometimes termed total costing, is probably the oldest system of cost accounting in operation. Even though it was introduced at a very early stage in the development of cost accounting methods, it is still widely used. Considerable problems are inherent in any application of absorption costing, as the author of this chapter recognises, and yet absorption costing continues to flourish. In fact, a partial adoption of absorption costing is recommended by the Accounting Standards Committee in its standard on stocks and work-in-progress. Since many firms still approach the pricing decision in terms of 'adding something on to total cost', full or total costing provides some information on which to base a selling price decision – but of an imprecise and significantly inaccurate nature, argues the author. The growing use of the contribution margin approach in performance measurement and cost analysis has led to an increasing use of direct or marginal costing for internal purposes, but the advocates of traditional absorption costing methods argue strongly that both variable and fixed costs are necessary to produce goods and, therefore, fixed cost overheads should be inventoried. Distinctions between variable and fixed costs are valuable for a range of managerial decisions, and the traditional absorption cost proponents recognise that value, arguing that such information is readily available from traditional financial statements. The issue to be resolved is one of timing. When should fixed factory overhead be released as expense? At the time it is incurred, as a period cost? Or at the time of sale of stock, as a cost of sale? The issue is narrowed, then, to one of whether or not fixed overhead should properly be part of inventory cost.

Conceptually, absorption costing is a simple and fundamental method of ascertaining the cost of a product or service. The direct cost of manufacturing a product – the cost of direct materials used, direct wages and any other expenses associated directly with the product – is calculated and to that figure is added an estimated amount to cover overheads and profit. Obviously, it is fairly easy to calculate the direct costs but more difficult to decide on equitable charge for overheads and profit. In fact, this problem of calculating overhead cost has proved a controversial topic for many years and has been highlighted by the introduction of an alternative system, known as marginal or direct costing, prior to the Second World War. During the First World War, a form of absorption costing called 'cost plus' costing was used extensively, particularly in government contracts for the supply of military equipment. That system was simple: a fixed percentage was added to total cost, to cover profit.

Following its introduction, it is perhaps surprising that marginal costing has not been adopted more extensively than has been the case to date. The problems inherent in absorption costing are so difficult to resolve that many proponents of marginal costing argue that any absorption costing 'solution' is conceptually invalid. Nevertheless, despite the opposition of the marginal costing enthusiasts, absorption costing continues to flourish – so much so, in fact, that the accounting standard on stocks and work-in-progress (SSAP 9) recommends that they be valued at that cost which includes production overhead.

Overheads include any costs not directly attributable to a product or service; in other words, any cost which is not a direct material, direct wage, or direct expense. Usually, such overheads can be divided into three categories: production; administration; selling and distribution. Where appropriate, however, further categories can be created, such as research and development. These categories are established for control purposes, so that costs can be identified for important functions in an undertaking.

The control of overhead expense is an increasingly important function of the management accountant. For many years, there has been a tendency for overhead costs to rise more sharply and more frequently than other cost elements. Reasons for this include:

1   Inflation, under which most expenses, but especially salaries, energy costs, rates and the like, have risen rapidly and considerably.
2   Improvements in control techniques, where the direct costs of materials and material-holding have been reduced.
3   Automation and mechanisation, where labour costs have been reduced but where increased installation, maintenance and operation costs have been incurred.

4   Specialist services, where industrial and commercial enterprises have increasingly resorted to outside specialists – such as market researchers, behavioural scientists, taxation advisers, etc.
5   Advertising and promotional costs and practices, with most enterprises being forced to meet increasing competition by more extensive and more frequent advertising and promotion.
6   Business size, where increases in the size and structural complexity of business enterprises have necessitated the institution and operation of effective and costly control systems.

ELEMENTS OF COST

The main elements of an absorption cost analysis are illustrated in Table 6.1; such a statement shows at a glance the cost of producing each product and the profit for the period.

When that kind of analysis is presented, it is easy to accept the data as a sound criterion for decision making. However, the problem arises: Are the figures reliable, or acceptable? Assuming that accounting records have been maintained accurately, it could be accepted that the sales row is correct and that the totals column is correct, though doubt must be expressed concerning the other figures and estimates in the statement.

Table 6.1
Absorption costing statement (£000s)

	A	B	C	Total
Direct materials	200	500	100	800
Direct wages	100	300	200	600
Direct expenses	20	50	30	100
Prime cost	320	850	330	1 500
Production overhead	180	350	270	800
Production cost	500	1 200	600	2 300
Administration overhead	120	260	170	550
Selling & distribution overhead	80	140	130	350
Total cost	700	1 600	900	3 200
Sales	800	2 000	1 200	4 000
Total cost	700	1 600	900	3 200
Profit	100	400	300	800

It is probably fair to say that the prime cost figures are relatively accurate, allowing for minor errors in charging out hours worked or materials used, but the overhead charges are, at best, arbitrary. This area has caused the greatest part of the controversy between absorption and marginal costing, so it is appropriate to explore the systems of charging overheads to product costs.

The recovery of overhead in production costs is a tedious and far from simple operation. Clearly, much will depend on the nature of the business or industry. If a company produces one type of aircraft at the rate of one a month, this is a different proposition from a company which produces dozens of different types of food products, at least one of which has an output of several hundreds of thousands of cans a day. Each category of overhead has to be considered separately, so that production cost can be ascertained.

PRODUCTION OVERHEAD

Included in production overhead would be all items of indirect materials, indirect labour and indirect expenses. It is easy to establish the amount of production overhead incurred during an accounting period; the difficult part is to relate those costs to specific production costs. It is proposed that the task should be undertaken in three stages: allocation; apportionment; absorption. The first two stages are concerned with charging overheads to the department or cost centre in which production is being carried out, so that the cost of production is ascertained in respect of each department, while the third stage is concerned with charging the cost incurred by a department to each product being manufactured.

A simple example will serve to illustrate this three-stage procedure. A factory has six manufacturing departments and its total production costs for one month are £1 000 000. The first stage is to allocate or charge direct to the departments wherever possible. For example, salaries of staff engaged exclusively in a department will be charged to that department, and the cost of a service used exclusively by one department will be charged direct to that department. Much of the production overhead cost cannot be allocated in this simple, direct way. The larger part of such cost will have to be apportioned between cost centres.

The apportionment of overheads depends very largely on managerial discretion and corporate policy, but a number of traditional basis are employed. The nature of the overhead will usually determine the choice of apportionment method. The most common methods use floor area, plant value, employee numbers, material values, and technical estimates.

Such overhead costs as rent and rates can be apportioned according to the floor areas of departments. In our example, if the annual rent of the factory amounts to £50 000 for a total floor area of 10 000 sq ft, and if Department 3 occupies 2 000 sq ft, the amount charged to that department in respect of rent will be £10 000 a year.

Overhead costs like insurance or depreciation can be apportioned according to relative plant values. For example, with an annual insurance charge of £10 000 for machinery and plant valued at £400 000 and with Department 2 using plant valued at £100 000, the amount charged to that department in respect of insurance would be £2 500 a year.

Canteen subsidies, health and welfare costs, sports facilities costs and the like can be apportioned according to relative employee numbers. For example, if total annual canteen costs for a factory with 10 000 employees are £100 000 and if Department 4 contains 3 000 employees, the amount charged to that department in respect of canteen facilities will be £30 000 a year.

Material values can be used to apportion the costs of storage and warehousing. If total annual costs for storage amount to £200 000 in respect of £3 000 000 of used materials and if the goods released from storage to Department 6 are valued at £600 000, the amount charged to that department in respect of storage costs will be £40 000 for the year.

Sometimes it may be necessary to consult specialists for guidance on the apportionment of certain overheads. For example, if departments do not receive individually metered supplies of electricity, it may be necessary to ask an electrical engineer to estimate departmental consumptions based on machine power, number of appliances, and so on.

When production overheads have been allocated and apportioned to departments or cost centres, management can be presented with a report of the costs incurred by each cost centre. It must be emphasised, however, that these cost figures will not be wholly accurate. If the apportionment has been carried out realistically, though, they will be at least representative. Accuracy can never be achieved in absorption costing, and even if it were possible the process would be much too costly and time consuming. Nevertheless, the information generated provides management with a useful guide to the cost of operating each department.

Unfortunately, such a report of the costs of overhead ascribed to each department does not mean that the procedure is completed. Our example assumed six manufacturing departments. Additionally, service or functional departments will usually have to be considered. Now, assume that there are two service departments to support the six manufacturing units. So far in the procedure followed, the two service departments would have been allocated or apportioned overhead cost in the same way as the manufacturing departments. However, the costs of service departments cannot be passed on to their end-products because, by their nature, such departments do not manufacture goods. Thus, costs of service departments must be borne by the manufacturing departments, necessitating a laborious process of re-apportioning service costs between production departments.

When a group has numerous service departments, that process may be particularly difficult and complex. For example, if one of the service departments is a canteen, the cost of operating it must be apportioned over all the manufacturing departments and other service departments. Furthermore, service departments may be interdependent; the canteen will feed the boilerhouse staff, while the boilerhouse will supply power to the canteen, and so on. There are a number of acceptable methods which can be used in an attempt to apportion service department costs to production departments, but perhaps the best is that of repeated distribution.

Table 6.2 presents the breakdown of apportioned total production overhead between the eight departments, and shows the estimated service provided by the two service departments to each of the other departments. Estimation of the proportionate service provision is perhaps the most difficult part of the procedure and might require

Table 6.2
Production overhead apportionment and estimated service provision

Departments	Apportioned production overhead	Estimated service provision Dept X	Dept Y
1	£120 000	10%	20%
2	£200 000	20%	5%
3	£100 000	5%	10%
4	£180 000	10%	20%
5	£140 000	15%	20%
6	£160 000	20%	15%
X	£60 000	–	10%
Y	£40 000	20%	–

the cooperation of experts in the field of each service department. The cost of a service department is apportioned to other departments according to the agreed percentage of service rendered. The process is repeated until the cycle is completed, as shown in Table 6.3.

It can be seen from the distribution summary in Table 6.3 that this re-apportionment of overhead is very arbitrary. However, using this approach does mean that all the overhead costs have been charged against production departments so that the final stage of absorbing the overheads into products manufactured in those departments can be completed. This stage is the essence of absorption costing, in that each product absorbs its estimated share of the production overhead.

Overheads must be recovered according to some estimated rate, normally based on a budget. In the majority of industries, it would be quite impossible to use actual recovery rates because the amount of expense incurred would not be known until after the event. It is estimated, therefore, to produce a forecast of the amount of overhead for a future period so that an estimated rate of absorption can be calculated.

Absorption rates

A variety of criteria have been used to decide a rate for the absorption of overheads.

The most common are:

1　a percentage of direct material cost;
2　a percentage of direct labour cost;
3　a percentage of prime cost;
4　a rate per unit produced;
5　a rate per labour hour;
6　a rate per machine hour.

Perhaps it is inadvisable to generalise and claim one of those methods to be the best. The circumstances of a particular situation must be considered before a choice is made. In broad terms, however, the fifth and sixth methods seem preferable to the others in most, if not all, cases.

Most overhead costs are incurred as a function of time – for example, rates, rent, salaries and depreciation occur with the passing of time – and so it is reasonable to suggest that, in the interests of consistency, overheads should be absorbed as a function of time. Thus, the hourly-based rates of absorption are to be recommended. Discretion must be exercised, of course, in determining where labour hours or machine hours are more appropriate.

125

Table 6.3
Production overhead distribution

Departments	Apportioned overhead	X1	Y1	Distributions X2	Y2	X3	Y3	Total
1	120 000	6 000	10 400	520	208	10	5	137 143
2	200 000	12 000	2 600	1 040	52	21	1	215 714
3	100 000	3 000	5 200	260	104	5	2	108 571
4	180 000	6 000	10 400	520	208	10	5	197 143
5	140 000	9 000	10 400	780	208	16	5	160 409
6	160 000	12 000	7 800	1 040	156	21	3	181 200
X	60 000	(60 000)	5 200	(5 200)	104	(104)	(2)	–
Y	40 000	12 000	(52 000)	1 040	1 040	21	(21)	–

Table 6.4
Production budget and job estimate

Department 5 – Production Budget 1983

Direct materials	£320 000
Direct wages	£240 000
Prime cost	£560 000
Production overhead	£160 000
Production cost	£720 000
Planned units of output	400
Planned labour hours	80 000
Planned machine hours	16 000

Job 99 – Estimate

Direct material cost	£510
Direct labour cost	£330
Prime cost	£840
Labour hours required	100
Machine hours required	25

To illustrate the production overhead absorption rate approach, consider the budget of Department 5 in the earlier examples. The cost estimate for a specific job is being prepared. The production data associated with that job are shown in Table 6.4, and the effects of the adoption of each of the six absorption rate methods listed above are shown in Table 6.5.

Under the first method, a percentage of direct material cost, it can be seen that the production overhead is 50 per cent of direct material cost, so the amount of overhead to be absorbed in Job 99 is £255. This

Table 6.5
Job overhead absorption rate methods

Absorption method	Prime cost	Production overhead	Production cost
% of direct material cost	£840	£255	£1 095
% of direct labour cost	£840	£220	£1 060
% of prime cost	£840	£240	£1 080
rate per unit	£840	£400	£1 240
rate per labour hour	£840	£200	£1 040
rate per machine hour	£840	£250	£1 090

method is normally unsuitable because overhead seldom varies in proportion to direct materials.

The second method, a percentage of direct labour cost, results in Job 99 bearing £220 of overhead cost, on the basis that production overhead is 66.7 per cent of direct labour cost. This method may be reasonable when one factory-wide wage rate applies, but it will not be suitable when wage rates differ from department to department.

Using the third method, a percentage of prime cost, the amount of production overhead to be absorbed by Job 99 is calculated at £240, representing 28.6 per cent of prime cost (on the basis that £160 000 is roughly 28.6 per cent of £560 000 – in the department's 1983 budget). This method is a combination of the first and second methods, and so shares the weaknesses of both.

The fourth method, using an absorption rate per unit of product, results in a charge of £400 per unit as an average of the estimated production overhead across the planned output of 400 units. This method looks the weakest of the six described, unless all the products being manufactured are of similar or equal value.

The labour hour rate approach, the fifth method, results in the apportionment to Job 99 of production overheads of £200 (on the basis that, in the department's 1983 budget, production overhead represents £2 per labour hour planned). If labour is a predominant factor in the production process, this method is preferable.

Under the sixth method, the machine hour rate approach, the production overhead burden for Job 99 is £250 (on the basis that production overhead in the budget represents £10 an hour). If machinery is a predominant factor in production, this method is preferable.

While the recovery of production overheads by means of a three-stage operation is important, it is essential that overheads should be controlled carefully. Results should be monitored by the use of budgetary control and standard costing systems. A budget for production overhead should be prepared, standard costs and standard recovery rates established, and deviations from the standards set should be analysed as variances.

The absorption of production overhead is central to absorption costing and is the most difficult part of the system. Once the production cost has been established, it forms the basis for calculating total cost. The other principal categories of overhead expense are administration overhead and selling and distribution overhead.

ADMINISTRATION OVERHEAD

All costs incurred in the administration activities of a business will be included in administration overheads, irrespective of whether such costs are materials, wages or expenses. A budget for administration overhead should be prepared so that actual results can be monitored. A monthly budget report should be presented to management giving details of each element of overhead and any significant variance should be analysed and explained.

In terms of expenditure, the control of administration overhead is similar to that of production overhead, that is, control is through budgets and the reporting of variance. Recovery of overhead is a different matter, however. The procedure followed with production overhead is not possible with administration overhead owing to the inherent difficulties of relating any administration expense with a particular product or department. A simple example will underline the difficulties. If the chief executive's secretary receives a salary of £8 000 a year, and the firm produces large numbers of each of dozens of products, how much should be charged to each product?

How, then, can administration overheads be charged to products? No sophisticated or scientific method is available, so a very arbitrary method is usually chosen – namely, charging administration overhead to products on the basis of their appropriate cost of production. The system works as follows.

A company manufactures four products – Alpha, Beta, Gamma and Delta – and incurs a total administration overhead cost of £500 000. The products incur total production costs as follows: Alpha – £200 000; Beta – £600 000; Gamma – £800 000; Delta – £400 000. On the basis that the four products incur respectively 10 per cent, 30 per cent, 40 per cent and 20 per cent of overall production costs, each product would be charged with those proportions of administration overhead; respectively £50 000, £150 000, £200 000 and £100 000.

SELLING AND DISTRIBUTION OVERHEAD

All costs incurred in marketing and distributing products will be included in selling and distribution overheads. Obvious examples include advertising, salesmen's wages and commissions, warehousing costs, transport costs and product brochures. Control of selling and distribution expense is normally exercised by a cost budget which may be analysed to show targets and results for months, divisions, products, or salesmen. Actual performance is monitored and deviations reported and investigated.

As with administration overhead, it is very difficult to charge selling and distribution overhead to products or departments. A straightforward and frequently used method is to treat selling and distribution overhead in the same way as administration overhead and charge it to products on a production-cost basis. Alternatively, the basis chosen could be production cost plus administration cost. Using the same results as in the previous illustration, the total cost could be calculated easily by this method. Assuming that selling and distribution overhead is budgeted at £1 000 000, then the four products would be charged with selling and distribution overhead as follows: Alpha – £100 000; Beta – £300 000; Gamma – £400 000; Delta – £200 000. That would give total costs for the whole product range of £3 500 000, attributable as follows: Alpha – £350 000; Beta – £1 050 000; Gamma – £1 400 000; Delta – £700 000.

Alternatively, selling and distribution overhead could be apportioned on a sales-mix basis. Assuming that total sales for all four products were expected to reach £4 600 000, of which Alpha would account for £552 000, Beta for £1 288 000, Gamma for £1 610 000, and Delta for £1 150 000, their selling and distribution overhead could be apportioned as follows: Alpha – £120 000; Beta – £280 000; Gamma – £350 000; Delta – £250 000. The four products would then bear total costs as follows: Alpha – £370 000; Beta – £1 030 000; Gamma – £1 350 000; Delta – £750 000.

It will be appreciated that these methods of charging overheads are simplistic, but absorption costing does not claim any high degree of sophistication. It attempts to analyse cost by products or departments, thereby providing management with a rudimentary guide for setting selling prices and determining costing and selling policies. Attempts have been made to take a more scientific approach to apportioning overhead costs to products, but they have often proved expensive and not significantly better than the 'rule of thumb' system. This is particularly true of selling and distribution costs.

Functional cost analysis can be used to analyse selling and distribution overhead by products or by product lines. Such costs as advertising, invoicing, warehousing, sales administration, and delivery could be apportioned to products in any one of a variety of ways. For example, delivery costs could be charged to products according to the weights of product units and the distances over which they are transported; advertising costs could be attributed directly or proportionately on a space basis to the products or lines being promoted. It is a difficult and tedious task. While statistical sampling techniques may be employed to reduce the time and effort spent on each such operation, there are any number of inherent difficulties. Nevertheless, it makes a challenging alternative to the simpler methods and could provide a useful means of establishing overhead burdens for each of a number of products.

Overabsorption and underabsorption

So far this discussion has concerned itself with the actual absorption of overheads into product costs. However, a further important aspect is the actual expense incurred. The overhead incurred in running a business is known with certainty, whereas the amount of overhead absorbed is based on prior estimates of the levels of production and overhead likely to be incurred during the period. Clearly, one of the most important factors to watch will be any difference between the budgeted overheads and the actual overheads incurred, and any departures from budgeted levels of expenditure should be investigated rigorously.

Overhead is absorbed or applied at a predetermined rate, and the resultant product cost consists of a mixture of essentially different elements: *actual* direct material cost, *actual* direct labour cost, *actual* direct expenses, and *applied* (or notional) overhead cost. To follow Horngren (1977), it is better that such a total product cost should be called a 'normal' product cost rather than an 'actual' product cost.

STOCKS

At the beginning of this chapter, the dispute between absorption costers and marginal costers was mentioned. That divergence is pointed up by stock valuation. The next chapter discusses the topic of marginal costing fully and at this stage it is sufficient to mention that while absorption cost includes overheads, marginal cost only includes those overheads which vary with output. Thus, when stocks of finished products and work in progress are being valued, notwithstanding the valuation method which is adopted (first in, first out or last in, first out, for instance), controversy arises as to whether this value should include a proportion of fixed overheads or exclude fixed overheads altogether.

Normally, stocks are described in one of three ways: raw ma-

131

terials, work in progress, and finished goods. No problem of overhead recovery arises in the valuation of raw material stocks although it would be tenable to argue for the apportionment of at least some warehousing costs. In the case of work in progress, the situation is quite different. Under an absorption costing system, production cost would be absorbed at each stage of the production process; stocks remaining at the end of a trading period will have been charged with an appropriate amount of production overhead. In some cases, administration overhead may have been charged to work in progress, but such a practice would not be in keeping with recommended accounting policies. Selling and distribution overhead should obviously not be charged to work in progress – unless, of course, some warehousing costs were apportioned.

Finished goods stock will have been charged with production overhead, may have been charged with administration overhead (even though this should not have been apportioned at this stage), and should not have incurred any selling and distribution overhead.

The problem of overhead recovery in stocks is concerned primarily with work in progress and attention should therefore be concentrated on that aspect of stock valuation. SSAP 9 explained that:

> In order to match costs and revenues, costs of stock and work in progress should comprise that expenditure which has been incurred in the normal course of business in bringing the product or service to its present location and condition. Such costs will include all production-related overheads, even though they may accrue on a time basis. The method used in allocating costs to stock and work in progress needs to be selected with a view to providing the fairest possible approximations to the expenditure actually incurred . . .

To illustrate the importance of stock valuation under both systems, Table 6.6 presents alternative profit and loss statements based on the essential principles of each system. The company works a 50-week year and produces one standard product at a normal level of 50 000 units a year. The product has a variable cost of £4 a unit and sells at £12 a unit. Budgeted costs per annum are: Production – £150 000; Administration – £80 000; Selling and distribution – £60 000. During Year 1, it is forecast that production will run at 100 per cent capacity but that sales will amount to only 60 per cent of production; in Year 2, production will only reach 60 per cent capacity, but sales will attain the target level of 50 000 units.

The question of which method has shown the operating position more fairly or more clearly is an open one, susceptible to subjective resolution. On balance, the marginal costing approach yields the better guide to what has happened and how the company stands at the end of each year. Consider, for example, the following. In Year 1, under the absorption costing approach profit was stated at £10 000; under the marginal costing approach a loss of £50 000 was reported. In Year 2, the absorption costing approach revealed a profit of £50 000; the marginal costing approach resulted in a profit of £110 000 being reported. When sales were low in Year 1, the mar-

Table 6.6
Alternative profit and loss statements (£000s)

Absorption Costing Approach			*Marginal Costing Approach*		
Year 1			*Year 1*		
Sales		360	Sales		360
Marginal cost	200		Marginal cost	200	
less Stock	80		*less* Stock	80	
		120			120
		240			240
Fixed overheads:			Fixed overheads:		
Production	150		Production	150	
less Stock	60		Administration	80	
		90	Selling etc.	60	
Administration	80				
Selling etc.	60				
		230			290
Profit		10	Loss		(50)
Year 2			*Year 2*		
Sales		600	Sales		600
Marginal cost	120		Marginal cost	120	
plus Stock	80		*plus* Stock	80	
		200			200
		400			400
Fixed overheads:			Fixed overheads:		
Production	150		Production	150	
plus Stock	60		Administration	80	
		210	Selling etc.	60	
Administration	80				290
Selling etc.	60		Profit		110
		350			
Profit		50			

ginal costing approach reflected the true position: when sales are lower than budgeted levels, profit is low. In Year 2, when sales recovered, profits under marginal costing were high. As Harris (1936) commented:

> ... a manufacturing company cannot realize a profit until its products have been sold. It cannot make a profit merely by producing goods for inventory.

That still holds good today!

PRICING POLICIES

Many firms still seem to base their pricing policies on absorption or total costing. Harvey and Thompson (1980), quoting a survey by Atkins and Skinner (1975), summarised as follows:

> The main method of pricing appears to be adding a percentage to cost. A typical comment was, 'Though efforts are made to escape from the cost-based attitudes of pricing, we have no other starting points in most cases.' Costs are most often obtained by the use of absorption (or full) costing.

Absorption costing produces a means of determining selling prices, but in most cases accuracy cannot be achieved due to the nature of the overheads included in the calculations. Nevertheless, the method gives data which can help in decision making, and many firms operate such a system. The major alternative is marginal costing and this is considered in Chapter 7.

REFERENCES AND FURTHER READING

Anthony, R.N., 'The rebirth of cost accounting', *Management Accounting* (USA), October 1975.

Atkins, B., and Skinner, R., 'How British industry prices', *Industrial Market Research*, 1975.

Baxter, W.J., and Oxenfeldt, A.R., 'Costing and pricing: the cost accountant versus the economist', *in* Solomons, D. (ed.), *Studies in Cost Analysis*, London: Sweet & Maxwell, 1968.

Demski, J., and Feltham, G., *Cost Determination: a Conceptual Approach*, Ames, Iowa: Iowa State University Press, 1976.

Dobson, R.W., *Distribution Cost Accounting*, London: Gee, 1950.

Grinnell, D.J., 'The product costing role of committed and discretionary fixed overhead costs', *Cost and Management* (Canada), March–April 1970.

Harris, J.N., 'What did we earn last month?', *NACA Bulletin*, 1936.

Hart, H., *Overhead Costs: Analysis and Control*, London: Heinemann, 1973.

Harvey, M., and Thompson, T., 'The cost pricing fallacy', *Accountancy*, August 1980.

Horngren, C.T., *Cost Accounting: a Managerial Emphasis*, 4th edn, Englewood Cliffs, N.J.: Prentice-Hall, 1977.

Owler, L.W.J., and Brown, J.L., *Cost Accounting and Costing Methods*, Plymouth: Macdonald & Evans, 1978.

Patterson, R., 'Stock valuation since SSAP 9', *Accountancy*, April 1979.

Shank, J.K., *Matrix Methods in Accounting*, Reading, Mass.: Addison-Wesley, 1972.

Thomas, A., *The Allocation Problem: Part Two*, Sarasota, Fla.: American Accounting Association, 1974.

7

Marginal costing

J. Lewis Brown

Marginal or direct costing has been practised in one form or another for the past fifty years, having been introduced in the early 1930s. The controversy between marginal costing and absorption costing continues and looks set to continue for many years to come. It was only in the years after the Second World War that interest in marginal costing developed to a significant level. Marginal costing (which might perhaps be better named 'variable costing') applies only the variable production costs to the cost of the product. One of the principal conceptual differences between the two systems – absorption and marginal – is that marginal costing treats fixed overhead as a period cost which is charged directly against revenue rather than as a product cost which is assigned to the units produced and thereby included in stocks. Notwithstanding the views of both the accountancy profession and the revenue administrations in the United Kingdom and the United States, which hold that direct costing is not a generally accepted method of stock valuation, the proponents of marginal costing argue strongly that to incorporate fixed factory overhead in product cost is incorrect and improper. The fixed part of manufacturing overhead, it is argued, is a function of the capacity to produce rather than of the production of specific quantities of product. As Amey and Egginton (1973) summarised:

> *Absorption costing involves the averaging of costs over units of output whether the costs are fixed or variable. The result is a product cost which is an average of costs at a particular level of output: the cost figure gives no indication of the short-run cost of producing additional units . . . variable costing is used widely for internal management purposes, but rarely for product valuation in external reporting.*

As discussed briefly in Chapter 6, the alternative methods have widely divergent implications for performance and profit measurement. More important, perhaps, are the significant dangers of adopting too rigid an approach to the use of marginal costing. As the author concludes, the misuse of marginal costs could easily result in setting selling prices too low to allow the recovery of fixed overheads. Nevertheless, the growing interest and participation in marginal costing show an increasing awareness of the substantial advantages associated with this method and the concepts of the contribution approach to costing and the techniques of cost-volume-profit analysis.

There is a fair amount of controversy over the meaning of marginal cost. The prevailing accounting concept is that of 'variable cost'; that is those elements of cost which vary with output. Prime costs, such as direct material cost and direct labour cost, would be included, together with direct variable expenses. This accountant's concept is different from the economist's concept, which is that the marginal cost is the incremental cost of producing one additional unit of output. In comparing the economist's marginal costing model with that of the accountant, Sizer (1961) suggested that:

> the differences are not so great as is often implied – that is partly due to a lack of understanding and that the accountant's marginal costing techniques are a practical application of the economist's marginal cost and marginal revenue theory.

In 1961, following publication of two reports – one in the United States (National Association of Accountants) and one in the United Kingdom (Institute of Cost and Management Accountants) – professional interest in marginal or direct costing was heightened and the succeeding two decades have seen a considerable debate as to the merits or otherwise of marginal costing.

Wright (1962) has provided a succinct definition of marginal costing:

> Direct costing, then, is an accounting system that separates expenses that vary with volume from those that do not. In manufacturing companies, this requires that only direct manufacturing expenses be charged to inventory and then matched against revenue for the determination of realized income. Period expenses are charged directly to profit and loss for the period in which the money was spent.

This concept of charging period or fixed costs against profit, rather than absorbing them into products, is the central issue in the absorption costing versus marginal costing debate.

In marginal costing, overheads are classified as 'fixed', 'variable' or 'semi-variable'. From that approach, it is not possible to identify an amount of net profit per product but it is possible to identify the amount of contribution per product towards fixed overheads and profits. Contribution is an important component of a marginal costing system and it will be discussed more fully later, but a measure of its importance can be gained from a simple example. If a company manufacturing four products adopts an absorption costing approach, it might be seen that one of those products makes a net loss of £50 000 over a period. In that period fixed overheads totalled £835 000 and the aggregate profit came to £260 000. Adopting a marginal costing approach might reveal that the direct costs of that product were £200 000. If sales in the period of that product totalled £400 000, the contribution of that product would be £200 000.

In reviewing its product mix, the company might wish to abandon any loss making product. Then since it showed a net loss of £50 000 under the absorption costing method, the product described above would be a candidate for discontinuance. Consider, however, what would have happened in the period under review if that product had not been produced. The contribution of £200 000 would have been forgone and the total profit of £260 000 would have been reduced to £60 000.

It would be dangerous to give the impression that absorption costing gives the 'wrong' answers and marginal costing the 'correct' ones. Marginal costing is not a panacea for decision makers, but it can be argued that it provides a more appropriate base on which to found such decisions as pricing and volume levels.

COST CLASSIFICATION

Marginal costing has the essential task of grouping overhead costs into categories – fixed, variable, and semi-variable. In general terms, the semi-variable category costs can be analysed to separate its components into either fixed or variable elements; a simple example would be telephone charges, which are based on a fixed rental and a variable charge per call made. Costs can be represented graphically, as shown in Figure 7.1 which looks at the three categories of overhead cost on a total basis and on a unit basis. Those graphs illustrate a paradox of marginal cost, in that a fixed cost is fixed in total but is variable per unit, whereas a variable cost is variable in total but is fixed per unit. Of course, it has been assumed that a fixed cost is fixed, while a variable cost is variable with production. It is appreciated that this may be a little naive, in that a fixed cost may only be fixed in the short term. More plant may be required, for instance, which would increase depreciation charges, or more supervision may be called for; these developments would give rise to a 'stepped cost' situation, under which fixed costs are fixed for a certain range of production, rise markedly at some threshold point, and continue at a fixed rate for the next range of production, and so on. Similarly, a variable cost may change as economies of scale are gained, though seldom by any significant proportion. These refinements to the underlying concept will be discussed later.

The problem of analysing costs by category can prove difficult in practice, although a number of techniques have been adopted to effect such an analysis – the least squares method, the range method,

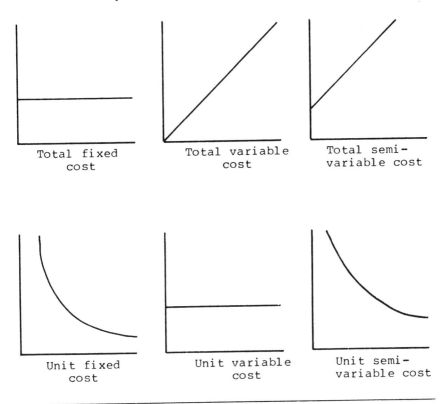

Figure 7.1   Total and unit cost graphs

Table 7.1
Maintenance costs

Budgeted data for five-month period

	Feb	Mar	Apr	May	Jun	Total
Running hours	4 800	4 000	3 600	4 400	3 200	20 000
Maintenance costs (£)	21 600	20 000	19 200	20 800	18 400	100 000

Least squares analysis

	Feb	Mar	Apr	May	Jun	Σ
Deviations from average hours (x)	+800	–	−400	+400	−800	–
Deviations from average cost (y)	+1 600	–	−800	+800	−1 600	–
x^2 (000s)	640	–	160	160	640	1 600
xy (000s)	1 280	–	320	320	1 280	3 200

the high-low value method, the scattergraph, and so on. At this stage it is not necessary to describe and discuss each of those methods, but consideration of the least squares method and the scattergraph will exemplify the analysis process. Both are based on the principle of the linear relationship presented by the equation

$$y = a + bx$$

where y is average total cost, a is the fixed element of that cost, b is the variable element, and x is a measure of activity. As an illustration, maintenance cost can be considered, in which the measure of activity, x, is machine hours.

An example

A company operates a number of machines of similar type and the budgeted operational data for a five-month period are shown in Table 7.1. Under the least squares method, the average total cost would be calculated as follows. The least squares criterion is employed in statistics to determine whether a line through a number of points provides the best possible fit and a full description can be found in most statistical textbooks – see, for example, Freund and Williams (1982). The least squares formula for calculating b, the slope of the average cost line, is

$$b = \frac{\sum xy}{\sum x^2}$$

and Table 7.1 also gives the relevant variables for calculating those quantities. From the values in the table, it can be seen that b = 3 200 000/1 600 000 or b = £2. Average monthly cost is £20 000, and therefore the following calculation can be made:

$$£20\ 000 = a + £2\ (4\ 000)$$

where average monthly operating hours are 4 000. From that statement, it can be calculated that a = £12 000.

Those data could be presented in scattergraph form – as shown in Figure 7.2 – from which it might be seen that the 'best fit' line through the five points C_1 to C_5 intercepts the vertical axis at a point equivalent to £12 000.

The assumption that fixed costs are fixed and variable costs variable with production is fundamental to such basic graphical presentations of marginal costing data. It is particularly useful in that a series of graphs can be assembled, providing readily understood information to assist in decision making. The principal value of such information is the speed with which it can be used rather than its precision.

BREAKEVEN ANALYSIS

Traditional methods like the breakeven chart and its analysis can show quickly and simply the estimated results of trading at various levels of activity. Such charts show fixed and variable costs and sales revenue so that profit or loss at any given level of production or sales can be ascertained. From the graph, a breakeven point can be determined – at which neither profit nor loss is made – as can the safety margin – the amount by which sales could fall before a loss is experienced. The graph shown in Figure 7.3 is based on the following simple data: period fixed costs – £300 000; variable costs per unit – £5; selling price per unit – £15; production and sales volume – 40 000 units.

The chart shows clearly the breakeven point and the margin of safety; the breakeven point is at sales of 30 000 units (or, alternatively, breakeven revenue is £450 000), and the margin of safety is 10 000 units (or, in revenue terms, £150 000).

Breakeven points can be calculated by formula, also. Such calculations require the derivation of the contribution per unit of product and the profit-volume ratio, which can be discussed briefly at this stage.

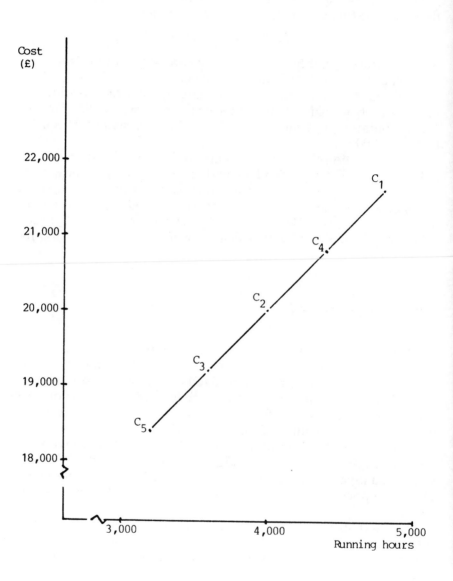

Figure 7.2   Maintenance costs

Contribution

Contribution is the amount which a product generates towards total fixed overheads and profits. It can be described as either sales revenue less marginal cost or fixed cost plus profit. In the simple example shown in Figure 7.3, contribution is £10 per unit (£15 sales revenue less £5 marginal cost).

Profit–volume ratio

Profit–volume ratios reveal the rate of contribution per product as a percentage of turnover; while it might better be called a 'contribution-sales percentage', the term 'profit–volume ratio' is now widely used. In the simple example shown in Figure 7.3, total contribution is £400 000 for total sales revenue of £600 000, giving a profit–volume ratio of 66.7 per cent (or, taking unit figures, £10 as a percentage of £15).

From these two relationships, the formulae for calculating breakeven points are constructed as follows. The volume breakeven point is derived from:

$$B_v = \frac{F}{C}$$

where F is total fixed cost and C is contribution per unit, and the revenue breakeven point is derived from:

$$B_r = \frac{F}{PVR}$$

where F is total fixed cost and PVR is profit–volume ratio.

For the earlier example, those two calculations would be as follows: B_v = £300 000/£10 = 30 000 units; B_r = £300 000/66.7% = £450 000.

So far, the assumption has been that fixed cost remains fixed for any level of production. If that assumption is relaxed, a more realistic picture emerges. If fixed costs are assumed to rise at certain levels of activity, the 'stepped cost' approach could be used to produce a graph such as Figure 7.4, which includes the possibility that a selling price might have to be reduced to meet competition. Additionally, variable costs may be reduced in the long run.

It can be seen from the graph that complications arise with changes in the factor, and that there will be more than one breakeven point, with more than one margin of safety. This refinement of the breakeven chart imports more realism into the analysis by graphical tech-

143

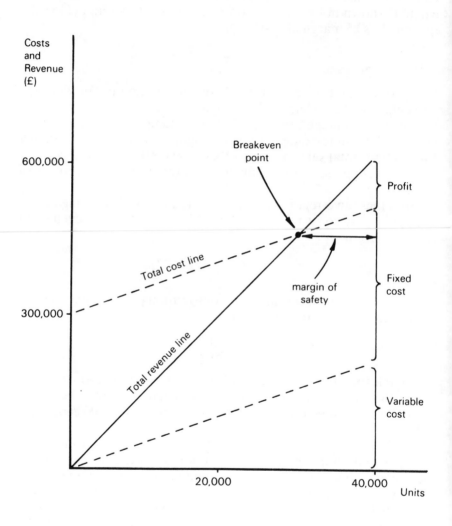

Figure 7.3 Breakeven chart

niques of marginal costs. A further development incorporates the 'relevant range' within which costs can be predicted with reasonable accuracy. Such a relevant range might be between the sales quantity points A and B indicated on the graph in Figure 7.4. The effect of such a narrowing of the field of concern is that it focuses the attention of management on particular levels of activity so that decisions can be taken more appropriately in a situation where predicted costs are more accurately portrayed.

Breakeven analysis has many limitations, but it provides a ready guide for decision making. The following limitations should be borne in mind:

1 fixed costs are not necessarily fixed in the long run;
2 variable costs are not necessarily strictly variable with output;
3 sales prices are not necessarily constant per unit;
4 capital employed is not taken into consideration.

KEY FACTORS

Marginal costing really shows its merit when scarce resources are being considered. Constraints or limiting factors inhibiting the production of sale of a product are key factors in a marginal cost analysis. Those factors can take a variety of forms – such as materials shortage, skilled labour scarcity, low sales demand, or insufficient capital. Where such scarce resources exist, the use of those key factors must be maximised so that contribution is as high as possible. Where only one key factor is experienced, a simple marginal costing statement can show the level of activity which would optimise contribution; where two or more such key factors obtain, however, a mathematical approach is essential – linear programming, for example, as described and discussed in Chapter 21. Graphical solutions are possible, of course, but they may not always be sufficiently precise.

Single constraint

The data presented in Table 7.2 relate to a manufacturing company which produces four products and reveal the individual contributions and profit–volume ratios for each of those products.

If the key factor or constraint were availability of direct materials, for instance, the appropriate criterion is contribution per direct material £; in the case of the four products, contributions per direct ma-

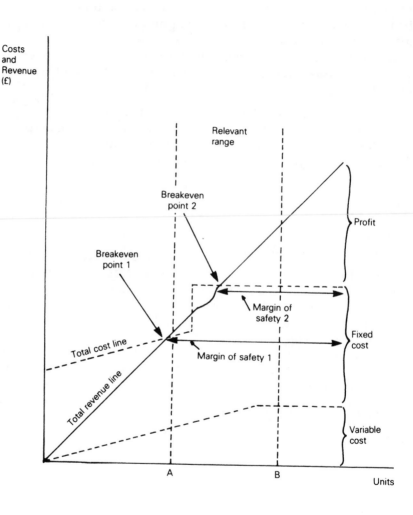

Figure 7.4   Breakeven chart – stepped cost and relevant range

terial £ are as follows: Product 1 – £2.00; Product 2 – £0.75; Product 3 – £1.25; Product 4 – £1.20. On that basis, Product 1 offers the highest contribution per limiting factor.

If the key or limiting factor were direct labour availability, the appropriate criterion would be contribution per labour £; in the example, those contributions are: Product 1 – £0.80; Product 2 – £2.00; Product 3 – £1.25; Product 4 – £1.50. On that basis, Product 2 offers the highest contribution per limiting factor.

If there are no scarce resources or limiting factors, the better product to concentrate on would be Product D, which offers the greatest contribution per unit. If, on the other hand, the criterion for measuring profitability (and thereby for concentrating production and effort) were the profit–volume ratio, the better product would be Product 3, which reveals a profit–volume ratio of £37.5 per cent.

Equally, of course, there may be upper limits on the quantities of any one product which can be sold in the market without altering the sales price and contribution relationships. In that situation, products would be ranked in order of their contribution, either in total or per limiting factor, or profit–volume ratio (whichever criterion was being employed). If, for example, sales demand is a further constraint, the problem moves from the relatively simple category of '-single constraint' to the more complex one of 'multiple constraints'.

Multiple constraints

When there are several limiting factors, the problem of contribution analysis and production level determination becomes very much more difficult. If only two products are manufactured and the num-

Table 7.2
Four-product manufacturing company

	Product A	Product B	Product C	Product D
Sales prices (£)	36	18	40	50
Variable cost (£):				
Direct materials	6	8	12	15
Direct labour	15	3	12	12
Variable overhead	3	1	1	5
	24	12	25	32
Contribution (£)	12	6	15	18
Profit–volume ratio	33.3%	33.3%	37.5%	36.0%

ber of constraints is also small, the optimal mix can be determined graphically. Three-dimensional graphs can cope with three products, but the complexities of that approach render the graphical solution impracticable; above three products, it is impossible to visualise graphical solutions and mathematical techniques are needed.

The simple graphical solution is illustrated in Figure 7.5, which represents the following data for a two-product manufacturing firm. Product A sells for £40.00 a unit; it requires 16 lbs of material costing £0.50 a lb; it takes 2 hours to go through the first stage of processing costing £3.00 an hour and 4 hours to go through the second stage costing £4.00 an hour. Product B sells for £48.00 a unit; it requires 19 lbs of material costing £1.00 a lb; it takes 3 hours in the first processing stage and 2 hours in the second.

In the coming period, the firm faces the following constraints. A maximum of 600 hours will be available in process stage 1 (P1) and 600 hours in process stage 2 (P2). There is a shortage of both types of raw material, so that only 1 920 lbs of material will be available for Product A (M1) and 3 420 lbs of material for Product B (M2).

These constraints may be plotted as shown in Figure 7.5, and a feasible production area determined – the hatched portion of the graph. The parameters of the feasible area are delineated by the constraint lines, and the nodal points (a) to (f) represent the feasible limits of each constraint. The contribution at each nodal point can be calculated as follows:

(a) 0 units of A = £0 contribution; 0 units of B = £0 contribution; total contribution = £0.

(b) 120 units of A = £1 200 contribution; 0 units of B = £0 contribution; total contribution = £1 200.

(c) 120 units of A = £1 200 contribution; 55 units of B = £660 contribution; total contribution = £1 860.

(d) 75 units of A = £750 contribution; 150 units of B = £1 800 contribution; total contribution = £2 550.

(e) 25 units of A = £250 contribution; 180 units of B = £2 160 contribution; total contribution = £2 410.

(f) 0 units of A = £0 contribution; 180 units of B = £2 160 contribution; total contribution = £2 160.

The optimal contribution is obtained, therefore, at a production of 75 units of A and 150 units of B.

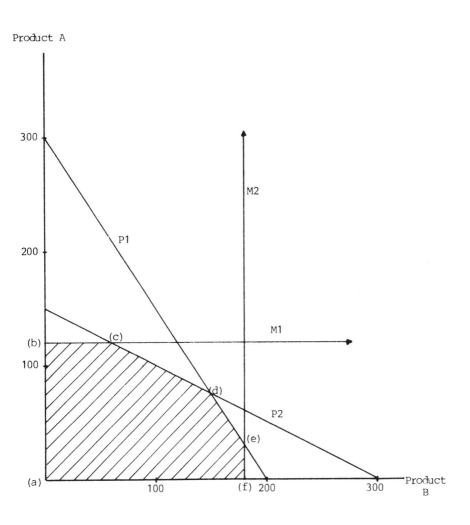

Figure 7.5   Two-product manufacturing firm

PRICING POLICY

As will be seen in Chapter 17, one of the most important functions of a marginal costing system is as an aid to pricing decision making. The marginal cost of a product is comprised of prime cost and variable overhead, so it is argued that marginal costs are relatively more accurate; prehaps it might be better to claim that, as marginal cost excludes all fixed overhead, it is less inaccurate than an absorption cost.

The application of marginal cost in the determination of prices can be exemplified by the familiar case of a special rail ticket. To attract football fans from Southbury to travel to Northbury to watch their team play in a cup match, the railway operators offer a return ticket at a special rate of £5, compared with the regular return price of £15. Clearly, the implications are that the marginal costs of providing an additional train will be covered; there may be some contribution also, but the fixed overhead would be recovered in the regular price of a ticket and there may be some shortfall there. The problem of basing selling prices on marginal cost is to make certain that sufficient contribution will be generated to recover all fixed overhead and to create an adequate profit. Pricing can be determined by considering what the market would pay or by calculations based on some profitability measurement, such as a profit–volume ratio.

In the former case, once the marginal cost is ascertained, it can be compared with the probable market price and the contribution determined. In the latter case, products would be appraised in terms of a desired profit–volume ratio.

A simple example may make the point clearer. A company produces six products, as illustrated in Table 7.3, which presents a pro forma profit and loss statement.

Table 7.3
Six-product manufacturing company

Forecast profit and loss statement (£000s)

	Product A	Product B	Product C	Product D	Product E	Product F	Total
Sales revenue	1 500	833	2 333	1 667	1 000	2 667	10 000
Marginal cost	900	500	1 400	1 000	600	1 600	6 000
Contribution	600	333	933	667	400	1 067	4 000
Fixed overhead							3 000
Profit							1 000

The company has forecast that it can produce the six items at the marginal costs shown and, at that level of output, fixed overheads are budgeted at the levels set out in the statement. If management determined that a minimum profit of £1 000 000 was required in the coming period, then a total sales revenue of £10 000 000 would be required. Those criteria would dictate a desirable profit–volume ratio of 40 per cent (£4 000 000 as a percentage of £10 000 000) and individual product sales revenue targets at levels consistent with profit–volume ratios of 40 per cent on average. Those targets and the forecast production levels will determine the individual product selling prices. The italicised figures in the pro forma statement represent these management estimates based on the marginal cost forecasts.

Obviously, in the real world, management would not aim at a uniform profit–volume ratio of 40 per cent for each of the six products, but would vary the individual ratios to suit market conditions, scarce resources usage, and so on. However, the average profit–volume ratio of 40 per cent provides a useful guide for setting individual product prices.

ADVANTAGES AND DISADVANTAGES

At various points, the advantages and disadvantages of marginal costing have been outlined as specific matters were discussed, and it may be helpful to summarise them briefly at this point. In most cases, because absorption costing and marginal costing are contrasting approaches rather than complementary ones, advantages of one approach are disadvantages of the other and vice versa.

The advantages may be summarised as follows:

1 Marginal costing management with more appropriate information for decision making.
2 The profit and loss statement is not distorted by changes in stock levels. Stock valuations are not burdened with a share of fixed overhead, so profits reflect sales volume rather than production volume.
3 Profit–volume analysis is facilitated by the use of breakeven charts and profit–volume graphs, and so on.
4 Pricing decisions can be based on the contribution levels of individual products.
5 The analysis of contribution per key factor or limiting resource is a useful aid in budgeting and production planning.

6 Responsibility accounting is more effective when based on marginal costing because managers can identify their responsibilities more clearly when fixed overhead is not charged arbitrarily to their departments or divisions.

Similarly, the disadvantages of marginal costing can be summarised as follows:

1 Difficulty may be experienced in trying to analyse fixed and variable elements of overhead costs.
2 Managers may find it difficult to adjust their thinking to profitability measurement in terms of profit–volume ratios.
3 Stock valuations (as, for example, under SSAP 9) may require the use of absorption costing methods.
4 The misuse of marginal costing approaches may result in setting selling prices which do not allow for the full recovery of overhead. This may be most likely in times of depression or increasing competition, when prices set to undercut competitors may not allow for a reasonable contribution margin.

REFERENCES AND FURTHER READING

Amey, L.R., and Egginton, D.A., *Management Accounting: a Conceptual Approach*, London: Longman, 1973.

Freund, J.E., and Williams, F.J., *Elementary Business Statistics: the Modern Approach*, 4th edn, Englewood Cliffs, N.J.: Prentice-Hall, 1982.

Hart, H., *Overhead Costs: Analysis and Control*, London: Heinemann, 1973.

Harvey, R., and Thompson, T., 'The cost pricing fallacy', *Accountancy*, August 1980.

Horngren, C.T., *Cost Accounting: a Managerial Emphasis*, 4th edn, Englewood Cliffs, N.J.: Prentice-Hall, 1977.

Institute of Cost and Management Accountants, *A Report on Marginal Costing*, London: ICMA, 1961.

National Association of Accountants, *Application of Direct Costing*, New York: NAA, 1961.

Owler, L.W.J., and Brown, J.L., *Cost Accounting and Costing Methods*, Plymouth: Macdonald & Evans, 1978.

Sizer, J., 'Marginal costing: economists v accountants', *Management Accounting*, April 1961.

Wright, W., *Direct Standard Costs for Decision-making and Control*, New York: McGraw-Hill, 1962.

8

Variance accounting

C. Stuart Jones

In this chapter, the author describes and discusses variance accounting techniques, demonstrating the presentation to management of periodic summaries of differences between actual results and predetermined budgets and standards. Such summaries are analysed by cause and responsibility. As the writer recognises, variances are most commonly associated with manufacturing industry, possibly because they were developed in that sphere of business activity, but variance analysis need not be confined to manufacturing activity. Any activity which is susceptible to definition and measurement before it takes place can be analysed for deviations. This is one of the attractive features of variance analysis, for it is sufficiently flexible for its principles to be applied to provide a great variety of variances to assist the managers of an enterprise to control its activities and plan future operations. The chapter concludes by discussing the use of variances in the processes of appraisal and decision making, and the writer draws attention to the problems associated with the use of variances derived from past performance to plan future outturn. Additionally, as Anthony and Reece (1979) and many others have emphasised:

> *. . . the terms 'favorable' and 'unfavorable' should be used with care; they denote the algebraic sign of a variance, not value judgments of managers' performance.*

Nevertheless, variance analysis is a welcome and straightforward technique for facilitating the better analysis of actual results, particularly when such analysis is conducted as promptly as practicable and reported as clearly and succinctly as possible.

The starting point for the analysis of variances is the standard cost for the product or service as derived from or used in the determination of

Table 8.1
Standard sales and costs (per unit)

	Product A		Product B
Standard sales price	6.00	Standard sales price	4.00
Standard costs:		Standard costs:	
Direct materials 2.00		Direct materials 1.50	
(6lbs X @ £0.25;		(4lbs X @ £0.25;	
1lb Y @ £0.50)		1lb Y @ £0.50)	
Direct labour 1.00		Direct labour 1.50	
(½ hr @ £2.00)		(¾ hr @ £2.00)	
	3.00		3.00
Contribution	3.00		1.00

the budget. The example in this chapter concerns a production department which constitutes a cost centre under the responsibility of a departmental manager. The department produces two products, A and B, using common resources and facilities, including two direct materials, X and Y, which can be partly substituted for each other. The standard cost for each unit of A and B is shown in Table 8.1 for the first three months of 1983.

Table 8.2
Budgeted departmental sales and costs

	Product A	Product B
Sales and production units	2 000	3 000
	£	£
Sales	12 000	12 000
Direct materials: X	3 000	3 000
Y	1 000	1 500
Direct labour	2 000	4 500
Total direct costs	6 000	9 000
Contribution	6 000	3 000
	9 000	
Fixed overheads	3 000	
Budgeted departmental profit	£6 000	

Initially, it is assumed that a marginal or variable cost system is employed and, consequently, no fixed overheads are allocated to individual products. This approach simplifies the analysis and provides particularly useful information for management. The complications that arise when absorption costing is used are discussed later.

The agreed budget for the first quarter of 1983 consists of the budgeted sales and production quantities of each product multiplied by that product's appropriate standard cost for the period, as shown in Table 8.2; for simplicity, production for stock has been ignored at this stage.

Table 8.3 details the actual sales achieved for A and B in the period, together with the actual costs incurred by the department for the three-month period. The actual cost information is compiled from source documents (wages analyses, timesheets, stores requisitions, invoices and so on), analysed in a form comparable with the detail given in the unit standard cost analysis (Table 8.1).

Table 8.3
Actual departmental sales and costs

	Product A	Product B
Sales and production units	2 500	2 800
	£	£
Sales value	12 500	11 900
Direct materials: X	3 125 (12 500 lbs @ 25p)	2 800 (11 200 lbs @ 25p)
Y	1 120 (2 800 lbs @ 40p)	1 080 (2 700 lbs @ 40p)
Direct labour	2 925 (1 300 hrs @ £2.25)	4 725 (2 100 hrs @ £2.25)
Total direct costs	7 170	8 605
Contribution	5 330	3 295

	8 625
Fixed overheads	2 900
Actual departmental profit	£5 725

155

NAIVE ANALYSIS

A comparison of Tables 8.2 and 8.3 shows that the actual profit is £275 less than that budgeted for the period (£6 000 – £5 725). It is tempting to explain this difference by comparing each of the elements of the budget and actual results so that, for example, material X reveals a saving of £75 (budget £3 000 + £3 000 as against actual £3 125 + £2 800). Direct labour reveals overspending of £1 150, and so on. A little thought, however, will reveal that the departmental manager is unlikely to be happy with an unfavourable labour variance based on budgeted output of 5 000 units when his department has produced 5 300 units.

Comparison of the fixed budget with the results in this way is naive and unsatisfactory. Nonetheless, it cannot be denied that the actual profit is £275 below budget. The final result of any more sophisticated analysis should explain the causes of that variation.

FLEXING THE BUDGET

The next step is to revise the fixed budget by 'flexing' each variable cost to reflect the changes in output. This involves multiplying each variable cost by the multiple

(budgeted cost/budgeted output) × actual output

where all that is being done, in simple terms, is multiplying the actual output for the period by the standard cost for the period. Table 8.4 presents an analysis on that basis, wherein flexed budget costs are compared with actual costs to provide a meaningful overview.

An important stage in variance analysis has been reached, because Table 8.4 provides a structural framework to which all subsequent detailed analysis can be related. Column (d) reveals the unfavourable sales price variance of £1 800, the favourable direct cost variances of £125, and the favourable fixed overhead cost variance of £100. Together, those variances explain why the actual departmental profit of £5 725 is £1 575 less than what might have been expected for the level of output achieved. The flexible budget in column (b) shows that a profit of £7 300 might have been expected in the circumstances.

However, there is a further, and more important, aspect to Table 8.4; clearly, there has been a change in the level of activity in the department compared with that anticipated when the fixed budget

Table 8.4
Calculation of variances – marginal costing

		a	b		c	d = b − c
		Fixed budget	Flexible budget		Actual	Sales price & cost variances
Unit sales:	Product A	2 000	2 500		2 500	
	Product B	3 000	2 800		2 800	
		£	£		£	£
Sales revenue:	Product A	12 000	15 000	(2 500 x £6)	12 500	
	Product B	12 000	11 200	(2 800 x £4)	11 900	
		24 000	26 200		24 400	1 800(U)
Direct materials and labour:						
	Product A	6 000	7 500	(2 500 x £3)	7 170	330(F)
	Product B	9 000	8 400	(2 800 x £3)	8 605	205(U)
		15 000	15 900		15 775	125(F)
Contribution		9 000	10 300		8 625	1 675(U)
Fixed overheads		3 000	3 000		2 900	100(F)
Department profit		6 000	7 300		5 725	1 575(U)

Sales volume or
   activity variance   £1 300(F)

Total profit variation   £275(U)

Notes: F = Favourable   U = Unfavourable

was set, and this is significant. The activity level achieved is of considerable concern to management, which determined the production targets after considering the sales potential for each product. A budget of 5 000 units was fixed (2 000 units of Product A and 3 000 units of Product B), with a profit expectation of £6 000. Management would be pleased to see that a production total of 5 300 units was achieved and would have expected to see a profit of £7 300 on that output. That favourable variation of £1 300 – the sales volume variance – represents the opportunity cost of the additional output and is simply the budgeted contribution which the changed activity represents.

Alternatively, it could be calculated on the following basis. An extra 500 units of Product A were involved, each with a standard contribution of £3.00 a unit, implying a total extra contribution of £1 500; there were 200 less units of Product B, each with a standard contribution of £1 a unit, making a total lost contribution of £200; in total, an extra contribution of £1 300 should have resulted.

The departmental profit variation from budget – an unfavourable variance of £275 – can be explained by the favourable sales volume variance of £1 300 being offset by the unfavourable cost and price variances of £1 575.

DETAILED ANALYSES

It is now possible to prepare a more detailed analysis of the variances to reveal the causes, using the standard cost and actual cost data provided in Tables 8.1 and 8.3. In practice, the extent of the analysis depends upon the information needs of management and the ability of the cost accounting system to collect and retrieve the necessary information. For instance, a record of man-hours spent on each product would be required to enable the calculation of a labour efficiency variance; such recording might call for the introduction of a special job or product progressing system. In designing cost systems, the accountant must be aware both of the needs of management and of the cost involved in capturing the data. These needs and costs will alter from time to time as management faces new problems and new techniques become available, so a flexible approach is desirable.

There are many approaches to the detailed analysis of variances and perhaps the easiest is the mechanistic substitution of new periodic variables in pro forma statements. While not gainsaying the importance of a proper understanding of the principles of variance analysis, a practical and systematic framework has a lot to recommend it.

Some ground rules for variance analysis statements can be summarised at this point. First, as can be seen from Tables 8.5 and 8.6, it is convenient to record the actual costs or sales information in the left hand column (a) of the analysis tables. The final column on the right hand side of the tables will show the parallel information in terms of the flexed budget. The differences between the first column and the final column will represent the total variance for each cost item and their values will correspond with column (d) in Table 8.4. Between the first and the final column, one variable is altered at a time – from actual to standard – to isolate the variance. It is axiomatic that having once changed a variable from actual to standard it should remain at standard in subsequent columns; if this is not done, two variances will be confused.

Labour cost variances

Labour costs are analysed first because, for most production situations, they are straightforward. The analysis in respect of products A and B is presented in Table 8.5.

Two labour cost variances are calculated: a labour rate variance (reflecting the difference between the budgeted wage rate per hour and the actual wage rate per hour), and a labour efficiency variance (reflecting the increased or reduced cost because the actual hours taken to produce the output achieved were greater or lower than the standard hours specified for that level of output).

In the example, there is an unfavourable labour rate variance of £850, which might have occurred for a variety of reasons: a national wage award, or the award of increases in excess of standard, or the engagement of a more skilled grade of labour, or changes in an incentive or productivity scheme. There is an unfavourable labour efficiency variance, which might have been caused by a range of factors: excessive labour turnover and the need to train new employees, or changes in working methods, or inferior working conditions, or plant breakdowns, or short production runs.

If sufficient information is available, a portion of the labour variances can be attributed to each cause. This is important because some of the causes are outside the control of the departmental manager and should not affect adversely the appraisal of his performance, while others may be partly the result of a positive decision made by the manager – the engagement of more skilled workers, for example.

Table 8.5
Analysis of labour cost variances

	(a) Actual Cost Actual rate × Actual hrs	(b) Standard rate × Actual hrs	(c)* Standard rate × Standard hrs for actual output
	£	£	£
Product A	(£2.25 × 1 300 hrs) = 2 925	(£2.00 × 1 300 hrs) = 2 600	(£2.00 × 2 500 units = 2 500 × ½ hr)
Product B	(£2.25 × 2 100 hrs) = 4 725	(£2.00 × 2 100 hrs) = 4 200	(£2.00 × 2 800 units = 4 200 × ¾ hr)
	7 650	6 800	6 700

Labour rate variance   (Col. b − Col. a) =   £850(U)
Labour efficiency variance   (Col. c − Col. b) =   £100(U)

Total labour cost variances   (Col. c − Col. a) =   £950(U)

*Column (c) is the flexed budget for labour costs and corresponds to the standard cost of labour for actual production

It is essential that the reasons for all variations are understood and the remedial action is taken and/or budgets and standards are revised.

Alternative labour variance calculation

As understanding of variance analysis is gained, the analyst will find that some of the simpler variances can be calculated without using any tabulation, thereby providing economy of effort and speed. For example, the labour efficiency variances can be approached as follows. The standard hours allowed to produce the actual output are compared with the actual hours taken and the difference is multiplied by the standard wage rate to produce either a favourable or unfavourable variance. For example, to produce 2 500 units of Product A should have taken 1 250 hours and to produce 2 800 units of Product B should have taken 2 100 hours, giving a standard total of 3 350 hours. The actual hours taken were 3 400 – a difference of 50 hours, which, at the standard wage rate of £2.00 an hour, gives rise to a labour efficiency variance of £100 (unfavourable).

Similarly, the labour rate variance could be calculated by comparing the standard rate of pay with the actual rate and multiplying the difference by the actual paid hours worked; for example, £2.00 was the standard rate, while £2.25 was the actual rate – a difference of £0.25 an hour for 3 400 hours, giving rise to a labour rate variance of £850 (unfavourable).

In formula terms, the labour variances may be represented as follows:

$$LRV = (SR - AR) \times AH$$

where LRV is labour rate variance, SR is standard rate, AR is actual rate, and AH is actual hours. In a similar fashion,

$$LEV = (SH - AH) \times SR$$

where LEV is labour efficiency variance, SH is standard hours, AH is actual hours, and SR is standard rate.

Material cost variances

The same approach is applied to the analysis of material cost variances as that used in analysing labour cost variances, and the variances themselves are also very similar. The material price variance is equivalent to the labour rate variance, while the material usage variance is equivalent to the labour efficiency variance.

161

The opportunity is now taken, however, to introduce two more advanced variances: the material mix variance and the material yield variance. These two variances are the two constituents of the material usage variance. Table 8.6 illustrates the analysis of material cost for products A and B.

The material price variance reflects the difference between the purchase price specified in the budget or standard cost statement and the actual price paid. For both products and both materials, the overall material price variance is £550 (favourable), but the total disguises the differences in type of material and product. For example, while the material price variance for material X used in Product A is £0, that for material Y used in Product A is £280 (favourable).

The material usage variance reflects the difference between the standard quantities of material allowed to produce the actual output achieved and the actual quantities used. Again, for both materials and both products, the overall material usage variance is £525 (favourable), indicating that the department has been efficient overall in the use of direct materials.

However, closer examination of Table 8.6 will reveal that the material mix variance for Product A is £153 (unfavourable), while that for Product B is £20 (favourable). The mix variance occurs because materials can be combined in different proportions to manufacture the product. In the example used, materials X and Y are partial substitutes for each other and discretion can be exercised during production.

The mix variance becomes particularly important when several ingredients are combined, as in steelmaking for example. To obtain a certain quality of steel, adjustments would have to be made to the mix of molten metal because of variations in the grade of scrap, pig iron and other ingredients. The possible combinations to produce a particular quality of steel are numerous and it would be impracticable to calculate a standard cost for all of them.

The material yield variance is a portion of the material usage variance and is due to the difference between the standard quantities of materials allowed to produce the actual output and the actual quantities used, other than that difference attributable to mix. Table 8.6 shows that the material yield variance for Product A is £628 (favourable), suggesting that considerable economy has been achieved during manufacture, which may have been aided partly by a more expensive mix of materials.

Table 8.6
Analysis of material cost variances

	(a) *Actual cost* Actual price × actual quantity at actual mix		(b) Standard price × actual quantity at actual mix		(c) Standard price × actual quantity at standard mix		(d)* Standard price × standard quality at standard mix	
		£		£		£		£
PRODUCT A:								
Material X	25p × 12 500lbs = 3 125		25p × 12 500lbs = 3 125		25p × (6/7 × 15 300 = 3 279		25p × 2 500 × 6lbs = 3 750	
Material Y	40p × 2 800lbs = 1 120		50p × 2 800lbs = 1 400		50p × (1/7 × 15 300 = 1 093		50p × 2 500 × 1lb = 1 250	
	15 300	4 245		4 525		4 372		5 000
PRODUCT B:								
Material X	25p × 11 200lbs = 2 800		25p × 11 200lbs = 2 800		25p × (4/5 × 13 900 = 2 780		25p × 2 800 units × 6lbs = 2 800	
Material Y	40p × 2 700lbs = 1 080		50p × 2 700lbs = 1 350		50p × (1/5 × 13 900 = 1 390		50p × 2 500 units × 1lb = 1 400	
	13 900	3 880		4 150		4 170		4 200
		8 125		8 675		8 542		9 200

Material price variance (Col. b – Col. a):
Product A   280(F)
Product B   270(F)   550(F)

Material mix variance (Col. c – Col. b):
Product A   153(U)
Product B   20(F)   133(U)

Material yield variance (Col. d – Col. c):
Product A   628(F)
Product B   30(F)   658(F)

Total material cost variance (Col. d – Col. a)   1 075(F)

*Column (d) corresponds to the standard cost of material for actual production

£525(F) material usage variance

Alternative material variance calculations

Material variances can be calculated also in the more direct fashion described earlier for labour variances. The material price variance can be represented as follows:

$$MPV = (SP - AP) \times AQ$$

where MPV is material price variance, SP is standard price, AP is actual price, and AQ is the actual quantity of material. Similarly, the material usage variance can be represented as:

$$MUV = (SQ - AQ) \times SP$$

where MUV is material usage variance, SQ is standard quantity, AQ is actual quantity, and SP is standard price.

The material mix variance may be calculated as:

$$MMV = (AQ_s - AQ_a) \times SP$$

where MMV is material mix variance, AQ_s is actual quantities of material inputs in standard proportions, AQ_a is actual quantities of material inputs in actual proportions, and SP is standard price.

In like fashion, the material yield variance can be represented as:

$$MYV = (AQ_s - AQ_o) \times SP$$

where MYV is material yield variance, AQ_s is actual quantities of material inputs in standard proportions, AQ_o is actual quantities of material outputs in standard proportions, and SP is standard price.

Direct cost variances

The main variances calculated so far can be recapitulated as follows: LRV £850 (unfavourable), LEV £100 (unfavourable), giving an overall labour cost variance of £950 (unfavourable); MPV £550 (favourable), MMV £133 (unfavourable), MYV £658 (favourable), giving an overall material cost variance of £1 075 (favourable).

As shown in Table 8.4, there is a total direct cost variance of £125 (favourable), but that variance masked important information which needed to be made available to management. Furthermore, the analysis of the detailed variances raised many more points meriting managers' attention. Some of those were within the control or responsibility of the departmental manager, while others were clearly outside his control – and, indeed, outside the control of the company.

A diagrammatic illustration of the procedure of variance analysis is given in Figure 8.1, which presents a graphical comparison of actual and standard cost for either direct material or direct labour. The graph is drawn on the assumption that the actual cost is greater than the standard cost for actual production and all variances are unfavourable.

Direct expenses and variable overhead variances

For clarity of illustration, neither direct expenses nor variable overhead was included in the earlier statements for products A and B. In practice, both categories of cost are likely to be present and will occasion two types of variance.

First, an expenditure or spending variance, which is very similar to the material price variance and is calculated in the same way, is calculated to reflect changes in the price paid. Second, where an expense varies with man-hours or machine-hours instead of unit output, an efficiency or usage variance can be calculated. It indicates the standard cost value of any difference between the standard number of man-hours allowed for the actual output produced and the actual

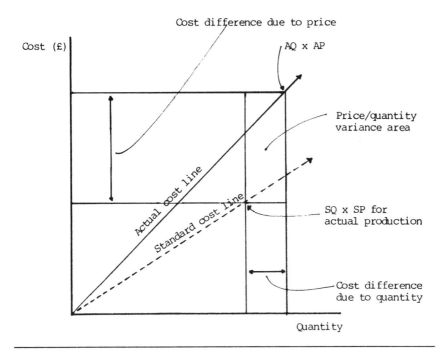

Figure 8.1 Cost comparison graph

number of man-hours worked, or machine hours where appropriate. The method of arriving at the variance in hours worked was explained earlier, and this variation is multiplied by the standard cost of the particular expense to provide a value for the variance.

A simple addition to the data provided earlier in connection with products A and B will make this explanation clearer. The budget variable overhead for the three-month period was estimated at £1 625; on the basis of a total labour utilisation of 3 250 man-hours (for 2 000 units of A and 3 000 units of B), variable overhead per man-hour was budgeted at £0.50. The actual variable overhead expenditure was £1 870, and 3 400 man-hours were worked.

On that basis, the variable overhead expenditure variance can be calculated as follows:

$$VSV = (SR - AR) \times AH$$

where VSV is variable overhead expenditure variance, SR is standard variable overhead rate per man-hour, AR is actual variable overhead rate per man-hour, and AH is actual man-hours worked. In this instance, the calculation would be:

$$VSV = (£0.50 - £0.55) \times 3\ 400$$

giving a variable overhead expenditure variance of £170 (unfavourable).

Similarly, the variable overhead efficiency variance can be calculated by:

$$VEV = (SH - AH) \times SR$$

where VEV is variable overhead efficiency variance, SH is standard man-hours for output produced. AH is actual man-hours worked, and SR is standard variable overhead rate per man-hour. In this case,

$$VEV = (3\ 350 - 3\ 400) \times £0.50$$

giving a variable overhead efficiency variance of £25 (unfavourable).

The flexed budget for variable overhead would have been calculated at £1 675 (being £0.50 an hour for the standard 3 350 man-hours for the actual production output achieved – 2 500 units of A and 2 800 units of B); the difference between actual variable overhead and flexed budget variable overhead is, therefore, £195 (that is, £1 870 – £1 675).

Sales variances

Sales variances may be calculated in two ways: related either to the

166

effect on turnover or sales revenue or to the effect on contribution. In explaining the change in profit between budget and actual (see Table 8.4) from £6 000 to £5 725 as an unfavourable variance of £275, the latter basis must be used.

Three variances arise under either method, but with different values depending on the approach. Sales managers tend to think in terms of turnover or revenue and this approach is perhaps the more appropriate for them.

The three variances that can be calculated are: sales price variance, sales mix variance, and sales volume variance. Table 8.7 illustrates the calculation of these variances as related to turnover and it can be seen that the approach is similar to that adopted for material variances. Two points should be noted, however. First, each column is deducted from the immediately preceding left hand column in order to give the correct 'sign' for the variance; this is opposite to the procedure for deriving cost variances. Second, the resultant total sales turnover variance of £400 (favourable) cannot be related to the analysis in Table 8.4 since the variance explains turnover rather than profit changes.

Table 8.8 illustrates the sales variances calculated on a contribution basis. Because Table 8.4 adopts a marginal cost presentation, the analysis of the sales variances is related to contribution rather than profit. The changes in contribution provide extremely useful tools for management decision making because they approximate opportunity cost; their significance is discussed later in this chapter. Suffice it to say at this point that if absorption costing is used, then a proportion of fixed overhead is included in the direct product costs and sales variances are then calculated using profit rather than contribution. The methodology is the same, but the variances will be smaller.

The sales price variance of £1 800 (unfavourable) is the same under either turnover or contribution or profit calculation methods. The sum of the sales mix and sales volume variances in Table 8.8 is £1 300 (favourable), which is, of course, the sales volume variance or activity variance shown in Table 8.4.

A sales volume variance can be analysed further, into a market size variance and a market share variance. Again, a simple example will serve to demonstrate the calculation and interpretation of the variances. Taking the earlier illustration, for products A and B, it is assumed that the market for products A and B has grown during the period from an expectation of 50 000 units demanded to 54 000 units demanded, and that the company's share of the market has fallen from 10.0 per cent to 9.815 per cent. The change in turnover due to

Table 8.7
Turnover-based analysis of sales variances

	(a) *Actual Sales* Actual price × actual quantity at actual mix	(b) Standard price × actual quantity at actual mix	(c) Standard price × actual quantity at standard mix	(d) Standard price × budgeted quantity at standard mix
	£	£	£	£
Product A	£5 x 2 500 = 12 500	£6 x 2 500 = 15 000	£6 x 2 120* = 12 720	£6 x 2 000 = 12 000
B	£4.25 x 2 800 = 11 900	£4 x 2 800 = 11 200	£4 x 3 180* = 12 720	£4 x 3 000 = 12 000
	5 300 24 400	26 200	5 300 25 440	24 000

Sales price variance (Col. a – Col. b):

$$\text{Product A} \quad 2{,}500(U)$$
$$\text{B} \qquad\quad 700(F) \;\Big\}\; 1\,800(U)$$

Sales mix variance (Col. b – Col. c)   760(F)
Sales volume variance (Col. c – Col. d)   1 440(F)
Total sales turnover variance   400(F)

*Actual sales unit of 5 300 split in the ratio budgeted:

Product A $5\,300 \times \dfrac{2\,000}{5\,000}$ = 2 120 units

B $5\,300 \times \dfrac{3\,000}{5\,000}$ = 3 180 units

     5 300 units

Table 8.8
Contribution-based analysis of sales variances

	(a) Standard contribution × actual quantity at actual mix	(b) Standard contribution × actual quantity at standard mix	(c) Standard contribution × standard quantity at standard mix
	£	£	£
Product A	£3 x 2 500 = 7 500	£3 x 2 120 = 6 360	£3 x 2 000 = 6 000
B	£1 x 2 800 = 2 800	£1 x 3 180 = 3 180	£1 x 3 000 = 3 000
	5 300 10 300	5 300 9 540	5 300 9 000

Sales price variance
Product A   2 500(U)
B   700(F)   1 800(U)

Sales mix variance (Col. a – Col. b)   760(F)
Sales volume variance (Col. B – Col. c)   540(F)   £1 300(F)

Total sales variance   500(U)

the increase in market size is calculated as follows:

$$MTV = MT_c \times MS_b \times BP_b$$

where MTV is market size variance, MT_c is change in total market size, MS_b is budgeted market share, and BP_b is budgeted price at budgeting mix, giving

$$MTV = 4\ 000 \times 10\% \times £24\ 000/5\ 000$$
$$= \text{favourable variance of } £1\ 920.$$

Similarly, the change in turnover due to reduced market share is calculated as follows:

$$MSV = MS_c \times MT \times BP_b$$

where MSV is market share variance, MS_c is change in market share, MT is total market size, and BP_b is budgeted price at budgeted mix, giving

$$MSV = -\ 0.185\% \times 54\ 000 \times £24\ 000/5\ 000$$
$$= \text{unfavourable variance of } £480.$$

Those two variances combine to give a favourable sales volume variance of £1 440 (as shown in Table 8.7). They can be calculated also on contribution basis, by multiplying the variance expressed in turnover terms by the budgeted contribution per £ of sales at budgeted mix.

For the market size variance, the calculation is:

$$£1\ 920 \times £9\ 000/£24\ 000$$

giving a variance of £720 (favourable). For the market share variance, the calculation is:

$$£480 \times £9\ 000/£24\ 000$$

giving a variance of £180 (unfavourable). Aggregated, the £540 (favourable) variance corresponds with the sales volume variance on a contribution basis (as shown in Table 8.8).

Fixed overhead expenditure variance

This variance is sometimes called the budget or spending variance, and is calculated as follows:

$$OSV = AFO - BFO$$

where OSV is fixed overhead spending variance, AFO is actual fixed overhead expenditure and BFO is the flexed budget fixed overhead expenditure. The £100 (favourable) variance shown in Table 8.4 may mask several significant but compensating variances. In practice, therefore it is important to calculate and report variances for each classification of expense.

The important question of fixed overhead variances is considered in more detail later in this chapter.

STANDARD COST ACCOUNTS

The departmental operating account shown in Table 8.9 is the pivot of standard cost accounts and is introduced at this juncture to re-inforce the analysis described so far. A separate account is opened for each cost centre which is the responsibility of a manager. It is debited with the value of direct materials used, actual labour cost incurred, actual overhead costs incurred, and, if absorption costing applies, with apportioned overheads from service departments and general overhead accounts. It is credited with the standard cost of production, consisting of both finished production and any work-in-progress; both are valued according to the standard cost of the work performed. If marginal costing is used, the standard cost credited excludes any fixed overhead, whereas with absorption costing fixed production overhead and certain administration overhead are included.

The balance of the account should represent variances which are under the control of the departmental manager. At the end of the period, variances are transferred out of the operating account to the profit and loss account, and thereby written off in the period in which they are incurred.

Table 8.10 illustrates the format of the profit and loss account used for internal purposes when a standard costing system operates. It supports the principle of 'management by exception' by high-lighting the impact of variances in changing the profit from that budgeted to that achieved. All the figures used can be traced to the analyses described in this chapter, and it is interesting to note how the sales variances on both profit and turnover bases are included in an informative manner.

FIXED OVERHEAD VARIANCES UNDER ABSORPTION COSTING

When an absorption costing system is used, the analysis of fixed overhead variances, with the exception of the spending or expendi-

Table 8.9
Departmental operating account

	£	£		£	£
Opening work-in-progress valued at standard marginal cost incurred		Nil	Finished production valued at standard marginal cost:		
Actual costs incurred:			Product A 2 500 units @ £3 = 7 500		
Direct material X	5 925		B 2 800 units @ £3 = 8 400		15 900
Y	2 200	8 125	Closing work-in-progress		Nil
Direct labour		7 650	Budgeted fixed overheads debited		
Controllable fixed overheads		2 900	to profit and loss account		3 000
Favourable variances credited			Unfavourable variances debited		
to profit and loss account:			to profit and loss account:		
Material price	550		Labour rate	850	
Material yield	658		Labour efficiency	100	
Fixed overhead			Material mix	133	1 083
expenditure	100	1 308			
		19 983			19 983

ture variance, becomes more complicated and the sales volume variance alters also. The reason is that absorption costing includes fixed overhead in the valuation of stock and work-in-progress – the method prescribed by SSAP 9. This leads to an underrecovery or overrecovery of budgeted fixed costs as production levels vary from those budgeted, giving rise to a fixed overhead volume variance which may be further split into an efficiency variance and a capacity variance.

Table 8.11 is a revision of Table 8.4 to reflect the adoption of an absorption costing approach. The first important difference is the flexing of fixed overhead in column (b) to reflect the recovery of fixed overhead (£3 093) included in the valuation of the actual output. It is assumed that the fixed overhead is recovered in product costs on the basis of hours worked. The budgeted fixed overhead rate per hours is thus £0.923 (that is, £3 000/3 250 hours) and the fixed overhead standard cost for Product A is £0.462 (£0.923 × ½) and for B £0.692 (£0.923 × ¾).

This step increases the total fixed overhead variance to £193

Table 8.10
Profit and loss account

	Sales £	Margin £
Budgeted sales and margin	24 000	6 000
Add (subtract) sales variances:		
Price	(1 800)	(1 800)
Mix	760	760
Volume	1 440	540
Actual sales	24 400	
Subtract standard cost of actual sales	15 900	
Subtract fixed overheads	3 000	
Standard profit of actual sales		5 500
Add (subtract) cost variances:		
Labour rate	(850)	
Labour efficiency	(100)	(950)
Material price	550	
Material mix	(133)	
Material yield	658	1 075
Fixed overheads spending		100
Actual profit for period		5 725

Table 8.11
Calculation of variances – absorption costing

		a	b	c	d=b−c
		Fixed Budget	Flexible Budget	Actual	Sales price & cost variances
Unit sales:	Product A	2 000	2 500	2 500	
	Product B	3 000	2 800	2 800	
		£	£	£	£
Sales revenue:	Product A	12 000	15 000	12 500	
	Product B	12 000	11 200	11 900	
		24 000	26 200	24 400	1 800(U)
Direct materials and labour:					
	Product A	6 000	7 500	7 170	330(F)
	Product B	9 000	8 400	8 605	205(U)
		15 000	15 900	15 775	125(F)
Fixed overheads		3 000	3 093*	2 900	193(F)
Total cost of production		18 000	18 993	18 675	318(F)
Department profit		6 000	7 207	5 725	1 482(U)
Sales volume or activity variance		£1 207(F)			
Total profit variation			£275(U)		

*Actual output @ standard fixed overhead cost per unit:
   Product A £0.462 x 2 500 units = £1 155
       B £0.692 x 2 800 units = £1 938
                   3 093

(favourable) by introducing the volume variance of £93 (favourable); at the same time, the sales volume variance is reduced by £93 because this is now calculated at the profit level and not the contribution level. The calculation of the detailed variances is shown in Table 8.12.

A volume variance can be calculated for any category of fixed overhead, but it is customary to restrict it to fixed factory or production overhead. Most administration, selling, distribution, and research and development fixed overheads are normally written off to the profit and loss account in the period in which they are incurred and so receive treatment similar to production overhead under the marginal convention.

Alternative approaches

The calculation of overhead variances can be conducted in a number of different but essentially cohesive ways, and several writers have advocated alternative approaches – the three-part or four-part overhead variance analysis, for example. Amerman (1953 and 1954) gave several examples of using a number of reference points to produce alternative combinations and subdivisions of fixed overhead variances. Solomons (1968) provided a further analysis of the variation of fixed overheads.

By way of illustration, Figure 8.2 presents a taxonomy of sales, production and overhead variances.

Table 8.12
Analysis of fixed overhead variances

			£	
(a)	Actual expenditure		2 900	
(b)	Budgeted expenditure		3 000	
(c)	Actual direct labour hours worked standard cost per hour $(3\ 400 \times \dfrac{£3\ 000)}{3\ 250}$		3 138	
(d)	Actual man-hours produced standard cost (3 350 hrs £0.923)		3 093	
Fixed overhead expenditure variance b – a			100(F)	
Fixed overhead capacity c – b			138(F)	volume
Fixed overhead efficiency variance d – c			45(U)	variance £93(F)
Total fixed overhead variances			193(F)	

Difficulties

If management by exception is to be useful, the significance attached to variances must be clear and unambiguous. Management must have confidence that the majority of figures which are not emphasised in reports are correct and that the reported variances have been calculated from reliable information. If credibility is to be maintained, the underlying cost accounting systems must be of a high order. Frequently, when challenged because of unfavourable variances, a manager will criticise the information recording system.

Obviously a balance has to be struck between the cost of analysis and the provision of reliable management information. This problem is heightened if the firm is in a turbulent environment with quickly changing information requirements.

The manner in which costs vary is a further problem. For illustration purposes it has been easy to assume that direct material, direct labour and direct expense costs vary directly with output; in

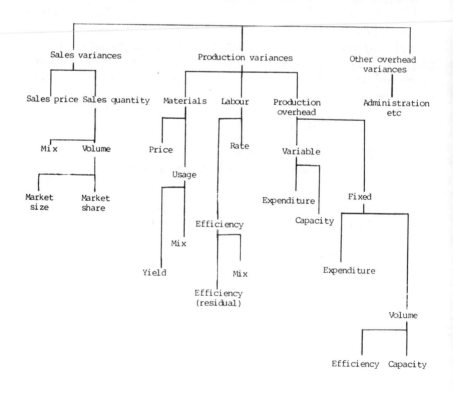

Figure 8.2   Standard cost variances

practice, separating costs to reflect their true relative variability is extremely difficult. However, this has to be attempted if meaningful variances are to be reported. To illustrate the point further, it is customary for variable overhead to be regarded as a function of a single variable such as machine hours, whereas the facts of cost behaviour belie any such single assumption. The introduction of several bases of cost behaviour greatly increases the complexity of analysis, although the general principles remain unchanged.

INTERPRETATION AND ACTION

The manner in which variances are interpreted and acted upon is important if they are to be valuable for management control. Unfortunately, the cause of a particular variance may not be obvious. Material price variances may be caused by errors in forecasting price movements or by shifts in world prices following political changes in supplier countries or because ordering patterns have become uneconomic or because of the substitution of higher priced materials. Clearly, some reasons are within the control of the firm with the responsibility being borne by different managers, but many are outside the firm's control.

The reasons for variations are complex. It is vital that they be researched thoroughly, understood clearly and acted upon in a reasonable manner. The temptation to use unfavourable variances as a 'weapon' for criticising subordinate managers must be resisted. Such unwise use of variances would have a distinct demotivating and sub-optimising effect on most managers.

It is possible for management to define limits for variances, within which no action is needed – in a similar manner to statistical quality control. In practice, such an approach is rare and investigation is usually arbitrary. Some firms leave it to each manager to investigate his 'own' variances as he feels necessary to improve future performance. Other firms favour more formal arrangements, with managers meeting to discuss variances and determine remedial action.

Generally, it is less than helpful to prescribe rigid limits (such as variations of more than £X or X per cent), since some variances will be persistently over the limit for the same reason every period. Other variances may be small but herald increasing problems.

There can be no substitute for an intelligent and flexible approach to variances if they are to be used effectively to control critical areas of a business. The same applies to the frequency with which variances are reported.

Variances are reported normally in money terms, although back-up statistical data are often very useful. For instance, a production foreman may find an awareness of man-hours gained or lost more meaningful than a simple statement of the money value of the labour efficiency variance. Efficiency, activity and capacity ratios can be used effectively alongside the money variances. An efficiency ratio can be constructed as the percentage relationship between the standard hours for the output and the actual hours worked; an activity ratio may be calculated as the percentage relationship between the standard hours for the actual output and the budgeted standard hours; a capacity ratio may be calculated as the percentage relationship between the actual hours worked and the budgeted standard hours.

SIGNIFICANCE OF VARIANCES

Most variances have economic significance, since they represent a real gain or loss to the enterprise, but the variance analysis of fixed overhead volume cannot be commended on that ground. Many writers have attacked the real significance of the overhead volume variance – notably Dopuch et al. (1974), who argued that the variance is meaningless for management in the short run. The variance merely balances the books when absorption costing is used. When the variance is expressed in non-financial terms, such as actual departmental or direct labour hours compared with budget, or production units compared with budget, the difficulties of interpretation do not arise.

The loss of a unit of production has an immediate and tangible meaning for operational managers and implies the loss of all the benefits that could have derived from that unit. The measurement of capacity utilisation has to be much wider than a simple consideration of volume variance.

The fixed overheads which comprise capacity costs represent important resources which management should seek to use in the most efficient manner possible. Since these are, by definition, largely a function of the passage of time rather than of output, it follows that their efficient use should take the form of maximising contribution in the time available to the stated objective of the firm. Jones (1980) and others have emphasised this opportunity cost approach to variance analysis. A close approximation to that opportunity cost of the change in the use of production capacity can be derived from the sales activity variance calculated at the contribution level – see Tables 8.4 and 8.8, for example, where such a variance is set at £1 300 (unfavourable).

If, however, absorption costing operates, the sales volume variance of £1 207 (favourable) – see Table 8.11 – will be calculated at the profit level, and this no longer measures the opportunity cost. However, if that variance is combined with the fixed overhead volume variance of £93 (favourable) in Table 8.12, the total is £1 300 (favourable), which is an approximation to the opportunity cost.

It will be an approximation provided the opportunity exists to sell the output or it makes economic sense to produce for stock in anticipation of future sales. Also, it will only be an approximation in the sense that the contribution used represents existing product contributions which may not reflect the optimal mix or optimal opportunities that really exist for that capacity. Nevertheless, for planning purposes at a senior level in the firm, the contribution measure of opportunity cost represents a useful starting point.

The significance of variances for decision making must be considered also. Variances relate only to past events and nothing can be done about them; they are sunk costs or benefits. Furthermore, the standards used to produce such variances are at best only *ex ante* estimates which represent the dynamic business situation by a static model and ignore the decision alternatives implied by the actual conditions encountered. Such estimates are likely to include random errors and slack, and they can quickly become irrelevant. A dynamic environment will tend to frustrate comparison.

A partial solution to some of these drawbacks may lie in superimposing actual prevailing conditions on to the standards, thereby providing a more realistic measurement of performance. Such an approach was used, for example, in introducing market size and market share variances based on the actual market size for the period under review.

Because traditional variance analysis relies upon comparisons of actual experiences with *ex ante* standards, it generally ignores decision alternatives implied by the actual conditions encountered. A more comprehensive solution proposed by Demski (1967), using linear programming techniques, extends the traditional analysis to include all inputs to the decision model by revising the original decision based on deviations encountered. That enables an *ex post* optimum to be determined from additional information acquired during implementation of the *ex ante* programme.

The difference between the *ex ante* and the *ex post* situations is a crude measure of the firm's forecasting ability, while the difference between the actual results and the *ex post* optimum reveals the opportunity cost to the firm of failing to use available resources to their fullest advantage. The difference between the *ex ante* budget, actual performance, and the *ex post* optimum can be analysed using traditional or conventional variance analysis techniques.

The prime intention of this approach is that the provision of the opportunity cost impact of deviations facilitates learning and taking remedial action. The system is not without its critics – see, for example, Amey (1973) – because of the difficulty of determining an *ex post* optimum for the complicated operations of a typical firm. Additionally, that optimum cannot be calculated until all the events anticipated in the original decision model have occurred. The longer the decision period, the more difficult it becomes to attach any meaning to the *ex post* optimum.

REFERENCES AND FURTHER READING

Amerman, G., 'The mathematics of variance analysis', *Accounting Research*, July 1953, October 1953, January 1954.

Amey, L. R., 'Hindsight v expectations in performance measurement', *in* Amey, L. R. (ed.), *Readings in Management Decision*, London: Longman, 1973.

Anthony, R. N., and Reece, J. S., *Accounting: Text and Cases*, 6th edn, Homewood, Ill.: Irwin, 1979.

Bromwich, M., 'Standard costing for planning and control', *The Accountant*, 19 April 1969, 26 April 1969, 3 May 1969.

Dearden, J., *Cost and Budget Analysis*, Englewood Cliffs, N.J.: Prentice-Hall, 1962.

Demski, J. S., 'An accounting system structured on a linear programming model', *The Accounting Review*, October 1967.

Dopuch, N., Birnberg, J. B., and Demski, J. S., *Cost Accounting*, 2nd edn, New York: Harcourt Brace Jovanovich, 1974.

Dyckman, T. R., 'The investigation of cost variances', *Journal of Accounting Research*, Spring 1969.

Jones, C. S., 'Fixed overhead volume variance: an opportunity cost approach', *Management Accounting*, May 1980.

Kaplan, R. S., 'The significance and investigation of cost variances: survey and extension', *Journal of Accounting Research*, Autumn 1975.

Solomons, D., 'The analysis of standard cost variances', *in* Solomons, D. (ed.), *Studies in Cost Analysis*, London: Sweet & Maxwell, 1968.

9

Costing for planning

Michael Bromwich

Above all else, information presented to management for decision-making purposes must be useful, and there must be a continual effort to improve the methods of preparing, submitting and interpreting such information. Professor Bromwich argues that the traditional variance calculations of budgetary control and standard cost systems can be made much more useful for decision making. Switching the emphasis of such systems from their traditional preoccupation with control to concentrate upon planning will aid management in a difficult task. The chapter reviews the usefulness of conventional variances for planning and appraisal in relation to both inefficiency in operation and the inaccuracy of original plans and standards. It shows how better information can be derived than that given by the usual variance computations. The author believes that variances of the kind discussed in his chapter can be much more useful to management than the ritual calculation of all-purpose textbook variances. As he argues, it is by no means clear that variances designed for one purpose can be used effectively for another, variances intended to aid planning processes cannot often serve as motivational devices, for example.

Contemporary changes in general purchasing power, major alterations in specific prices, and the seemingly extra variability and uncertainty of today's economic environment, among other things, make it imperative to improve the information available to management for decision making. In one particular area, that of variance analysis, traditional emphases can be switched from a predominant concern with control to a more effective concern with planning.

The model used in standard costing approaches compares actual and expected results, significant deviations being identified and isolated for remedial action or reformulation by management. Devices of that type are known as 'feedback' systems, in which the outputs of the system themselves become inputs to the adjustment process designed to ensure that the outputs of the system are those specified originally. Such a typical 'engineering' control system can be depicted as in Figure 9.1. Outputs are given, the process is easily contained, inputs are specified and are relatively few. The outputs are monitored and can be controlled by the regular making adjustments to the inputs. Probably the best known feedback model is the conventional central heating system, where differences between actual and desired warmth are used as signals for automatically changing boiler activity.

The model is readily incorporated in the management accountant's control process. If the output of the information system is actual material prices paid, then the error signal becomes a price variance and the regulator becomes the responsible manager. The usual analogue drawn between standard costing and budgetary control systems and feedback control devices illustrates the traditional preoccupation of budgetary and standard costing practitioners with control. Any management accounting textbook will also give clear evidence of this heavy emphasis on control aspects.

The feedback approach to standard costing does, however, bring out very clearly the link between planning and control. In the central heating system, for example, past performance is monitored and, on the assumption that any past error will continue unless corrective action is taken, a planning decision is made about fuel input. Similarly, standard cost variances can only be used to guide future actions, for any mistake is a sunk cost. If a purchasing manager who lost £15 000 last month is sacked, this is due less to his past error than to fears that he may continue to make such mistakes in the future.

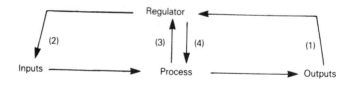

(1) feedback
(2) adjustment of inputs
(3) information flow directly from the process
(4) adjustment to the process

Figure 9.1 Feedback control system

Unfavourable control variances (better called 'appraisal' variances because of the emotive connotations of the word 'control') are planning variances which serve to highlight the need for improved performance or planning in the future.

One area of feedback theory rich in potential applications to accountancy, involves the use of variances as inputs into planning models and future decisions – that is, feeding forward such variance information.

CAUSES OF VARIANCES

One of the most important differences between simple feedback systems and those of the management accountant is the latter's need to consider the cause of any error signal. In the central heating system, the remedy is clear and the cause is usually of little importance. In the management accountant's system, the cause may be of paramount importance; very different responses may be required to variances resulting from different factors. Indeed, many variances cannot be eliminated, but must be taken into account when replanning; for example, a price variance following a change in foreign exchange rates.

There are two major causes of variances between standard and actual performances:

1 inefficiency in operation; failure to obtain a reasonable standard in the prevailing circumstances, whether through inability in one form or another or through lack of motivation;
2 incorrectness of original plans and standards; invalidation of original plans and standards through environmental change.

Under the second set of circumstances, reporting variances may result in a revision of plans and the one thing that should not be encouraged is adherence to the original, wrongly-based plans. The process of variance analysis should prove educational in this respect.

Variances calculated from these causes and with the circumstances of the business explicitly in mind will be more useful to management than the ritualistic textbook all-purpose variances. A different kind of variance might then be used for each cause. As Stedry (1967) said, it is not obvious that variances designed to aid planning can also serve as motivational devices.

VARIANCES FOR PLANNING AND APPRAISAL

The present chapter, therefore, reviews the usefulness of the conventional variances for planning and appraisal in relation to the two principal causes mentioned earlier, and shows that information obtained in that way can be more meaningful than that derived from the usual variance computations. The variances highlighting the first cause (inefficiency and poor motivation) may be called 'appraisal' variances. At present, it does not seem possible to suggest an analytical approach to split the appraisal variance between the two underlying causes and a detailed investigation of actual specific variances appears the only solution. However, recent work has contributed substantially towards understanding the motivational effects of accounting methods of planning and control. By isolating off-standard results due to those causes, it is possible to learn something about a manager's past performance. In other words, given the environment faced by the manager and the decisional variables over which he had authority or control, how near did he come to optimum performance?

Both for self-appraisal by the manager and for senior management review of subordinates, only controllable variances are pertinent. Thus, where the environment has changed, performance should be compared with a standard reflecting those changed circumstances, showing how well the manager has grasped new opportunities or coped with an unfavourable environment. The major difficulty lies in the definition of optimum performance; but it can be shown that some useful approximations exist. Any attempt to define optimum performance for changing circumstances introduces a greater element of subjectivity into variance analysis than is usually present, but the associated difficulties are likely to be offset by the provision of more meaningful information to management.

Variances monitoring the second principal cause (poor or inappropriate plans and standards) may be called 'planning' variances – being used to evaluate plans and standards rather than operational performance. When used in conjunction with the variance between original plans and the current appraisal standard (which reflects the prevailing environment), a comparison between unadjusted original plans and actual results can provide a useful check on forecasting skill and ability. Further, and more important, an unfavourable trend in a planning variance could be fed into the decision process for the next period and might suggest revisions of original plans; a persistently favourable variance might hint at new opportunities for the firm.

The subsequent sections deal separately with individual variances on the assumption that many price, wage and overhead variances are not controllable by operating managers. Indeed, many may not be controllable by anyone within the organisation. This is true, for example, of many material prices, where the buying organisation does not have substantial purchasing power, and of many public sector price increases. In such cases, it is not clear that reporting price increases to operating managers serves any useful purpose. Often, even the enterprise's purchasing managers cannot be held responsible for price increases. Price variances, then, can only be used sensibly in re-planning and revising decisions.

It is not clear, either, that information concerning this type of price increase dictates the detailed alterations to standard costing systems that are being attempted by many firms. Indeed, it can be suggested that in situations of rapidly changing prices, such as those caused by major and continual currency fluctuations, many operating managers would be better served if their performance reports emphasised physical quantities. This is one reason why there are doubts about the wisdom of incorporating a current cost 'cost of sales adjustment' (as recommended by SSAP 16) into management accounts in any general way. It might be less confusing to report relevant price changes only to those concerned to decide the enterprise's response to such changes. These doubts are magnified when the 'monetary working capital adjustment' of SSAP 16 is considered, especially since it is difficult to see how the normal methods recommended for its calculation can yield a measure of the real cost of financing the enterprise's operating activities. It might also be better to consider issuing special reports for those concerned with such activities as stockholding, credit management, and short term financing.

As exemplified below, price variances might serve two crucial roles: to monitor forecasting ability, and to aid decision making concerning the enterprise's future responses to the underlying price changes they reflect. The traditional view of variance analysis seems to be that all variances require action within the organisation to regain the original planned state (see Institute of Cost and Management Accountants (1980) and Chapter 8 in this handbook for instance). This concentration on control may lead to neglect of the vital contribution that variance analysis can make towards strategic re-planning. Furthermore, when considering non-controllable variances, an attempt to use them solely for control purposes robs variance analysis of any contribution whatsoever, other than the possible negative impact of distorting decisions. This neglect of variances which reflect non-controllable factors deprives variance analysis of its potentially unique role in providing a formal framework for scanning and understanding the environment. Planning variances, as defined above, can reveal a great deal about changes in the environment.

The remainder of this chapter seeks to justify the above view of standard costing by considering the relevance of several familiar and well used variances to planning and decision making. The suggested procedures should not be applied to all variables in the system; but should be confined to those items considered of special significance to decision making. The variances are considered in three categories: direct cost variances; sales variances; fixed overhead variances.

DIRECT COST VARIANCES

Conventionally, these are categorised as follows:

1   material price variances;
2   material usage variances;
3   mix variances;
4   labour rate variances;
5   labour efficiency variances;

and the following sections examine and discuss each in turn.

Material price variances

The usual price variance – actual material price less standard material price times actual material usage for actual performance – may be of little use for appraising the performance of the purchasing agent or officer, since price changes may be due to a market forces outside his control. For instance, oil prices uncontrollable by operational buyers; local authority rate charges and public utility prices offer further examples. In such cases, a more meaningful variance may be derived by comparing the actual price paid with the best available estimate of the market price prevailing at the time of actual purchase. A favourable variance would indicate the buyer's ability to 'beat the market', either by bulk buying or by special arrangements.

A major weapon of the market beating buyer is speculative purchasing, though his ability to engage in this strategy depends on the market in which he buys, the finances of the firm, and his management's attitude. Many salutary experiences in recent years warn against the reckless pursuit of this kind of 'entrepreneurial' behaviour – as witness the costly mistakes made by the cocoa buyers in several large chocolate manufacturing organisations! Various approximate measures of speculative 'success' can be suggested. Where the buyer is ordering quantities larger than seem economically necessary and above those called for in the normal production process, his policy might be justified by a claim that prices were about to increase. By calculating the variance between the prices which actually obtain in the later period (in which those items would otherwise have been purchased) and the buyer's earlier estimates of those prices, his forecasting success can be measured. The profitability of his speculative activities can be gauged by deducting from the actual later prices the lower prices paid plus the holding costs incurred – to which special attention should be paid in times of high interest rates. Given the variability of financing costs, consideration might be given to issuing special reports on the opportunity costs of holding current assets, rather than attempting to incorporate this information in general all-purpose information reports.

The above description illustrates the general point that variances for appraisal purposes should show how well managers did in the prevailing circumstances and should abstract from non-controllable environmental changes.

As a check on forecasts and standards, the usual price variance may be helpful for planning purposes, particularly if used in conjunction with the appraisal variances outlined above. Further, were an appropriate external forecast of prices available, an assessment of relative forecasting skill could be obtained by comparing the mistakes of the general market index with the firm's internal index. Such an external index may be valuable as an approximate measure even if it covers a much wider range of goods or services than the firm uses.

Price variances play a major role as indicators in assessing whether the trend in prices necessitates a change in existing plans – such as to raise final output prices or to change production methods. Here a rate-of-change variance, namely a comparison showing the trend in the price variance over time, may be more helpful than the conventional computation.

It is suggested, therefore, that the usual price variance should be split in two – a planning variance and an appraisal variance. The planning variance shows how the market price differed from that previously assumed, and the appraisal variance measures the buyer's ability in the conditions that actually prevailed.

The planning variance formula is

$$(p_c - p_s) \times mX$$

where p_c is the general market price at the time of purchase (based on external indicators), where p_s is the original standard price, and where mX is the standard material usage for the actual output (where m is the standard usage per unit of output and X is the actual number of units produced).

The appraisal variance formula is

$$(p_a - p_c) \times mX$$

where p_a is the actual price paid. Material usage is evaluated in these cases at standard usage per unit of output in order to avoid complications that arise from the presence of the joint variance.

The usefulness claimed for planning variance is general and is not restricted to those concerned with price changes. The value of these variances for planning may be extended by classifying them in terms of the responses gained. The most extreme type of uncontrollable change is that to which management can respond only by altering future activity in a given way. The only response that a profit maximising management can make to such changes is to alter its future plans to reflect their effects. An extreme example of this type of environmental change would be a new legislative requirement, the provisions of which could be followed only by quitting the enterprise's existing area of activity – if, for example, the manufacture of cigarettes were made illegal.

A further category incorporates those environmental changes that can be modified or exploited by managerial action, even though their occurrence is beyond the influence of management. Many instances of this second type of expectational change could be given. For example, it is unlikely that a firm could influence the world trend in steel prices, but it may escape many of the consequences of such price changes by stockholding in the short run and by using substitute materials in the long run. The higher taxation of 'high tar' cigarettes and the expected decline in the market for such cigarettes might be exploited by a concentration on 'low' or 'medium tar' cigarettes.

The third type of change that might be monitored separately is that generated by alterations to factors within managerial control. This category can be subdivided at least once. One element of the subdivision would then indicate the expected change if no action were planned to correct past inefficiencies; a second, on a similar basis, would indicate the effects of incorrect original forecasts of factors within management's control.

It is recognised that none of the above classifications can be delineated precisely. However, at least some of the advantages claimed for the proposed system should prove relatively robust and insensitive to considerable inaccuracy. These ideas merely extend the concepts underlying existing standard costing and budgetary control techniques and procedures. The variance between the original and revised levels of the variable in question, in so far as those variances could be assigned to uncontrollable factors, would give a further indication of the uncertainty surrounding the enterprise's activities, particularly when calculated over successive periods to produce a time series of variances.

Further analysis of such variances into those which management could meet only with a change of plan and those which could be offset by appropriate action within the existing plan would point up the nature of the uncertainties facing the firm. In so far as such variances were controllable and could be analysed into those due to errors in earlier planning and those due to errors in execution of the plan, they would highlight the need for management action to improve efficiency.

Even such modified variances reflect only part of the buyer's responsibility. By bulk purchasing, he may show a favourable price variance – but at the expense of inventory holding cost. Some attempt should be made to lay down inventory standards so that such effects could be detected. Similarly, provided that the information obtained is worth its cost, standards could be set for the buyer's other responsibilities; for example, a transport cost variance would highlight the cost of rush orders and could be charged to the responsible department. One could argue that management accountants have been dilatory in extending their activities in such ways.

Material usage variances

This variance is less likely than the price variance to be affected by uncontrollable changes in the firm's environment; even so, such cases can easily be imagined. For example, poorer quality labour than expected may be used, owing to shortages of skilled workers. Then, for appraisal, actual material usage should be compared with an adjusted standard. However, if the use of inferior labour is due, say, to poor performance in the personnel department, then, in principle, the responsible manager should incur a variance equal to the difference between the revised and the original standard.

In such a situation, where the use of lower grade labour is due to general economic conditions and is therefore non-controllable, the modified variance suggested above should be used for appraisal, but the conventional variance should be used for appraisal, but the conventional variance should be used in conjunction with it for re-planning. A conventional usage variance that becomes increasingly unfavourable over time may indicate a need for more capital-intensive methods. This suggests reporting a rate-of-change, as mentioned earlier.

Mix variances

Substitutions between materials (and, indeed, between materials and other factors, and between other factors such as labour and capital) may also be profitable. This may often be the only way of responding to uncontrollable price changes. If such decisions are possible technically, the responsible person should be given an indicator that tells him when they would be profitable. The normal material usage variance gives no such hints to the production manager, since usage is evaluated at standard prices to avoid contaminating the variance with items beyond the manager's control. This may be reasonable – provided signals are given elsewhere in the management accounting system to indicate the profitability of substitution decisions. In general, material usage is priced at standard throughout the system and, consequently, operational management is not informed when it would be profitable to change material proportions.

It might be expected that the mix variance would highlight the possibility of substituting cheaper materials for more expensive ones. However, it cannot do so, since it is priced at standard cost. The variance generally serves the far less important role of an appraisal variance, denoting the cost of changes in mix at given constant relative prices. Furthermore, owing to the implicit assumptions about feasible material substitutions, it does not even do that very well.

Ideally, for planning there should be 'on the shelf material usage plans for different relative prices – that is, usage recipes giving mixes for different various relative material prices. Depending on prices, some materials will feature in some recipes but not in others, or larger quantities of any specific material will appear in some recipes than in others. These recipes can be used to calculate a planning variance called a 'substitution' variance. For each material actual use is compared with 'off the shelf' optimal usage for the relative prices that actually held in the period, and the difference is valued at the actual price for the period of that material. These components are then summed over all materials to give the total substitution variance. For each material, the following comparison is made:

$$(m - m^*) \times p_a^* X$$

where the new symbols, m^* and p_a^*, are, respectively, the optimal usage for each material and its current price, where m is the actual usage of material per unit of finished output, and where X is the actual number of units produced.

An unfavourable substitution variance would suggest that the use of different material proportions should be considered. This may seem a costly exercise, but it can prove an extremely valuable one. A number of industries such as the oil and chemical industries, follow this procedure. A cake manufacturer, for example, could employ alternative recipes depending on the relative prices of jam, sugar, and other ingredients.

The concept of having different recipes for different relative prices is not restricted to materials and can be applied to any number of factors – capital and labour come to mind, as do alternative energy sources, recipes for both depending on expectations of relative prices in the long run.

Apart from serving as a planning variance, the substitution variance is useful for appraising the executive responsible for decisions of that type. This is an instance of the same variance being used for both planning and appraising. However, if this revised mix variance is to be helpful for appraisal, the reasons for any substitution must be known. For example, there may have been a departure from the optimal mix as a result of a failure in the buying department, rather than any inefficiency in production. For appraisal purposes, the optimal usage, m^*, should represent the best operating management could do in the light of the purchasing department's failure. A separate comparison based on the difference between this optimum (which is available to the production department) and the optimum which should have been attained but for the inefficiency of the purchasing department indicates the cost of the latter. This cost would be useful in appraising the purchasing department's performance and may underline a need for re-planning.

In their usual form, mix and yield calculations give no clear guidance to the correctness of the original technical specifications and, therefore, worthwhile revisions may not be made. The only remedy seems to be routine engineering studies of existing technical specifications.

For these reasons, it seems doubtful whether the calculation of the conventional mix and yield variances would be worthwhile. It can also be shown that many of the above difficulties and reservations could be applied to sales price and mix variances.

Labour rate and efficiency variances

Criticisms of the conventional material price variance also apply forcefully to the labour rate or price variance – actual wage per hour less standard wage per hour times actual hours worked to produce actual output. Indeed, the staffing department may be even more at the mercy of the outside market than the buying department. The conventional labour rate variance may be useful for planning, but it is less likely to make a good appraisal variance.

The conventional formula for labour efficiency variances – actual hours worked less standard hours estimated for actual production times standard wage per hour – is generally regarded as an appraisal variance, any deviations from standard reflecting adversely on the production manager. This is reasonable if the standard reflects the environmental conditions prevailing during the period. If, for example, owing to conditions in the labour market, less than skilled labour had to be used, the standard for appraisal purposes should be adjusted to reflect that fact.

A rate-of-change variance may be useful for appraisal purposes, as the responses of both senior management and the individual responsible manager depend closely on whether any unfavourable variance is expected to persist. Watching the trend in labour, and other appraisal variances, may be helpful in validating standards; a persistent trend should signal a thorough study of existing targets.

In calculating labour efficiency variances (and, indeed, all variances), attention should be paid to all that are mutually dependent. For example, by allowing higher than standard material waste, greater labour efficiency may be obtained; labour efficiency and material usage variances cannot usefully be studied in isolation. The efficiency (appraisal) variance based on current attainable standards and the uncontrollable efficiency variance (planning) due to changes in environmental conditions together explain deviations from forecast capacity due to labour inefficiency. They may suggest that management should employ more capital-intensive methods, consider price increases, or consider switching to a product needing less skilled labour. The two variances together are thus relevant for planning.

Cost of labour inefficiency

The conventional efficiency variance, even when adjusted to take account of attainable standards, may understate the cost of excess labour usage. This cost variance is taken to be the wage payments for which standard performance was not obtained, whereas the true cost is the opportunity cost of production lost due to inefficiency – approximately, the lost total contribution to fixed overheads and profits.

A simple example may help to explain this. Assume that 100 labour hours were taken to produce 90 units of output; the standard output for one hour of labour was one unit. The standard wage rate was £2.50 an hour. The conventional efficiency variance would price the ten extra hours at £2.50, giving an unfavourable variance of £25.00. If the selling price was £25.00 and the standard contribution to fixed costs and profits was £7.50, the real loss associated with those ten hours was the forgone contribution from the ten units that might have been produced – an unfavourable opportunity cost variance of £75.00.

Under the above assumptions, the true cost of labour inefficiency is the conventional variance (provided that the inefficiency was controllable by the manager in question) plus any lost contribution.

On the other hand, the conventional variance reflects accurately the cost of inefficiency if idle capacity is expected in the future and if unsatisfied demand in any period can be carried forward and satisfied in future periods. If overtime has to be worked to make up lost units, however, the cost of such overtime should be included in the variance as a cost of excess wage payment.

The approach suggested above, which entails a forecast of the future effects of past inefficiency, is more subjective than the usual calculations. However, it shows more clearly the effect of substandard performance and illustrates the need to consider its likely impact.

SALES VARIANCES

These may be considered in the following categories:

1   sales volume variance;
2   sales price variances.

Again, these will be considered in terms of their applicability to planning and appraisal and in terms of the real costs of such inefficiences as are identified, bearing in mind lost opportunities and forgone profits.

Sales volume variances

In conventional terms, the sales volume variance is calculated as the difference between actual sales and standard or budgeted sales priced at the standard or budgeted contribution per unit. All such a variance reveals is whether a sales manager has sold more or less than expected. What would be of more interest would be to know how well he has performed. If, for example, the market was such that many more units could have been sold than were actually sold, the sales manager has underperformed (provided production capacity was such that it would have allowed him to market those extra units). In the prevailing circumstances, the sales manager should have sold more.

A simple example will help to emphasise the point. A sales manager for a motor vehicle manufacturer is set a target of 2 000 saloon cars to sell in the coming three months. Each saloon car generates a contribution of £1 750 to fixed overheads and profits. The sales manager actually sells 2 500 saloon cars. However, examination of market trends suggests that, given the increased demand for cars of the type in question, the manager could have sold 3 000 such cars during that quarter. Those details are reproduced in Figure 9.2, which reveals that the budgeted contribution for the period was £3.5 million, whereas the actual contribution was £4.375 million. Conventional sales volume variance analysis would hint at a 'good' variance of £875 000 extra contribution.

Taking an opportunity cost view of the sales manager's performance, however, would reveal a forgone contribution of £875 000. Rather than significantly overperforming, the sales manager had underperformed markedly. The question of whether or not he had beaten an obsolete target is irrelevant. Even though the management accountant's conventional variance has suggested that the sales manager had performed well, the cost to the company of the neglected opportunities – that is, the failure to sell the additional 500 saloon cars – is a true measure of the extent to which he failed.

Equally, if the market for saloon cars of the type in question had declined, the sales manager should be assessed against a more realistic lower standard. To calculate such an appraisal variance precisely would call for better demand information than most firms possess. Here again, however, a close enough approximation may be made to produce useful information. Trend analysis is of considerable assistance in such an approximation, as will be discussed in Chapter 21 of this handbook.

Other, perhaps more qualitative information may also help considerably. Properly weighed, appraisal variances of this type will consistently provide better information than their conventional counterparts. Original plans can be compared with the adopted appraisal standard to give a planning variance. As discussed earlier, such a variance will reveal useful information about forecasting abilities, shifts in the environment, and the need for revision of plans – particularly if used in conjunction with a rate-of-change variance.

In following the usual rule for pricing lost sales, care needs to be taken to take realistic account of those opportunity costs. It is assumed, in that context, that any such lost sales are lost forever. But to take the saloon car example again, the 500 unsatisfied customers might be prepared to wait for delivery, rather than buying another make or model. In those circumstances, the 'real' opportunity cost to the company would be any loss in the value of money occasioned by

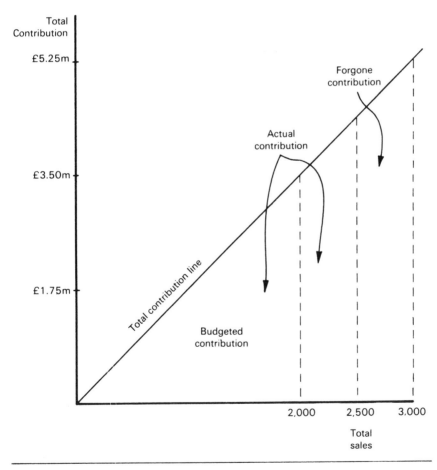

Figure 9.2   Sales performance

the defined actual cash flows generated by the sales. Equally, concomitant opportunity costs may be occasioned by being unable to use that £850 000 now rather than in one or two months' time.

Sales price variances

Typically, the sales price variance is calculated as the difference between the actual sales price and the standard sales price times the actual sales volume. Realistically, however, it is not particularly meaningful to consider a sales price variance on its own. In any relatively stable economic environment, an unfavourable sales price variance will tend to be associated with a favourable sales volume variance; equally, perhaps, the higher the actual sales price, the lower the actual sales volume. Little may be gained, therefore, from splitting the overall sales variance.

It is, after all, unrealistic to expect to sell more than the standard or budgeted quantity without some associated reduction in selling price. The better approach to calculating valuable sales variances is to decide an adjusted selling price upon which to base the variances. Such an adjusted selling price would be derived from an assessment of the price that would have been expected for the actual volume of sales achieved. The adjusted price should be used also for recalculating the standard or budgeted contribution.

When a marked change has taken place in the external environment, the above procedures are of little use, since both price and volume variances may be favourable for reasons beyond the control of management or even despite management's actions. The variance analysis in those circumstances becomes very much more subjective, depending upon estimates of the best attainable performance in the changed conditions facing the firm during the period in question. Important clues for such a solution would be, for instance, changes in market share and in inventory levels.

FIXED OVERHEAD VARIANCES

Routine treatments of overhead variances encompass the calculation of overhead under- or over-recovery and its division between overhead capacity variance and overhead efficiency variance. In the context of this chapter, it would be better to consider overhead variances from rather more practical viewpoints – those of the opportunities lost through inefficient use of available resources.

In many instances, conventional overhead variance data are redundant, since most will be reported elsewhere as either sales or direct cost variances – being the results of either failing to sell the budgeted quantity or of inefficiencies in production. Perhaps more important, fixed overheads are the current consequences of previous decisions on investment, of labour supply constraints, of public utility policies, and so on, and are by definition fixed for any volume of production within a given range. Overhead recovery rates treat such overheads as variable with production, which is patently unrealistic and at best confusing – particularly as the different, acceptable methods of calculating overhead rates all lead to different answers, all arbitrary and each misleading.

That latter point argues forcefully against incorporating a replacement cost depreciation adjustment (of the type recommended in SSAP 16) into management accounting performance reports. Generally, depreciation expenses are not controlled by operating managers; they become no more controllable when based on the so-called replacement cost of assets.

Unless depreciation is affected by asset usage, those expenses are determined by the investment decision concerning the asset in question. No useful additional information to that obtained by monitoring the investment project as it proceeds is yielded by reporting depreciation expenses.

The need for more useful methods for planning and controlling such overheads represents a major challenge to the management accounting profession. The importance of the task is being increased by several factors which tend to boost the proportion of total costs represented by fixed overheads. Such influences include increasing capital intensity reflecting technological advances, and those changes in employment law and practice which inhibit flexible staffing arrangements.

One approach to this task which seems to show some promise is the establishment of cost centres for major items of fixed overheads. The budgets for such centres recognise that these costs alter with some causal factors, rather than with short run production levels. Assuming that this difficult task can be accomplished, at least in part, the approach advocated so far in this chapter can be used to control and plan those factors normally treated as fixed overheads. The costs of many of those factors are not usually susceptible to bargaining by the firm, however, and this renders the calculation of planning variances for such items of crucial importance, especially if such variances highlight the responses available to the firm to price increases for those factors. Variances for use in appraising the performance of those charged with managing what are normally regarded as fixed overheads require that both the benefits the organisation hopes to obtain from their use can be determined and the factors which cause the amounts of those benefits to vary can be identified. As argued above, appraisal variances should be limited to those causal factors which lie within the firm's influence or control.

When the budget is prepared, the level of expected benefits needs to be determined for each major item of fixed overhead. Setting budgeted amounts of benefit from each overhead item implies a total expenditure on each of those items, assuming certain standards of performance relative to those causal factors which are within the firm's control.

Appraisal variances will measure the degree of achievement of those performance levels. However, it is likely that most variances associated with what are normally regarded as fixed overheads will be of the planning variety – leading to new forecasts of enterprise profitability and to consideration of alternative methods of achieving the desired level of benefits in the changed environment.

Figures for fixed overheads under-recovered owing to production inefficiencies reveal little or real value. For example, if a firm's planned production for a period is 7 000 units, each requiring 30 minutes labour, and if total fixed overheads are budgeted at £28 000 for the period, the conventional overhead recovery rate will be set at £4.00 a unit or £8.00 per labour hour. If actual production is only 6 000 units, the overhead under-recovered is calculated at £4 000 (on the assumption that budgeted and actual labour hours worked are the same). All that reveals, essentially, is that the figure of under-recovery can be explained by inefficiency in the use of labour.

But what is the real loss? It is the cost of the opportunities lost due to the inefficient use of labour – in other words, the labour efficiency variance discussed earlier. If the 1 000 units are 'lost' forever, it is the value of the lost contribution plus the wages paid to inefficient labour (500 hours at the wage rate). If the units could not be sold anyway, the cost is only the labour cost.

Idle capacity cost

In order to check the accuracy of forecasts used in the past to justify investments and to highlight the opportunity cost of unused facilities and help to plan better usage in the future, it is helpful to have a ready measure of the cost of idle capacity.

The best measurement of forecasts and monitoring their validity can be achieved by a simple comparison analysis of planned and actual cash flows and sales volumes. Again, an appraisal standard would be helpful, comparing the levels used to justify an investment and the optimal levels which might have been achieved.

Ascertaining the opportunity cost of idle capacity is more difficult, as choices must be made between a variety of measures of capacity. Due to economies of scale, under which it might be worthwhile to invest in a plant of far greater capacity than is actually required, the notion of technical capacity is inappropriate in many circumstances.

As a first step, management should be provided with an estimate of expected idle capacity for the coming period. That estimate can then be compared with tue actual variance caused by idle capacity. Both variances, one for planning and one for appraisal, should be costed at their opportunity cost – the profits forgone due to idle capacity. Spare capacity could, perhaps, be rented out, or it could be used to manufacture another product. If no alternative use is possible, idle capacity has no cost.

The usual overhead efficiency variances can be both misleading and redundant; the traditional overhead capacity variances are not a true measure of idle capacity; only the conventional overhead expenditure variance is useful in the context of this chapter's arguments. Even then, such a variance needs to be pruned of non-controllable items or influences.

(Editorial note: This chapter is an edited version of a paper presented to a technical symposium of the Institute of Cost and Management Accountants at Pembroke College, Oxford, in January 1981, and parts rely on ideas in the author's series of articles on standard costing for planning and control in The Accountant *in April and May 1969. The permission of the publisher to reprint parts of those articles is gratefully acknowledged.)*

REFERENCES AND FURTHER READING

Beyer, R., and Trawicki, D., *Profitability Accounting for Planning and Control*, 2nd edn, New York: Ronald Press, 1972.

Bromwich, M., 'Standard costing for planning and control', *The Accountant*, 19 April 1969, 26 April 1969, 3 May 1969.

Dearden, J., *Cost and Budget Analysis*, Englewood Cliffs, N.J.: Prentice-Hall, 1962.

Horngren, C. T., 'A contribution margin approach to the analysis of capacity utilization', *The Accounting Review*, April 1967.

Institute of Cost and Management Accountants, *Terminology of Management and Financial Accountancy*, London: ICMA, 1980.

Solomons, D., *Divisional Performance: Measurement and Control*, Homewood, I11.: Irwin, 1965.

Solomons, D. (ed.), *Studies in Cost Analysis*, London: Sweet & Maxwell, 1968.

Stedry, A. C., 'Budgetary control: a behavioral approach', *in* Alexis, M., and Wilson, C. Z., (eds), *Organizational Decision-Making*, Englewood Cliffs, N.J.: Prentice-Hall, 1967.

10

Relevance in controls

David Allen and Roger Cowe

This chapter considers the practical difficulties in matching financial control systems to managerial responsibilities. The basic notion of Responsibility Accounting that planning and control should reflect responsibility appears to be widely accepted. But defining the scope of managerial responsibilities is not always as easy as it might seem, and as organisations adapt to meet changing needs it becomes necessary to adapt control systems accordingly.

The authors briefly consider the issue of assigning responsibility in large, diverse organisations and comment on the current desire of a number of organisations to push profit measurement down the organisation, thus creating profit-responsible managers at lower levels than previously.

In this context the chapter continues with a review of Responsibility Accounting and the notion of cost, profit and responsibility centres. The authors note that these attractive concepts cannot always be implemented neatly, especially in matrix organisations where profit centres are not merely aggregations of cost centres. In such circumstances there is likely to be a considerable element of shared cost, and in some cases revenue, thus exacerbating the issue of whether or not to allocate between profit centres.

There does not appear to be any simple solution in such complex circumstances, but the chapter concludes with a proposed range of solutions for different types of cost.

Many issues affect the design of financial control systems. One important consideration is achieving a fit between the control system and the organisation's aims. This chapter considers the practical aspects of how financial control systems can be made most relevant in that context.

Focusing on organisations' financial aims, maximising long-term profitability can be considered a primary goal of all commercial organisations, converted into a series of policy objectives through a strategic planning process. Planning and control systems can then be seen as a tool to build commitment to those policy objectives and to try and ensure appropriate objectives are pursued across the organisation.

In the pursuit of profitability trade-offs are inevitably made, for example between conflicting objectives, between competing business opportunities and between current spending for future revenues and immediate profitability. Planning and control systems can be seen as a way of managing those trade-offs to try and ensure that optimal decisions are made and followed.

For these purposes a simplified planning and control environment can be represented as in Figure 10.1.

In this simplistic representation strategic direction flows down from corporate to operational managers, who draw up detailed plans and are responsible for detailed control of their operations. Their performance is monitored by corporate management.

If such a planning and reporting system is to be used to motivate individual managers to work towards corporate goals, and to control managers' performance, the control system needs to match the organisation structure, relating financial performance with individual managers' responsibility.

From time to time it may be necessary to change the organisation structure to provide for more effective pursuit of organisational goals. This may be prompted by changes in the environment such as the emergence of new markets or new competitors, or by influences within the organisation such as new technology. It will then be

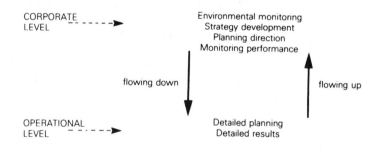

Figure 10.1   Representation of planning and control system

necessary for planning and control systems to change to meet the demands of the new organisation structure.

In the simplest organisation structures, represented in Figure 10.2, matching planning and control systems to organisation structure is relatively easy.

A simple functional organisation can divide responsibilities between functional specialists, with each function being allocated functionally-defined targets – for example, sales volumes and prices, production levels and costs. Trade-offs between functions can be made at board level, where the profit focus is located.

DISAGGREGATION OF THE ORGANISATION

Such a structure is satisfactory for small organisations, in which it is feasible to monitor performance of functions closely from board level and so avoid sub-optimal decisions at lower levels in the organisations. But as the organisation grows it becomes increasingly difficult to manage the enterprise as a single unit and disaggregation becomes necessary. This might take the form of geographical or product-based divisions, each effectively managed as a separate smaller business within the whole, and each having a structure similar to that depicted in Figure 10.2.

In some cases such disaggregation of the organisation is seen as inadequate, with important consequences for planning and control systems. A number of pressures have led some organisations to conclude that a traditional functional structure within geographical or other divisions does not provide a suitable context in which to identify and pursue profitable market opportunities.

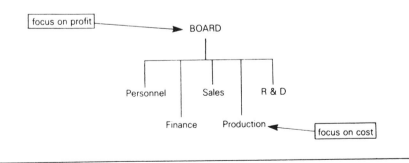

Figure 10.2   Simple functional organisation

Companies that are unhappy with such a position may perceive too much functional specialisation inhibiting a fuller business awareness at operational levels, making it difficult to pursue corporate profitability objectives coherently.

A greater marketing awareness, together with increased competitive pressures, has suggested to such companies the need for business decisions to be taken lower down the organisation than has previously been the case. Top management is seen as being too distanced from the market place to take many market-related decisions in a fast-changing environment, so such decisions must be delegated to operational managers. Those operational managers are perceived as previously having been concerned too narrowly with their functional specialism. Thus production managers have been over-concerned with technology, and sales managers with sales volumes rather than with profitability.

It is also recognised that in functionally-organised operations it is often difficult to take profit-oriented decisions at an operational level because of the detachment between costs and revenues. For example, if functional managers only have cost information, it is difficult for them to know whether or not spending money on overtime working would be justified by increased revenues. A business manager responsible for the product involved, on the other hand, would have the information to put the cost/revenue equation together and thus take a *business* decision based on profitability rather than a narrow cost-oriented decision based on cost budgets.

The consequent development of profit-responsible managers at lower levels in organisations is depicted in Figure 10.3.

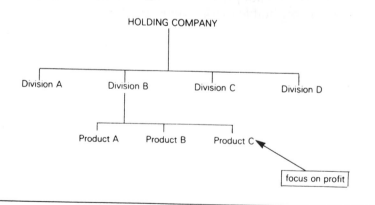

Figure 10.3 Pushing profit down the organisation

IMPLICATIONS FOR PLANNING AND CONTROL

The major consequence for financial control systems of pushing business decisions down the organisation in this way is the need to measure profit at lower levels in the organisation. Whereas previously operational managers were required to operate within cost and volume budgets, fuller business responsibilities require profit measures instead.

Budgetary control and standard costing has traditionally formed the basis of routine financial control in functionally-organised companies. The emphasis of financial control systems, originating with standard costing, was on manufacturing, with much concern for product costs but little attention paid to distribution, marketing and other expenses except so far as allocating them to products was concerned, and relatively little attention paid to revenues.

The growth of divisionalised companies led to wider control measures being introduced so that central management could monitor the performance of divisions and subsidiaries. Thus divisions became sub-sets of the corporate whole and attempts were made to measure their performance in ways which reflected the ways in which the company itself was measured, e.g. ratios such as return on capital.

But within those semi-autonomous divisions the emphasis of financial control was still on manufacturing operations. The consequent emphasis on costs resulted in profit measures only being applied at a fairly high level in organisations, just as traditionally profit was relevant only at board level, while below that level concern was for manufacturing costs and overhead expenses.

Pushing business decisions and therefore profit measures down the organisation requires a re-orientation of the planning and control system to match the new organisation. This poses tricky problems of identifying where costs lie and how the corporate profit can be disaggregated. These problems can partly be addressed by techniques which have been developed within the concept of Responsibility Accounting.

RESPONSIBILITY ACCOUNTING

Responsibility Accounting is a concept which aims to help achieve a fit between planning and control systems and managerial responsibilities. It suggests the superficially-attractive proposition that financial systems should provide information on the activities directly controlled by a manager, excluding costs and revenues under other managers' control. But while attractive in relatively simple organisation structures, the concept poses difficulties in less straightforward circumstances.

Responsibility Accounting has been defined by Horngren (1984) as:

> a system of accounting that recognises various responsibility centres throughout the organisation and reflects the plans and actions of each of these centres by assigning particular revenues and costs to the one having the pertinent responsibility

In other words, the accounting system generates information on the basis of managerial responsibility, allowing that information to be used directly in motivating and controlling each manager's actions. The concept suggests that product managers, for example, should receive information relevant to their own product areas, and their performance should be judged only by reference to events within their control.

This concept of controllability is central to Responsibility Accounting. It is a highly attractive concept which seems to make sense in practice. It is difficult to argue with a notion which says that someone should not be held responsible for events over which they are not supposed to have any control, but should be judged on what they have been asked to do. Specifically, a product manager who controls prices and a sales force can be held responsible for margins. But if this manager has no control over manufacturing or procurement the responsibility is not for actual margins but for margins on standard cost. Whoever is responsible for manufacturing should answer for manufacturing variances.

The simplicity and general acceptability of the concept hides major problems of attaching cause to financial results, however. If sales were below budget, was it the responsibility of the sales force for not selling well enough or not adequately predicting demand, or of the factory for not producing the required quality, quantity and mix of product?

The equation becomes even more complex with more complex organisation structures. For example, if a common sales force sells several brands the product managers are then not responsible for sales, and may not have sole responsibility for setting selling prices. Whose responsibility is it if turnover is down? Matrix organisations can make it even more difficult to identify clear responsibilities for results and consequently to develop appropriate control systems.

Such limitations of responsibility accounting should not obscure certain benefits, however. The concept can usefully be applied to specific problems. For example, it would suggest that the cost of after-sales service due to poor quality should be charged to the factory rather than the sales force. Similarly, the cost of production disruptions due to unreasonable demands from the sales force should be charged to the sales force rather than the factory. In the first case the factory manager should be prompted to pay more attention to quality. In the second case the sales force is likely to be more careful about making outrageous demands on the factory.

Responsibility accounting can also be credited with ending many sterile debates over arbitrary allocation of costs. In the example above, conventional accounting would be forced to try and allocate the cost of the sales force between the various products, producing a profit statement following the outline shown in Table 10.1.

Table 10.1
Profit statement with fully allocated overheads

	Product A	Product B	Product C	Total
Sales	£200	£300	£500	£1 000
	directly attributable to each			
Manufacturing costs	£150	£250	£350	£ 750
Margin	£ 50	£ 50	£150	£ 250
Overheads (allocated)	£ 30	£ 20	£ 30	£ 80
Profit	£ 20	£ 30	£120	£ 170

In this case the product managers can rightly claim that they have no responsibility for overheads, so the profits calculated are not 'their' profits.

The usual Responsibility Accounting solution is not to allocate shared costs. This can be seen as a similar approach to the concept of using contribution rather than gross margin. Just as fixed costs should not be allocated arbitrarily to products, it is argued, so shared overheads should not be allocated arbitrarily to product groups or responsibility centres. (In this case we assume that manufacturing costs can be attributed directly to each product group – as if each were manufactured in its own factory.) The outline profit statement is then as shown in Table 10.2. This table shows overheads attributed to products where possible, and not allocated where direct attribution is not possible. This process can be continued through various

Table 10.2
Profit statement with no allocation

	Product A	Product B	Product C	Total
Sales	£200	£300	£500	£1 000
	directly attributable to each			
Manufacturing costs	£150	£250	£350	£ 750
Margin of contribution	£ 50	£ 50	£150	£ 250
Attributable overheads	£ 20	£ 15	£ 15	£ 50
Net contribution	£ 30	£ 35	£135	£ 200
Other overheads – no longer allocated				£ 30
Profit	calculated only in total			£ 170

levels, so building up various levels of contribution, as in the following examples, showing the breakdown of results to the lowest level (see Table 10.3). The overheads shown in Table 10.3 are only those directly attributable to Product A. Only those directly attributable to sub-groups are allocated within Product A.

The same process can be used to break down the results of each sub-group as shown in Table 10.4.

Table 10.3
Product profit statement

	Sub-group 1	Sub-group 2	Sub-group 3	Total Product A
Sales	£100	£40	£60	£200
	directly attributable to each			
Manufacturing costs	£ 80	£30	£40	£150
Margin	£ 20	£10	£20	£ 50
Attributable overheads	£ 8	£ 2	£ 5	£ 15
Group net contribution	£ 12	£ 8	£15	£ 35
Other Product A overheads. Not allocated to sub-groups				£ 5
Net contribution for Product A (as above)				£ 30

Table 10.4
Sub-group profit statement

	Model alpha	Model beta	Model delta	Total Group 1
Sales	£20	£50	£30	£100
	directly attributable to each			
Manufacturing costs	£15	£35	£30	£ 80
Margin	£ 5	£15	–	£ 20
Attributable overheads	£ 2	£ 2	£ 1	£ 5
Group net contribution	£ 3	£13	£(1)	£ 15
Other Group 1 overheads. Not allocated to sub-groups				£ 3
Net contribution for Group 1 (as above)				£ 12

COST, PROFIT AND INVESTMENT CENTRES

This approach to cost allocation and profit measurement is associated with a concept of describing managerial units according to the extent of responsibility pertaining to them. Three broad areas of responsibility are usually identified: the lowest being cost only, then in ascending order, costs and revenues, and finally costs, revenues and investment. These three levels coincide with the notion of cost centres, profit centres and investment centres.

These terms are more or less self-explanatory. A cost centre is an individual activity or group of similar activities for which costs are accumulated. Unlike a profit centre it has no revenues attached to it. A profit centre differs from an investment centre in that while revenues can be identified with this group of activities, assets cannot be. An investment centre, on the other hand, is an activity which can ostensibly be financially segregated completely from other parts of the business, from both a balance sheet and a profit statement point of view.

Cost centre managers therefore only have control over costs, profit centre managers control revenues as well, while investment centre managers control costs, revenues and investment (including working capital) and can take full business decisions for their responsibility area.

In a manufacturing environment, therefore, a cost centre would be a manufacturing operation or group of machines, a profit centre might be a production line or perhaps no lower than the whole factory, while a product operation (incorporating several factories) might be an investment centre. There might be many layers of cost or profit centres, cost centres aggregating to departments, for example, and profit centres aggregating to product groupings.

In this environment profit centres can normally only be established at a fairly high level, contrasting with a retailing operation, in which each department within a shop could be a profit centre.

The differences between profit and investment centres are relatively slight. In practice many profit centre managers are measured by return on investment, among other measures, even if they do not have full control over investment in their profit centre. And few managers of investment centres have absolute control over investment in their business, with no interference from the corporate level.

The main differences are between cost centres and profit centres. Cost centres are the financial building blocks of the organisation, while profit centres represent business units to which both costs and revenues can be assigned. It is a key argument of this chapter that many companies are seeking to lower the level at which profit centres exist, pushing profit measures further down the hierarchy and thus creating profit centres at a lower level than previously.

Clearly it is not possible to attach revenues to every cost centre unless a complex internal charging mechanism is used throughout the business, or cost centres are created at a higher level than would normally be the case.

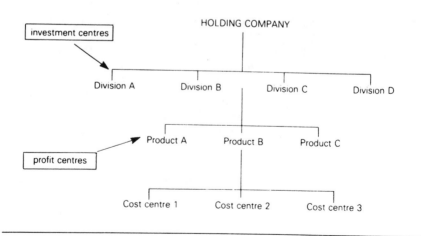

Figure 10.4   Investment, profit and cost centres

Figure 10.4 represents the relationship of cost, profit and investment centres to the kind of organisation structure we have discussed previously.

In this example profit centres constitute collections of cost centres, minimising the problem of allocating shared costs since a large proportion of costs can be attributed directly to each profit centre. In some cases profit centres are created by overlaying functional organisations with product responsibilities, making the allocation question more important. In this more complex situation the profit centres will not merely be aggregations of cost centres, as we have so far described. On the contrary, profit centres will possibly share considerable resources, probably including direct, variable costs as well as overheads. Cost centre managers will therefore serve a number of product masters in what is a matrix organisation, as depicted in Figure 10.5.

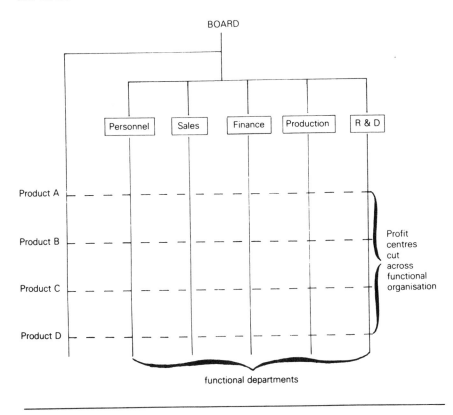

Figure 10.5 Profit centres in a matrix organisation

This might appear to be an unnecessarily complex structure but it is not uncommon in many organisations. It represents, for example, the position of brand or product managers *vis-à-vis* common manufacturing and sales organisations, as is frequently found in many consumer products businesses. It also depicts the position in a number of integrated businesses in which there are managers with overall responsibility for lines of business but without direct control over manufacturing or sales operations, which remain common. This situation can be found, for example, in transport operations, where route managers might have profit responsibility but use common vehicles and sales teams, computer manufacture and the motor industry.

This kind of structure adds to the problem of apportioning costs to products. Where profit centres do not have dedicated cost centres such apportionments are inevitable if the aim of introducing low-level profit measures is to be achieved. Apportionment will inevitably cover a greater proportion of costs than in a more straightforward structure.

Such a situation demands much of the financial control systems. In particular it demands a robust cost centre structure that is logical in the context of the operation of the various functions. Like any cost centre approach within the context of Responsibility Accounting it will therefore have to relate to managerial responsibilities at the lowest relevant level. This is essential to be able to relate spending back to its source, a necessary part of any financial control system. Without this ability it is inevitably difficult to control costs, since it is impossible ultimately to establish the 'what, where and why?' of spending.

The cost centre therefore remains the building block of the financial control system, despite the emphasis on profit measures. As we have said, there comes a point as the financial control system penetrates further down the organisation that revenues and costs can no longer be matched. The point at which this disconnection occurs is bound to vary from organisation to organisation, but wherever it occurs it is important to establish and maintain a link between the cost centre and profit centre structure.

Criticisms of responsibility accounting

The concepts of Responsibility Accounting and cost/profit/ investment centres can provide a useful framework within which to design financial control systems. These concepts suggest that cost centres exist where managers only have cost responsibility, while profit centres can be introduced where managers have profit responsibility. But as we argued at the beginning of this chapter, a number of organisations are seeking to create profit centres at lower levels than previously, and this poses problems for profit measurement.

In particular it raises the question of how to deal with shared cost. Many companies seem loathe to implement responsibility accounting fully. Instead they wish to allocate some shared costs, usually as great a proportion as possible. This desire is perhaps particularly prevalent among companies which have created profit centres in a matrix organisation, as shown in Figure 10.5. In such cases the profit centres will tend to share a much greater proportion of costs than in a more conventional organisation where a profit centre constitutes a collection of cost centres, heightening the desire to allocate as much of that cost as can reasonably be done.

Such companies argue that the pressure on costs is so high, and the scale of shared/fixed cost is so great, that it cannot be 'ignored' but must instead be brought within one or other areas of profit responsibility, ideally at the lowest possible level. It is argued that it may not be possible to attribute costs directly to profit centres, but it is possible to assign responsibility. Thus one manager can be given a lead role in managing particular costs, as the prime user of that service.

This attitude appears at first sight to exhibit a misunderstanding of Responsibility Accounting. It is no part of the concept that shared costs should be ignored. Rather it is suggested that the responsible manager for shared costs is the manager responsible for the services being provided, i.e. the sales manager in the example quoted earlier where the sales force was common to various products. Thus the product managers are held responsible for their net contribution (or segment contribution as it is sometimes described), while the managers of services are held responsible for the cost of their function.

Given this understanding, however, it can be argued that functional managers responsible for such shared overhead will face only limited pressure on their performance if they are not directly and continually accountable to profit-responsible managers. It can also be argued that the purpose of giving managers total profit responsibility is to enable them to take a total business view, which must inevitably include as much of shared costs as is feasible. Functional managers are also likely to face conflicting objectives which are difficult for them to resolve within the context of cost budgets. Technical managers are likely to pursue technical excellence, for example, often at considerable expense. One purpose of pushing profit responsibility down organisations might be to enable the balance between technical and financial requirements to be struck at lower levels – by profit-responsible managers.

It is not true to say that functional managers will face no pressure on costs where those costs are not allocated, but that pressure is likely to be indirect and occasional, rather than direct and continuous. Pressure will arise during preparation of the budget, for example, as acceptable cost and revenue levels are determined, and it may arise from time to time if results during the budget year are disappointing, especially if functional costs are above budget.

On the other hand, if costs are allocated and product managers are held responsible for profits, not net contribution, it is more likely that product managers will continually be concerned with costs charged against their profits. And while this concern may be exhibited in the sterile form of arguments about allocation, it will perhaps also appear as a valuable concern about the level of total cost being allocated.

There are dangers in both approaches. Allocating costs runs the risk of energy being dissipated in internal arguments about allocations which hinders a concern with total costs. But if no costs are allocated there is a risk of not asking important questions about functional costs often enough.

Perhaps the choice is between pressure on functional managers from a central source, presumably a central finance function, and pressure from profit-responsible product managers. A strong financial scrutiny of functional costs can substitute for the 'market' pressures of the product managers. Thus a strong central finance function operating zero-based budgeting and other such techniques (described in Chapter 5) might maintain pressure on functional costs. But this approach clearly incurs additional investment in control systems, which to some extent negates the aim of minimising overheads that produces the desire to maintain pressure on such costs in the first place.

UNDERSTANDING COST BEHAVIOUR

It is clear that the establishment of the kind of control system described here rests fundamentally on a good understanding of cost behaviour.

Three dimensions are important in examining how far down the structure profit measurement can be pushed, in planning and in focusing attempts to control the business on those aspects which are controllable by the responsible managers. These three dimensions are controllable/uncontrollable, variable/fixed and direct/shared.

The main distinction normally drawn is between variable and fixed costs. This is indeed important in planning and in tactical decision making of the make-or-buy variety, where it is crucial to understand this aspect of cost behaviour to assess the likely outcomes of various courses of action. But for control purposes the other two dimensions are perhaps more important.

We have already argued that there is no clear winner in the debate about allocating fixed costs or sticking at contribution. Particularly in organisations with very high fixed costs it may be dangerous to remove such a large element of cost from the direct and continuing scrutiny of profit-responsible managers.

Fixed costs are an increasingly high proportion of most organisations' costs. Even with a growth in bought-in services the element of variability in many companies' costs is limited. Direct labour in manufacturing operations has traditionally been described as a classic variable cost, on the rather old-fashioned assumption that if production drops so does the direct labour cost, and vice versa. While this is true in the broadest sense and over a lengthy timescale it certainly is not true on the short term, which is what we are concerned with in the context of financial control. Only simple piecework systems result in high variability of labour costs in the short term.

Similar dangers exist in concentrating controls only on what is 'controllable'. Since in the short term very little is controllable it is tempting to dismiss variations from plan as environmentally-influenced and therefore to be ignored. Such an attitude to control, however, diminishes the role of managers. Identifying a variation as 'uncontrollable' should merely be to say that it was not within the direct control of the responsible manager. It is necessary to go on from there to ask what can be done that is within the manager's control to rectify the situation.

The most important distinction is perhaps between direct and shared costs, and in drawing that distinction, to acknowledge that 'shared' can range from minimal sharing to total jointness. In the matrix structure which we discussed earlier many costs will be shared. Indeed some revenues might also be shared, in circumstances where products are sold jointly.

SOME COST CONVENTIONS

It seems to us that rather than there being a clear alternative between a contribution and an allocation approach in determining profit responsibility, there is in fact a continuum, as depicted in Figure 10.6.

This continuum represents a range of approaches for dealing with different classes of cost. On the left, specific costs pose no problem. They can be attributed directly to profit centres. Moving towards the right of the spectrum costs become less and less specific and hence more general and shared. A number of conventions can be applied to such costs, depending on the extent to which they are shared.

The 'committed resource' convention can be applied to costs which are identifiable in the main with particular profit centres but where there is a limited element of sharing between profit centres. Under this convention profit-responsible managers commit themselves to a given level of service for a specified period, contracting formally or otherwise with functional managers for that level of service. Only by removing cost entirely, or by agreement with another profit centre, can a manager improve the cost position.

This approach ensures that managers know the level of cost which will be incurred on their behalf, and ensures that changes in the pattern of demand of one profit centre do not affect another. In a conventional allocation system, for example, a drop in usage of a service by one profit centre could result in a greater allocation to another. Under the Committed Resource convention, a profit centre incurs the committed cost level until a new agreement is reached.

A 'prime user' approach can be applied to costs which are even less readily identifiable with one profit centre, but where costs can be adjusted in line with management decisions about the level of activity. Such costs therefore fall into the 'controllable' or 'variable' categories. It still avoids totally arbitrary allocations.

NATURE OF COST	Directly attributable	Committed resources	Prime user approach	Joint indirect	Admin/ General
TREATMENT	no allocation required	majority directly identifiable	responsibility assigned where costs cannot be	ZBB and incremental budgeting 'sole user'	allocations and emphasis on central control

Figure 10.6 A continuum of cost assignment

216

Under this convention the major responsibility for a cost is assigned to the prime user of a service even though costs cannot be directly identified with users. The prime user of the service is therefore given a lead role in managing that cost, although not all costs are assigned to that profit centre. Costs are allocated by asking how much cost would be avoided if only the prime user were served. Those avoidable costs are then charged to the secondary profit centre. This approach can deal with any number of profit centres sharing a service, cascading down from major to subsidiary users eliminating costs at each stage.

It will be most difficult to identify shared costs at all closely with profit centres towards the right end of the spectrum. Even the most vigorous supporters of cost attribution might accept that it serves little purpose to try and attribute some such shared general expenses. In such cases zero-based and incremental budgeting might be applied to try and exert the pressure on costs which will be missing from failing to involve profit-centre managers in management of these costs.

A 'sole user' approach is similar to the 'prime user' philosophy, applied to fixed costs. It starts from the same point – asking which is the major user, but then focuses on capacity-related costs. The capacity requirements and associated costs of the prime user are identified first, with secondary users bearing only the additional costs required to run their additional service. This 'sole user' approach can be particularly useful in the case of discretionary costs, for example equipment renewals. But in the case of continuing expenditure the sole user analysis can be compared with existing provision to identify areas of potential surplus. This means of identifying surplus capacity is a strength of this approach.

At the far right of this continuum lie those costs such as central management which can only sensibly be controlled centrally, and which are therefore not allocated at all or allocated on traditionally arbitrary bases.

CONCLUSION

We have not attempted here to prescribe in detail how relevant controls can be established for organisations. What we have attempted is to describe some key alternatives in ascertaining relevance.

It would seem important to integrate financial control structures with those required in a planning context. Some measure of profitability of major product groupings may logically be demanded in the planning process, which can only be derived by the application of something close to full cost allocation. Applying a similar approach for all reporting purposes provides profit centre managers with 'bottom line' results which, even if not wholly actionable by those managers, creates a working ethos of profit orientation throughout the organisation. It is possible that in some circumstances, particularly with large matrix organisations, cultural gains might outweigh intellectual reluctance to accept allocation conventions.

We have discussed the familiar problem of measuring managers on their net contribution or on profits after cost allocations. Classically this debate concerns the role of fixed and variable costs. We have suggested a more relevant distinction might be between direct and shared costs. We have suggested that a trend towards developing low-level profit measures suggests that more shared costs will have to be allocated. Otherwise it will not be possible to assign low-level profit responsibility.

Finally we have suggested that a pragmatic approach to these problems might result in using different approaches along a spectrum dealing with the range of cost types from specific costs, which can be attributed directly, to general expenses, which cannot satisfactorily be attributed other than by arbitrary allocation.

REFERENCES AND FURTHER READING

Coase, R. H., 'The nature of costs', in Solomons, D. (ed.), Studies in Cost Analysis, London: Sweet & Maxwell, 1968.

Demski, J. S., 'Uncertainty and evaluation based on controllable performance', Journal of Accounting Research, Autumn 1976.

Fremgen, J., and Liao, S., The Allocation of Corporate Indirect Costs, New York: National Association of Accountants, 1981.

Horngren, C. T., Introduction to Management Accounting, 6th edn, Englewood Cliffs, N.J.: Prentice-Hall, 1984.

Kaplan, R., Advanced Management Accounting, Englewood Cliffs, N.J.: Prentice-Hall, 1982.

Tomkins, C. R., Financial Planning in Divisionalised Companies, London: Haymarket, 1973.

11

Divisional performance measurement

David Fanning

Many management accounting texts assume simple manufacturing operations carried on within straightforward organisation structures. Real business life, of course, is rarely so clean. The complexities of formal organisational structures pose considerable difficulties for those trying to design and maintain planning and control systems.

This chapter considers the requirements for financial measures of divisional performance. It begins with a thorough examination of the two major measurement methods – return on capital and residual income. The author demonstrates that the popular return on capital concept can lead to divisional managers basing judgements on too short a time horizon. Residual income can also lead to a short-term perspective but can help to direct divisional managers to follow corporate goals. Including a charge for the use of capital can also lead to divisional managers paying more attention to the control of working capital.

Having considered these two methods of assessing divisional performance the author considers the criteria by which measurement devices should be judged, in the context of the purposes for which divisional reports are prepared.

The final section of the chapter considers the wider issue of divisional control, and the thorny question of delegation to divisional managements.

In many textbooks on managerial accounting, decentralisation and divisionalisation are regarded as synonymous labels for the same process. However, clear and important distinctions must be made between the two processes. Decentralisation implies the delegation of decision making and relaxation of the constraints and strictures governing managerial freedom. Both benefits and costs associate with decentralisation, and the extent to which any firm adopts the process is dictated by the perceived net difference between those costs and benefits. The benefits of decentralised management have been well described by many writers – see Horngren (1977), for example – and can be summarised as follows: the optimisation of decision making, the dispersal of the burden of decision making, the heightening of managerial freedom and motivation, the better development of managers, and the closer monitoring of transfer prices and effective activities. On the other side of the equation, the costs include the dangers of suboptimisation and dysfunctional behaviour, the additional costs of gathering, presenting and analysing performance data, and the likelihood of duplication of activities in separate divisions.

Divisionalisation is one form of decentralisation, in which a divisional manager is given responsibility for all the operations and outcomes of a division – planning, implementation, production, marketing, costs, revenues, profits. Such a division may be an operating unit of a company, a subsidiary company of a holding company, or a group of operating companies within a conglomerate. Divisions can be delineated on product or market lines, by geographical criteria or in any way beneficial to the establishing corporation.

The process of divisionalisation gives rise to two major problems. First, as Child (1977) and others have argued, the very process of divisionalisation is divisive in organisational terms. The creation of operating divisions leads to the dilution of corporate loyalty. A divisional identity develops instead; managers belong to, and owe allegiance to, a division. Decisions may not be taken in the best interests of the organisation as a whole, particularly where divisional and corporate interests conflict. There are strong pressures on divisional managers to act in their own best interests – given greater strength by the adoption of accounting yardsticks as measurement devices.

Second, and perhaps more fundamental, full divisional autonomy is virtually impossible to achieve. There can be no such thing as a fully independent division. The corporation is formed, owned and judged as a whole; central management and corporate directors are held responsible for group performance, in which divisional performances play a crucial role. The concept of full responsibility has to be replaced, if a realistic view is to be taken and realistic judgements made of managerial performance, and the most amenable substitute is the notion of controllability, as discussed later in this chapter.

The test of a skilful central management is the extent to which its decentralisation and divisionalisation practices succeed. Control must be maintained, despite the force of motivational freedom;

divisional contribution to corporate wealth must be maximised, despite the spur autonomy gives to profit making for divisional benefits alone. These are daunting obstacles in the path of any organisation wishing to decentralise and divisionalise its operations, and overcoming them is one of management's most difficult tasks.

PERFORMANCE MEASUREMENT

Most yardsticks used to judge managerial performance are founded on accounting information, and those used to appraise divisional performance offer easy and attractive measures of the success or failure of divisional activities. The strengths and weaknesses of such accounting yardsticks have been described and discussed by many writers in recent years – notably Solomons (1965) and Tomkins (1973). Two methods of appraisal or measurement have been adopted by companies, although other less attractive and flexible tests have been advanced. It can be argued that neither method is wholly acceptable, but the fact of their widespread use makes it sensible to present their main characteristics and discuss their implications. The two most common methods are: return on investment and residual income. Each is examined in turn.

Return on investment

The most common form of performance evaluation in divisionalised companies is the return on investment method (see Mauriel and Anthony (1966) for a discussion of the identification of responsibility centres and methods in a sample of divisionalised companies). In this context, return on investment is calculated as a ratio of net divisional profits (before tax) to the net assets (at book values) employed in the division.

By employing such a simple yardstick, the assessor concentrates on the percentage return: the divisional objective is to maximise that percentage return, and little attention is given to absolute values. Table 11.1 presents the income statements and summarised balance sheets for two operating divisions in a multiproduct company. Adopting the simplistic return on investment approach (that is by expressing net profit before tax as a percentage of net capital employed in the division) the return on investment for Division A can be calculated at 39.4 per cent, and that for Division B at 50.2 per cent. Taking a slightly more realistic approach, by making a notional charge against each division for corporation tax (say at a rate of 52 per cent), would reduce each division's profits to £137 280 and £38 750 respectively. On that basis, the return on investment for Division A would be calculated at 18.9 per cent and that for Division B at 24.1 per cent.

The next step in appraisal is to relate those calculated returns on investment to the company's cost of capital or some other measure of required rate of return for divisional profits. Even where firms use an investment hurdle rate or internal rate of return for appraising capital investment projects, the rates will be determined in very different ways from the calculated rate of return on investment – a point discussed below. A comparison between the two will be misleading, as will the view that the highest rate of return is always the best. A better approach is to compare the rate of return after tax for each division with the excess of those earnings over different costs of capital. Solomons (1965) applied this technique to the evaluation of the alternative merits of various investment opportunities, but the procedure can be used just as effectively to appraise divisional operating results.

Table 11.2 illustrates this procedure, where the firm's cost of capital has been set at 12 per cent, 16 per cent and 20 per cent, respectively. It can be seen that a straightforward appraisal of Division B as being more profitable, as measured by its superior rate of return on investment, will not be the better judgement for all costs of capital. If the firm's cost of capital is 20 per cent, for example, then Division B

Table 11.1
Divisional income statements and balance sheets

	Division A	Division B
	£	£
Sales revenue	858 000	236 050
less Cost of goods sold	405 000	101 500
Gross profit	453 000	134 550
less Operating expenses (including allocated overheads)	167 000	53 820
Net profit before tax	286 000	80 730
Net fixed assets	630 000	139 550
Net current assets	95 000	21 250
Net capital employed	725 000	160 800

is clearly the better performer. However, for costs of capital of 12 per cent or 16 per cent, Division A generates greater excess returns. The actual cutoff point between the division is, of course, close to 18.9 per cent as a cost of capital.

This analysis highlights one of the major drawbacks to the adoption of a return on investment criterion. The manager of Division B, aware that his activities are earning a return of 24.1 per cent on investment and rewarded on that basis by central management, will act to ensure the continued 'superiority' of his division. For circumstances where the firm's actual cost of capital is less than 18 per cent or so, the manager of Division A is performing better in the interests of the firm as a whole, although his division's rate of return on investment of only 18.9 per cent will lead, on this approach, to an unfavourable comparison with the manager of Division B.

A further problem with the straightforward return on investment approach is that it is constrained by accounting practices and procedures. Simply by the imposition of depreciation charges, a manager's return on investment will increase over time, even if his actual profitability remains static or declines slightly. For instance, if the manager of Division B depreciated his fixed assets by some 15 per cent per annum on a straightline basis, and if the average life of those assets is 6 years or so and if the assets in the balance sheet in Table 11.1 are three years old at that balance sheet date, the depreciation charge for the next period will be around £38 000. If the division's profits decline to some £32 000, the calculated rate of return on investment will be 26.1 per cent (£32 000/£122 800) – an apparent increase in divisional profitability, but in the absence of any real improvement.

Table 11.2
Divisional earnings

	Division A	Division B
Net capital employed	£725 000	£160 800
Net profit after tax	£137 280	£38 750
Rate of return on capital invested	18.9%	24.1%
Excess of net profit after tax over cost of capital		
at 12%	£50 280	£19 454
at 16%	£21 280	£13 022
at 20%	(£7 720)	£6 590

Table 11.3
Divisional project

Initial investment:	£20 000	Required return:	20.0%
Cash flows: Year 1	£3 000	Return:	15.0%
2	£3 300		16.5%
3	£3 600		18.0%
4	£11 000		55.0%
5	£12 100		60.5%
6	£13 310		66.6%
Net present value (at 20%)	£1 499	Internal rate of return:	22.3%

Allied to that problem is the further one that such rates of return are calculated in relationship to balance sheet book values – whether opening, closing, or average values. The values may bear little or no relation to real underlying values, especially in the absence of any adjustments to take account of changing prices or replacement costs.

The rate of return on investment is calculated on short run fixed period returns, ignoring any consideration of the time factors involved. Hurdle rates and internal rates of return are calculated in respect of capital investment projects over the lifetimes of those projects and have considerable regard for time factors. Flower (1971) has proposed a mechanism for overcoming the problems generated by picking balance sheet values at a fixed point in time, and there are obvious mechanisms for overcoming the disparate approaches of the rate of return on investment and the internal rate of return for projects or capital investment opportunities – as discussed above and illustrated in Table 11.2.

For the group as a whole, the rate of return on investment criterion lends itself to short term judgements and will act as a dysfunctional influence on divisional managers so judged. If, for example, a divisional manager is required to obtain a rate of return on capital employed of greater than 20 per cent and if he is presented with an investment opportunity such as that outlined in Table 11.3, his short run decision will be to reject the proposal. The rate of return in the first three years is less than his required rate of return and his immediate reaction will be to avoid the possibility of being judged adversely. The short run view of what should or should not be undertaken will ignore the real benefits to be gained over the lifetime of the project.

Residual income

According to Mauriel and Anthony (1966), about one-third of the companies they surveyed used the residual income approach either on its own or in combination with the return on investment yardstick, to measure divisional performance. The residual income technique deducts a charge for the use of assets from divisional profits, and bases this charge on the company's cost of capital. The emphasis of the residual income approach is to determine an absolute value for divisional income, as adjusted, rather than a percentage value.

The significant feature of the residual income method, as exemplified by Solomons (1965), is the notion of controllability – one of the criteria for divisional performance measures discussed later in this chapter. If a division is to be charged for the use of capital and some measure of residual income derived, it is reasonable to expect that the profit figure adjusted for that capital charge should be one which reflects all items subject to any substantial degree of control or influence by the divisional manager – and that items over which the divisional manager has little control should not be included. Such an approach can be applied to the income statement for Division A given in Table 11.1; adjusted to distinguish between controllable and non-controllable items of expenditure, the income statement would appear as in Table 11.4. It can be seen that such a statement would appear as in Table 11.4. It can be seen that such a statement reveals three possible measurements of divisional profit: net profit before tax; contribution margin; controllable profit. Which should be used? The arguments advanced by Solomons (1965) and later writers held that divisional income statements should clearly reveal a figure of controllable operating profit against which would be set a charge for use of capital in the division during the period, based on the corporate cost of capital. Such a statement, described as a divisional residual income statement, is presented in Table 11.5. The corporate cost of capital has been estimated at 18 per cent, and the division employed a net capital of £725 000 during the period (see Table 11.1), leading to a charge on controllable investment of £76 500 – calculated on the basis that net current assets represented controllable capital invested in the division and that controllable fixed assets had a net book value of £330 000 (being plant and equipment), whereas non-controllable fixed assets had a net book value of £300 000 (being land and buildings). Accordingly, as shown in the table, controllable residual income for Division A was calculated at £286 500, representing a rate of return of 67.4 per cent on controllable capital invested in the division; net residual income before tax

225

Table 11.4
Divisional income statement

		£
Sales revenue		858 000
less Variable cost of goods sold	405 000	
Variable divisional selling and administration expenses	27 300	
		432 300
Variable profit		425 700
less Controllable divisional overhead		62 700
Controllable profit		363 000
less Fixed non-controllable divisional overhead		41 700
Contribution margin		321 300
less Allocated extradivisional fixed non-controllable expenses		35 300
Net profit before tax		286 000

Table 11.5
Divisional residual income statement

		£
Sales revenue		858 000
less Variable costs		432 000
Variable profit		425 700
less Controllable divisional overhead		62 700
Controllable profit		363 000
less Interest on controllable investment		76 500
Controllable residual income		286 500
less Interest on non-controllable divisional investment	54 000	
Fixed non-controllable divisional overhead	41 700	
Allocated extradivisional fixed non-controllable expenses	35 300	
		131 000
Net residual income before tax		155 500

was calculated at £155 500, representing a rate of return of 21.4 per cent on capital invested in the division. Taking a similar approach to the activities of Division B produced a controllable residual income figure of £92 300 (after a charge of £29 700 on controllable investment), representing a rate of return of 55.9 per cent on controllable capital invested in the division; net residual income before tax was calculated at £31 230, representing a rate of return of 11.4 per cent on capital invested in the division.

The most obvious outcome of such a revision of divisional earnings measurements is that the relative positions of Divisions A and B are reversed. Division A is estimated to have the higher rate of return, by either definition of capital invested, as shown in Table 11.6. From being significantly 'worse' than Division B, Division A is now seen to perform much better. The figures derived can be adjusted further, by making a notional tax charge (based on a rate of 52 per cent), as shown in the table – there Division A's rate of return on capital employed is 10.3 per cent and Division B's is 5.5 per cent. Taking the further refinement shown in Table 11.2, those rates of return can be compared for different costs of capital. In those circumstances, both divisions have significant shortfalls at all rates of cost of capital.

A number of writers – notably Amey (1969) – have criticised the inclusion of a charge for interest on capital employed in the calculation of residual income. Amey's criticism was founded on the belief that operating divisions have little actual control over capital investment in their divisional activities. None the less, the evidence that the measure is used, as adduced by Mauriel and Anthony (1966), tends to negate Amey's criticism. He argued also that the inclusion of a charge for interest did little to encourage the maximisation of the rate of return on capital and, if it was designed to encourage the maximisation of divisional profits, would have a marked dysfunctional effect since managers would be instructed to maximise residual income. The arguments against these criticisms have been marshalled by Samuels (1969) and by Mepham (1980), and as Solomons (1965) demonstrated clearly, residual income has marked beneficial effects as a divisional performance measurement yardstick.

Amey considered that the firm's corporate objectives would be served best if divisional managers had no control over their own capital investment. The cost of capital in Amey's argument was a fixed cost, and as such should play no part in either divisional investment decision making or, more important, in divisional performance measurement. Emmanuel and Otley (1976) reviewed these arguments and criticisms and came down conclusively in favour of

Table 11.6
Divisional residual incomes

	Division A	Division B
Controllable capital employed	£425 000	£165 000
Controllable residual income	£286 500	£92 300
Rate of return on controllable capital invested	67.4%	55.9%
Net capital employed	£725 000	£275 000
Net residual income before tax	£155 500	£31 230
Rate of return on capital invested	21.4%	11.4%
Net residual income after tax	£74 640	£14 990
Rate of return on capital invested	10.3%	5.5%

residual income as a measurement tool. That divisional managers are knowledgeable in matters of investment for their own areas of responsibility is one of the more cogent arguments for divisionalisation. Equally, capital invested in a division includes working capital, or net current assets, and so comes under the close, day to day control of divisional managers. Any charge for interest will be comprised of two elements, therefore, and will tend to act as a powerful motivational force in the improvement of divisional performance.

The residual income approach, like the return on investment method, concentrates on short run results in fixed periods, but the calculation of residual income after levying a charge for the use of capital takes account of the cost of capital and involves consideration of the time value of money and present values. In such circumstances, divisional decisions are likely to be more in keeping with corporate decisions. The data in Table 11.3 ignore depreciation, and it might be useful to bring that into this discussion. Charging depreciation would reduce book values (that is, capital invested) and would result in a reducing charge for interest on capital invested in the division. Under the residual income approach, there would be a positive increment to residual income in each year of the project's life and this factor would aid its acceptance by the divisional manager, with concomitant long run benefits.

A beneficial effect of the employment of the residual income approach is that it encourages divisional managers to be take more notice, and even to become aware of, the real costs of using capital. The motivational impact of the inclusion of an actual charge for capital use is likely to be far greater than the recognition of a percentage rate of return on capital. Arguably, if managers have to pay for the use of capital, that capital will be used more effectively and efficiently. The appreciation of the actual cost of retaining under-used capital resources will prompt a rationalisation of capital requirements, thereby releasing funds or assets for use elsewhere.

MEASUREMENT CRITERIA

Having examined the two leading measurements and discussed their advantages and disadvantages, we can now compile a list of the criteria by which such measurement devices should be judged. Shillinglaw (1961 and 1962) suggested that there are three criteria against which divisional profit measurements must be judged before they are considered acceptable:

1 Divisional profit should not be increased by any action that reduces total company profit.
2 Each division's profit should be as independent as possible of performance efficiency and managerial decisions elsewhere in the company.
3 Each division's profit should reflect all items that are subject to any substantial degree of control by the division manager or his subordinates.

The first rule is clearly in the best interest of the firm as a whole. It can be shown convincingly in any discussion of transfer pricing, for example, as in Chapter 18 of this handbook, that 'selfish' profit seeking actions by divisional managers will reduce overall contribution. Central management will take action to restrain divisional managements found to be price cutting or operating suboptimising transfer pricing practices. The various accounting practices followed in a firm – for instance, in relation to depreciation or absorption costing – may induce conflict between divisional interests and those of the firm as a whole. Dearden (1960 and 1961) has discussed a number of these related problems, and Solomons (1965) has provided the simplest solution:

> . . . unwise rules of divisional profit measurement may cause a division to act against the best interests of the company. They are really all manifestations of a single defect. In every case there is a failure to make a division bear the true cost to the company of the division's action – the true cost of using capital, of administrative services, of scrapping equipment and so on.

Once those defects are recognised, there is every chance of devising a system which will rectify matters.

229

The second and third criteria advanced by Shillinglaw are concerned with the independence of divisions and with the contention that divisional managers should be judged only on the results of those activities over which they have full control. As discussed before (in Chapter 10, for instance) the notion of absolute control is not realistic; a more acceptable criterion is that of significant influence. Shillinglaw's view of divisional performance reports was that they should only include those items over which the manager had control. To include and identify controllable items is one thing, and thoroughly commendable at that, but to exclude and thereby ignore other aspects of divisional performance is clearly naive and undesirable.

Alongside Shillinglaw's criteria, it is valuable to examine the purposes for which divisional reports will be drawn up. They have three principal roles:

1   the guidance of divisional management in making decisions;
2   the guidance of corporate management in making decisions;
3   the appraisal of divisional management by corporate management.

Those three roles have two different orientations. Decision making guidance relates to the future, whereas appraisal relates to the past. In the one case, profit figures, however derived or defined, have limited value for forecasting future outcomes and making decisions. In the other, profit figures may be the only information available for assessment of managers' endeavours and the appraisal of their results.

In those circumstances – and it must be remembered that all classes of profit figure are surrounded with qualifications and misgivings as to their accuracy, usefulness and relevance – the residual income approach seems to offer better and more appropriate information to both divisional and corporate management.

For divisional managements in the process of taking decisions, the controllable residual income before tax figure (see Table 11.5, for example) offers the better guide; for corporate managements in the process of making decisions concerning investment, the net residual income figure before tax offers a more appropriate guide, although the incidence of tax and its allocation to divisions may make the after tax figure a better criterion in certain circumstances.

For corporate managements wishing to appraise the performance of divisional managements, the controllable residual income figure represents the more effective and amenable yardstick of divisional performance. No account should be taken of factors outside the divisional manager's control or influence when appraising that manager's performance. For that reason, the measurement of controllable residual income, free of all cost elements outside the divisional manager's control, offers the better yardstick for performance measurement.

DIVISIONAL CONTROL

As discussed elsewhere in this handbook, control is best exercised through the use of budgets; controllable residual income will form a part of any divisional operating budget or profit budget, if that is the yardstick adopted. Divisional managers report the congruence, or lack of congruence, between budgeted results and actual outcomes, and support such reports with explanations and analyses of variances, current plans and proposed actions to rectify or eliminate shortcomings.

Corporate management can take action as appropriate on the basis of those budget reports, as described and discussed in the chapter dealing with responsibility accounting (Chapter 10), but special problems inhibit the effectiveness of budget reports as control mechanisms or evaluatory devices.

These have been described by Anthony and Dearden (1976) as falling into three principal categories:

1 the degree of discretion available to divisional managers;
2 the degree to which critical performance variables can be controlled by the divisional manager;
3 the degree of uncertainty associated with the critical performance variables.

The greater the degree of discretion allowed to a divisional manager, the harder it becomes to set precise goals or targets. The greater the number of choices available to a divisional manager, the more difficult it is to decide which of those choices will be best for the firm in the long run.

The greater the degree of control of the divisional manager over the critical performance variables by which he is to be judged, the easier it is to set quantified and effective budgetary control systems.

The greater the degree of uncertainty surrounding those critical variables, the harder it will be to set satisfactory goals and to measure subsequent performance. In general terms, the higher the level of uncertainty associated with a division's operations, the lower the controllability of the divisional manager, especially where the greater proportion of any uncertainty will surround variables external to the division and the firm.

Additionally, the problem of the time span of both managerial activities and performance measures becomes acute when divisional managers are engaged in making decisions regarding long term projects. Managers of innovative or experimental divisions may not be fairly judged in such cases. Equally, however, the results of current performance are influenced by the impacts of previous decisions, so substantial compensating influences may be at work.

Delegation – tight or loose?

Control devices are needed over and above the profit budget, and their importance will vary with the degree of delegation adopted by corporate management. That aspect of divisional control can be examined by considering the two extremes: tight delegation and loose delegation.

It is frequently said that one of the marks of a 'bad' manager is his inability to delegate efficiently. Such a manager delegates only routine tasks, maintains a close watch over their progress and participates in the planning and execution of any delegated tasks which he considers important or attractive. In much the same way, corporate managements practise tight delegation procedures, taking the view that divisional managers work best within a clearcut and short period, and when corporate management shares important decision making exercises. Advocates of tight delegation argue that managers work better when they are committed to a relatively short term role – that is, for example, within a one-year budget period. Equally, it is argued that although divisional managers make day to day decisions, the participation of corporate management in those decision processes will increase the scope for making better and more profitable decisions.

Under conditions of tight delegation, it is necessary to augment the budget control process by two further control mechanisms. There will need to be a much closer involvement of corporate and divisional management in the budgeting and reporting system, encompassing regular meetings, systematic analyses of divisional reports, and much deeper insights into the detailed facets of divisional operations. Additionally, the existence of a structure of tight delegation will call for a competent, experienced and alert infrastructure of accounting and budgeting staff. In other words, the management accounting team's role becomes crucial.

In conditions of tight delegation, the divisional manager will be judged by his adherence to budget plans, and that process of evaluation by proximity to targets will lead to some of the dangers discussed earlier in this chapter: the encouragement of uneconomic actions and the subsequent incorrect evaluation of the manager. The control devices built on to the budget system can help to alleviate those weaknesses. Corrective actions can be discussed and evaluated more logically and in greater detail, and appraisals of divisional managements will be made more in terms of personal observation than report interpretation.

Loose delegation practices use the budget as a planning and communication device, rather than as a measurement and performance appraisal device. The philosophical tenet of loose delegation is that divisional managers are good managers, experienced and efficient, and should be left to get on with their delegated tasks. In such circumstances, central management would be negligent if it took the naive view that such divisional managers could be left completely to their own devices. Some kind of early warning system must give clear signals when divisional managements are performing unsatisfactorily or ineffectively. In complex organisations, such as most business enterprises, the accounting and budgeting systems offer only limited assistance in that direction. By their nature, such systems depend on historical data, and evaluations of past performance, and fail to offer sufficiently early warnings of poor managerial performance. Personal observation by experienced managers is probably the only sensible way of operating such an early warning system; Stewart and Stewart (1982) gave valuable insights into detecting, understanding and remedying poor performance.

Non-financial control measures

There seems to be general agreement that profitability alone is inadequate to measure the performance of divisional managers. The General Electric Company adopted eight measures of divisional performance when it decentralised in the 1950s:

1 profitability;
2 market position;
3 productivity;
4 product leadership;
5 personnel development;

6   employee attitudes;
7   public responsibility;
8   balance between short range and long range goals.

Anthony and Dearden (1976) argued that, as a minimum, divisional managements should be judged by market and product performance and development, employee performance and development, and social or public responsibility. Those measurements can be formalised and incorporated in a structured system of management by objectives, or they can be informal and unstructured.

CONCLUSION

Notwithstanding the very large problems associated with both the return of investment and residual income approach to divisional performance measurement, the two methods underlie any system of divisional measurement and control. As such, the main task for the coming years is to refine those methods and tailor their structure more closely to the enhanced measurement of divisional performance.

Fundamental difficulties must be overcome to design and implement control systems which will recognise the influences and impacts of accounting, behavioural, decisional and organisational differences on divisional performance, and there is a clear need for wider research into these areas from the viewpoint of divisional performance measurement and evaluation.

In appraising a divisional manager, there is a danger that the importance of the profitability yardstick will overshadow other, and perhaps equally crucial, yardsticks and measurement devices. Corporate management must take a balanced but realistic view of divisional performance, and there is a need for researchers and practitioners to develop suitable mechanisms and approaches to make that realistic view more accessible. The ability of central management to control divisional operations depends on its ability to recognise, encourage and reward 'good' performers and to identify, understand and cure 'poor' performers.

REFERENCES AND FURTHER READING

Amey, L. R., 'Divisional performance measurement and interest on capital', *Journal of Business Finance*, Spring 1969.

Anthony, R. N., and Dearden, J., *Management Control Systems: Text and Cases*, 3rd edn, Homewood, Ill.: Irwin, 1976.

Child, J., *Organisation: A Guide to Problems and Practice*, London: Harper & Row, 1977.

Dearden, J., 'Problem in decentralized profit responsibility', *Harvard Business Review*, May–June 1960.

Dearden, J., 'Problem in decentralized financial control', *Harvard Business Review*, May–June 1961.

Emmanuel, C. R., and Otley, D. T., 'The usefulness of residual income', *Journal of Business Finance and Accountancy*, Winter 1976.

Flower, J. F., 'Captim – a bright idea from Bristol', *Accountancy*, December 1971.

Horngren, C. T., *Cost Accounting: A Managerial Emphasis*, 4th edn, Englewood Cliffs, N.J.: Prentice-Hall, 1977.

Mauriel, J. J., and Anthony, R. N., 'Misevaluation of investment center performance', *Harvard Business Review*, March–April 1966.

Mepham, M. J., 'The residual income debate', *Journal of Business Finance and Accountancy*, Summer 1980.

Samuels, J. M., 'Divisional performance measurement and interest on capital: a contributed note', *Journal of Business Finance*, Autumn 1969.

Shillinglaw, G., *Cost Accounting: Analysis and Control*, Homewood, Ill.: Irwin, 1961.

Shillinglaw, G., 'Toward a theory of divisional income measurement', *The Accounting Review*, April 1962.

Solomons, D., *Divisional Performance: Measurement and Control*, New York: Financial Executives Research Foundation, 1965.

Stewart, V., and Stewart, A., *Managing the Poor Performer*, Aldershot: Gower, 1982.

Tomkins, C., *Financial Planning in Divisionalised Companies*, London: Haymarket, 1973.

12

Management auditing

Janusz Santocki

Auditing might seem a strange subject for a management accounting handbook, but as the author of this chapter quickly emphasises, management auditing can be an important tool in the management accountant's task of analysing corporate performance and prospects.

The chapter begins by defining what is meant by the term 'management audit' and its synonyms, and drawing distinctions between this approach and financial auditing. It continues by exploring the scope of this technique and the benefits it can produce. The remainder of the chapter is then devoted to explaining the nature of management auditing assignments and the methods of carrying out such an audit. There are five essential elements: information, knowledge, techniques, analysis and reporting, and each of these is considered in turn.

The author concludes that interest in this concept is justified by the practical benefits it can produce for organisations, especially the constant direction of attention at improving performance, even when there are no specific and obvious problems to be addressed.

Management audit is not a new concept. What is new is the greatly increasing interest in the techniques and function of a management audit shown during the past two decades. The earliest recorded evidence of the concept seems to be that given by de Roover (1963), who described how an auditor was sent to the London branch of the Medici Bank in 1948:

> with instructions to audit the books to ascertain whether the manager had made wise investments and operated within the scope of the policies established by the managing partners.

As a further example of early interest in management audit, a leading work was published in London in the early 1930s (Rose, 1932).

Empirical research in management auditing was being conducted in Europe and the United States during the 1950s and early 1960s.

The description of the Medici Bank auditor's brief sets out well and simply the objective of management audit. The assumption is that the manager's duty is to make 'wise investments' and that it is for the auditor to check whether or not that duty has been discharged efficiently and to report accordingly. It is accepted that the manager has the duty not only to operate within the scope of the policies and rules of an organisation, but also to attempt to make the optimal use of resources under his control.

The philosophy of management audit refuses to accept that the management of an organisation cannot be improved. Equally, it is false to hold that directors are born with the qualities required for successful management and that those qualities cannot be developed. Acceptance of these tenets means that directors and managers are prepared to open their managerial process and the resulting performance to somebody else's appraisal. That appraisal should comprise two elements: the review, and the recommendations. These should assist management through reporting on weaknesses in performance and recommend ways of minimising, if not eradicating, those weaknesses.

MEANING OF MANAGEMENT AUDIT

Several definitions have been advanced in attempts to set out the meaning of the management audit function. The Dutch accountants' institute (Nederlands Instituut van Registeraccountants, 1979) saw management audit as a:

> recurrent comprehensive investigation into apparently healthy organisations with the object of achieving an insight into the state of the organisation – and also its environment – so as to be able to form an opinion on future prospects whereby specific action can be taken to arrive at a better control of the operations of the organisation.

Another definition was provided by Dombrower (1972), who saw management auditing as:

> a concept which will assist management in developing its own resources more effectively by adopting an independent and objective analytical approach to (a) the organization, (b) the controls, and (c) the functions of the entire operation. The results

of this review are then compared to the objectives and standards of the organization with specific reference to generally accepted management and operational concepts. Usually a sound operational audit department will be preventive in its approach, since it will attempt to detect problem areas while they are in their early stages of development.

Campfield (1967) defined management audit as follows:

> Management auditing is an informed and constructive analysis, evaluation, and series of recommendations regarding the broad spectrum of plans, processes, people and problems of an economic entity.

These definitions share a marked degree of common ground. Santocki (1976) defined management audit as an objective, independent, informed and constructive appraisal of the effectiveness of managers or teams of managers in their achievement of corporate targets and objectives, identifying existing and potential strengths and weaknesses at all levels in the organisation and in all functions and operations of the organisation. Presentation of recommendations designed to rectify weaknesses and potential weaknesses featured prominently in this context.

Probably the most important aspect of management auditing is the intention to assist management to improve performance. Through that assistance, the management auditor can help to increase productivity and profitability. The function is advisory, however, in the management consultancy tradition, and not executive. The management audit draws management's attention to what needs to be done to make the best use of the resources available. Management audit is intended neither to replace management nor to curtail its responsibility for decision making and control. The role of management auditing is to provide relevant and timely information on the basis of which management can make decisions.

The management auditing process is a system of investigation, analysis and appraisal. It is not the 'doing' function; its objective is to conduct the audit and produce the recommendations that will lead to the 'doing'. The description of management auditing as 'preventive medicine' is an apt one. It is important for management auditors to report in the early stages of each project, before problems have the chance to get out of hand.

The management auditor must be independent and his function must be, and be seen to be, 'external'. A management audit team must not form part of the management team of the department which is being appraised. The team must be independent of those being audited – and this happens in most organisations, where the management audit team is responsible to a chief executive or controller.

Confusion has arisen in the literature as to the meanings of apparently synonymous names for the process. Among others, the terms 'management audit', 'performance review', 'operational audit', and 'efficiency audit' have been used interchangeably. The distinction between an operational audit and a management audit, advocated by some writers, deserves a brief discussion. The former is said to be a purely internal function to serve the needs of an organisation's management; the latter is an 'external' function serving the needs of a wider audience – such as the shareholders, for instance. Those refinements seem unnecessary. Management auditing is the more popular term, and it can be for management (the internal role) and for shareholders (the external role). There seems little point in labouring what is a relatively unclear distinction.

THE APPROACH

'An auditor is a watchdog' is an apt description of the role of the statutory financial audit, and still represents the legal view of the auditing function. An outsider checks the administration of an entity for a period, with a view to detecting errors or omissions in financial statements. Mistakes could be either intentional or accidental. Intentional errors include such actions as the falsification of accounts or the embezzlement of property. Unintentional errors arise from incompetence of staff or imperfection of systems and controls.

The watchdog is the guardian of conventions and orderliness, and this is accepted as an important function. The role of the statutory financial auditor can be described as essentially protective, that is ensuring that the rules are observed. The limitations of such a function are that its main contribution to the wealth of an organisation and its owners is to minimise losses incurred through dishonesty or negligence, and that it attests only to the reliability and accuracy of certain kinds of published financial information. With the adoption of auditing standards by the main professional bodies, those limitations are reinforced by the narrowing field of relevance of the auditor's opinion. Considerable disquiet has been expressed about the value of the financial auditing process – and, let it be said, the increasing cost of that process (see, for example, Briston and Perks, 1977).

The fundamental philosophy in the auditing process should be to increase the wealth of an organisation, as well as to protect it. That requires a more constructive and dynamic approach. The underlying assumption is that an organisation's management has not yet reached its optimum performance, realises that fact, and is open to suggestions as to how to improve performance and attain the optimum.

Both kinds of auditor – financial and management – may use the same or similar techniques. The ways in which each uses those techniques will differ, however, because the objectives differ. Management auditing is a comparatively new 'philosophy' and, as such, requires a different attitude of mind in its implementation. A description of some typical questions will illustrate and explain the differences in approach of the two kinds of auditor. Table 12.1 presents examples of financial auditing and management auditing questions.

The difference between the two groups of questions is fundamental and demonstrates that the need for a management audit is derived from the extended meaning of management's accountability. Attention turns from the verification of the compliance of management with regulatory frameworks and of the accuracy and reliability of the financial information to the assessment of underlying causes, related management practices, and resulting managerial performance. Public demands for improved accountability continue to grow and the legalistic approach of the statutory financial auditor is inadequate for the discharge of the extended accountability of management.

Table 12.1
Financial audit v management audit

Financial audit	Management audit
Has the entity kept proper accounting records?	Is the data provided to management accurate and timely and relevant?
Was the transaction properly authorised and is there acceptable evidence?	Has management satisfied itself that the price paid was the most economical, and how did it do so?
Are salaries paid to key employees within the limits imposed by the entity's regulations?	Is there a staff development programme adequate to replace retiring key employees and to cater for future likely requirements?
Do the balance sheet and profit and loss account show a true and fair view?	Is management well informed of existing and potential weaknesses and limitations in planning and budgetary controls?
Have decisions been made within the formal powers of the directors?	Can the processes leading to decision making be improved?

Scope of management auditing

The areas of management auditors' involvement described and discussed here are those for which there is reasonably good evidence of practical application and resulting benefits.

First, there must be an appraisal of the business's organisational structure, with special reference to the effective use of all the resources employed, physical and financial and human, and to the degree of support for the aims and objectives of the business. The management auditor reviews the organisation's structure by analysing its components and relating those to the corporate aims. Too elaborate a structure is cumbersome, ineffective and costly; idle capacity is wasteful; shortages and bottlenecks are expensive of time and resources; and so on.

Second, there is the appraisal of management's processes and procedures for determining organisational objectives and policies. Frequently better and more effective ways will be available, and a thorough analysis and evaluation of existing processes will lead to the identification of aspects susceptible to improvement.

Third, there is the appraisal of management systems of planning and control, with a view to determining whether those systems are adequate, whether they are reviewed and updated regularly, and whether they are understood and used continuously by all employees. To be effective, any system must be clearly understood by those using it and must be reviewed regularly to ensure its continued relevance and feasibility.

Fourth, there is the appraisal of management control techniques, to determine whether relevant, timely and accurate information reaches all levels of management, whether such information is acted upon, and whether the information contains budgetary control and standard costing data. The importance of relevant information being available to management at the right time has been emphasised by other contributors to this handbook and there can be no substitute for timely and useful information.

Fifth, there is the appraisal of technical competence, to determine the abilities of staff to achieve the organisation's objectives and to examine the scope and effectiveness of staff development and training schemes and the nature and extent of staff recruitment. The management auditor is concerned to discover whether the organisation possesses the resources necessary to achieve its objectives efficiently and effectively. Does management appreciate the technical and resource environment in which it operates, and is it aware of the problems and dangers ahead? Proper management requires an appreciation of both short term and long term needs and opportunities.

Sixth, there is the appraisal of management planning and control systems in the terms of the communication systems which they incorporate, so that effective systems transmit relevant and timely information. This aim of management auditing goes further than the appraisal of management control techniques, and it refers to the effectiveness of the entire communication system throughout the organisation. The question to decide is whether a proper monitoring procedure ensures that all concerned receive timely, accurate and adequate information. Intuition and hunch are not the best foundations for decision making and control; relevant information is crucial. A management auditor with experience and skill can make a significant contribution to the resolution of any problems in this area.

Seventh, there is the appraisal of results, with a view to determining whether or not the firm's objectives and policies are appropriate to the business and its environment, are attainable, and are being met. Ideal objectives and policies are easy to proclaim, but the frustration caused by failing to achieve such ideal targets can be most demotivating and dysfunctional. The management auditor's review and assessment will bring a sense of reality to the process of determining objectives and policies. Once appropriateness and feasibility are established, the determination of actual attainment levels can follow smoothly.

Management training and performance

Management auditing can contribute markedly to the management training scheme of an organisation. Typical responses to a survey conducted by the author included the following:

> The most difficult problem at present is retaining the people in the [management audit] team and recruiting suitable replacements. We had over 100 per cent labour turnover last year due to members of the team moving into operating companies as line managers. . .

and other respondents indicated that a period with the management audit team was an integral part of managerial training programmes.

It is perhaps a high commendation for the management auditing process that it contributes significantly to the development of line managers, even to the extent of forming a pool of managerial talent from which line managers can be recruited.

Management auditing contributes also to the development of standards for the evaluation of managerial performance. Teach-ins and staff seminars conducted by a management audit team can assist greatly in the acceptance by managers of a system of managerial assessment. Performance standards must be both properly based on the organisation's activities and clearly understood by those to be evaluated; management auditing helps markedly in those respects.

AUDITING ASSIGNMENTS

The typical management audit assignment is not a single 'problem' or area; of routine, a management audit takes full account of all facets of an organisation's activities. Table 12.2, however, presents some specific areas of concern, drawn from the management audit programme of a leading UK public company.

They are examples of an audit programme for one period of three months, and are drawn from Santocki (1979). The management audit programmes of many companies have life cycles of three or four years, during which all aspects of operations are reviewed more or less automatically. Additionally, from time to time a number of further assignments are imposed or requested.

Once an established management auditing function exists within

Table 12.2
Typical management auditing assignments

To review and report upon labour turnover at a number of different locations

> An imposed assignment from the board of directors, deriving from a realisation that turnover rates at certain locations were very much higher than at others.

To review and report upon certain cost centres

> Part of a regular random audit assignment.

To review and report upon the distribution methods and procedures of a regional depot

> An audit assignment from line management, concerned that one regional depot was out of line with other depots.

To investigate and report upon all aspects of operations at a specific location

> A comprehensive audit assignment from senior management.

To review the staffing position of the production planning department

> An assignment prior to the decision whether or not to approve a request for additional staff in the production planning department.

an organisation, access to it is generally available to senior and line management, as the examples in the table demonstrate.

Method of working

There are three fundamental questions which the management auditor will pose in connection with most, if not all, assignments, and which will influence the chosen method of fulfilling the assignment:

1 Does the organisation know what it wants to achieve? The ambiguity of objectives and policies should be resolved before other aspects can be examined properly.
2 Is the organisation capable of achieving what it wants to achieve? Targets which are too demanding or unrealistic are worse for staff motivation and optimising behaviour patterns than no objectives at all.
3 Are the organisation's structure and methods efficient and effective enough to allow it to pursue those objectives and policies? This aspect of the investigation requires the greatest amount of effort in a management audit.

Answers to those three preliminary questions will lead to two further questions:

4 Are there any ways in which the management auditor can assist management in its pursuit of the organisation's objectives and policies?
5 Can the management auditor assist management to improve processes and procedures for the attainment of those objectives and policies?

There are five essential elements of the management auditing process: information, knowledge, techniques, analysis, and report.

Information

Information plays a key role in any management audit. The past affects the present and the two together influence the future; for each phase, information is needed. The management auditor may face two particular problems in respect of information provision. First, staff may volunteer information, and the management auditor should be conscious of the motives behind such voluntary disclosure. Second, staff may be too guarded in their dealings with the management auditor and reveal little information or make its acquisition difficult. A more careful explanation to staff, describing the need for a

244

management audit and the scope of its findings and recommend-ations should go some way towards alleviating that problem. Above all else, a management auditor should try to collect information ob-jectively, reducing the impact of subjective personal judgements.

Knowledge

The management auditor should get to know the available manage-ment methods and practices which are appropriate to his work. Managerial planning and decisions making processes should be understood clearly, and the management auditor should be able, when necessary or appropriate, to see matters as a practising line or functional manager would.

He must also possess a sound knowledge of the particular organis-ation or department and its operations. This knowledge will ensure that he will begin his work from a favourable position; it may also, of course, impart a degree of prejudice, in that the auditor will not be wholly impartial, but an experienced management auditor will be sufficiently skilful to discount any such special bias.

Techniques

Among the management auditing techniques in common use are the following. A well-conducted interview is unavoidable since other techniques of eliciting information are unlikely to be so effective. Such an interview must be planned and structured, and the interview must be conducted in a disciplined and professional manner.

Direct observation is a further essential technique for manage-ment auditing, and it will generally disclose information which is difficult to recover or collect by other means. Staff relationships, for example, can best be assessed by observation; attitudes can be discerned; operational styles and preferences can be appraised. The study of internal documentation – staff manuals, organisation charts, operational memoranda, and so on – will reveal a great deal more about an organisation and its management than might be thought likely. The management auditor will need to familiarise himself with the budgets, forecasts and internal accounting reports of the subject entity.

In some instances, a questionnaire approach may be followed with good effect, especially where an anonymous response can be elicited on various otherwise sensitive topics. As in any other use of ques-tionnaires, the management auditor needs to satisfy himself about the validity, truthfulness and relevance of both questions and answers.

245

Ratio analysis and trend analysis are two commonly used techniques which the management auditor will use to evaluate the performance and status of the unit being audited.

Analysis

Analysis can be considered in two ways: from the point of view of the adequacy of the information available, and from that of the interpretation of the information.

A management auditor does not need to know all the facts; sufficient relevant information is all that is required. Total and absolute data are expensive, both in their collection and in their interpretation. The management auditor should seek out significant and relevant information, rather than accept all that is offered or available.

The interpretation of that information must be conducted sensibly and in a structured way. The first important task will be to separate facts from opinions. The measurement of management performance is discussed elsewhere in this handbook (see Chapter 11 for example), and there are a number of popular and apposite standards by which to judge managerial performance – for instance, return on capital employed or rate of growth. Other measures may be more or less apposite, depending on the nature of the audit assignment – for instance, profit per employee or labour turnover or direct material cost. As discussed in Chapter 10, responsibility centres and responsibility accounting practices will go a long way towards assisting in the evaluation of managerial performance.

Statistical sampling techniques and other quantitative methodologies have a role in the management audit processes, although care must be taken not to overlook the vital qualitative aspects of an audit of this nature.

Report

Reporting completes the assignment and the management auditor, as explained earlier, is not concerned with the actual implementation of his recommendations. The report should figure largely in the management auditor's mind throughout the whole audit process. In that way, a more disciplined investigation may be undertaken with constant attention to the purpose of the assignment.

Management auditors usually report to management, though sometimes reports are made to shareholders or employees' representatives. The report always features the management of the enterprise, but the emphasis and detail may vary from one type of recipient to the other. Typically, reports to management are more comprehensive and more detailed than those to other parties. It should be noted that management auditing for third parties is not legally required or enforceable in the United Kingdom, and it is essential that the terms of reference for such a reporting task should be determined clearly at the beginning of the investigation. In general terms, also, reports for management are prepared by internal teams, whereas reports for outsiders are prepared by external auditors.

One of the cardinal rules of management audit reporting is that – unlike, say, the consultants' report on the London Transport undertaking – the final report should not be a surprise to those being audited. The discussion and appraisal of a draft report, involving those reported upon, will have beneficial effects, and at the very least appropriate managers should receive copies of the management audit report.

PROCEDURES AND PROBLEMS

Santocki (1975) reported the results of an examination of the ways in which typical management audits were conducted, and the following description exemplifies the general approach:

> It is not stereotyped but is adopted according to the nature of the audit. However the most frequent procedure [is]: (i) initial informal interviews with senior management (after a general review of accounting information available at H.Q.); (ii) then development of a questionnaire, usually sectionalized, eg marketing, finance, production, etc; (iii) this is followed by visits to units where appropriate and other interviews with relevant personnel; (iv) audit reports are then developed from the above and the principal points are discussed with the unit, before a report is submitted. . .

The view is almost unanimous that a successful management audit team must be a multidisciplinary one, and the strong (but not dominant) presence of accountants is supported almost as vigorously. The legalistic approach of statutory financial auditors diminishes their effectiveness as members of a management audit team. Equally, the preoccupation with costs and budgets may lessen the effectiveness of 'traditional' management accountants. Nevertheless, each has the potential for making a worthwhile and crucial contribution to the management audit team. Other specialists and professionals to complement the accountant in a team would include economists, psychologists, engineers, personnel managers, data processing experts, marketers, and so on.

The greater difficulty facing the management auditor is ignorance – that is, the ignorance of management at all levels in an organisation. Senior management must understand and believe in the value of management auditing for it to have a good chance of success. There is ample evidence, especially from North America, of the successful application of management auditing, and there are many instances of quantifiable benefits arising from its endeavours. What is needed is the effort to adopt the practice and work from its results. An understanding of management audit processes and their implications will remove unjustified fears of its adverse effect on line managers and their subordinates. Some critics argue that the process of management auditing curbs managerial initiative and removes individual manager's decision making and controlling functions. For that reason and others, the introduction of management audit to an established business must be undertaken carefully and in a planned fashion, preceded by initial discussions and explanations throughout the organisation.

CONCLUSION

Management auditing is neither a new nor a purely academic concept. It is an essential and practicable component of a sensible organisation structure. The Dutch institute's report (Nederlands Instituut van Registeraccountants, 1979) demonstrated the need for management auditing:

> The demands being made on the enterprise by the many parties involved are no longer of a financial nature only. . . . During a period of frequent bankruptcies, supervision of payments and business closures, it is to be expected that interested parties will take a more critical attitude towards management. . . . The following questions then arise; why were we not earlier involved in the problems; was this unavoidable? . . .

The need for management audit is always present; it becomes more acute at a time of economic pressure or constraint.

The importance of management audit is that it directs senior management to constantly appraise the effectiveness and efficiency of their areas of operations, whether or not they are currently the subject of management audit. In many cases an early indication or warning of bad management or potential difficulties has resulted in remedial action being taken to good effect.

The quality of the management auditor is vital to the success of the practice, rather than his professional orientation or training. Management auditing is primarily an attitude of mind; the knowledge and the techniques are available, waiting to be employed.

REFERENCES AND FURTHER READING

American Institute of Management, *The Appraisal of Management*, New York: Harper, 1962.

Briston, R. J., and Perks, R. W., 'The external audit – its role and cost to society', *Accountancy*, November 1977.

Campfield, W. L., 'Trends in auditing management plans and operations', *Journal of Accountancy*, July 1967.

de Roover, R., *The Rise and Decline of Medici Bank*, Boston: Harvard University Press, 1963.

Dombrower, D., 'The professional accountants' formula for survival – operational auditing', *Canadian Chartered Accountant*, December 1972.

Greenwood, W. T., *Management and Organizational Behavior Theories: An Interdisciplinary Approach*, Cincinnati: South-Western Publishing, 1965.

Greenwood, W. T., *A Management Audit System*, Rev. edn, Carbondale, Ill.: Southern Illinois University, 1967.

Leonard, W. P., *The Management Audit*, Englewood Cliffs, N.J.: Prentice-Hall, 1962.

Nederlands Instituut van Registeraccountants, *Management Audit* (English translation), Amsterdam: NIVR, 1979.

Rose, T. G., *The Management Audit*, London: Gee, 1932.

Santocki, J., *Auditing: A Conceptual and Systems Approach*, Stockport: Polytech, 1979.

Santocki, J., *Case Studies in Auditing*, 2nd edn., Plymouth: Macdonald & Evans, 1978.

Santocki, J., 'Management audit from the inside', *The Accountant*, 28 March 1974.

Santocki, J., 'Management audit – is it myth or reality?', *Management Accounting*, September 1973.

Santocki, J., 'Management performance – how the British measure their managers' efforts', *Accountants Weekly*, 13 June 1975.

Santocki, J., 'Meaning and scope of management audit', *Accounting and Business Research*, Winter 1976.

Secoy, T. G., 'A CPA's opinion on management performance', *Journal of Accountancy*, July 1971.

Part Three
Beyond Manufacturing

OVERVIEW

Parts One and Two of this handbook dealt with management accounting for planning and control in a general context. In common with other management accounting literature a manufacturing environment was generally assumed. This assumption does not invalidate the preceding chapters for those working in non-manufacturing organisations, and should not be taken to imply that management accounting is only or even mainly of use in manufacturing operations.

It is not always recognised that as the manufacturing sector shrinks it becomes less and less appropriate for management accounting to focus on product costing, variance accounting and factory budgeting. This part of the handbook is devoted to redressing the undue balance in favour of manufacturing, stemming from management accounting's roots in cost accounting – an almost exclusively manufacturing-based discipline.

This part of the handbook deals with two aspects of the non-manufacturing environment – first those functions which are beyond the factory and second organisations which are not engaged in manufacturing.

The first category includes marketing, and physical distribution, two important functions often neglected by management accountants but vital to the success of the organisation. Chapter 13 considers issues concerned with the measurement of the effectiveness of marketing operations. It deals with both the measurement of past marketing performance and planning future operations, in keeping with the nature of management accounting as a forward-looking discipline, based in data about the past.

The author points out that effective interaction of marketing and management accounting experts requires that each understands the other's discipline and approach. Accordingly the chapter begins with a discussion of the nature of marketing. But the bulk of the chapter is concerned with the difficulties in applying management accounting to marketing activities, and how these difficulties might be overcome. This is supported by comprehensive examples.

The following chapter deals with distribution costs. The author explains how management accounting can be applied in this area, explaining the various elements of cost and the importance of understanding the behaviour of each of these elements. He shows how this knowledge can be used in decisions on issues such as depot locations and the use of external contractors.

The final chapter in this part considers the role of management accounting in organisations beyond the private sector where profitability is not the prime motivation. Such not-for-profit organisations exist throughout the public and voluntary sector. Their lack of profit objective does not invalidate management accounting, even though the discipline is usually based in a commercial environment.

But there are many important differences between private sector and not-for-profit organisations. Corporate goals, ownership, power and management are all significantly different. The reduced impact of market forces calls into question some basic assumptions of management accounting, as does the lower level of accountability. The author shows, however, that management accounting does have a role to play in such organisations, and illustrates techniques such as cost–benefit analysis and programme budgeting.

It is hoped that this part of the handbook emphasises not so much the separateness of the non-manufacturing world as the areas of commonality between manufacturing and non-manufacturing. Management accounting has a significant role to play in both areas.

13

Marketing and the management accountant

Richard M. S. Wilson

Management accounting's traditional concern with and roots in manufacturing has resulted in insufficient attention being paid by accountants to marketing activities. Where there has been contact between accounting and marketing it has commonly been in the context of conventional cost control. As a result of this it is not uncommon to find considerable antipathy between the two functions, which has then made it more difficult for a more positive relationship to develop.

In this chapter Richard Wilson argues that such a position can only hinder organisational effectiveness. He points out that more and more businesses are adopting a market-led stance, accepting that performance is affected more by external interaction with markets than by internal factors such as existing technology. In that context it is even more important that the gap between management accounting and marketing is bridged, and that controllers provide a more useful service to help in analysing, planning and controlling the marketing activities of the business.

Wilson identifies a number of differences between marketing and production environments which mean that the familiar techniques and attitudes appropriate in a manufacturing context cannot simply be transplanted. One fundamental difference is the relationship between the level of cost and the level of activity. He stresses that marketing expenditure leads rather than follows results, so that cost minimisation is not appropriate in marketing as it is in production. The right level and mix of costs for any given level of activity are much more a matter of judgement than is the case in manufacturing, where the lowest cost is normally the best position.

There are many difficulties in applying management accounting to marketing but that need not mean it should not be attempted. Wilson goes on to show how management accounting can help in cost–volume

–profit analysis, marketing cost control and in monitoring marketing productivity and effectiveness. The first step, he suggests, must be to understand marketing cost behaviour. The familiar classifications of fixed/variable and controllable/uncontrollable can be applied to marketing costs, but it is dangerous to attach these labels without careful thought since the relationship between cost and activity is not necessarily as it will be assumed by production-oriented management accountants.

A fundamental problem of dealing with marketing costs is the difficulty of understanding the effect on costs and revenues of alternative courses of action. Wilson discusses methods of learning more about these important relationships, through marketing experimentation and a 'missions' approach. The outcome, he suggests, should be a better understanding of the benefits from each option, and therefore more effective marketing.

Finally he illustrates a system for variance analysis appropriate to marketing activities, arguing that standard costing can be applied to marketing, but cannot simply be transferred from manufacturing without making allowances for the major differences between these two environments.

If business enterprise succeeds through the creation of utilities, it seems rather anomalous that the background of the typical management accountant reflects an introspective fixation with production (and the utility of form) rather than a broader concern with marketing (and the creation of the utilities of time, place, and ownership).

Given that we are effective to the extent that we achieve what we set out to achieve, and that we are efficient if we use minimum input to achieve a given output (or achieve maximum output for a given input), it can be suggested that measuring and improving the profitability and efficiency of marketing operations is an important element in increasing organisational effectiveness.

Measuring and improving the profitability and efficiency of marketing operations requires knowledge of the costs and revenues associated with marketing activities, which can be viewed from at least two directions:

1   the analysis of costs, revenues, and profits of *past* marketing activities – the *ex post* approach that is characteristic of an accounting orientation;
2   the assessment of the financial implications of *proposed* courses of marketing action (involving the prospective allocation of resources to opportunities that have been identified in the or-

ganisation's environment) – the *ex ante* approach that is characteristic of marketing orientation.

Rather than adopting one of these approaches to the exclusion of the other, it is essential to accounting–marketing integration to consider them together, but to relate them to a common set of problems. These problems are the nature and magnitude of marketing costs; the interaction of volume, costs, and profits; and the productivity of marketing actions.

By considering the problems of cost definitions and levels, the interrelationships of cost, volume, and revenue, and the productivity of marketing outlays, we have a base from which to promote better decision making, which is a prime determinant of organisational effectiveness. But this takes us into the consideration of a sequence of related matters.

Better decisions depend, *inter alia*, on better definitions of problems requiring solutions and on the generation of better potential solutions from which a choice (i.e. decision) must be made. Both these matters (problem definition and potential solutions) depend upon the availability of better information, which – at least in part – depends upon the techniques available (i.e. the state of accounting technology in this context) for supplying information.

At this point, it is as well to consider the 'specialised ears and generalised deafness' that Boulding (1956) stated to be so characteristic of the specialist world of the advanced economies. If accounting systems are to be designed to reflect the decision-making needs of marketing users, this suggests that accountants should seek an understanding of the problems and operating conditions facing marketing managers. Equally, of course, there is some onus on marketing managers to get behind the mystique that tends to surround accounting methods, statements, and terminology, and demand a comprehensible and useful service from their organisations' accounting functions rather than having to tolerate something 'designed' many years ago to suit accountants' convenience in discharging their stewardship role.

These issues are incorporated in Figure 13.1 which (working from the left hand side) suggests that functional specialists – whether in marketing or management accounting – will improve communications if they take active steps to learn about their counterparts' functions. Improved understanding coupled with more relevant information should lead to better marketing decisions. This in turn should lead to improved organisational effectiveness.

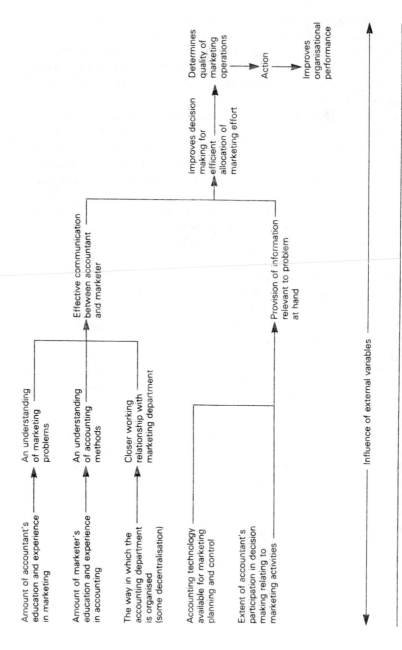

Amount of accountant's
education and experience
in marketing

An understanding
of marketing
problems

Amount of marketer's
education and experience
in accounting

An understanding
of accounting
methods

The way in which the
accounting department
is organised
(some decentralisation)

Closer working
relationship with
marketing department

Effective communication
between accountant
and marketer

Improves decision
making for
efficient
allocation of
marketing effort

Determines
quality of
marketing
operations

Action

Improves
organisational
performance

Accounting technology
available for marketing
planning and control

Extent of accountant's
participation in decision
making relating to
marketing activities

Provision of information
relevant to problem
at hand

Influence of external variables

**Figure 13.1   A framework for improved management accounting –
marketing interaction
(*Source*: Bancroft and Wilson, 1979, p.29)**

MARKETING DEFINED

There are many definitions of marketing, some highlighting the process, some the functional activities, and some the orientation of marketing. The Institute of Marketing accepts as its primary definition the following:

> Marketing is the management process for identifying, anticipating, and satisfying customer requirements profitably.

In essence marketing requires:

1 the identification of consumers' needs (covering *what* goods and services are bought; *how* they are bought; by *whom* they are bought; and *why* they are bought);
2 the definition of target market segments (by which consumers are grouped according to common characteristics – whether demographic, psychological, geographic, etc.);
3 the creation of a *differential advantage* within target segments by which a distinct competitive position relative to other companies can be established, and from which profit flows.

A differential advantage can be achieved by manipulating one or more elements of the *marketing mix*. This mix consists of the functional elements of marketing which are often referred to as the 'four P's' – product, price, promotion, and place. In a rather fuller way the mix consists of items listed in Table 13.1.

The increasing acceptance of the *marketing concept* (whereby the organisation looks outwards to the satisfaction of consumers' needs – and those of society – in establishing its competitive position, rather than looking inwards to its entrenched technology) has created a deeper interest in analysing marketing costs for the purposes of establishing marketing strategy and controlling marketing efforts in executing that strategy.

There are two sides to the study of marketing costs. The first of these is concerned with the costs of obtaining orders through such activities as selling, advertising and sales promotion. These costs tend to vary with changes in the level of sales, but sales volume will be the dependent variable and order-getting costs will be the independent variable. In other words, sales volume will respond to the level of order-getting costs, and variations in the level of order-getting costs will be made in anticipation of sales being at a predicted level. In this sense, positive management action is needed to permit order-getting costs to increase with increases in sales volume, and, in contrast to manufacturing circumstances, a policy of cost minimis-

Table 13.1
Elements of the marketing mix

Product management New product development Branding Packaging	PRODUCT
Advertising Sales promotion Public relations Personal selling Merchandising	PROMOTION
Pricing	PRICE
Channels of distribution Logistics/physical distribution Customer service	PLACE
Marketing research and intelligence Marketing management	

ation in marketing is unlikely to be desired because of the causal relationship between marketing outlays and sales levels. But the relationship between order-getting costs and sales volume may not be directly linear. For example, a company may increase the amount it is to spend on advertising when sales fall on the basis of the wholly reasonable argument that declining sales require counteractive promotional support to reverse an adverse trend. On the other hand, some companies may maintain the amount to be spent on advertising at some predetermined level (giving it the characteristics of a committed rather than a managed or programmed cost), while still others may unwisely raise advertising expenditure as the level of sales rises and decrease advertising expenditure as sales decline.

The other side of marketing expenditure relates to order-filling activities – warehousing, transport, shipping, invoicing, credit control, etc. These are dealt with in the context of physical distribution management in Chapter 14.

Whereas order-filling activities such as warehousing, transportation and materials handling have warranted substantial attention, perhaps because of their more systematic nature, order-getting activities (i.e. the problems of stimulating demand by advertising, selling and pricing in a way which attracts customers) are a relatively deficient area in marketing cost analysis. The following problems arise in dealing with these activities:

1 determining the objectives of advertising, sales promotion, personal selling (and pricing);
2 determining the promotion budget;
3 decisions relating to the allocation of the total marketing effort among varying marketing activities;
4 assessing the effectiveness of marketing effort;
5 identifying profitable/unprofitable marketing segments;
6 decisions relating to where and when a change in marketing effort is required;
7 identifying methods by which segment efficiency may be increased.

A COMPARISON OF MANAGEMENT ACCOUNTING FOR PRODUCTION AND MARKETING ACTIVITIES

In many companies, the costs of marketing greatly exceed factory overhead costs, yet very little attention has been given to the analysis of marketing costs compared to the extensive attention given to production costs.

It is instructive to consider some of the reasons for this state of affairs, and these include the following:

1 While the costs of productive labour and materials can be associated with specific machines, processes, and products, the costs of the elements of the marketing mix cannot be associated so readily with outputs (such as sales and profit levels).
2 Marketing activities tend to be less routine and repetitive than is the case with many standardised production activities.
3 The dependency of marketing activities on outside agencies distinguishes them further from the more internally-regulated and predictable manufacturing activities.
4 Marketing activities tend to be performed in many locations – often distant from each other – rather than on one site.
5 Within manufacturing there is the relatively simple choice to be made between using the product or the process as the cost object. In contrast, within marketing there are many more possible cost objects – such as the product line, product range, customer, customer/industry group, salesman, sales territory, size of order, channel of distribution, etc.
6 The cost behaviour patterns of many marketing activities are the reverse of those for manufacturing activities in the sense that

261

marketing costs tend to determine sales volume (hence manufacturing costs). Marketing costs are committed in anticipation of sales. Whereas manufacturing costs *necessarily* increase as sales volume rises, marketing costs must be *permitted* to increase. Thus, for a given level of activity, the lower the manufacturing costs the better, while the right level (and mix) of marketing costs is a matter of judgement. It can be argued that the 'best' approach is to focus on *technical efficiency* in relation to marketing outlays (i.e. to maximise the outputs for a given level of input), and on *economic efficiency* in relation to manufacturing outlays (whereby one aims to minimise the inputs for a given level of output). This indicates the analytical complexity inherent in accounting for marketing costs.

7   Since marketing costs are rarely included in inventory valuations (being treated instead as period costs) financial accounting principles, etc., provide little incentive for detailed analysis.

8   Manufacturing activities typically have a short-run focus whereas marketing operations must pay attention to long-run considerations. This also produces a conflict over financial accounting practice in that promotional outlays in a particular period are invariably matched with the sales achieved during that period notwithstanding the fact that much promotional expenditure (and other order-getting outlays) are in the nature of capital investment intended to stimulate sales over several time periods.

9   Personnel in manufacturing roles often have a greater cost consciousness and discipline than their marketing colleagues.

10 The risk of sub-optimisation (whereby one particular aspect is maximised to the possible detriment of the whole) is much greater in a complex marketing context than it is in manufacturing.

11 Many marketing activities have an intangible quality that distinguishes them from the tangible characteristics of production activities. Among the intangible factors is the psychological dimension of purchase predisposition.

PROBLEMS IN MANAGEMENT ACCOUNTING FOR MARKETING

It is invariably found that the costs stemming from marketing activities are difficult to plan and control. The lowest costs are not necessarily to be preferred, since these may not result in the effective attainment of the desired sales volume and profit. Most order-getting costs are programmed rather than variable, and tend to influence the volume of sales rather than being influenced by it.

The characteristics of marketing costs lead to problems in analysis. Such characteristics include:

1   Long-run effects (e.g. the effect of an advertising campaign lasts longer than the campaign, and is usually lagged).
2   The difficulty in measuring productivity, since standards are not easily determined. (Standards can be set for sales activities – e.g. cost to create £1 of sales, average cost of each unit sold, cost to generate £1 of profit, cost per transaction, cost per customer serviced. However, in product decisions, levels of performance may be expressed in terms of the minimum required level of sales per product, or the minimum profit contribution required.)
3   The non-symmetrical nature of costs. (For example, costs increase more in changing from regional to national distribution than would be saved by changing from national to regional distribution.)
4   Costs are frequently indivisible or joint costs, often intended to support a product group.
5   Some costs have discontinuities, or a stepped character shape.

Planning in the light of these characteristics must be based to a significant extent on past experience, knowledge of competitive activities, test marketing exercises, and the estimated expenditure that desired profits at various levels of activity will permit.

Accounting data in the more conventional form provides a point of departure for marketing cost analyses, but these data must be reworked on the basis of units that are subject to management control. (The relevant control unit will depend on the purpose of the analysis, but may be a product, product line, sales territory, marketing division, customer group, etc.).

But the difficulties of developing and successfully applying management accounting techniques in marketing are compounded by a multitude of further factors that are not primarily financial, among which are the following:

6   Plans must be based on sales forecasts. If the forecast of projected sales exceeds the firm's productive capacity, the firm may be required to expand its production facilities, raise prices (to ration available output) or sub-contract, only to find that the forecast was too high. Conversely, the forecast may predict insufficient sales to produce the desired ROI. In this event, the firm may alter its sales coverage, extend credit carelessly, introduce

inadequately tested new products, and so forth, in an attempt to increase the sales volume. Should the original forecast have been low, the actions taken subsequently may be against the firm's better interests.

7   The outputs of the marketing sub-system intimately affect the outputs of the firm's other sub-systems. In turn, the next outputs of these other sub-systems will affect the further outputs of the marketing sub-system. The solution can only come from a greater intra-organisational understanding of what is in the interests of the firm as a whole.

8   The enormous range of strategic possibilities makes it impossible to include all of them in a formal analysis. Any particular marketing strategy will involve a particular combination of the elements of the marketing mix, with particular assumed environmental conditions. The number of different possible combinations is vast. This does not mean that quantitative techniques are useless, but it does mean that measurement problems arise to complicate the issue.

9   The ever-changing environment – including the impacts of competitive activities, developments in technology, changes in consumer tastes, government action, and the other factors depicted in Figure 13.2 – makes planning difficult. As a result, control is made more difficult since it is no longer clear which variances were avoidable and which unavoidable.

10 In considering the range of possible strategies, the uncertainty that any one constituent factor may change at almost any time makes the question of choice even more difficult.

11 The effectiveness of costs (i.e. productivity or efficiency) is not easy to measure. The interdependent variety of elements involved and their varying long- and short-run effects are the cause of this difficulty. For example, the respective contributions of advertising and direct selling activities to the sales level are not readily separable.

12 The tendency towards 'conglomeration', with its attendant diversification of activities and sheer size, results in an increasing complexity that challenges the best efforts in securing control.

13 The interface of the marketing sub-system with external agencies is fraught with difficulties. The firm's control over the performance of these agencies (such as wholesalers, shippers, and advertising agents) depends upon the degree of independence of each, and the nature of the relationship.

14 The human element (in the form of salesmen, product managers, and other marketing personnel, added to the all-important con-

sumer) creates further problems. Marketing is centred upon this human factor, while production is centred upon more inanimate factors.

15 Finally, problems arise in connection with special marketing projects, such as the development of a new product, a major advertising campaign, or entry into a new territory. The problem is the usual one of correctly evaluating the profit and cost aspects of the project, and then keeping within budgeted expense limits and time schedules.

Although these problems are many, they do not mean that no attempts should be made to successfully plan and control marketing activities. However, there is evidence to show that most accountants are not yet in tune with marketing thinking. First, accountants lack the knowledge and understanding of the information requirements necessary for the marketing function. Second, accountants do not accept marketing as a distinct and separate managerial function. This seemingly blind attitude was found in a survey (reported by Williamson, 1979) to be well ingrained and is an appalling indication of the failure of accountants to see the real essence of business activity (i.e. product–market interactions) and of a misplaced arrogance in looking down on a group whose purpose and function they so clearly misunderstand. Lastly, organisational design may impede adequate

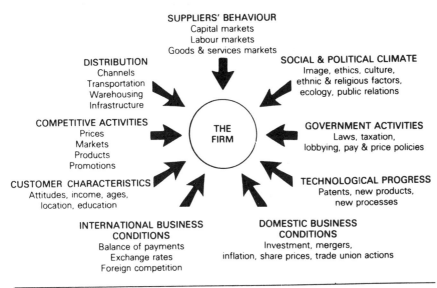

Figure 13.2 The influence of external factors
(*Source*: Wilson, 1983, p.209)

communications between functions. This could (and does) happen to such an extent that the accounting and marketing departments may be geographically diverse from one another, although marketing *activities* are geographically diverse in any event.

A long-established organisational design could also hinder a new pattern of resource allocation. It may be such that available resources are channelled towards the order-filling production and distribution functions rather than to the order-getting processes such as advertising, sales promotion and selling. Allocating to the former in preference to the latter is tantamount to saying that a firm can sell what it can make – the old sales concept – rather than the marketing concept of making what the consumers want.

The practical consequences of these inhibitions manifest themselves in the following ways:

Schiff and Mellman (1962), in an almost isolated empirical study, noted deficiencies of the accounting function in supplying marketing with sufficient information in certain areas, such as:

1 lack of effective financial analyses of customers, channels of distribution and salesmen;
2 an over-emphasis on net-profit based reporting (or the full cost allocation approach);
3 inadequacies in marketing cost classification (e.g. little distinction was made between fixed and variable costs or between controllable and non-controllable costs);
4 return on investment was rarely used; and
5 there was a general lack of integration between the accounting and marketing functions.

Goodman (1970) in a later study found that accounting did not appear to have made much progress in satisfying the needs of marketing planning. These areas of failure he saw as being:

1 non-use of sufficient return-on-investment criteria;
2 insistence on using the traditional full-costing for decision analyses;
3 inability to separate the reporting obligation of accounting from the service function;
4 imperfect understanding of the marketing concept;
5 lack of minimum acceptable goal criteria; and
6 disregard for the implications of working capital.

As various authorities have observed, there are fundamental differences between accounting and marketing. For example, accounting builds from an analysis of internal financial data whereas marketing builds from the diagnosis of external market situations. The respective perspectives are literally poles apart. (See Simmonds' Foreword in Wilson, 1981). Thus the marketing view that profit stems from a firm's position relative to its competitors (i.e. reflecting its differential advantage) and is not a function of arbitrary financial periods is not likely to meet with full-blooded approval – or even understanding – by the average accountant who invariably fails to link his own profit measures to either market share or changes in market size.

THE CLARIFICATION OF COST CATEGORIES

Many of the costs of marketing are not satisfactorily identified since marketing *functions* are not always carried out by the marketing *department*. (It could be argued that any members of an organisation who deal with customers, for example, are carrying out a marketing function even though they may not be recognised in any formal sense as members of the marketing staff.) This is one definitional problem, but not the only one.

In their training management accountants are almost indoctrinated to think, for example, of variable costs as being *manufacturing* costs that fluctuate with the level of *production* output, or to define direct costs as those that can be readily traced to units of *production* output, and so on. It is imperative that a broader view be taken in order that the analysis of marketing costs might be tackled.

In this general sense we can define costs in the following ways:

1   A *fixed cost* is one that does not vary in relation to changes in the level of activity (however defined) within a given period of time.

2   A *variable cost* is one that varies in proportion to changes in the level of activity (however defined).

This distinction facilitates flexible budgeting, permits cost–volume–profit analysis, and gives a basis for flexible pricing. However, the further distinction between *avoidable* and *unavoidable* costs needs to be considered since it cannot safely be assumed that a fixed cost is inevitably unavoidable. Much will depend on whether a particular fixed cost is 'committed', 'managed', or 'discretionary': the latter could almost certainly be avoided in the short term if a better use for the resources in question was available, although a committed fixed cost would not be easily avoided other than in the long run.

The base (i.e. level of activity) to be used in determining cost behaviour patterns must be carefully selected and have a clear casual relationship with the level of cost in question. In this regard it must not be assumed that sales volume *causes* order-getting costs. Let us consider some examples:

a) advertising and sales promotion costs are not caused by sales volume since sales volume is the dependent (rather than the independent) variable. The advertising budget is likely to be a fixed sum per period of time representing a programmed, managed, or discretionary cost.

b) personal selling costs are rather more complicated: commissions will tend to vary with sales volume (or value); salaries will be a fixed cost of a managed type that is independent of sales volume within any given financial period; and expenses will be a mixture of fixed and variable costs that are also independent of sales volume. Suitable bases for determining cost behaviour patterns may be number of calls made, number of customers, distance travelled, etc.

3 A *direct cost* is one that can be specifically traced to a cost object. In a marketing context, as mentioned earlier, this object may be any one of several alternatives *other than the product*. Thus, in an analysis of sales territories, the salaries, commissions, and expenses of sales personnel working exclusively in one territory constitute direct costs of that territory.

4 An *indirect cost* is one that cannot be traced to a specific cost object on anything other than an arbitrary basis.

The more specific a cost object is (e.g. a customer, or a product line), the greater will be the proportion of costs that are indirect, whereas the more broadly-based is a cost object (e.g. a sales territory), the greater will be the proportion of costs that can be traced directly to it. It should be borne in mind, however, that direct costs can be fixed or variable in nature (and similarly with indirect costs), so directness should not be linked in any general way with variable costs alone – whether in a marketing or any other setting.

5 A *controllable cost* is one that can be influenced by an individual whose performance is being measured by reference to such costs. Thus a sales manager will be held accountable for his sales team's expenses on the grounds that he can influence – hence control – their rate of incurrence. Controllable costs, then, usually originate in the sphere of organisational responsibility under consideration.

6 An *uncontrollable cost* is one that cannot be influenced by a par-

ticular individual (e.g. a manager cannot specify his own salary, so this is an uncontrollable cost from the viewpoint of his level of authority). It would, in general terms, be unreasonable to judge an individual's performance by reference to significant amounts of uncontrollable costs.

Controllable costs will often – but not always – be variable in nature. However, it is unusual for any fixed costs to be controllable in the short run unless they are clearly discretionary or programmed (which will frequently include some order-getting costs, such as advertising appropriations that have not yet been irrevocably committed).

It is not usually considered reasonable to hold an individual accountable for apportioned costs – such as may relate to head office services to divisions. Nevertheless, if one is interested in the performance of the division (rather than its manager) it may be appropriate to make cautious allocations of uncontrollable costs. (This is the basis of productivity analysis which will be discussed in the section starting on page 274.)

7 A *standard cost* is one that represents the efficient performance of a repetitive task. This will include the direct labour and material inputs in a manufacturing situation, but it is by no means limited to the production arena. Distribution activities as well as certain clerical tasks are amenable to cost standards, and a range of marketing cost standards can also be developed. (This topic will be covered later (see the section starting on page 282), and was referred to in the section starting on page 262 above.)

Yet another definitional problem concerns the focus that the management accountant should adopt in seeking to render a service to his marketing colleagues. If the management accountant perceives his terms of reference as stemming from the traditional accounting preoccupation with product costing, thereby emphasising the attributes of what is currently being made, he will fail to offer analyses that emphasise patterns of consumer preferences and competitive positioning by market segment. The attributes of market segments – from which profit derives – are fundamentally different from those attributes that characterise the production process. Any analysis that is based on product cost will inevitably generate insights that are limited by their origins, thereby failing to support marketing orientation.

The usual approach of accountants has been termed 'data-oriented': the recording, analysing, and reporting of data is determined by what is available. Such an approach neither answers nor asks the critical questions concerning the problems of the market place that require diagnosing and solving. The remedy is to redefine the management accountant's role in terms of an 'information-orientation' by which marketing problems are examined to determine information needs, from which the required information can then be generated to assist marketing managers.

MARKETING COST ANALYSIS: AIMS AND METHODS

Control in marketing can be seen to be concerned with the allocation of total marketing effort to segments, along with the profitability of these allocations. It is generally found, however, that companies do not know the profitability of segments in marketing terms. Useful computations of marketing costs and profit contributions in the multiproduct company require the adoption of analytical techniques that are not difficult in principle but which are not widely adopted on account of, *inter alia*, the preoccupation with factory cost accounting that exists.

It is clearly essential for management to know the cost implications of different courses of action if the best is to be selected. In the pricing decision, for example, products may be priced in such a way as to give a specified rate of return. However, if costs are inappropriately allocated to products, then some products will be overpriced and some underpriced. (This is not intended to be an argument in favour of cost-plus pricing.)

The fact that most companies do not know what proportion of their total marketing outlay is spent on each product, area, or customer group may be due to the absence of a sufficiently refined system of cost analysis, or it may be due to vagueness over the nature of certain costs. For instance, is the cost of packaging a promotional, a production, or a distribution expense? Some important marketing costs are hidden in manufacturing costs or in general and administrative costs, including finished goods inventory costs in the former and order-processing costs in the latter.

Since few companies are aware of costs and profits by segment in relation to sales levels, and since even fewer are able to predict changes in sales volume and profit contribution as a result of changes in marketing effort, the following errors arise:

1 Marketing budgets for individual products are too large, with the result that diminishing returns become evident and benefits would accrue from a reduction in expenditure.

2   Marketing budgets for individual products are too small and increasing returns would result from an increase in expenditure.
3   The marketing mix is inefficient, with an incorrect balance and incorrect amounts being spent on the constituent elements – such as too much on advertising and insufficient on direct selling activities.
4   Marketing efforts are misallocated amongst products and changes in these cost allocations (even with a constant level of overall expenditure) could bring improvements.

Similar arguments apply in relation to sales territories or customer groups as well as to products. The need exists, therefore, for control techniques to indicate the level of performance required and achieved as well as the outcome of shifting marketing efforts from one segment to another. As is to be expected, there exists great diversity in the methods by which manufacturers attempt to obtain costs (and profits) for segments of their business, but much of the cost data is inaccurate for such reasons as:

1   Marketing costs may be allocated to individual products, sales areas, customer groups, etc., on the basis of sales value or sales volume, but this involves circular reasoning. Costs should be allocated in relation to causal factors, and *it is marketing expenditures that cause sales to be made* rather than the other way round: managerial decision determines marketing costs. Furthermore, despite the fact that success is so often measured in terms of sales value achievements by product line, this basis fails to evaluate the efficiency of the effort needed to produce the realised sales value (or turnover). Even a seemingly high level of turnover for a specific product may really be a case of misallocated sales effort. (An example should make this clear: if a salesman concentrates on selling product A which contributes £5 per hour of effort instead of selling product B which would contribute £12 per hour of effort, then it 'costs' the company £7 per hour he spends on selling product A. This is the *opportunity cost* of doing one rather than another and is a measure of the sacrifice involved in selecting only one of several alternative courses of action.)
2   General overheads and administrative costs are arbitrary (and erroneously) allocated to segments on the basis of sales volume.
3   Many marketing costs are not allocated at all as marketing costs as they are not identified as such but are classified as manufacturing, general, or administrative costs instead.

Distribution cost accounting (or analysis) has been developed to help overcome these problems and aims to:

1   Analyse the costs incurred in distributing and promoting products so that when they are combined with production cost data overall profitability can be determined.
2   Analyse the costs of marketing individual products to determine their profitability.
3   Analyse the costs involved in serving different classes of customers and different areas to determine their profitability.
4   Compute such figures as cost per sales call, cost per order, cost to put a new customer on the books, cost to hold £1's worth of inventory for a year, etc.
5   Evaluate managers according to their actual controllable cost responsibilities.
6   Evaluate alternative strategies or plans with full costs.

These analyses and evaluations provide senior management with the necessary information to enable them to decide which classes of customer to cultivate, which products to delete, which products to encourage, and so forth. Such analyses also provide a basis from which estimates can be made of the likely increases in product profitability that a specified increase in marketing effort should create. In the normal course of events it is far more difficult to predict the outcome of decisions that involve changes in marketing outlays in comparison with changes in production expenditure. It is easier, for instance, to estimate the effect of a new machine in the factory than it is to predict the impact of higher advertising outlays. Similarly, the effect on productive output of dropping a production worker is easier to estimate than is the effect on the level of sales caused by a reduction in the sales force.

The methodology of distribution cost analysis is similar to the methodology of product costing. Two stages are involved:

1   Marketing costs are initially reclassified from their *natural* expense headings (e.g. salaries) into *functional* cost groups (e.g. sales expenses) in such a way that each cost group brings together all the costs associated with a particular element of the marketing mix.
2   These functional cost groups are then apportioned to control units (i.e. products, customer groups, channels of distribution, etc.) on the basis of measurable criteria that bear a causal relationship to the total amounts of the functional cost groups.

While costs can be broken down in a microscopic manner, there are dangers and limitations which should not be overlooked as they can hinder the control of marketing costs. If the outcome of functionalising all marketing costs is to compute a unit cost for every activity, then this can be misleading. At the least a distinction should be made between fixed and variable costs, and the focus should be on the *purpose* for which a particular cost is to be derived and not simply on the *means* by which a figure is computed. Thus costs and units can be looked at separately, thereby avoiding myopic confusion.

An important distinction to make in distribution costs analysis – beyond the basic fixed-variable split – is that between separable fixed costs and non-separable fixed costs. A sales manager's salary is a fixed cost in conventional accounting, but in so far as his time can be linked to different products, sales territories, customers, etc., his salary (or at least portions of his salary) can be treated as being a separable fixed cost attributable to the segments in question in accordance with time devoted to each. In contrast, corporate advertising expenditure that is concerned with the company's image is not specific to any segment, hence it is non-separable and should not be allocated. Any non-specific, non-separable cost allocations would inevitably be very arbitrary, and such costs should therefore be excluded from all detailed cost and profit computations.

If one is concerned purely with measuring profit by segment, then even separable fixed costs should be omitted from the calculations since they are not direct deductions from the sales revenue of specific segments. However, distribution cost analysis is concerned also with the most effective use of marketing effort, and this form of analysis requires the inclusion of separable fixed costs. (This highlights the important difference between product costing and distribution cost analysis: the former is very much concerned with the task of simply compiling product costs whereas the latter is concerned with the cost and revenue implications of different marketing actions and activities.)

There are many different bases for analysing and apportioning marketing costs to control units, but it is important to observe that some costs vary with the characteristics of one type of control segment only. Thus inventory costs depend on the characteristics of the products rather than on those of the customers, whereas the cost of credit depends on the financial integrity and number of customers rather than on sales territory factors. Accordingly, all functional costs should not be apportioned indiscriminately to products, customers, territories, etc., but only to whichever segments exhibit a cause-and-effect relationship with the cost factor in question.

The financial control of marketing activities can now be seen to depend on the generation and analysis of information to attach costs and revenues realistically to the activities to which they relate. This in turn constitutes the basis on which the margin of contribution may be calculated – the size of which will tend to determine whether or not the activity under consideration is deemed satisfactory.

AN ILLUSTRATION OF SEGMENTAL ANALYSIS

In Figure 13.3 a number of segments are illustrated for a hypothetical engineering company, ABC Ltd. It is possible to measure the costs and revenues at each level in order to highlight the profit performance of each segment. Thus, for example, the profit performance for the calculator market may be measured along the lines shown in Table 13.2.

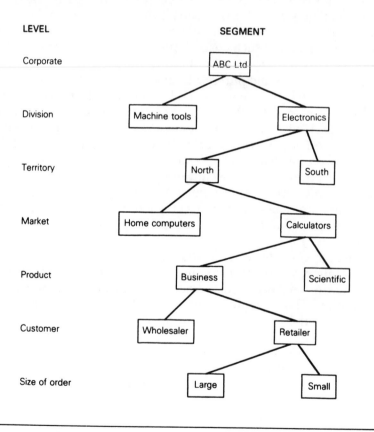

LEVEL	SEGMENT
Corporate	ABC Ltd
Division	Machine tools / Electronics
Territory	North / South
Market	Home computers / Calculators
Product	Business / Scientific
Customer	Wholesaler / Retailer
Size of order	Large / Small

Figure 13.3 Segmental levels

274

The approach adopted in Table 13.2 is a *contribution approach*, with costs and revenues being assigned to segments on bases that are essentially direct. Common costs have not been assigned to segments at all.

Although the contribution approach avoids the controversies surrounding the apportionment of indirect costs to segments there can be benefits in carrying out apportionments – provided the bases are clearly thought out and have a causal connexion with cost levels. This approach gives the foundation of *marketing productivity analysis*.

The steps to be followed in carrying out productivity analyses were hinted at in the section starting on page 270. They are:

1 determine the analysis to be made;
2 classify costs into appropriate categories (as discussed in the section starting on page 267);

Table 13.2
Segmental contribution statement

Product: Calculators	North Territory (£)	South Territory (£)	Total (£)
Net Sales	xxx	xxx	xxxx
Variable manufacturing costs	xx	xx	xxx
Manufacturing contribution	xx	xx	xxx
Marketing costs			
Variable:			
Sales commissions	x	x	x
Selling expenses	x	x	x
Variable contribution	xx	xx	xxx
Assignable:			
Salesmen's salaries	x	x	x
Manager's salary	x	x	x
Product advertising	x	x	x
Product contribution	xx	xx	xx
Non-assignable:			
Corporate advertising			x
Marketing contribution			xx
Fixed common costs:			
Manufacturing			x
Administration			x
Net Profit			xx

3 select bases for apportioning indirect costs to functional activities;
4 allocate revenue and direct costs to the chosen segment;
5 apply indirect costs to the segment;
6 summarise (4) and (5) into a statement showing the net profit of the segment.

It is vital to recognise that this net profit approach to segmental analysis can only raise questions: it cannot provide any answers. (The reason for this, of course, is that the apportionment of indirect costs clouds the distinction between avoidable and unavoidable costs, and even direct costs may not be avoidable in the short run.)

The application of the above steps to a company's product range may produce the picture portrayed in Table 13.3.

The segment could equally be sales territory, customer group, etc., and after the basic profit computation has been carried out it can be supplemented (as in Table 13.4) by linking it to an analysis of the effort required to produce the profit result. (Clearly this is a multi-variate situation in which profit depends upon a variety of input factors, but developing valid and reliable multi-variate models is both complex and expensive. As a step in the direction of more rigor-

Table 13.3
Segmental profit statement

Product	% contribution to total profits
Total for all products	100.0
Profitable products:	
A	43.7
B	35.5
C	16.4
D	9.6
E	6.8
F	4.2
Sub-total	116.2
Unprofitable products:	
G	–7.5
H	–8.7
Sub-total	–16.2

ous analysis one can derive benefits from linking profit outcomes to individual inputs – such as selling time in the case of Table 13.4.)

From Table 13.4 one can see that product A generates 43.7 per cent of total profits, requiring only 16.9 per cent of available selling time. This is highly productive. By contrast, product E produces only 6.8 per cent of total profits but required 10.2 per cent of selling effort. Even worse, however, is the 24.8 per cent of selling effort devoted to products G and H which are unprofitable.

A number of obvious questions arise from this type of analysis. Can the productivity of marketing activities be increased by:

1   increasing net profits proportionately more than the corresponding increase in marketing outlays?
2   increasing net profits with no change in marketing outlays?
3   increasing net profits with a decrease in marketing costs?
4   maintaining net profits at a given level but decreasing marketing costs?
5   decreasing net profits but with a proportionately greater decrease in marketing costs?

If these analyses are based purely on historical information they will provide less help than if they relate to plans for the future. One

Table 13.4
Segmental productivity statement

Product	% contribution to total profits	% total selling time
Total for all products	100	100
Profitable products:		
A	43.7	16.9
B	35.5	18.3
C	16.4	17.4
D	9.6	5.3
E	6.8	10.2
F	4.2	7.1
Sub-total	116.2	75.2
Unprofitable products:		
G	–7.5	9.5
H	–8.7	15.3
Sub-total	–16.2	24.8

way of overcoming the limitations of historical information is to plan and control the conditions under which information is gathered. This can be achieved through *marketing experimentation*.

MARKETING EXPERIMENTATION

In a marketing experiment attempts are made to identify all the controllable factors that affect a particular dependent variable, and some of these factors are then manipulated systematically in order to isolate and measure their effects on the performance of the dependent variable.

It is not possible, of course, to plan or control all the conditions in which an experiment is conducted: for example, the timing, location, and duration of an experiment can be predetermined, but it is necessary to measure such uncontrollable conditions as those caused by the weather and eliminate their effects from the results. Irrespective of these uncontrollable influences, the fact that experiments are concerned with the deliberate manipulation of controllable variables (i.e. such variables as price and advertising effort) means that a good deal more confidence can be placed in conclusions about the effects of such manipulation than if the effects of these changes had been based purely on historical associations.

Studies of marketing costs can provide the ideas for experiments. Questions such as the following can be answered as a result of marketing experimentation:

1   By how much (if any) would the net profit contribution of the most profitable products be increased if there were an increase in specific marketing outlays, and how would such a change affect the strategy of competitors in terms of the stability of, say, market shares?

2   By how much (if any) would the net losses of unprofitable products be reduced if there were some decrease in specific marketing outlays?

3   By how much (if any) would the profit contribution of profitable products be affected by a change in the marketing effort applied to the unprofitable products, and vice-versa, and what would be the effect on the total marketing system?

4   By how much (if any) would the total profit contribution be improved if some marketing effort was diverted to profitable territories or customer groups from unprofitable territorial and customer segments?

5   By how much (if any) would the net profit contribution be increased if there were a change in the method of distribution to small unprofitable accounts, or if these accounts were eliminated?

Only by actually carrying out properly-designed marketing experiments can management realistically predict with an acceptable degree of certainty the effects of changes in marketing expenditure on the level of sales and profit of each differentiated product, territory, or customer segment in the multi-product company.

Experiments must be conducted under conditions that resemble the real-life conditions of the market place (in so far as this is possible). It is pointless, for example, carrying out an experiment to prove that the sale of £1's worth of product X in Southampton through medium-sized retailers adds more to profit than does the sale of £1's worth of product Y through small retailers in Newcastle if the market for product X is saturated and no re-allocation of marketing resources can change the situation. This points to the danger of confusing what is happening now with what might happen in the future: ascertaining that product X is more profitable than product Y may be the right answer to the wrong question.

The correct style of question should be: 'what will happen to the dependent variable in the future if the independent variables are manipulated now in the following way?'. If the concern is with the allocation of sales effort, the aim of an experiment may be to show how changes in the total costs of each sales team can be related to changes in the level of sales. In such a simple case in which only one type of marketing effort is being considered, this effort should be re-allocated to those sales segments where an additional unit of effort will yield the highest contribution to net profits and overheads.

The experiment can be designed to show which sales segment produces the highest value when the following equation is applied to each in turn:

$$\frac{\text{Additional sales} - \text{additional variable costs}}{\text{Additional expenditure}}$$

If an additional budget allocation of £1 000 to the London sales force results in extra sales of £5 000 with additional variable costs amounting to £2 000, then the index of performance is

$$\frac{5000 - 2000}{1000} = 3$$

279

It may happen that the same index computed for the Midlands sales force of the same company has a value of 4, in which case selling effort should be re-allocated to the Midlands *provided* due consideration has been given to the expected level of future demand.

As a result of the high costs involved, experiments must usually be conducted with small samples of the relevant elements. This is generally valid so long as the samples are properly determined and representative. However, it is believed by some that marketing experimentation is not a feasible means by which information can be obtained as a basis for making important decisions.

There are certainly a lot of difficulties to be overcome in planning and executing experiments, and the need to keep special records and make repeated measurements is both expensive and time consuming. The risk is always present that the results of an experiment will not be of any value because they may not be statistically significant. A further risk is that even temporary and limited experimental variations in the marketing mix may damage sales and customer relationships both during and after the experiment.

RECENT DEVELOPMENTS: THE MISSIONS APPROACH

In an attempt to develop the relatively simple (hence somewhat deficient) approach of segmental analysis (see page 274) in a way that

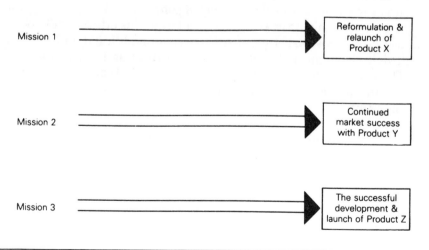

Figure 13.4   Marketing missions
(*Source*: Wilson, 1983, p.209)

captures some of the flavour of the complexity of marketing processes the *missions approach* has been suggested. (Barrett's work is notable in this field.)

A 'mission' in the present context may be defined as the provision of a product or range of products at a particular level of service to a particular customer or customer group in a particular area. Figure 13.4 illustrates three possible marketing missions.

If we take the analysed cost and revenue flows suggested in Figure 13.5 (in what has been termed a 'modularised data base approach'), we have a basis for determining the costs, revenues, and profits attributable to each mission.

The next step is to superimpose the (horizontal) missions over the (vertical) functional flows in order to produce a missions matrix (as shown in Figure 13.6).

This matrix focuses attention on the purposes to be served (as shown by the missions) and the cost and revenue (hence profit) consequences of carrying out each mission. Within this framework it is

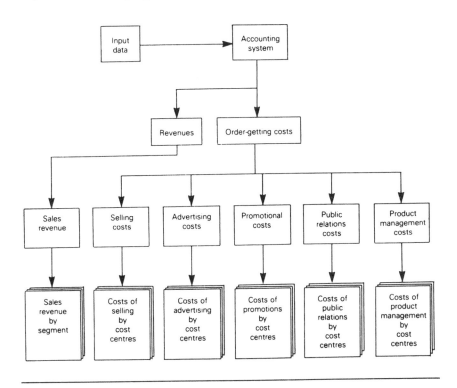

Figure 13.5   Marketing missions

possible to consider trade-offs between one course of action and another in a way that was outlined in the sections on segmental analysis and on marketing experimentation. For example, what might be the impact on mission B's performance of an increase in direct sales effort and a decrease in promotional expenditure? Because each mission is multi-dimensional (see Figure 13.7) the risk of information loss is much less than in the two-dimensional case shown in Table 13.4 above.

In effect, reports derived from a missions approach will give information that cuts *across* segments rather than giving it *by* segments.

PERFORMANCE MEASUREMENT AND CONTROL

Marketing managers tend to view their success or failure in terms that are different from the criteria that are characteristic of accountants' reports. As mentioned earlier, the introspective concern with cost data and transactions on the part of the accountant is in marked contrast to the marketer's interest in competitive position (as indicated by relative market share, potential for market growth, and product life cycle patterns).

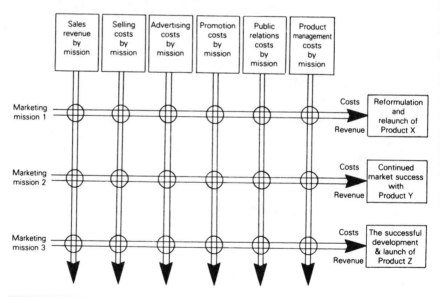

Figure 13.6 A framework for missions analysis

282

From the point of view of cost control, given a particular organisation structure, individual categories of marketing expenditure can be divided into fixed and variable types, their behaviour patterns can be established, and standards can be set via budgets or standard costs. It is therefore possible for comparisons to be made between actual outlays and desired (or standard) outlays as in any other area of cost control. A general understanding of cost behaviour, cost–volume–profit relationships, and relevant costing is a fundamental prerequisite to the control of any category of cost. Within the marketing sphere, however, the influence of external factors is more strongly felt and this raises measurement problems relating both to the prediction of outcomes in the face of very many internal–external interactions, and to the identifying of causal relationships when attempting to evaluate, for instance, the effectiveness of advertising outlays. The key to controlling marketing activities lies in the very careful planning of marketing activities, provided that plans are flexible and drawn up in accordance with the principles of contingency planning. (For example, if it is expected that product X will secure a 10 per cent share of its market segment which, in total, is expected to amount to sales of 100 000 units during the next period, a detailed plan should be compiled that not only gives consideration to this size and share but which also considers 'what if . . . ?' questions. What if the market demand is 75 000 units, or 125 000 units? What if our share with product X is 12 per cent or 8 per cent?)

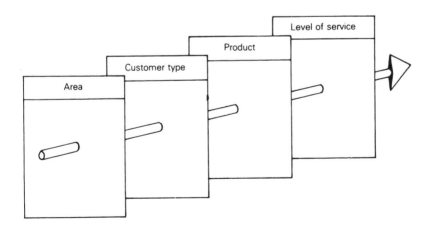

Figure 13.7   Multi-dimensional mission characteristics
(*Source*: Barrett, 1980, p.143)

The example just given highlights the importance of sales forecasting in the planning of order-getting cost levels. Order-getting budgets are also affected by:

1   Specific marketing objectives that must be achieved.
2   Anticipated competitive behaviour.
3   Other anticipated environmental factors.
4   Past experience.
5   Funds available.

This final point – the money available with which to carry out a plan – is widely used for budgeting advertising and promotional outlays. It can be derived as follows:

Expected sales revenue		£250 000
Works cost	100 000	
Administration and other overheads	75 000	
Required profit	50 000	
		225 000
Money available for promotions		£25 000

Behind this simplistic approach is a belief that advertising is more important in achieving success than is manufacturing, but it is an unsatisfactory approach for reasons other than this. It places too much emphasis on the *residual* amount (i.e. the funds remaining after all other costs have been covered) rather than on the amount that is required to achieve a specified result, and it fails to consider adequately the *effectiveness* of the expending of this amount. Cost control must look at both the actual and the desired patterns of expenditure *and* the effectiveness (which is equivalent to quality) of the expenditure, and this is far from being an easy task. To what extent, for example, is a given level of sales due to the ability/personality of the salesman, the characteristics of the customer, features of the product itself, competitive offerings, general business conditions, or the effect of advertisements and other promotional activity?

Moreover, to what extent is marketing expenditure in the nature of capital investment rather than revenue expense? This is a grey area (see Wilson, 1986). In the case of investment in manufacturing capacity, by contrast, there is widespread agreement on the range of items to be included in the investment base but, in building marketing capacity (e.g. via research studies, product development, promotional activities, and training programmes), there is a tendency to treat costs as being *current* (to be charged immediately against revenue) rather than *capital* outlays (which have earning potential over a longer period), thereby suggesting that markets have no value. (The obvious exception, arising in take-over situations, is goodwill, which represents the capital value of an enterprise over and above the value of its physical and net financial resources. But, as a realistic measure of marketing investment, it is unhelpful – not least of all because it is measured by accountants' simplistic formulae rather than by focusing on the underlying marketing determinants.)

However, it is primarily through its marketing investment that an enterprise is able to justify investment in production and distribution facilities, and so the question of defining marketing investment is worthy of attention in order to help managers evaluate resource allocation choices *ex ante* and to give a reference point for measuring performance *ex post*. (In particular, marketing investment is the independent variable on which sales volume depends, whereas manufacturing investment is dependent upon sales volume, so a clearer understanding is most desirable.)

Any investment base must be linked to a measure of profit if performance (in terms of a rate of return on investment) is to be assessed. Managers in general are *au fait* with this approach for organisations as a whole, but work is needed in relating appropriate measures of marketing investment and marketing profit to determine marketing profitability. This may be done for marketing activities *in toto*, or for particular elements (e.g. sales operations, channel activities, product lines). For each, it should be possible to define the attributable investment base (including, say, stocks, debtors, cars, training, consumer research, and promotions in the case of a sales region), and to relate to this a measure of marketing profit for that element.

If the measure of performance for an element is given by

$$\frac{\text{Profit}}{\text{Investment}} \times 100$$

it follows that this can be improved (i.e. productivity can be increased) by either increasing profit or reducing investment. The major difficulty lies in linking specific outcomes (profit) to specific inputs (the investment), especially over long future periods.

If resources allocation (and subsequent utilisation) in marketing (and hence its contribution to society as a whole) is to be improved, the aim must be to direct marketing effort (investment) into marketing activities (sales areas, advertising campaigns, etc.) to the point where further effort would yield no additional benefit (i.e. where the resources would be better employed elsewhere). The difficulty again is one of relating investment to profit as one develops and executes marketing strategies.

Over the past 15 years or so work undertaken in the USA on what is called the PIMS study (profit impact of market strategy) has suggested that (historically at least) there is a positive statistical association between market share and profitability in the largest US companies. It follows that control effort needs to be devoted to both these aspects of performance, and Simmonds (in Chapter 2 of this volume) addresses these issues.

By way of summary it can be noted here that the PIMS project found three factors to be significantly associated with return on investment (ROI). These were:

1   *Market share*
    – ROI increases steadily as market share increases
    – companies having relatively large market shares tend to have above-average rates of investment turnover
    – the ratio of marketing expenses to sales revenue tends to be lower for companies having high market shares
2   *Investment intensity*
    – the higher the ratio of investment to sales the lower the ROI
    – companies having high investment intensity tend to be unable to achieve profit margins sufficient to sustain growth
3   *Company factors*
    – ROI varies amongst companies due to differences in size, diversity, etc.
    – diversified companies appear to achieve good results as effective generalists
    – specialist companies also appear to achieve good results

The key to control is *not* to go for high market share at all costs, but to manage a balanced portfolio of products (by which the heavy cash demands of new products and heavily-competitive products are balanced by the cash inflows of established products).

Against this background what can be suggested to help the management account in developing budgets to facilitate performance evaluation and the control of marketing activities?

As a starting point the senior managers of the organisation must specify the desired outcomes for both marketing and financial performance. This will include a specification of, *inter alia*:

Return on investment ⎤
Liquidity   ⎬ Company-wide
Leverage   ⎦

Market share   ⎤
Sales volume   ⎥
Inventory turnover   ⎬ By segment
Profit contribution   ⎦

Such benchmarks as these facilitate more detailed budgeting, and in this task it is possible to make use of cost standards.

Standards can be developed for repetitive activities, and it is possible to determine standards in a marketing context for the following illustrative activities:

cost per unit of sales
cost per sales transaction
cost per order received
cost per customer account
cost per mile travelled
cost per call made

The degree of detail can be varied to suit the particular requirements: thus 'cost per unit of sales' may be 'advertising cost per £ of sales revenue for product X' and so on.

It is clearly more difficult to establish precise standards for most marketing activities than is the case in the manufacturing or distribution functions. Physical and mechanical factors are less influential; psychological factors are more prominent; objective measurement is more limited; personal judgement is more conspicuous; tolerance limits must be broader; and the range of segments for which marketing standards can be developed is much greater. But the discipline of seeking to establish standards can generate insights into relationships between effort and results that are likely to outweigh any lack of precision.

It is possible for an organisation to develop marketing standards by participation in an inter-firm comparison scheme (such as the one run by the Centre for Inter-firm Comparison). As Westwick (1973) has shown, integrated sets of ratios and standards can be devised to allow for detailed monitoring of marketing performance.

When budget levels and standards are being developed it is vitally important to note the assumptions on which they have been based since it is inevitable that circumstances will change and a variety of unanticipated events will occur once the budget is being implemented. Bearing this in mind let us work through an example. Table 13.5 illustrates an extract from a marketing plan for product X (column 2), with actual results (column 3) and variances (column 4) being shown for a particular operating period.

The unfavourable contribution variance of £150 000 shown at the foot of column 4 is due to two principal causes:

1   a variance relating to sales volume; and
2   a variance relating to contribution per unit.

In turn, a variance relating to sales volume can be attributed to differences between:

3   actual and anticipated total market size; and
4   actual and anticipated market share.

Therefore a variation between planned and actual contribution may be due to variations in price per unit, variable cost per unit, total market size, and market penetration.

In the case of product X we have:

1   *Profit Variance*
$$(Ca - Cp) \times Qa = £(0.35 - 0.40) \times 11\,000\,000$$
$$= (£550\,000)$$

2   *Volume Variance*
$$(Qa - Qp) \times Cp = (11\,000\,000 - 10\,000\,000) \times £0.40$$
$$= £400\,000$$

3   *Net Variance*

Profit variance	£(550 000)
Volume variance	£400 000
	£(150 000)

Where:

Ca = Actual contribution per unit
Cp = Planned contribution per unit
Qa = Actual quantity sold in units
Qp = Planned quantity of sales in units

However, (2) can be analysed further to take into account the impact of market size and penetration variations.

4   *Market Size Variance*
$$(Ma - Mp) \times Sp \times Cp$$
$$= (30\,000\,000 - 25\,000\,000) \times 0.4 \times 0.4$$
$$= £800\,000$$

5 *Market Share Variance*
$$(\text{Sa} - \text{Sp}) \times \text{Ma} \times \text{Cp}$$
$$= (0.367 - 0.40) \times 30\ 000\ 000 \times 0.4$$
$$= £(400\ 000)$$

6 *Volume Variance*

Market size variance	£ 800 000
Market share variance	£(400 000)
	£ 400 000

Where:

Ma = Actual total market in units
Mp = Planned total market in units
Sa = Actual market share
Sp = Planned market share

In summary, the position now appears thus:

Planned profit contribution		£4 000 000
Volume Variance:		
Market size variance	£800 000	
Market share variance	£(400 000)	
		400 000
Profit variance		(550 000)
Actual profit contribution		£3 850 000

Table 13.5
Operating results for product X
(Adapted from Hulbert and Toy, 1977, p. 13)

Column 1 Item	Column 2 Plan	Column 3 Actual	Column 4 Variance
Revenues:			
Sales (units)	10 000 000	11 000 000	1 000 000
Price per units (£)	1.00	0.95	0.05
Total revenue (£)	10 000 000	10 450 000	450 000
Market:			
Total market size			
(units)	25 000 000	30 000 000	5 000 000
Share of market (%)	40.0	36.7	(3.3)
Costs:			
Variable cost per			
unit (£)	0.60	0.60	–
Contribution:			
Per unit (£)	0.40	0.35	0.05
Total contribution	4 000 000	3 850 000	(150 000)

289

But this is not the end of the analysis! Variances arise because of unsatisfactory performance *and* unsatisfactory plans. It is desirable, therefore, to distinguish variances due to the poor execution of plans from those due to the poor establishing of plans. In the latter category are likely to be found forecasting errors reflecting faulty assumptions, and the estimates of total market size may constitute poor benchmarks for gauging subsequent managerial performance.

It is difficult to determine categorically whether market share variances are primarily the responsibility of forecasters or those who execute the plans based on forecasts. On the face of it the primary responsibility is likely to be attached to the latter group.

In interpreting the variances for product X it can be seen that the favourable volume variance of £400 000 resulted from two variances relating to market size and market share. Both of these are undesirable since they led to a lower contribution than intended. Had the forecasting group correctly anticipated the larger total market it should have been possible to devise a better plan to achieve the desired share and profit contribution. The actual outcome suggests that competitive position has been lost due to a loss of market share in a rapidly-growing market. This is a serious pointer.

Lower prices resulted in a lower level of contribution per unit, and hence a lower overall profit contribution. The reasons for this need to be established and future plans modified as necessary.

As an approach to improved learning about the links between effort and results – especially in the face of active competitive behaviour – it is helpful to take the above analysis further and to evaluate performance by considering *what should have happened* in the circumstances (which is akin to flexible budgeting in a manufacturing setting).

At the end of the operating period to which Table 13.5 refers it may become known that a large company with substantial resources made an aggressive entry into the market place using lots of promotions and low prices. Furthermore, an unforeseen export demand for product X may have arisen due to a prolonged strike in the USA's main manufacturer. On the basis of these details it becomes possible to carry out an *ex post* performance analysis in which the original plans are revised to take account of what has since become known.

A clearer distinction can be made via *ex post* performance analysis along these lines since a distinction can be made between:

1   planning variances due to environmental events that were
    (a) foreseeable,
    (b) unforeseeable;

2 performance variances that are due to problems in executing the plans.

The situation is summarised in Figure 13.8.

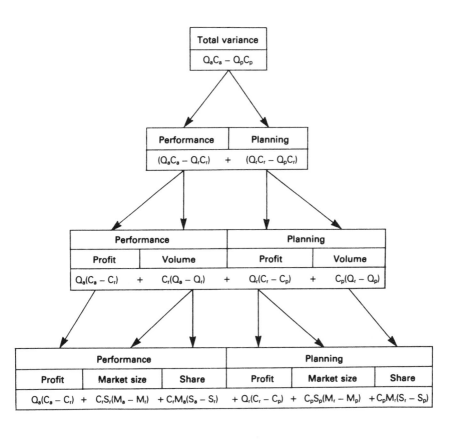

LEGEND

Subscripts	Variables
a=actual	Q=Quantity
p=planned	C=Contribution margins
r=revised	S=Share
	M=Market

Figure 13.8   Ex post performance analysis
(Adapted from Halbert and Toy, 1972, p.20)

CONCLUSION

The part that the financial controller can play in helping to control the marketing function is only gradually being accepted. The controller has, in fact, been looked upon either with suspicion or doubt as someone who only considered figures, when marketing men were convinced that people were more important. At best this made him a mere recorder of history – at worst, a positive barrier to progress.

Enlightenment will increase as the profit awareness of marketing management increases further, accompanied by an emphasis on the controller's service function. This service aspect of the controller's work requires that he be fully aware of the firm's products, its markets, the marketing organisation, and the particular problems that marketing management faces. Only when he has this knowledge can the financial controller begin to develop the appropriate control and information systems.

No matter how great his abilities may be in other directions, if the marketing manager lacks an understanding of financial concepts he will be unable to appreciate fully the end results of his planning, and the actions that must be taken to bring these about. In addition, these actions will be beyond his control.

The financial skill required is largely that of being able to compare the financial outcomes of different courses of action, and appreciating the significance of cost–volume–profit interrelationships.

The techniques to help in bringing management accounting and marketing closer together already exists – and have done for many years in one form and another. Recent developments such as the missions approach and the design of modularised data bases now supplement the established methods of marketing experimentation and distribution cost analysis.

It must be remembered when using distribution cost analysis that any cost allocation involves a certain degree of arbitrariness, and this means than an element of error is contained within each apportionment. Furthermore, it remains necessary to supplement the analysis of distribution costs with other relevant information and with managerial judgement. Distribution cost analysis is the joint responsibility of the financial controller and the marketing manager, with the former supplying most of the information and the later supplying most of the judgement. Nevertheless, the marketing manager must be fully aware of the methodology and limitations of distribution cost analysis in the same way that production managers should understand product costing.

The high costs involved in establishing and maintaining a distribution costing system are justified by the benefits derived from increasing the efficiency of marketing effort. The risks involved in adopting a full system of distribution cost analysis before the benefits have been demonstrated can be reduced by initially confining the analysis to a sample of products, customers, or territories, and by making periodic rather than continuous analyses.

However, technique is not the most critical ingredient in bringing management accounting into marketing in order to improve organisational effectiveness. The organisation of the accounting function must be designed in the most appropriate way. One can envisage a range of alternative approaches to the marketing–accounting interface, such as:

1 no organised accounting support for marketing;
2 marketing accountants located within the accounting department;
3 marketing accountants located within the marketing department.

Progress from (1) to (3) is likely to be evolutionary as both functions learn about how best to interact, and time is also needed to develop the accounting systems whereby the marketing function may be assisted.

But, above all, management accountants must acquire an understanding of the nature of marketing and the need to look outwards to the challenges of the environment.

REFERENCES AND FURTHER READING

References

Bancroft, A.L., and Wilson, R.M.S., 'Management Accounting for Marketing', *Management Accounting*, Vol. 57, No. 11, pp. 25–30, December, 1979.

Barrett, T.F., 'Modular Data Base System', *International Journal of Physical Distribution and Materials Management*, Vol. 10, No. 4, pp. 135–146, 1980.

Boulding, K., 'General Systems Theory – The Skeleton of Science', *Management Science*, Vol. 2, No. 3, pp. 197–208, April, 1956.

Goodman, S.R., *Techniques of Profitability Analysis*, New York: Wiley, 1970.

Hulbert, J.M. and Toy, N.E., 'A Strategic Framework for Marketing Control', *Journal of Marketing*, Vol. 41, No.2, pp. 12–20, April, 1977.

Schiff, M., and Mellman, M., *The Financial Management of the Marketing Function*, New York: Financial Executives Research Foundation, 1962.

Westwick, C.A., *How to Use Management Ratios*, Epping: Gower Press, 1973. (See especially Ch. 6, pp. 112–141, 'Ratios for Marketing Management'.)

Williamson, R.J., *Marketing for Accountants and Managers*, London: Heinemann, 1979.

Wilson, R.M.S. (compiler), *Financial Dimensions of Marketing – A Source Book* (2 volumes), London: Macmillan, 1981.

Wilson, R.M.S., *Cost Control Handbook*, 2nd edn, Aldershot: Gower Publishing, 1983. (See especially Ch. 17, pp. 493–545, 'Marketing – Order-Getting')

Wilson, R.M.S., 'Accounting for Marketing Assets', *European Journal of Marketing*, Vol. 20, No.1, pp. 51–74, 1986.

Further Reading

Barrett, T.F., *The Design of Marketing Accounting Systems: Issues and Influences*, 55 pp., November, 1983. (Unpublished paper available from Marketing Accounting Research Centre, Cranfield School of Management, Bedford MK43 0AL.)

Barrett, T.F., *Mission Costing*, 21 pp., no date. (Unpublished paper available from Professor Barrett at Department of Accounting, Queen's University of Belfast.)

Goodman, S.R., *The Marketing Controller*, New York: AMR International, 1972.

Mossman, F.H., Crissy, W.J.E., and Fischer, P.M., *Financial Dimensions of Marketing Management*, New York: Wiley, 1978.

Ratnatunga, J.T.D., *Financial Controls in Marketing: The Accounting-Marketing Interface* (Canberra Series in Administrative Studies – 6), Canberra: Canberra College of Advanced Education, 1983.

Sevin, C.H., *Marketing Productivity Analysis*, New York: McGraw-Hill, 1965.

Wilson, R.M.S., *Management Controls and Marketing Planning* (revised edn), London: Heinemann, 1979.

Wilson, R.M.S. with Bancroft, A.L., *The Application of Management Accounting Techniques to the Planning and Control of Marketing* (pp. 240), London: ICMA, 1983.

Wilson, R.M.S., 'Financial Control of the Marketing Function', Ch. 12, pp. 130–153 *in* Hart, N.A. (ed.), *The Marketing of Industrial Products* (2nd edn), London: McGraw-Hill, 1984.

14

Physical distribution

Gordon Hill

The aim of this part of the book is to show how management account-ing can be applied to non-manufacturing operations, and distribution is a major non-manufacturing operation in many organisations.

Traditionally such costs may have been lumped together as 'selling and distribution overheads', 'general administration overhead' and treated as a fixed, non-controllable cost. Distribution cost is a signifi-cant component of the cost of doing business for many organisations, however, and relegating it in such a fashion is likely to lead to excessive cost in this area, so reducing the scope for improving overall perform-ance.

In this chapter Gordon Hill shows how distribution cost can be ana-lysed and management accounting principles applied to it. He explains the elements of cost involved and the importance of understanding the behaviour of each element of cost. Such an understanding can be used to develop journey costs and delivery costs. Hill considers each of the factors influencing each of these approaches.

Having analysed the cost factors in distribution the next section of the chapter then considers how this information can be used to im-prove distribution performance. In particular, delivery strategies and depot location are considered. Finally the option of using transport contractors is discussed.

The author concludes that managers must understand the cost im-plications of their proposals, that management accountants are well-placed to take an integrated view of distribution cost and so provide relevant information to the management of physical distribution func-tions.

In this chapter the principles of management accounting are applied to the costing of road transport. Emphasis is given to the costing of transport operations associated with the physical distribution of manufactured goods. Essentially, such distribution involves two types of transport operation: that known as trunking, and that known as local delivery. Trunking involves, typically, the point-to-point movement of relatively large consignments over long distances. Local delivery, on the other hand, is concerned with the delivery of relatively small consignments to such outlets as private dwellings, retail shops and institutions. Such consignments could consist of just one parcel or of several packages weighing several tons, and typically several deliveries will be made each journey. There are both similarities and significant differences between the two types of transport operation and the way in which they are costed.

COST ELEMENTS

The objective of a well managed physical distribution function is to deliver the goods to the customers in such a manner as to minimise cost, so far as this is consistent with predetermined customer service standards. It is essential, therefore, that the behaviour of each element of cost, and the factors influencing that behaviour, are understood clearly. Particular attention is paid in this chapter to the costing of road transport, but the points made are of general significance and other aspects of physical distribution are considered.

Conventionally, transport costs tend to be quoted in terms of tons carried or tons delivered. From the viewpoint of the manufacturing company, this is convenient because the cost per ton can be converted into the cost per unit product. Thus, the transport element of the total cost of goods sold can be established. However, such calculations can be extremely misleading, since only average transport costs can be used. Such averages disguise the range and magnitude of the actual costs associated with transport and delivery. For example, a vehicle which undertakes a 250-mile round trip to make an urgent delivery to a customer would incur almost exactly the same actual transport costs whether the order delivered weighed 10 tons or 100 kgs.

To say that transport costs are independent of tonnage would be inaccurate. Equally, to say that there is a simple relationship between tonnage carried and cost would be grossly misleading. In order to understand transport costs more clearly, we must examine the cost elements and the factors affecting their behaviour.

Vehicle operating costs

The costs of operating a vehicle fall into two groups which, consistent with conventional management accounting principles, are fixed costs and variable costs. The fixed costs are referred to as the 'standing charges'; these are time-dependent costs which will be incurred whether the vehicle is driven or not. The variable costs are referred to as the 'running costs'; these can be related directly to the distance the vehicle is driven.

Nine elements of cost constitute the range of standing charges for a vehicle. An operator's licence fee must be paid annually for most goods vehicles over 3.5 tonnes maximum permissible gross weight. Additionally, excise duty is payable on all goods vehicles. The rate of duty payable depends on the way in which the vehicle is used, its unladen weight, and the way in which it is constructed.

Insurance premiums are influenced by such factors as the nature of the cover contracted and the insured operator's claim record. The operators of small fleets of vehicles usually seek comprehensive insurance cover, whereas the larger fleet operator may choose to bear some or all of the costs of accident repair charges. The cost of such repairs would be set against the saving on insurance premiums. While it could be argued that the vulnerability to accidents is directly related to the mileage travelled, insurance is an annual cost, independent of the extent to which the vehicle is used. Most goods vehicles are required to be tested annually at an approved heavy goods vehicle testing station to ensure that they meet the legal requirements for mechanical condition and safe operation.

It is now common to treat the wages of the driver (together with associated employment costs) and any crew as an annual cost. In the event that no work is available, it may be possible to allocate the crew of a vehicle to other duties. In that case, proportionate recognition would need to be taken of the extent to which that occurred.

The operation of a fleet of vehicles will incur overhead costs which cannot be attributed directly to any specific vehicle. Such costs will include the costs of transport management, traffic management, parking and garaging space, and so on. It is important that these additional costs are recognised and taken into account when operating costs are being calculated.

Financing charges accrue also: leasing, for example, gives rise to specific charges. Depreciation should also be included in the 'standing charge' category. It could be contended that depreciation is a running cost, on the basis that the decline in value of a vehicle is influenced greatly by the intensity of its use. However, the value of a vehicle is as much dictated by its age as by any other factor. The treatment given to depreciation must be decided in the light of experience, but it is more common for this element of cost to be included as a fixed cost or standing charge. Typically, the value of a new vehicle can be expected to decline by some 90 per cent or so over the first five years of its life.

Interest should be included, either as the actual expense of interest paid on capital borrowings to finance the purchase of the vehicle or as the opportunity cost of capital. This cost is overlooked more often then not, even though it represents a large portion of realistic standing charge totals.

By way of illustration, Table 14.1 presents the estimated standing charges and running costs of two typical vehicles – a 16-ton van and a 32-ton articulated tractor and box trailer. From the examples, an impression can be gained of the relative significance of each element of cost; generally, the costs quoted are those obtaining in late 1986.

Table 14.1
Standing charges and running costs

	Rigid van	Articulated tractor and trailer
Carrying capacity	10 ton	21 ton
Gross vehicle weight	16 ton	32 ton
Capital cost	£25 000	£45 000
Residual value (after 5 years)	£2 500	£4 500
STANDING CHARGES (annual):		
Depreciation (20%)	£4 500	£8 100
Excise duty	£900	£2 500
Operator's licence	£20	£20
Insurance	£650	£1 285
MOT	£25	£40
Interest	£1 955	£3 455
Driver's wages	£14 000	£16 100
	£22 050	£31 500
RUNNING COSTS (pence per mile):		
Fuel	12.0	17.0
Lubricants	0.5	0.6
Tyres	4.0	7.1
Maintenance	8.5	9.3
	25.0	34.0

Standing charge per journey

The decision as to the proportion of the annual standing charges of the vehicle that should be attributed to each journey made merits some attention. It is influenced by several considerations.

1 *Availability of the vehicle:* Routine servicing is undertaken normally during the day, with the result that the availability of the vehicle for operation is limited. Additionally, it is prudent to anticipate that the vehicle will be off the road for some of its working life as a result of accidental damage or breakdown. Experience will indicate the extent to which maintenance requirements reduce the availability of the vehicle; a conservative estimate would be between 10 per cent and 12½ per cent over its working life. This estimate implies that a fleet of nine vehicles would be needed to ensure the availability of eight operational vehicles each day. In such a circumstance, the standing charges of the eight operating vehicles should be increased by one-ninth to cover the standing charges of the other vehicle.

2 *Availability of the driver:* Unless provision is made to cover for the driver in the event of holiday or sick leave absence, the operational availability of the vehicle will be reduced. The extent is likely to be of the order of 8 per cent to 10 per cent. It is unlikely that the driver's absence could be precisely coordinated with the non-availability of the vehicle for maintenance reasons. It would be prudent to plan on the assumption that those two considerations will not coincide. If a fleet operator finds that the annual holidays of the drivers cannot be staggered appropriately, it might prove necessary to make special provisions for relief or temporary drivers. As an example, the effective standing charge for each vehicle in a company fleet could be calculated as follows. The company regularly operates 14 articulated tractors and trailers; it has a fleet of 16 such vehicles and employs 17 full-time drivers. The standing charge, excluding driver's wages, for each vehicle is calculated at £15 400 a year; drivers' wages average £16 100 each a year. The effective standing charge for each vehicle operated each day is £31 500: standing charge excluding driver's wages = £15 400 × 16/14 = £17 600; driver's wages = £16 100 × 17/14 = £19 500.

3 *Availability of transport work:* If there are some days, or even longer periods, during which no transport work is available, a correspondingly greater standing charge must be attributed to the days on which work is undertaken. An example of such a situation might be that of a fleet of ice-cream distribution vans, of which hardly any would be used in the winter months. The extent of such an additional standing charge could be offset to some degree by careful scheduling of vehicle maintenance and drivers' holidays.

4 *Intensive vehicle use:* In accordance with EEC rules, the time that a driver may drive between appropriate periods of rest are defined precisely. The vehicle, on the other hand, is available for twenty-four hours each day. In some circumstances, it may be possible to use the vehicle intensively by employing several drivers on a shift basis. The effect would be to increase the overall cost of drivers, but there would be a significant reduction in the standing charge attributable to each hour of operation and to each journey. Another way in which it is possible to use vehicles intensively is by articulation. For instance, the use of articulated vehicles enables trailers to be switched speedily and easily at the end of a journey, thus avoiding the expense of waiting time during the unloading/reloading process. An example of a situation where that arrangement works well is between a company's factory and its finished goods warehouse. In this particular case, storage space at the factory is limited and goods are loaded direct from the production line on to a trailer; when the trailer is fully loaded, a tractor is coupled up and the goods are taken the ten miles to the company's warehouse. This arrangement calls for one tractor and three trailers – one being loaded at the factory, one being unloaded at the warehouse, and one on its way between the two points. Under such arrangements, the standing charges for the vehicles involved can be spread over a significant amount of activity and, as a consequence, the cost of transport is kept to a relatively modest amount.

Running costs

Table 14.1 gave details of the estimated running costs per mile for the two typical vehicles described; these costs fall into four main categories – fuel, lubricants, tyres, and maintenance. Maintenance refers to both mechanical and bodywork maintenance. In addition, there is a periodic need to clean the vehicle, since a clean appearance is considered by many operators as a reflection of corporate image.

JOURNEY COSTING

The cost of a journey is the aggregate of the standing charges for the period of the journey and the running costs for the distance of the journey. Two simple examples will serve to illustrate the points made earlier.

The articulated tractor and trailer unit referred to in Table 14.1 was used on 225 days in the year. On one of those days, it made a round trip of 210 miles to make a delivery of 14 tonnes to a customer. The journey cost was computed as follows: standing charges = £31 500/225 = £140.00; running costs = 210 × £0.34 = £71.40; journey cost = £211.40.

The unit was used later on to make a round trip of 490 miles to make a delivery of 10 tonnes to a customer; the journey took two days and the cost was computed as follows: standing charges = £31 500/225 × 2 = £280.00; running costs = 490 × £0.34 = £166.60; driver's overnight allowance = £20.00; journey cost = £466.60.

In evaluating the cost of local delivery, it is again necessary to take account of both standing charges and running costs. A local delivery journey could involve more than 100 drops, but for delivery to retail stores the total number of drops would be nearer 10. The problem is to determine the extent to which journey costs should be allocated to each delivery. To solve that problem, it is necessary to examine the work involved in making the journey.

By way of illustration, Figure 14.1 depicts a typical analysis of the nine-hour working day of a local delivery driver. The analysis involves six elements, each of which merits some explanation.

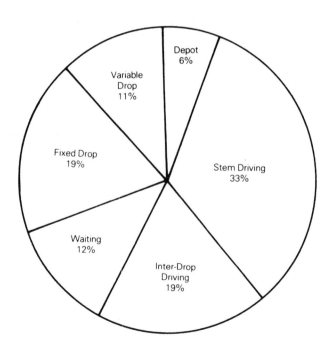

Figure 14.1   Delivery journey time analysis

Depot time is the time spent by the driver at the depot at the beginning and the end of the journey. Some duties are the specific responsibility of the driver and must be undertaken before the journey begins. These include the routine daily check of the vehicle and the collection of instructions and documents related to the work on the journey. The duties undertaken at the end of the journey may include such tasks as paying in cash and writing a journey report. Where practicable, it is beneficial for warehouse staff to load and unload the vehicle during the driver's off-duty time, thereby increasing the journey time available to the driver.

Stem driving time is the time devoted by the driver to travelling to and from the delivery area to be serviced. That driving is likely to be on main roads and, therefore, at a higher average speed than inter-drop driving.

Inter-drop driving time is the time devoted to driving between delivery locations. It is possible that this will be mainly urban driving, and average speeds may be fairly low.

Waiting time is the time, in excess of that which is normal and reasonable, that the driver spends waiting his turn to deliver at a delivery point.

Fixed drop time is the time required at the delivery location to perform all the tasks associated with making the delivery – except the time taken to actually unload the vehicle and, if necessary, deliver the goods into the customer's premises. Fixed drop time includes the normal waiting time as well as that required to position the vehicle, open the doors, and hand over the goods and documents, close and secure the vehicle, and depart.

Variable drop time is the time actually spent on unloading the vehicle and moving the goods into the customer's premises. This represents a fairly small proportion of the driver's day; it is, however, the only time during that day when revenue is being generated! Any steps, therefore, which result in an increase in this proportion of the driver's day must be beneficial.

DELIVERY COSTING

Trunk transport is usually costed by journey. For many such journeys, the total consignment is destined for one delivery location; in such cases, the journey cost equates to the delivery cost. However, because local delivery journeys can involve a multiplicity of deliveries, the question arises as to how each such local delivery should be costed.

A common approach is to approximate certain charges on the basis of time standards. Depot and stem driving times are not identifiable with any particular delivery drop and should therefore be allocated equally to each delivery made. Waiting time should be attributed directly to the delivery locations at which it occurs. Using time standards, it is possible to allocate the inter-drop driving time and the fixed and variable drop times to the delivery locations serviced. However, for most purposes, it is sufficiently accurate to average these elements of cost. Hence it is relatively simple to obtain a satisfactory approximation to the cost of each delivery.

For example, the rigid van described in Table 14.1 was used for delivery on 225 days in a year. On one of those days it made a local delivery journey involving a driving distance of 90 stem miles and 22 inter-drop miles; eleven deliveries were made, totalling 390 cases of merchandise. That situation is shown diagrammatically in Figure 14.1 and the analysis of the costs involved is given in Table 14.2.

Table 14.2
Delivery journey cost

	Standing charge (%)	Standing charge (cost) £	Running cost @ 25p per mile £	Total £
Depot	6	5.88		5.88
Stem driving (90 miles)	33	32.34	22.50	54.84
Inter-drop driving (22 miles)	19	18.62	5.50	24.12
Waiting	12	11.76		11.76
Fixed drop	19	18.62		18.62
Variable drop	11	10.78		10.78
	100	98.00	28.00	126.000

The cost per delivery is calculated on the basis that the total journey cost is attributable to the time spent in the delivery area. Accordingly, the cost of waiting time can be calculated as follows: waiting time cost = £126.00 × 12/61 = £24.79. The cost of each delivery is found as follows: delivery cost = (£126.00 − £24.79)/11 = £9.20. Therefore, the cost of delivery involving waiting time (as defined earlier) is £33.99, while the cost of each normal delivery is £9.20.

From the analysis it can be seen that the cost of the variable drop time is a modest proportion of the total cost and that even for delivery journeys involving no stem driving the cost would, in that case, be only 14 per cent of the total. The general conclusion is that local delivery costs are, for practical purposes, independent of the size of the delivery. The major cost is in putting the vehicle in a position to make the delivery.

Factors affecting cost per delivery

A number of factors have a direct influence on delivery cost. The following merit particular attention:

1 *Waiting time:* As can be seen from the above example, the cost attributable to waiting can be significant. Even more important, the time devoted to waiting reduces the time available to make deliveries. The cost of the normal deliveries on the journey is increased and, worse still, a second journey to the delivery area may be necessary. If the example of the rigid van mentioned earlier is used again, in the absence of waiting time it might have been possible to make twelve deliveries rather than ten. Those extra deliveries might have involved further inter-drop driving of five miles. The journey cost would be calculated as follows: original journey cost = £126.00; additional mileage = 5 × £0.25 = £1.25; total journey cost = £127.25. On the other hand, had it been necessary to make a second journey to the delivery area, for customer service reasons perhaps, to make the final two drops, and if the vehicle had been used exclusively for that purpose on the day in question, the total journey cost would have been much greater. The costs of waiting time could be assessed as follows: first journey (ten deliveries) cost = £126.00; second journey (two deliveries) – standing charge = £98.00; running costs = 95 × £0.25 = £23.75; journey cost = £121.75. The total journey cost for the twelve deliveries over two days would have been £249.00. Against that, the journey cost for making twelve deliveries on the one day would have been £127.25. The cost of waiting time on the first can be evaluated, therefore, at £121.75. Accordingly, great care should be exercised in computing waiting time. It is particularly relevant for assessing whether or not the trading terms with customers to whom delivery usually involves waiting are appropriate and reflect adequately the costs associated with servicing them.

2 *Receiving time restrictions:* The effectiveness of the use of the time spent by a local delivery vehicle in a delivery area is directly influenced by the hours during which consignees are prepared or able to receive deliveries. For example, retail butchers prefer deliveries in the morning, retail store managers prefer deliveries early in

the week rather than on Fridays, social club stewards are only available to accept deliveries at certain times of the day, and so on. Other more general causes of restriction include lunch breaks, half-day closing, pedestrianised area vehicular access times, and so on. Increasingly, consignees require transport operators to 'pre-book' delivery times. This practice is acceptable if such timed drops can be integrated into an operable sequence of deliveries. Costly operational problems can occur, however, if preceding delays result in late arrivals and subsequent refusals of deliveries. In such cases a second attempt must be made to effect the delivery.

3 *Vehicle carrying capacity:* The weight capacity of a vehicle is dictated by its official licence; the volume capacity will be determined by the configuration and physical dimensions of the body. In situations where the weight or cubic capacity of the vehicle limits the number of vehicles that can be planned for a journey and results in a greater number of journeys than would otherwise be necessary, consideration should be given to the use of a larger vehicle. It is recognised that there might be a restriction on the size of vehicle which could gain access to a delivery location, but this situation does not arise frequently. In the examples given in Table 14.1, doubling the carrying capacity results in a 43 per cent increase in standing charges and a 36 per cent increase in running costs. By using a large vehicle, comparatively modest additional operating costs are incurred but the result could be that fewer journeys are made. That would reduce total operating costs. An example will make the point more clearly, perhaps. Ten deliveries totalling 12 tons in weight have to be made in a delivery area which is 45 miles away from the depot. The only ve-

Table 14.3
Delivery costs for different stem distances

Stem distances (miles)	10	30	50	70	90
Deliveries possible	17	14	11	8	5
Total inter-drop distances (miles)	43	35	28	20	13
Standing charge (£)	98.00	98.00	98.00	98.00	98.00
Stem driving cost (£) (25p per mile)	5.00	15.00	25.00	35.00	45.00
Inter-drop driving cost (25p per mile) (£)	10.75	8.75	7.00	5.00	3.25
	113.75	121.75	130.00	138.00	146.25
Cost per delivery (£)	6.69	8.70	11.82	17.25	29.25

hicle available has a 10-ton carrying capacity. Two journeys will, therefore, be necessary. The costs would be estimated as follows: standing charges = £98.00 × 2 = £196.00; stem driving costs = 90 × 2 × £0.25 = £45.00; inter-drop driving costs = 27 × £0.25 = £6.75; total journey cost = £247.75. Had a 12-ton vehicle been available, only one journey would have been necessary. The standing charges and running costs for that 12-ton vehicle are estimated to be 10 per cent higher than those for the 10-ton vehicle. On that basis, the journey costs would be as follows: standing charge = £107.90; stem driving costs = 90 × £0.275 = £24.75; inter-drop driving costs = 27 × £0.275 = £7.42; total journey cost = £139.97. Use of the larger vehicle would result in a cost saving of £107.78, a reduction of some 43 per cent.

Stem distance and delivery cost

As can be seen from Figure 14.1, there are two main elements of the work associated with a local delivery journey. First, there are the tasks undertaken outside the delivery area, the depot duties and stem driving; second, there are the tasks undertaken within the delivery area, the inter-drop driving and the tasks at each delivery location.

It follows that the greater the distance from the depot to the delivery area, the greater will be the proportion of the driver's time devoted to stem driving. In turn, this reduces the time in the delivery area and the time available for making deliveries. The greater the stem distance, the greater also will be the running costs for the journey. To examine this problem more clearly, the estimates presented in Table 14.3 can be made. The significance of those calculations becomes clearer when represented graphically, as in Figure 14.2. As the stem distance increases, the cost per delivery rises at a disproportionately greater rate. The figure also shows the relationship between the cost per delivery and stem distance for a two-day journey. It has been assumed in drawing those curves that the size of the deliveries and the nature of the merchandise being delivered is such that the carrying capacity of the vehicle is not exceeded. It is not unusual to find, as in this case, that the cost per delivery on a two-day journey is less than for a one-day journey, even for journeys involving a modest stem distance from the depot. Clearly, substantial economies can be achieved if sufficient deliveries can be accumulated to justify one two-day journey rather than two separate one-day journeys. For greater stem distances, journeys of even longer duration may be justifiable.

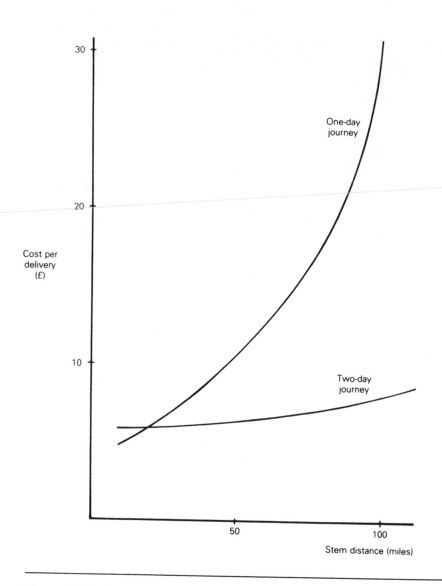

Figure 14.2   Stem distance and cost per delivery

Second deliveries

As a customer service, many companies adopt the procedure that any items which are not available when a customer's order is being despatched become the subject of a balance order. In that way, the unavailability of one or more specific items does not hold up delivery of the bulk of the order. An objective of such companies will be to so manage finished goods stocks that most goods will be available when ordered.

As has been shown earlier, the delivery of a small order costs virtually the same as the delivery of a large one. Hence, the delivery of a balance order costs almost as much as the delivery of the main order. Thus, a small shortfall in order fulfilment can result in a significant increase in total distribution costs. Commercially, that may be tolerable, but it must be recognised that some of the items in balance orders may cost more than the gross margin on those items. It would be advisable, therefore, for such companies to consider the adoption of a policy which requires that balance orders of less than a specified value will be cancelled, the customer having the option of re-ordering such items with his next regular order.

Balance orders give rise, of course, to other costs in addition to those associated with delivery. For instance, there would be extra clerical and administrative costs, extra order assembly costs, and extra packaging and despatching costs. A balance order for goods with a gross margin of 20 per cent, involving transport costs of £10 and other costs of £7, would need to be worth at least £85 to break even.

Delivery frequency

In the same way that balance order policy has a direct impact on delivery costs, so does order frequency. If each order placed by a customer gives rise to a delivery, then order frequency directly influences the number of deliveries to be made. It follows, therefore, that if, for example, it were commercially acceptable to deliver once a fortnight to a customer rather than once a week, and if the delivery size doubled as a consequence, delivery costs would be halved. Coupling this with all the other costs associated with processing and filling an order, it becomes clear that substantial cost savings can be made from reducing delivery frequency.

In some circumstances, order frequency is directly associated with the frequency of salemen's or representatives' calls. The discriminate selection of customers, whose business is inadequately contributing to corporate profits, for servicing at a reduced frequency could result in a marked improvement in the profits earned.

DEPOT LOCATION

Having discriminated between the two types of transport, trunking and local delivery, the problem remains of deciding where trunking should end and local delivery begin. The easy answer, of course, is at the depot where local delivery vehicles are based. That could be a 'stocked' depot or a 'cross-docking' depot at which goods are transferred directly from trunking vehicles to local delivery vehicles. If demountable bodies are used, the depot may be little more than a concreted area where the bodies can be interchanged between the two vehicle types.

Further questions then arise. These involve deciding how many depots are required, where they should be located, and which delivery areas should be serviced from each depot. The resolution of these problems requires trading-off three costs:

1   the cost of operating trunking vehicles from each of the sources of goods – factory locations or ports of entry;
2   the cost of operating the depots – building and occupancy costs, storage costs, stockholding costs, and so on;
3   the cost of local delivery from the depots to the customers in each delivery area.

Those three costs must be aggregated for each possible combination of depot locations, to determine the combination which gives the lowest total operating cost.

Additionally, operational data are needed for the assessment of each option. Such data include:

1   the number of delivery areas to be serviced;
2   the identification of a focal point (city or main town) in each delivery area;
3   the rate at which goods have to be moved from each source to the customers in each delivery area;
4   the number of deliveries each year that each tonnage quantity represents;
5   the number of potential depot locations;
6   an operating cost profile for depots of varying tonnage through-put rates;
7   a matrix of costs per delivery for each delivery area from each potential delivery depot location;
8   a matrix of costs for operating trunking vehicles from each source to each potential depot location.

The results of these trade-off evaluations can be shown graphically, as depicted in Figure 14.3, which shows the minimum total operating cost for networks of depots from one to ten in number. It does not follow, of course, that the particular depots featured in any one optimal network will necessarily be the same as those featured in the optimal network which is one depot greater in size.

Figure 14.3 reveals that, in the situation on which the graph is based, the minimum total operating cost corresponds to a network of five depots. However, if it were thought that a network of seven depots was desirable (perhaps from customer servicing considerations), such a graph would help to determine the additional cost that would be incurred in providing that level of service. Such a move is revealed by the two horizontal dotted lines on the graph; to move from five depots to seven depots would cost a further £400 000 a year.

USING TRANSPORT CONTRACTORS

The nature of the transport costs incurred by own-account operators and by transport contractors are essentially similar. The differences lie in the interpretation of those costs. That interpretation is heavily dependent upon the size and nature of the consignments carried, the opportunities for operational economies, and the level of service required.

If an own-account operator makes a long distance journey to deliver a 20-ton consignment to a customer, it is most unlikely that there would be a return load from that customer. The vehicle will return empty and the operator will incur the whole cost of the round trip. Had the same consignment been transported by an outside contractor, it is possible that he would have been able to arrange a return load from another shipper. So, although the contractor will require a suitable profit margin on the round trip, he has two possible sources of revenue and could probably quote attractive freight rates to both shippers as a result. The contractor may not be able to transport the goods as speedily as the original shipper would like or require, as it may tke time to arrange a suitable return load. In those circumstances, a commercial decision is required as to whether the delivery can be delayed to take advantage of the outside contractor's lower transport rate or whether an own-account vehicle should be used to provide quicker, but more costly, service.

In the case of local delivery, a similar kind of commercial decision may be necessary. If the shipper has sufficient orders for delivery in a

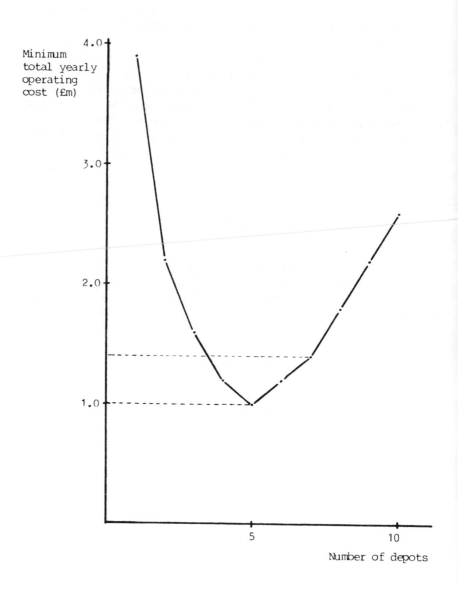

Figure 14.3   Depot numbers and total operating cost

particular area to permit an efficient (that is, cost effective) journey to be planned, the cost per delivery will be known and the company will retain control over the timely delivery of the goods. A transport contractor might be able to make the deliveries more economically, but it is unlikely that he would match the company's own vehicle plans for speed.

None the less, contractors frequently quote rates on a weight carried basis, reflecting the economies of consolidation. When these rates are compared with own-account delivery costs, it may be found that some deliveries could be made less expensively by using the services of outside contractors. This is particularly likely in the case of deliveries to remote areas and those to which insufficient quantities of goods are consigned. Discriminating use of contractors can, therefore, be most beneficial.

Looked at from the contractor's viewpoint, the key to success is the ability to have access to, and to be able to coordinate, sufficient consignments to make the best use of his vehicles. For trunking, this means ready access to return loads; for local delivery, it means the accumulation of sufficient traffic to each delivery area. Both these requirements call for effective systems and methods of communication to facilitate the required coordination.

Additional advantages accrue from the facility to avoid complex and ever-increasing legal requirements, and from the opportunity to avoid extensive capital investment in vehicles and support facilities – see Dowsett (1981) for a practical analysis of the advantages of using outside carriers for the transport of parcels.

CONCLUSION

The physical distribution manager can achieve worthwhile and substantial savings by taking a structured view of transport costs and alternatives. Directly, the manager can achieve better cost control by planning the more effective use of drivers, by getting the number and mix of vehicles right, and by selecting the most appropriate and effective network pattern for depots and support facilities.

The physical distribution manager will be constrained in his decisions by a number of factors outside his direct control; customer service standards, demand and order patterns, delivery frequencies, and trading terms.

It is essential that such managers understand the cost implications of their activities so that they can contribute effectively to the decision making processes in the organisation. The management accountant, in his turn, is well placed to take an integrated view of the cost of distribution and to encourage senior management to take a corporate view of all the functions involved in the physical distribution of manufactured goods and products.

REFERENCES AND FURTHER READING

Aylott, D.J., and Brindle-Wood-Williams, D., *Physical Distribution in Industrial and Commercial Marketing*, London: Hutchinson, 1970.

Bowersox, D.J., Smykay, E.W., and LaLonde, B.J., *Physical Distribution Management*, New York: Macmillan, 1968.

Christopher, M., Walters, D., and Gattorna, J., *Distribution Planning and Control: a Corporate Approach*, Farnborough: Gower, 1977.

Christopher, M., and Willis, G. (eds), *Marketing Logistics and Distribution Planning*, London: Allen & Unwin, 1972.

Cox, B., 'Transport costs', *Management Accounting*, February 1981.

Dowsett, B., 'Outside carriers for parcels', *Management Accounting*, October 1981.

Frain, J., *Transportation and Distribution for European Markets*, London: Butterworth, 1970.

Gattorna, J. (ed.), *Handbook of Physical Distribution Management*, 3rd edn, Aldershot: Gower, 1983.

Glendinning, R., 'Management of physical distribution', *Management Accounting*, February 1981.

Institute of Directors, *The Director's Guide to Storage, Handling, Freight and Distribution*, London: Institute of Directors, 1980.

Longman, D.R., and Schiff, M., *Practical Distribution Cost Analysis*, Homewood, Ill.: Irwin, 1955.

Sawdy, L.W.C., *The Economics of Distribution*, Epping: Gower, 1972.

15

Not-for-profit organisations

Duncan Bennett

Most of the other contributions to this handbook have been concerned, at least implicitly, with the planning, management and control of the activities of profit-seeking enterprises. However, a significant part of the economic activities of most countries is accounted for by not-for-profit organisations – central and local government, charities, educational establishments, and the like. For the most part, the processes of planning and control in not-for-profit organisations are the same as in profit-oriented concerns. There are, however, a number of important differences. The prime difference, of course, is in the pursuit of an objective other than the profit or wealth-maximising aim of industrial and commercial organisations. Organisations in the not-for-profit category exist to provide a service and their effectiveness is measured by the nature and quality of that service and the costs and benefits to the community in which they operate. Further, there are huge differences in the areas of ownership, power and management. Ownership is generally in public hands – governments, local authorities, hospitals or education authorities, trustees, and so on. Management is by professionals, and there is a general lack of adequate management controls, although that situation has been changing for the better over the past few years. Generally, not-for-profit organisations operate in monopoly markets, and the market place assumes a much less important role in the planning and strategic processes of the organisation. Not-for-profit organisations tend to be controlled and directed by politically-oriented persons or to operate subject to the oversight and control of political masters. All in all, the management and control of not-for-profit organisations pose several challenging questions for management accountants anxious to control costs, to perform effectively and efficiently, and to measure performance.

All organisations, whether or not they are attempting to trade, have a common need for funding in order to maintain themselves. They share another feature: each has an objective which it was set up to attain.

Control of any organisation depends upon the information which is available to the controller. The more timely and relevant that information is, the better the controller's ability to design decisions likely to attain the organisation's objective. Thus, there can be no fundamental difference in the role of the management accountant as intelligence officer to management in either type of organisation, profit seeking or otherwise. Management must be provided with accurate, timely and relevant information and must make decisions based on that information, using the skills, experience and judgement available.

Not-for-profit organisations comprise a very wide spectrum, ranging from central government and local government, through charities, friendly societies, and clubs to miscellaneous voluntary organisations. Central government practice is unique and is outside the scope of this chapter.

For broad discussion purposes, then, not-for-profit organisations can be classified in two main groups. The first category requires initial capital outlay and is self-funding thereafter. Such an organisation, having been set up by a capital payment for premises, land, fittings and equipment, makes a charge for its services at a level which sustains it without leading to an unallocated financial gain. An independent college is a good example. Income from fees may well exceed the cost of providing the service given, but any surplus will be used to further the aims of the college rather than to reward an entrepreneur or investors.

The second group is supported by regular contributions or grants, rather than by selling a service. This group includes central and local government, supported by taxes, rates, levies, duties, and so on – largely of a compulsory nature. Additionally, other members of the group, such as charities, churches, private health services, and the like, are supported by voluntary contributions.

Support of central and local government organisations is backed by the concept of equity. The individual contributor has the right to a say in the creation and execution of policies; he or she has a vote which can be used to exert some influence on the policies and practices of national or local government, albeit at arm's length. Other organisations in the not-for-profit sector may, or may not, grant some form of participation to supporters.

A unifying theme in the sector is that its members exist to provide a service – running buses, rescuing mariners, housing pensioners, educating students, researching diseases, building roads. It is here that the management accountant will find the most difficult aspects of his work in this field. Allowing for all the problems of defining and measuring profit, it is still a clear enough item and it is measurable. Services are not susceptible to such clear-cut analysis, and the degree of successful provision is not so easy to measure or report. Equally, there is a distinct lack of available guidance on the application of management accounting and control techniques to not-for-profit organisations. The controller has to depart from the traditional practice of measuring a quantifiable profit and adopt a cost–benefit approach to the organisation's activities. Dobbins and Fanning (1981) described the case of a university of medium size, regularly in a position of operating deficit, because costs always exceed income. Table 15.1 illustrates the income and expenditure statement for such a university. Its activities resulted in a deficit of £400 000. The university can and should be seen, however, in a social context. What benefits does it produce for society, and what are the associated costs to society? The alternative statement presented in Table 15.2 shows one way of approaching the quantification of such a judgement. Some not-for-profit activities are not susceptible to such an analysis, however.

Table 15.1
University income and expenditure

	£
Income:	
Tuition fees	2 800 000
Research grants	860 000
Government grants	7 610 000
	11 350 000
Expenditure:	
Teaching costs	6 890 000
Research costs	780 000
Student and staff facilities costs	200 000
Maintenance, equipment and miscellaneous costs	2 670 000
Administration costs and loan charges	1 210 000
	11 750 000
Deficit:	400 000

Table 15.2
University benefits and costs

	£
Benefits:	
Increased value of students	X XXX XXX
Value of research	X XXX XXX
	XX XXX XXX
Costs:	
Teaching costs	6 890 000
Research costs	780 000
Administration and other costs	4 080 000
	11 750 000
'Social' profit:	X XXX XXX

DISTINCTIONS

Gross and Warschauer (1979) identified five principal accounting differences between commercial organisations and not-for-profit undertakings, and a brief discussion of these distinctions will point up the nature of the problems facing a manager and controller of the latter. The first difference is that accounting in not-for-profit organisations is for cash, ignoring accruals and payments in advance, for instance, and most records are of receipts and payments. Secondly, fund accounting is adopted as a usual practice by many not-for-profit organisations, such funds as 'general', 'capital', or 'endowment' being set up to account for the particular resources made available for those purposes. The third accounting difference is in the treatment of fixed assets. Many organisations in the not-for-profit sector write off fixed assets on acquisition. Where assets are donated, they will not be depreciated and may not appear in the organisation's accounts. Fourthly, not-for-profit organisations make transfers between separate funds, or make appropriations to funds for future purposes, thereby departing significantly from commercial accounting practices. The final distinction is in the treatment of outstanding income. For the commercial organisation, debtors are treated in an unequivocal way; owing money is factual and enforceable. In not-for-profit organisations, the enforceability of a pledge may be doubtful; its subsequent collection will be a matter of hope rather than probability.

Distinctions of a more urgent kind have been identified by Anthony and Herzlinger (1980), and those differences are more meaningful for management accountants and controllers than mere book-keeping differences.

The distinctions arise from the nature of a not-for-profit organisation and the essential differences in its objectives and policies. Each of the distinctions presents significant difficulties in a management control context.

Absence of profit measure

There is no profit motive in the not-for-profit organisation; the motive is to provide a service as effectively and efficiently as possible and at a level consonant with the needs and criteria of those for whom the service is intended. In those circumstances, some outputs can be quantified – so many bus routes, so many graduates, so many hospital admissions, and so on. Other outputs, however, cannot be quantified so easily; and even where it is possible to quantify outputs it will be impossible to find a single measure of organisational effectiveness. There is no 'bottom line' figure to use as an indicator. There is no profit measure, and the absence of such a measure renders the management control process exceptionally difficult.

There is no single criterion for evaluating alternative courses of action, since there is no single objective function for a not-for-profit organisation. Decision making becomes a much more complicated and less clear-cut process than in a commercially oriented undertaking. As Anthony and Dearden (1976) commented:

> The management team of a nonprofit organization often will not agree on the relative importance of various goals; members will view a proposal in terms of the importance that they personally attach to the several goals of the organization.

In essence, profit is the difference between the costs of the organisation's inputs and the results of its outputs. As such it offers a tangible measure by which benefits and costs can be compared. While the inputs (that is, costs) of a not-for-profit organisation can be ascertained and measured in precisely the same way as those of a profit-oriented organisation, the outputs are seldom susceptible to measurement in a manner which facilitates comparison between inputs and outputs.

There is, therefore, no single measure of performance in a not-for-profit organisation, and it is virtually impossible to compare organisational units or separate organisations in an effective and realistic way.

319

Reduced impact of market forces

The activities of a commercial, profit-oriented organisation are governed by the demands of the market in which it operates. It must act within the demand and supply constraints created by the market place. Its goods must be wanted, acceptably priced, and competitive. Most not-for-profit organisations have little cause for worry from competition, and most offer the services they think best rather than those the consumers would like.

Again, as Anthony and Dearden (1976) emphasised:

> In a profit oriented organization . . . the new client is an opportunity to be vigorously sought after; in many nonprofit organizations, the new client is only a burden, to be accepted with misgivings.

For an airline, the pursuit of more passengers is a profitable objective; more patients for a clinic is a costly outcome. More customers generate fresh resources for a commercial undertaking, whereas more clients consume existing resources in a not-for-profit organisation.

One of the principal influences in the market place is that of competition. In the presence of competition resources must be used effectively and efficiently and managers will be judged, and motivated, by considerations of how effectively and efficiently they use the resources entrusted to them. By contrast, the not-for-profit sector provides no such incentive, and managers are motivated by considerations of a personal and qualitative nature.

Competition does exist, of course, in one important way: there is competition for funds, both between organisations and between departments or units within an organisation. In those circumstances, managers are rewarded (in the sense that they get the resources they want) as a result of their status and political skills rather than for their effectiveness or performance.

Comparative absence of accountability

The archetypal commercial organisation has to account for its actions and their outcomes to its owners and, to some extent, its creditors. Shareholders expect that the company will be run in their best interests and they demand regular reports of the results of that operation. Additionally, they expect sufficient profits to be generated to pay dividends to shareholders, interest to lenders, taxes to government, and so on, and to provide funds for future activities or investment.

Not-for-profit organisations, on the other hand, are characterised by a comparative lack of accountability. There are no owners, except in the general sense that the community owns central and local government or that club members own a social club. Power in not-for-profit organisations is not exercised in the same way as in profit-oriented concerns. Additionally, by their nature, most not-for-profit organisations are 'governed' by part-time, often unpaid, elected or nominated amateurs. The need for a strong, effective, experienced and specialist board is much greater in a not-for-profit organisation; paradoxically, the reverse is more often the case in practice. That creates severe problems for management control, and makes effective planning and strategic analysis much more difficult.

Having less rigorous control mechanisms, and being largely traditionalist, the majority of not-for-profit organisations have neglected to adopt comprehensive and sophisticated management accounting and information systems. The advances in theory and practice in the areas of management planning and control have been ignored by their managements, which tend to see their role as a fiduciary one, keeping the system relatively honest, rather than a stewardship one, managing the resources effectively and beneficially.

BUDGETING

The performance of an organisation can be monitored only in the knowledge of what should have been achieved. Some elements of budgeting must be present in any organisational planning, especially in not-for-profit organisations where there are seldom profits to be maximised but where costs must be minimised. One cannot say 'good' of something without being aware of what 'bad' is; there must be some form of standard against which performance can be measured.

The budgeting processes for a not-for-profit organisation follow the same paths and take the same directions as those for commercial, profit-oriented enterprises (see Chapter 5 for a discussion of budgeting), and there are few integral differences. The first step is to estimate the amount of revenue that will be received for operating purposes during the coming period. Budgeted expenses are calculated to match revenues; expenses measure the extent to which the organisation is filling its role in society, since, broadly speaking, society will provide what it regards as sufficient revenues to produce a desired level of service. To have revenue surpluses is to have spent too little, to have provided a lower standard of service. The budget will be formulated in terms of responsibility centres (see Chapter 10 for a description of responsibility centres and responsibility accounting), and centre managers will generate their own budgets subject to any guidelines from senior managers and consistent with the attainment of the objectives of each centre.

Generally, such budget estimates will be based on current levels of expenditure, but occasionally budgets will be prepared on a programme basis rather than a centre-by-centre basis. The concepts of the programmed budgeting process have been discussed elsewhere in this handbook, as they apply equally to profit-conscious organisations and not-for-profit entities. In a narrower sense, programme budgets will refer to the budgeted costs of a specific programme of action over the coming period or periods. Table 15.3 gives a budget projection for a three-year period for a programme designed to reduce injuries and deaths caused by motor vehicle accidents in which driver drunkenness is a contributory factor. The costs and the components of the programme are fictitious, as is the programme itself. The personnel costs are based on an average number of employees engaged full time earning an average salary of £11 000 a year in 1984, increasing by some 9 per cent annually thereafter. Advertising costs are expected to rise by 10 per cent annually, publication and administration costs by 12 per cent, and monitoring costs by 5 per cent. In-

Table 15.3
Three-year programme budget

	1984	1985	1986
	£	£	£
Personnel costs	242 000	264 000	288 000
Advertising costs	1 250 000	1 375 000	1 512 500
Publication costs	300 000	337 500	379 700
Monitoring costs	100 000	105 000	110 300
Administration costs	250 000	281 300	316 400
	2 142 000	2 362 800	2 606 900
Discounted present value (10%)	1 947 078	1 951 673	1 957 782
Total estimated actual cost over three years			7 111 700
Total estimated discounted present value cost over three years			5 856 533

flation is expected to run at an additional average of 10 per cent over the three-year period. The total estimated actual cost over the three-year period is calculated at £7 111 700; discounted at 10 per cent, the total present value cost is calculated at £5 856 533. The programme would be funded by the government department responsible for transport and would be mounted by the accident prevention units within that department. Funds would be provided from the total departmental budget. Responsibility would be allocated to a senior civil servant who would be seconded from existing duties within the department and who would manage the programme on a full time basis.

As with any budget for an input-using operation, the most difficult part of the process would be to determine the estimated costs for different elements of the programme.

The preparation of the budget would be undertaken hand-in-hand with a cost–benefit analysis of the probable inputs required and the likely outputs derived from the programme. The outputs would be the number of injuries and deaths prevented, quantified in some amenable way. It might be possible to ascertain some quantifiable benefits and to attribute some monetary value to those benefits before attempting the detailed establishment of a budget, on the basis that an injury or death prevented had an intrinsic value which could be compared with the cost involved.

Cost–benefit analysis

Cost–benefit analysis is an ideal tool for the management accountant engaged in not-for-profit activity measurement. Typically, most government agencies have employed cost–benefit analysis techniques to justify proposals for new projects or programmes. The drawback is that such an analysis can only be applied to those outcomes which are susceptible of quantification. Most instances involve important qualitative considerations which cannot be encompassed in a numerical cost–benefit analysis. Equally, rendering considerations into quantitative elements of the analysis will tend to narrow the focus of management's judgement and concentrate decision making in too mechanistic a way on unimportant or misleading considerations.

In addition, there are significant dangers in employing cost–benefit analysis in too trusting a way. While the calculation of benefits and costs for one programme may prove realistic and sensible, there is a danger that other completely different programmes designed to attain different objectives will be judged together on the basis of their benefit–cost relationship. None the less, the systematic analysis of inputs and outputs will tend to improve the decision making process. The application of cost–benefit analysis can be illustrated by reverting to the example used in Table 15.3. The benefits of the programme will be the reduced injuries and deaths attributed to drunken driving. Those benefits can be quantified in a relatively straightforward way.

The first step is to determine the proportion of current injuries and deaths, and projected injuries and deaths, that might be avoided by implementing the programme. Table 15.4 presents estimates of projected road casualty figures for the period 1984–86; it is emphasised that these are hypothetical estimates and are not based on any official or accurate projections. The table also shows the estimated proportion of those casualties that might be averted by the programme's impact.

On that basis, it can be calculated that the programme will result in the reduction of injuries and deaths over the three-year period by a total of 14 300 (375 deaths and 13 925 injuries), at a total present value cost of £5 856 533 – an average present value cost of £409.55 per incident averted.

The analysis would proceed by calculating the present value cost in lost earnings and associated expenditure for each injury and each death. The calculation of those costs for injuries would be based on average lengths of off-work time, sickness benefits, employer opportunity costs, and the like; it would include an estimation of the costs of police, fire and ambulance services' involvement at the scene of accidents, legal and court costs of any subsequent proceedings, road repair and maintenance costs, vehicle repair or replacement costs, and so on. The underlying procedure can be illustrated by limiting

Table 15.4
Road casualty estimates and programmes impacts

	1984	1985	1986
Road users killed	7 500	7 700	7 900
of which due to driver drunkenness	750	770	790
Road users injured	350 000	380 000	410 000
of which due to driver drunkenness	26 250	28 500	30 750
Programme impacts:			
deaths averted	75	125	175
injuries averted	2 625	4 575	6 725
	2 700	4 700	6 900

the analysis at this stage to a consideration of the programme's effect on the occurrence of fatal injuries.

Table 15.5 shows the calculation of the probable 'savings' (that is, reduced costs) from averted deaths as a result of the programme's impact.

The values shown in Table 15.5, under the heading 'Discounted earnings', are derived from a consideration of the likely lifetime earnings of males and females of different ages, adjusted to take account of the likelihood of unemployment or removal from the labour force and for mortality rates due to other factors than road accidents. Those likely earnings were then discounted at 10 per cent. Taking the likely number of users saved from death and multiplying those numbers by the average discounted earnings of persons in the different age ranges, the resultant earnings figures were then discounted back to the base year, 1984, using a rate of 10 per cent, and the estimated discounted present values of the earnings of those whose lives would be saved are those shown in the table.

It can be seen that over the three-year programme, the present value of the lifetime earnings of all those whose lives would be saved is estimated at £60 150 000. The present value of the costs of the programme was estimated at £5 856 533. The present value of the savings from other sources (that is, reduced public service commitments to road accident attendance, vehicle repairs, road repairs, and so on) had been calculated at £6 500 per accident averted, giving a total benefit over the three-year period of some £2 437 500 in respect of fatal accidents averted.

The program cost per death averted was estimated earlier at £409.55; the savings per death averted averaged £166 900, giving a cost–benefit ratio of 407.5:1.

Table 15.5
Savings from averted deaths

Age of user	Numbers		Discounted earnings (£000)		
	Males	Females	Males	Females	Total
Under 14	25	15	2 500	1 125	3 625
15–24	40	20	6 000	2 250	8 250
25–34	55	30	9 900	4 200	14 100
35–44	40	20	8 400	3 300	11 700
45–54	35	20	7 175	3 100	10 275
55–64	30	10	5 700	1 200	6 900
Over 64	25	10	4 500	800	5 300
	250	125	44 175	15 975	60 150

Cost–benefit analysis can be undertaken even where there is uncertainty about the values or savings of outcomes. One of the American departments prominent in the advocacy of cost–benefit analysis displays the motto: 'It is better to be roughly right than precisely wrong'. If the outcomes or outputs cannot be quantified, it is still possible to employ cost–benefit analysis techniques. For example, if a local authority has two alternative social welfare proposals under consideration, each costing £525 000 in a full year, it can proceed by evaluating the likely qualitative benefits flowing from each proposal. If the money is spent on additional social workers, will that create more social benefit than spending the money on increased welfare facilities? Alternatively, which proposal would have the greater benefit to a university engineering department? A further full time lecturer at a salary of £11 000 or a new measurement machine costing £66 000 and having an expected life of six years?

MANAGEMENT MOTIVATION

In the absence of the profit measure and without such managerial performance yardsticks as return on investment or residual income (as discussed in Chapter 11), management must adopt different measures for appraising performance. Management by objectives is a more or less formal procedure that stresses goals and outputs and depends for its success on feedback and performance reports.

In the not-for-profit organisation, the objectives can be stated fairly clearly, and it may well be possible to express them in a quantified form – so many homeless families housed, for instance, or so many passenger/miles operated by local bus services. In that way, managers can be judged by their attainment or surpassing of the objectives set by them or for them.

In most not-for-profit organisations, the principal criterion is the level of service provided or the effects of the programs implemented. Costs are a secondary consideration in that context, although any measurement of managerial effectiveness must include an evaluation of cost control performance and adherence to budgeted levels of expenditure.

CONCLUSION

Not-for-profit organisations have many shared characteristics with their profit-oriented counterparts in the industrial and commercial sector, but equally they have many distinctive problems. The absences of the profit motive and a profit measure are formidable obstacles to a proper system of performance appraisal. None the less, the adoption of such techniques as cost minimisation and outcome maximisation will assist the management accountant in his role as management controller for such an organisation.

Cost–benefit analysis and a programmed approach to budgeting offer significant advantages to the controllers of not-for-profit organisations, and the motivation of managers may be achieved by following the 'management by objectives' approach.

Not-for-profit organisations are judged by the extent to which they contribute to the welfare of the community or interests they exist to serve. That measurement may be extremely difficult to make, and there are obvious dangers in adopting either a cost minimisation tactic or an outcome maximisation one, in isolation.

With notable exceptions, the particular problems of the not-for-profit organisation have been overlooked by writers and researchers and, by and large, by the professional bodies and the standard-setting authorities. The idea has been advanced (Charnes et al., 1980) that:

> Managerial accounting . . . will move away from its present almost exclusive emphasis on private enterprise decision making. That is, the movement will be toward perfecting and developing tools in these disciplines as aids for improved decision making and managerial evaluation in the large and continually growing sector of not-for-profit entity activities.

If so, the discussion in this chapter may go some way towards assisting that process.

REFERENCES AND FURTHER READING

Anthony, R. N., and Dearden, J., *Management Control Systems: Text and Cases*, 3rd edn, Homewood, Ill.: Irwin, 1976.

Anthony, R. N., and Herzlinger, R., *Management Control in Non-profit Organizations*, Rev edn, Homewood, Ill.: Irwin, 1980.

Canadian Institute of Chartered Accountants, *Financial Reporting for Non-profit Organizations*, Toronto: CICA, 1980.

Charnes, A., Cooper, W. W., and Rhodes, E., 'An efficiency opening for managerial accounting in not-for-profit entities', *in* Holzer,

H. P. (ed.), *Management Accounting 1980*, Urbana-Champaign: University of Illinois, 1980.

Dobbins, R., and Fanning, D., 'Social accounting', *in* Pocock, M. A., and Taylor, A. H. (eds), *Handbook of Financial Planning and Control*, Farnborough: Gower, 1981.

Gross, M. J., and Jablonsky, S. F., *Principles of Accounting and Financial Reporting for Nonprofit Organizations*, New York: Wiley-Interscience, 1979.

Gross, M. J., and Warschauer, W., *Financial and Accounting Guide for Nonprofit Organizations*, 3rd edn, New York: Ronald Press, 1979.

Hay, L. E., *Accounting for Governmental and Nonprofit Entities*, 6th edn, Homewood, Ill.: Irwin, 1980.

Henke, E. Q., *Accounting for Nonprofit Organizations*, 2nd edn, Belmont, Ca.: Wadsworth, 1979.

Henke, E. O., *Introduction to Nonprofit Organization Accounting*, Belmont, Ca.: Wadsworth, 1979.

Sizer, J., 'Developing quantitative and financial performance indicators in non-profit organizations', *in* Sizer, J., *Perspectives in Management Accounting*, London: Heinemann, 1981.

Sorenson, J. R., and Grove, H. D., 'Cost-outcome and cost-effectiveness analysis: emerging nonprofit performance evaluation techniques', *The Accounting Review*, July 1977.

Part Four
Special Issues in Management Accounting

OVERVIEW

This final part of the handbook brings together a number of individual issues and techniques which are important in all sectors of the economy but do not fit neatly into the areas of either planning or control. In general they are managerial issues in which management accounting has a major part to play, rather than matters of management accounting technique.

In the first chapter of this section Professor Groves considers a very important set of issues which are sometimes overlooked by a concentration on techniques. Organisational and behavioural considerations have by no means been ignored in previous chapters but in Chapter 16 they are considered explicitly and as a coherent set of issues rather than as an undercurrent in another context.

Professor Groves emphasises that management accounting exists in an organisational context and a management accounting system is part of a wider control system. He explains the development of management theories and taking the Contingency Theory position he proposes a contingency framework for management accounting, identifying a number of variables which can be expected to influence information system design.

His conclusion is an important warning for readers of this Handbook – it is unrealistic to expect to define simple, straightforward solutions or rules to most management accounting problems. In the organisational context as elsewhere, however, research findings can be helpful in guiding the design of management accounting systems.

For example pricing, which is the subject of Chapter 17, is often dealt with by managerial rules of thumb. Management accounting research, however, can help develop new approaches to this complex task. Whatever method a company uses for fixing prices the cost of the product is a consideration. Too often, perhaps, it is the sole consideration and too rigid a pricing formula is applied, based on a cost which may not be entirely appropriate. In such cases the trade-off between price and volume is often not addressed explicitly, and perhaps not even implicitly. However, that trade-off is a crucial aspect of a company's strategy and a major determinant of its profitability.

In Chapter 17 Professor John Sizer uses profit–volume charts to show how the price/volume trade-off can be analysed. He maps a contribution curve for a product to show how the optimum price and volume can be determined. While recognising practical difficulties in establishing demand curves, Professor Sizer points out that nevertheless useful conclusions can be drawn by making best estimates and by analysing trade-offs – an activity which is an intrinsic part of management. In the second part of this chapter the author shows how a contribution graph can be a useful and very practical way of identifying product profitability issues and highlighting how the different constituents of the marketing mix might be juggled to improve profitability. Finally he considers the impact of inflation on pricing.

Setting external prices sometimes seems to be child's play compared to the intractable problem of fixing transfer prices. Chapter 18 examines this issue, which is an inherent part of the continuing trend to divisionalisation and decentralisation. The scale of the problem varies depending on the extent of inter-trading between divisions within a group of companies, but it is common in most conglomerates and is a particularly difficult issue because of the motivational impact which transfer pricing practices can have. Transfer prices are clearly important in determining the measured performance of inter-trading divisions, and the dangers of maximising divisional profits at the expense of group profitability are often all too apparent.

In Chapter 18 Jeffrey Davies shows how an optimum output level for the group as a whole may not maximise individual divisions' profits and may therefore seem unsatisfactory to divisional managements. He examines the problems that arise in trying to set transfer prices and proposes a general rule which he argues should be used in the context of the company-wide planning and control system.

As Davies shows, an inappropriate transfer pricing system can affect overall group performance. But transfer pricing is concerned with the relationships between parts of the group, not the fundamentals of the business itself. Chapter 19 is concerned with examining the fundamental cost structure, through formal cost reduction procedures.

Few companies can afford the luxury of not being concerned with costs, and formalised cost reduction or profit improvement programmes seem to be becoming increasingly common, either as *ad hoc* exercises or as part of regular planning processes. Anthony

Hollis explains the scope for such procedures in all the functions of the business, not merely the production function which is usually the main focus of management accountants' attention.

Hollis stresses that behavioural considerations should be paramount, since the commitment of managers is essential to achieve long-lasting cost reductions, and that schemes invariably require changes in managerial behaviour. He identifies three common approaches to cost reduction which virtually guarantee failure, and argues that a coherent, structured approach is essential.

Despite the proclaimed distance between management and financial accounting, the vast majority of management accounting data usually comes from the financial accounting system and conventions adopted tend to be the same. Management accounts are consequently little more than detailed financial accounts, presented in the same kind of format and focusing on the same essential ingredients – notably accounting profit.

In Chapter 20, however, Bernard Cox puts the case for using value-added statements both internally and externally, suggesting that value added can provide a more meaningful measure of corporate performance than conventional accounting profit. The concept can be particularly useful for employee relations purposes, both by avoiding the emotive term 'profit' and by focusing on wealth created rather than the surplus after payments to labour.

Cox examines the problems in preparing value added statements for both external and internal purposes, showing how a value added statement can be prepared from standard management accounts. Finally he discusses value added incentive schemes, a major application of this interesting concept.

Few management accountants have a mathematical background, and the advance of computers removes the need for much calculation effort. But mathematical techniques can be important in a number of areas of management accounting and even though computers can perform the actual calculations it is necessary for the management accountants to understand the process so that it can be applied intelligently. The final chapter of the book explores the use of mathematical models in three specific applications – purchasing, production and investment. Professor Groves warns of the limitations and drawbacks of the methods he explains, but emphasises that despite the constraints such techniques can be important in planning and control.

16

Organisational and behavioural issues

R.E.V. Groves

The subject of management accounting is commonly considered as a collection of techniques. This is perhaps unavoidable, given the environment of examination syllabuses in which management accountants learn their trade, and the pressures of business life that condition managers' perceptions of management accounting. However, it is insufficient to consider the subject as a collection of theories and techniques, as though it were a science being applied to inanimate objects.

Management accounting exists only in the context of organisations, which constitute collections of individuals rather than rigid hierarchies of positions represented in organisation charts. Management information systems are part of wider control systems designed with the intention of influencing the behaviour of people within the organisation.

Despite this context most books on management accounting focus on technical issues. This Handbook has ostensibly followed that pattern, although implicit in many of the chapters has been a recognition that the techniques must be considered within the fluid organisational environment in which they will have to operate. Similarly, most managers seem to recognise organisational and behavioural implications in the managerial process, while not necessarily stating them explicitly.

It is, however, important to consider these factors explicitly and that is the purpose of this chapter. Professor Groves emphasises that management accounting cannot satisfactorily be separated from its organisational context and goes on to consider the implications of this observation for the design of management information systems.

He briefly explains the development of management theory from the sterile approach of Scientific Management to the people-oriented views of the Participative Management school, and finally the less prescriptive Contingency theorists.

Taking the Contingency Theory position that no one management system can be prescribed for all organisations, Professor Groves then considers the factors which are likely to affect the design of a management accounting system. His contingency framework for management accounting aims to help managers and management accountants analyse existing systems and design new ones. It presents a number of major variables, grouped into contingent variables (which reflect the organisation's environment and organisation), organisational control networks (which define the nature of the control systems), and intervening variables (which reflect the crucial human element in the system).

Each of these variables is examined and Professor Groves explains how each has been found to be important in information system design. He concludes that research has produced what sometimes seem to be contradictory results, and is unlikely to define any simple or straightforward answers, but that it is essential to be aware of organisational and behavioural factors in designing management accounting systems.

Many texts on management accounting emphasise its technical procedures and mechanisms. This emphasis is manifested by setting out the rules for, and methods of, calculating the accounting information which it is hoped will aid managers in budgeting their resources, or controlling their staff. For example, the mechanisms for budget formulation and review are described at length and the reader is left in no doubt how to identify and measure variances from the targets formulated mechanically. Just as faithfully the computational methods necessary for the derivation of accounting information for use in decision making, such as in a make or buy situation, are explained clearly.

Unfortunately the detailed description and discussion of these techniques often does not mention the organisational, behavioural, and political processes that underlie the use of the techniques in the production of managerial information. This detachment of the technical processes from the environment in which they operate helps maintain the emphasis on the accounting procedures once readers attempt to practise what they have read. In reality it is not possible to unravel the organisational and technical aspects of budgeting because not only does the organisation's structure help form the budgetary process for a company, but also that same budgetary process has helped the structure of the organisation evolve over time.

A decision to market a new product could bring with it organisational changes such as a promotion of a salesman to product manager to oversee the new project's successful implementation, while the methods of selling also may require changes, including hiring additional sales personnel. In the technical accounting analysis that took place prior to that marketing decision it is doubtful if the organisational costs and benefits which accrued from that one decision would have been included.

Whichever aspect you take of management accounting (planning, control, or decision making) it is necessary to take a wider view of the aspect under consideration, because of the need to highlight the social, political, and economic structures as well as the technical procedures to arrive at the appropriate outcome. The budget, possibly the outcome of numerous arguments and debates involving all the appropriate personnel, or possibly the outcome of a dictat, is a reflection of the socio-economic and political structure of the organisation. A management accountant cannot exist on knowledge of technique alone.

Writing in 1979 Chandler and Daems felt that management accounting had developed primarily to enable activities in disparate and diverse organisations to be co-ordinated, so as to ensure that all sub-group performance was properly monitored whilst securing efficient allocation of funds to those sub-groups. However, management accounting should be viewed as part of the larger management information system which was for the benefit of all of the managers. It is therefore worth considering the three main theories of management which have developed since the turn of the century. Each theory in its way might provide some insight into which accounting techniques might be the most appropriate given the circumstances of a particular organisation.

SCIENTIFIC MANAGEMENT

The early theory of scientific management is based on the assumption that an individual's motivation is based on economic rewards and penalties, and that a person's goal is the maximisation of economic welfare. Taylor (1947) is thought of as the father figure of this approach.

Many of the accounting texts fit this model, suggesting that the accounting system is a 'goal allocation' device which permits management not just to select, divide and distribute its operating objectives throughout the firm, but to provide a control device aimed at identifying and correcting undesirable performance. There was a belief that there was sufficient certainty, rationality and knowledge within the system to permit accurate comparisons of results, enabling the identification of both the responsibility for performance and the ultimate benefits or costs of that performance. The accounting 'system' was felt to be neutral in its evaluation model – the system was assumed to be objective and thus personal bias was eliminated.

Within this theoretical framework the essence of management control is authority from above. Management accounting systems and techniques described in the management accounting texts and offered as prescriptions for success could easily be placed within the context of this model; for example, optimal production plans, stock models, investment strategies, formal systems for recording information such as standard costing, job or process costing. These are all impersonal techniques aimed at ensuring the achievement of the corporate goals of top management.

PARTICIPATIVE MODEL OF MANAGEMENT

The second model of management that has influenced thinking in management accounting is the participative model, or as Caplan (1966) called it, the behavioural approach.

Whereas the scientific model is based on formal systems and bureaucracy, the participative or behavioural model is based on the concept that organisations are coalitions of individuals. The assumptions are that as individuals are not mindless, though organisations are, they get together formally and informally. Through the co-ordination of these groups, and the individuals within them, the corporate objectives are set up and the entity managed.

This co-ordination comes about through the participative approach to the goal selection, planning, control and review. For example, Likert (1967) suggested the splitting up of organisations into smaller group structures so that they would provide greater support to the individuals who were its members. Thus, through the use of small groups, participation can be fostered. The small groups can be co-ordinated again in a participative way but without reducing the benefits of decentralised decision making. This is based on the idea that participative management is in the long-run interests of the entity (McGregor's theory X vs. theory Y; 1960). This is almost the antithesis of the bureaucratic formality of the scientific approach.

Under the participative approach the inclination is to try and obtain an organisational structure which allows for participation, and keeps as wide as possible both the individuals' and groups' autonomy and powers of discretion. This is not an easy task because, on the one hand there is the attempt to decentralise decision making as much as possible whilst on the other, co-ordination between these autonomous sub-groups is still needed so as to ensure that the corporate goals are achieved. So it is still necessary to have some of the trappings of bureaucracy such as rules, plans, etc. even though that could be considered scientific management! It is worth remembering that management accounting systems are part of a larger management information system (MIS) of an entity.

Formal management accounting systems based solely on the participative model of management are not well developed. Even those management accounting systems for decentralised ventures, which were intended to encourage departmental or divisional independence, still require flows of information back to Head Office and usually have rigid rules to help maintain both the system and Head Office's ultimate authority. It is in other parts of the information system where the participative approach has been tried usefully. Evidence would suggest that it can be used beneficially through informal information systems (Galbraith, 1973; Clancy and Collins, 1979) and in the budgeting process (Hofstede, 1968; Swieringa and Moncur, 1975).

CONTINGENCY MODEL OF MANAGEMENT

The fact that neither of those two theories provided the complete answer led to development of a contingency theory, which now will be described and discussed in some detail since it is believed that it is beneficial for management accountants to consider the issues highlighted. Consideration of these issues in a practical context can help accountant managers in the review or design of the accounting information system of which they are part.

The major premise of the contingency approach is that 'there is no one optimum type of management system' (Burns and Stalker, 1961, p. 125). Therefore the relevant management system for an organisation depends on a number of factors facing the specific firm. These factors include the socio-economic and political environment the firm is in, the technology of its products, its present organisational structure and so on. As Dermer (1977) says, when designing any planning and control system it should be 'situationally specific'.

Contingency theory, then, has moved towards an open systems approach to organisation theory, and away from the universalism of the scientific and participative models of management. This has led in the academic literature to an increased focus on effective system design so as to achieve specific organisation objectives (Bruns and Waterhouse, 1975; Gordon and Miller, 1976; Hayes, 1977; Otley, 1978; Lowe and Tinker, 1976; and Waterhouse and Tiessen, 1978, to name but some.) Practising management accountants would, in many instances, argue that that is how their accounting information system had been designed. But, many of those practising accountants might also be prepared to agree that their systems, though technically satisfactory, may not be organisationally or environmentally satisfactory. The normative appeal of the contingency theory is that it provides a framework for choosing between management theories and information system designs. So it is possible under certain circumstances for control to be best achieved by the use of the application of scientific management as is discussed later.

A contingency framework for management accounting

The organisation map of the accounting network of divisions, profit centres, cost centres, etc. highlights the roles that the financial planning mechanisms have to play, and have played, in the building of the corporate organisation. It is possible to try and present a framework for a contingency theory of management accounting. By setting out the framework it is hoped that the reader will gain an insight into the various variables that influence both the theoretical and practical formulations of management accounting information systems. At the same time some of the empirical research results will be described and interpreted.

In Figure 16.1 my views of contingency framework for management accounting are presented. This framework is based upon two pieces of work: one by Otley (1980) and the other by Likert and Bowers (1968). Otley suggested a 'minimum necessary contingency framework' whilst Likert and Bowers discussed the concept of intervening variables and their implications. The purpose of the framework is to help accountants explain the existing system that they have or to help determine a new system that they are trying to incorporate. It can show the different types of variables that will affect the design of the system under investigation. For example, the technology of the industry that the company is in, along with the economic and social environment that the company is working in, will have implications as will the existing organisational network. Notwithstanding all that, the system has to be made to work with the individuals who are presently working for the company and each individual has his or her own set of intervening variables. The primary causal relationships start from the contingent variables through organisational control packages and the intervening variables, these two sets being interactive since the intervening variables pertain to the individuals who make up the groups, sections, etc. which constitute the systems of the control packages. From the efforts of the individuals we get the output which the end result variables measure. Selection of the end result variables will be affected by both the contingent variables and the organisational control network in operation or to be introduced. The dynamic process continues through the feedback loops operating in the interactions both within the entity and between it and the

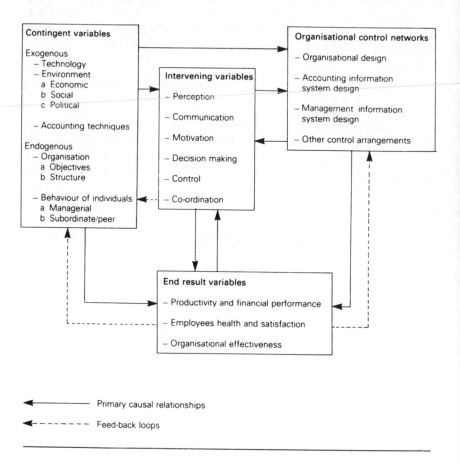

Primary causal relationships

Feed-back loops

Figure 16.1   Contingency framework for management accounting

external environment. Figure 16.1 is only the skeleton of the contingency approach to management accounting; it is now appropriate to put some flesh on it by explaining the elements in the framework and their implications for management accountants.

CONTINGENT VARIABLES

Each management accounting information system is an individual system in its own rights and when one looks at the behavioural aspects of each system this becomes very apparent. However, the scientific or participative theories were generalised theories which would not necessarily apply to some of the systems that can be found. For example, Otley's research in the coal industry on the manner in which budgetary information was used in evaluation of individuals conflicted with the findings of Hopwood's earlier work in a steel company. These alternative and conflicting findings are confusing if one wants to generate a general theory concerning evaluation styles of management. However, they just indicate how it is possible for different pieces of research to provide different explanations. This example is just one of many that can be found in the behavioural literature where researchers have shown how situational differences have brought about differences in the behavioural aspects of the system and in the processes that are used within it. The only generalised thing one can say then about the contingency theory is that there is no general theory concerning behavioural aspects of accounting information systems, unlike the suggestions propounded by the scientific or participative researchers.

It is therefore necessary in each situation to identify those variables that impact upon the system and to monitor and measure their effects. This will help explain the processes that one presently finds in a system or will help one explain the reasons why the system that is being proposed is being proposed. The framework in Figure 16.1 is set out with the idea that these are the main variables which researchers have found to have a bearing upon the design and explanation of systems. The systems are thus contingent upon the underlying variables found in the environment and which the system has to satisfy. The main contingent variables can be split into two groups: exogenous and endogenous. We shall deal the exogenous variables first since those tend to have the more major impact on accounting techniques used within an accounting information system.

Technology

It has long been known that production technology has influenced the accounting techniques used in assessing the results produced under different production technologies. For example, all one needs to do is to look down the chapter headings of the general management accounting texts to see the descriptions such as 'job costs', 'contract costing', 'process costing', 'contribution costing', etc. Yet it was not until 1965 that Woodward's work on organisation structures helped make people more aware of the link between organisational structure and the industrial technology of the company which was being organised. Woodward found that the better companies, in the three groups of technology that she identified, tended towards similarity of organisation and that there are also differences between the organisations found in the three groups. The three groups that she had investigated were unit/small batch manufacturers, large batch and mass production and processing companies.

In process costing the bulk of the costs are incurred jointly by a mix of products and may require considerable financial processing based on allocation rules which are not completely objective and probably will have been laid down by the accountant, another contingent variable. In job-costing situations the production measure is well defined. So this will only require a limited amount of allocation and processing, because the majority of the costs are due entirely to that specific job.

It is not just the accounting techniques that are influenced by the technology but also the financial control structure that is used. For example, the design of an information system could be effected by the variety of tasks that management had to undertake and the degree of knowledge of the task that management had. These results were propounded by Daft and MacIntosh (1978) which were in line with some findings of Piper (1978) who showed how different levels of complexity in technology would have a bearing on financial control structure that ought to be used. If the work is to be done efficiently and effectively, then Perrow (1967) suggested that the structure should be allied to the task involved because this would allow great co-ordination and control of work and so of necessity it would be related to the technology of the product and its manufacture or of the service that was being provided.

It would seem misguided to conclude that the application of scientific management and participative theories are no longer valid. They are still useable, but in specific contexts. Where there is little or only small changes in an organisation's technological environment then probably control is best exercised through the application of scientific management. Organisations that are mass-producing standard products using well-defined technology and preferably in an unchanging market could try to build similar stable organisations. Standard procedures, clearly defined lines of communication and responsibility could be used with the management performance being judged against consistent and well-defined standards. This need not deny the opportunity of representation and participation within the system, but changes within the system would not be frequent nor would they be the subject of continual review by management.

On the other hand, when the entity is involved in situations of high variety, where technological and economic conditions are unpredictable or even novel, then a very different kind of management system is appropriate. There is a need for an 'organic' system where creativity and commitment are crucial. If production is often faced with unexpected requests, either in terms of volume or types of product, or the product market is changing rapidly, or the technological base of the company is changing, then inflexibility and inability to react appropriately to change are likely if the system attempts to stick to rigid well-defined standards and processes. High technology companies such as those in the computer and micro-chip businesses and research organisations are examples that come to mind. It is hoped that by introducing a participative control system, increases in productivity, job commitment, and improvements in the quality of the job done should follow. Empirical results in this area have been somewhat contradictory, so it is difficult to generalise from them because of the difference in the underlying circumstances (Coch and French, 1948; Fleishman, 1965; French, Israel and As, 1960; Hofstede, 1968; Morse and Reimer, 1956; Vroom, 1960). Nevertheless, the consensus is that commitment both to the task and the organisation is enhanced, and that is important if the 'organic system is to succeed.

These comments indicate how neither the scientific nor the participatory approach are universally successful. Rather it is better to take the contingency approach so that the main task of management is to interpret the organisation's situation in terms of its predictability. It has been suggested by Lawrence and Lorsch (1967) that management should attempt to identify the rate of change over time of environmental conditions, the certainty of information concerning conditions at any point in time, and how fast the feedback is on the results of the decisions taken. Their view was that the greater the change rate, the more uncertain the conditions and the slower the feedback facing an organisation the greater the need to develop an organic organisation which would naturally be reflected in a similar style of accounting information system.

Environment

The latter paragraphs of the foregoing section show how difficult it is to isolate specific influences on both the organisation and the accounting information system. Certainly the economic, social and political environments faced by firms are different and changing over time, and have been shown to influence the choice of accounting systems used by the firms. Some managers and entities operate in very competitive environments while others have an easier time. Otley (1978) found that if a requisite feature of an accounting system was the accuracy of its budgets then different budget types and management styles were needed for the differing levels of competition faced by the organisations. Otley had researched a large entity with several physically separate operating units which were managed and treated as individual entities and faced very different trading conditions. He found that using a flexible type of budget provided the most accurate budget estimate in a liberal environment, but in a tough environment the most accurate estimate came from using a rigid style of use. Otley quite fairly suggested the need for further testing of this hypothesis.

Khandwalla's (1972) study had shown how different types of competition, price, product or changes in other elements of the marketing mix, had very different impacts on the use made of accounting controls within a manufacturing organisation.

Perhaps it goes without saying that the information system required by a small company of plastic injection moulders would be different from that needed by a large civil engineering concern, as in both instances the economic environment that firms in these industries face is changing and is bringing with it a need to reflect that change in the type of accounting controls used by the organisations. Companies are facing increased competition leading to the view that information must be more timely, more appropriate, and thus perhaps less accurate than say ten years ago. In addition, the introduction of computers has changed what was once infeasible to what is now common place. Again using civil engineering as an example, because of environmental pressures the time taken to prepare quotes is shorter than it was, the quotations are more precise and more competitive, which means possibly that margins are smaller. As soon as margins get pinched then companies feel the need for deeper and more frequent investigation of actual results as compared to forecasts, as well as the systematic and ongoing review of methods used in the everyday operations for the selection of the most cost effective way of dealing with problems as and when they arise. All these elements bring with them considerable changes in accounting information systems, the personnel who are working in them and the techniques that are being used by them.

The social and political aspects of the external environment also affect the budgetary style, for example it may be quite in order to run a corporate unit at a loss in one or more geographical regions because it is politically and socially expedient. Take the operation of unprofitable branch lines by British Rail or 'uneconomic' coal mines by the National Coal Board. The accounting information system used, and the management actions with its outputs must ensure that all geographical regions, and thus all pits within each region, are trying to be as efficient and effective as possible in their operations. Nevertheless, if the political masters allow for the continued running of uneconomic pits because the social and political consequences of the alternative are too great to contemplate, then the entity has to get on and manage accordingly.

In 1985 considerable publicity was given to the fact that the National Coal Board were using accounting information to define uneconomic pits and thus using this information in the decision as to whether or not to close such pits. There was some considerable discussion both in general articles and published reports as to whether or not the NCB were using the correct information in their management decision taking. It could be argued that their selection of indicators were politically inspired. Whether this be true or not, it is not for this author to judge, but it is quite often the case that corporate politics play a significant role in the selection of accounting indicators, which are used for judging the staff within the company. There are without doubt numerous anecdotes of indicators which favour one division over another division in a company and which were incorporated into the formal assessment so as to help boost the standing and stature of the manager of the first division. The selection of accounting variables for the assessment profile could have been due to the political influence of that manager. Thus accounting techniques become one of the contingent variables one has to look at when trying to decide on the system to be incorporated.

Accounting techniques

There are numerous alternative accounting techniques that a manager can use within the accounting information system to measure, analyse, record or report an event. They learn some of the accounting techniques such as how to pad out budget estimates ('budget slack'), so as to provide leeway during budget negotiations, or in safe-guarding potential under-estimates of expenditures. Similarly, through the use of provisions they learn how to provide for, so called, 'anticipated' expenditure in order to increase 'actual' expenditure for a period, or the reverse, to relinquish provisions for expenditure no longer required so as to improve the net profit position. For some managers, their actions can be thought of as part of the game of budgetary control (Hofstede, 1968).

Organisations have to decide whether to use historical cost accounting or current cost accounting as the basis for their budgets. They have to select a method to value inventory, allocate overheads, write off depreciation and so on. It is a moot point whether the use of one accounting method as opposed to another will produce different management decisions, though it is certainly true that absorption cost accounts present different pictures from profit and loss accounts based on variable costs. For example, head office may require subsidiary companies to account for stock and WIP using SSAP 9 in their monthly accounts, which for a manufacturing subsidiary is somewhat similar to an absorption cost approach and which can have a smoothing effect on the monthly profit figures. If other members of the group are service companies or factors, then they will not have any stock or WIP whose value is dependent on production levels and thus their reports will be sales based as in a variable cost based profit and loss account. Comparisons between subsidiaries of the two different types would be invidious. The studies by Dyckman (1964), Bruns (1965) and Jensen (1966) were not at all conclusive.

Amigoni (1978) tried to assess the appropriateness of a range of accounting control tools, including ratio analysis, financial simulation models as well as financial accounting. He concluded that, by adding new accounting tools to those already in use, an organisation can adapt to the increasing structural complexity of the entity in its relations with the environment, but if there is increasing disturbance and discontinuities in the environment the old tools cannot continue in use and must be replaced by new ones. But he added that there was a dearth of accounting tools that might be useful when organisations are faced with very complex situations and high levels of environmental discontinuity.

Organisation – objectives

Turning inwards now to those contingent variables that influence the accounting information system. The objectives of the organisation are obviously very important in the formulation of an accounting information system as well as being the target for comparison when checking organisation effectiveness. Not-for-profit organisations have different needs from profit dominated entities, while public sector organisations may have a different set of objectives from those in the private sector. The budget which is a detailed plan of the enterprise's future course of action should reflect, develop and enshrine the corporate objectives. The reflection of the objectives in the budget will be dependent upon the belief in these objectives by the organisation members as well as the political strength of those members. Debate and deliberation will have taken place to produce both the objectives and the budget, and the results will arise out of the political processes that permeate organisational life as well as the particular structure of the organisation.

Pendlebury (1986) has shown how local authorities in preparing their budgets have their objectives dominated by the political pressures of their locally elected members. They also have their budgets affected by the requirements of the central government grant and aid. The process of preparing the budget in spite of the increased pressures for spending cuts has not changed particularly over the past five years so the organisation that is being used in the finance department remains unchanged. With the role of a budget not being quite the same as that in the private sector, Pendlebury shows that the size of the authority can have an affect on the organisational structure and the role that the budget plays in the managerial process of the spending departments. The smaller authorities tend to use the budget more as a sanctions or administrative list of money that can be spent. Then when the departments wish to spend some money they can check whether it has been sanctioned by the budget, something they discover by or through conversations with the finance officer, who will then give them the go-ahead, if that be the case. Thus the finance officer is able to keep a very close eye on the major items of expenditure of each of the spending departments, and his role is not that of adviser but more of an auditor of spending. The larger authorities, partially because they have more revenue earning facilities such as leisure services, are now using budgets more as a management tool.

Organisation – structure

The structure of an organisation and its information system are usually entwined. It is often stated that the structure should be organised into responsibility centres, that is the command of an individual should be only over those items for which he or she is held responsible and the financial analysis of an individual's activities should only be based upon the costs, revenues and investments, wherever appropriate, over which the individual has control. For example, in company with various divisions it has been recommended that the company be split into these various divisions and control of each division be handed to a manager who will then be held responsible for the activities of that said division. His performance and that of the division will be monitored with care. Thus if the division is a manufacturing division with no external markets for its products the manager will only be assessed upon the costs that he has control over other than revenues. If he is given responsibility for the purchase of assets then he should be monitored on the performance of those assets in one way or another. Thus any budgetary system or any total information system should take these points into account. Bruns and Waterhouse (1975) produced evidence that the budget related behaviour of a manager depended upon certain aspects of the organisation structure such as the amount of autonomy or centralisation, or the degree to which the activities over which he has control are structured. Lip service is generally paid to the concept of decentralisation on the grounds that organisations so structured provide the managers of these subdivisions the opportunity to behave as if they were masters in command of their own ship and thus gaining greater satisfaction from their jobs. This in turn is perceived to generate improved performance from management. Again in turn the accounting information system has to be designed to satisfy that organisational structure, though there have been long debates in the accounting literature as to what form some of the reporting mechanisms should take. For example, whether divisional performance should be measured through the use of return of investment or residual income. Unfortunately there is no hard evidence to support the use of one in preference to the other, only the conceptual arguments put forward by the various protagonists (see Chapter 11).

There have been two conflicting pieces of work by Hopwood (1972) and Otley (1978) which were investigating the effect of different styles of management evaluation. Hopwood's study was based in an American integrated steel works which was split into cost centres which had considerable interdependence, whilst Otley's study was based in the English coal mining industry where the units were virtually independent of each other and were profit centres. Both studies looked at different styles of subordinate evaluation through the use of accounting information and found that there were different conclusions. For example, Hopwood concluded that in his environment those managers with a short-term perspective were associated with colleagues who would bring about the manipulation of accounting data, had poor relationships with their peers, subordinates, incorporated dysfunctional behaviour in their operations, and where there was considerable job-related tension. On the other hand, Otley found managers with the same evaluation style where these particular effects did not occur, in fact good performance was the outcome of the rigid short-term style of management. This was due to the highly competitive nature of the environment in which those specific managers were operating.

This emphasises the dangers of generalising from one or two pieces of work. It is necessary to investigate the number of variables that will impinge upon the information system before deciding upon the particular form that should be used.

Behaviour of individuals

The financial practices cannot operate in isolation of the management practices if they are to be effective. For example, the style of managerial leadership influences the organisational climate which in turn affects the subordinate and peer relationships (Likert, 1967; Hopwood, 1972). Managers with high authoritarian needs responded less positively to a system set up for high levels of participation than did managers with low authoritarian needs, according to Vroom (1960) though Tosi (1978) disputes that. How can the performance and motivation of subordinates be affected?

House (1971) argued that a leader should attempt the increase of the personal pay-off to the subordinate from working in his department. The leader could try to simplify the subordinates job by reducing or removing the obstacles that lie ahead, or by increasing the opportunities for personal satisfaction. Should the leader's behaviour produce positive motivational responses, the subordinate's view of his role will be less ambiguous. The leader's behaviour will change over time depending on whether he or she is dealing with a 'raw recruit', an 'old faithful', or a new job or activity that the department has been given, and so on. Similarly the behaviour patterns of the subordinates, being peers in the organisations, will be affected by the intervening variables and the design of the organisation.

There is a feedback loop from the organisational control networks through the intervening variables to the contingent variables. The patterns of organisational segmentation and the practices of regular performance reporting and evaluation are some of the mechanisms within the networks which will be perceived and evaluated and thus communicated back to the individuals and the managers in the organisation. Perhaps the feedback will be through some of the end result variables such as employee satisfaction and organisational effectiveness. This in turn will influence the style and patterns of leadership and behaviour in the organisation.

INTERVENING VARIABLES

Individuals respond to cues and stimuli, and their actions or responses are based on their perceptions of these cues and stimuli. In a work environment the budget itself as well as the budgetary process are sets of stimuli. The perceptions are affected by the environment, the contingent variables, and take into account the communication mode used as well as the individual's motivation in a particular decision-making or control situation. From this perception the individual provides a particular response. So the response will have been influenced by the combined interaction of all the factors mentioned above plus others not mentioned. The budget and the budgetary process will produce cues and stimuli which will affect the perceptions of the individuals who are working within the process and needing the information from an accounting information system. Clearly then it would be helpful to try and identify what these stimuli and cues are likely to be so that they can be monitored and measured in studies so as to help accountants when they are attempting to build new information systems.

Argyris (1952) highlighted some of these relationships in his anecdotal study. Swieringa and Moncur (1975), and Irvine and Brennan (1979) went further, identifying that individuals perceived something called budget pressure which affects their behaviour on the job. They defined budget pressure as the consequence of the perception by a person of the frequency of stimuli coming directly or indirectly from budgeting activities. The major form of pressure was of a general nature, coming from general discussions of budget matters, next most important was pressure from higher management, next was pressure from active involvement in supervision, and finally the pressure from investigation and control of budget variances. Each of these are general descriptions of pressures based on a set of individual stimuli. The more frequently these stimuli occurred the greater the perceived pressure.

These stimuli are such things as a person's immediate supervisor talking to him about budget variances, or direct action by people other than the person and his supervisor to correct budget variances, or when his supervisor has personally checked on matters related to the ability of the man's department to perform as budgeted, and so on. Naturally enough an individual's perceptions of stimuli such as these affect his performance, the design and continued operation of the organisational control networks, as well as the feeding back and effects on the contingent variables.

It is appropriate at this stage to mention studies on how humans process information, generally known as HIP, human information processing. A good review of literature can be found in Libby and Lewis (1977). To date the research has been undertaken in unrealistic circumstances. However, it has shown that individuals in their information processing tend to use simplifying heuristics rather than deal with the whole mass of information that is probably available to them. This obviously has implications concerning the quantity and quality of information that should be processed in any one system and dealt with by any one individual.

Turning to the motivational levels of individuals, it has been shown how these vary both at the amount of what is desirable and at the level of what can be achieved. Stedry (1960, 1962), Stedry and Kay (1966), Locke (1968) and Likert (1967) all found that up to a point setting higher goals or aspirations led to the achievement of higher targets, but as Stedry and Kay (1966) and Hofstede (1967) pointed out there is a perceived level of difficulty above which an individual will tend to give up. This 'switch-off point' obviously depends on the work environment as well as the individual. Combining individuals into an organisation brings together their different interests, motivations, and perspectives of life, and as objectives or goals may not always be provided, but rather emerge through the organisational interactions, it is often helpful to try and categorise the decision-making process so as to provide guidance in the design of the organisation control networks.

ORGANISATION CONTROL NETWORKS

The goals that individuals are working towards in an organisation will have been arrived at after considerable debate and possibly discord, so that within the entity there may be some uncertainty over the objectives as to whether or not they are feasible and whether or not they are acceptable. The greater the uncertainty in the external environment, and also within the organisation, the greater the uncertainty over the objectives. Similarly, there is a scale of uncertainty over the consequences of the actions prescribed to achieve the objectives.

By drawing up a matrix it is possible to identify the decision-making processes for the different combinations of uncertainty levels for objectives and uncertainty levels for the consequences of the prescribed actions. Earl and Hopwood (1980) used the theories of Thompson and Tuden (1959) to devise a simple 2 × 2 matrix. On the one axis they had High and Low uncertainty of objectives and on the other axis they had High and Low uncertainty for the action consequences that had been prescribed to achieve those objectives. From the four combinations it was possible to derive the general nature of the type of information and control system that is necessary for the organisation under that combination of circumstances.

For example, in a relatively stable environment where both objectives and the action consequences necessary to achieve those objectives are known with reasonable certainty, then the recommended decision would probably be based on a computation. Examples of this would be stock control models, credit control routines, or linear programming models used in a refinery for the allocation of the blending or refining. Effectively, these are a form of answer machines because they can easily and accurately compute the consequences of the actions and decide whether or not the goals that have been set can be achieved. Thus, here, the information system that would be set up would be a relatively straight forward one not requiring any participation between individuals but rather just a number of inputs derived from the normal data collection process of the organisation. Naturally, as the amount of uncertainty over either the objectives or the consequences increase then the process has to become more complex. For example, if there is some uncertainty about the required objectives and also a small amount of uncertainty of the consequences, then as the results of alternative actions are reasonably clear it becomes a political process as to which alternative is chosen. Thus the information system has to provide possible solutions for each of the scenarios that would achieve the possible objectives. In the end the decision will be taken by compromise and thus the political process of achieving it will be extremely important.

For many companies the objectives are relatively certain but there is considerable uncertainty concerning the outcomes of the decisions that they take and therefore the decision is based upon a considered judgement. This means that the information system has got to provide answers to the demands of the decision makers. For example, in a credit control system where the objective is to obtain payment by debtors as soon as possible or certainly not later than 90 days, there are times when a judgement has to be taken as to whether or not a solicitor's letter is sent after two months because further information is known about the customer. Were the customer to receive the solicitor's note at this stage of the trading cycle then it is possible that a valuable customer could be lost for a long time. Thus here a system should not only be informing the decision taker of the time a debt has been outstanding, but also the state of credit that the customer is in, and whether any of the debt is in dispute. The system should also be able to provide historical information of the payments profile that has occurred in the past so that any previous disputes or outstanding payments etc. can be brought to the notice of the decision taker.

In a situation where there is some uncertainty of outcome but reasonable certainty of desired objectives, then it is quite possible that companies will be preparing a series of flexed budgets rather than a single budget. However, this will obviously depend upon the environmental circumstances within the company.

Where bargaining is the process of arriving at a decision, then there is a need for information ammunition to help the participants. The management accounting mechanism should be able to provide useful information to be able to bargain effectively. Likewise where decision making is made via the judgemental mode then the use of probability and risk analysis in a budgetary context could be introduced since though there is relative certainty concerning the objectives there is considerable uncertainty concerning the consequences.

The building up of budgetary control processes, as well as other management accounting mechanisms, do help to cement relationships and reduce organisational uncertainty, though it tends to be in a one-way direction – namely downwards, because that is the direction of the power and the visibility. The subordinates do not get much opportunity to review the leader and this tends to reinforce the centralised co-ordination of activities.

Where the decision making is predominantly of an inspirational nature, the information system will probably be geared towards producing information that helps the managers rationalise their decisions.

From this it is possible to see that the technical practices of budgeting etc. can be adapted to meet the circumstances. The uses and sources of budgetary control and management accounting are diverse and complex, though this is not fully apparent until attempts to probe the underlying organisational processes are made. Wildavsky (1974) and Pendlebury (1986) are good sources of information on insights into the budgetary practices in public organisations. See also

Rosenberg, Tomkins and Day (1980) for further insights into specific aspects of this.

END RESULT VARIABLES

The standard performance measures used in organisations have tended to be financial ones – the outputs of the budget control process, e.g. profit, return on capital etc. However, it is worth questioning whether these measures are appropriate in monitoring the organisation's effectiveness in achieving its goals. Profit and return on capital are not related to the satisfaction of human needs, except in a very narrow and restricted sense, that of shareholders whose cash income is dependent on the firms' dividends for their own survival.

One thing is clear from what has been said earlier in this chapter, which is, that during the evaluation of members of an organisation they will feel pressure and one should be attempting to select end result variables that help minimise that pressure. In addition, the end result variables should help to achieve the task that the personnel are trying to achieve. For example, budgeting information should help them in their control of whatever it is they are managers of. Similarly, any decisions that have to be taken will be serviced by pertinent information. A further point that has been to borne in mind is that during the human processing of information an individual does not absorb more than the limited number of variables and so the selection of what is appropriate is crucial since there is no point in a system presenting information that will not be used. Likewise, one should never forget that the information that you are presenting as measuring a certain thing actually does do what it purports to do. For example, the profit of a division should not be struck after the arbitrary head office charge has been included if one is trying to assess the effectiveness of the divisional manager in his or her role.

The question of who the managers are working for will not be debated here, but obviously the answers will be pertinent to the selection of the output variables. Obviously what is important here is that the end result variables must measure what they purport to measure, whether it be the physical output of a production process, the financial return from a department, the profits generated through a manager's division, etc. By reviewing the needs of the system, that is whether to measure an individual or an entity, it is possible to then move on to reviewing financial and nonfinancial measures which for the group of individuals and their role playing needs will be appropriate, but which cannot be listed here since they are far too numerous and are once again as Dermer says 'situational specific'.

CONCLUSIONS

Building an accounting information system is a considerable and dangerous task. It is considerable because of its size and complexity, and dangerous because of the effects on the organisation and its individuals, that a system may have once erected. Hopefully the reader is by now aware of the complex relationships between the practices of budgeting, financial planning and control and the organisation. The budgetary process of an enterprise may have been introduced in order to enhance economic efficiency of that entity, but its functions will probably ensure the creation of particular patterns of political and social as well as economic power. This budgetary process may reinforce and legitimise the present organisation practices, which may or may not be a good thing.

What I have tried to do in this chapter is to indicate some of the behavioural problem areas and influences that can help managers identify what is happening in their existing systems and at the same time help those who wish to try and install other systems. It is hoped that it will bring a greater awareness of the behavioural problems involved in accounting information systems. Hopefully it has also pointed out the need to use the research findings of others but only where they are applicable to the situation in which the manager finds himself.

This uncertainty concerning the benefits of changing organisational practises through the introduction of financial planning or other means highlights the need for much more research in this area. There is a need to appreciate that any probing is unlikely to produce simple or straightforward answers, nor are they likely to remain the same over the passage of time. This should neither deter the continued attempts to improve the accounting information systems presently operating nor the building of systems about to be incorporated. One way improvements can occur is through the introduction of an appreciation of the organisational and behavioural implications of the financial craft to the accountant.

REFERENCES AND FURTHER READING

Amigoni, F., 'Planning Management Control Systems', *Journal of Business Finance and Accounting*, 1978, pp. 279-291.

Ansari, S. L., 'An Integrated Approach to Control System Design', *Accounting Organisations and Society*, 2.2, 1977, pp. 101-112.

Anthony, R.N., *Planning and Control Systems: A Framework for Analysis*, Cambridge, MA: Harvard Business School, 1965.

Argyris, C., *The Impact of Budgets on People*, Controllership Foundation, 1952.

Argyris, C., 'Organizational Learning and Management Information Systems', *Accounting, Organizations and Society*, 1977.

Banbury, J., and Nahapiet, J.E., 'Towards a Framework for the Study of the Antecedents and Consequences of Information Systems in Organisations', *Accounting, Organisations and Society*, 1979, pp. 163-177.

Baumler, J.V., 'Defined Criteria of Performance in Organizational Control', *Administrative Science Quarterly*, September, 1971.

Berry, A.T., and Otley, D.T., 'The Aggregation of Estimates in Hierarchical Organizations', *Journal of Management Studies*, May 1975.

Boland, R., 'Control, Causality and Information System Requirements', *Accounting, Organizations and Society*, 1979.

Bonini, C.P., *Simulation of the Information and Decisions Systems in the Firm*, Englewood Cliffs, N.J.: Prentice-Hall, 1963.

Bruns, W.J., 'Inventory Valuation and Management Decisions', *Accounting Review*, April, 1965, pp.354-357.

Bruns, W.S. and Waterhouse, J.H., 'Budgetary Control and Organization Structure', *Journal of Accounting Research*, 1975.

Burchell, S., Clubb, C., Hopwood, A., Hughes, J., and Nahapiet, J., 'The Role of Accounting in Organizations and Society', *Accounting, Organizations and Society*, 1980.

Burns, T., and Stalker, G., *The Management of Innovation*, London: Tavistock, 1961.

Caplan, E.H., 'Behavioural Assumptions of Management Accounting', *Accounting Review*, July 1966, pp. 496-509.

Chandler, A., and Daems, H., 'Administrative Co-ordination, Allocation and Monitoring: A Comparative Analysis of the Emergence of Accounting and Organization in the USA and Europe', *Accounting, Organizations and Society*, 1979.

Cherns, A.B., 'Can Behavioural Science Help Design Organizations?', *Organizational Dynamics*, 1977.

Cherns, A.B., 'Alienation and Accountancy', *Accounting Organizations and Society*, 1978.

Child, J., 'Organizational Structure, Environment and Performance – The Role of Strategic Choice', *Sociology*, 1972.

Child, J., 'Management and Organizational Factors Associated with Company Performance – Part I', *Journal of Management Studies*, 1974.

Child, J., 'Managerial and Organizational Factors Associated with Company Performance – Part II', *Journal of Management Studies*, 1975.

Clancy, D. and Collins, F., 'Informal Accounting Information Systems: Some Tentative Findings', *Accounting, Organizations and Society*, 1979.

Coch, L. and French, J.R.P., 'Overcoming Resistance to Change', *Human Relations*, vol. 1, no. 4, October 1948, pp. 512-532.

Cooper, D., 'A Social and Organisation View of Management Accounting' in *Essays in British Accounting Research*, (ed.) Bromwich M. and Hopwood. A.G., London: Pitman, 1981, pp. 178-205.

Daft, R.L., and MacIntosh, N.B., 'A New Approach to Design and Use of Management Information', *California Management Review*, 21, Fall 1978, pp. 82-92.

De Coster, D.T., 'An Intuitive Framework for Empirical Research in Participative Budgeting', in Previts, G.J. (ed.), *Accounting Research Convocation*, Alabama: University of Alabama, 1976.

Demski, J., and Feltham, G., 'Economic Incentives in Budgetary Control Systems', *Accounting Review*, April 1978.

Dermer, J., *Management Planning and Control Systems*, Homewood, IL: Irwin, 1977.

Dyckman, T.R., 'On the Investment Decision', *Accounting Review*, April, 1964, pp. 285-295.

Dyckman, T.R., 'The Effects of Alternative Accounting Techniques on Certain Management Decisions', *Journal of Accounting Research*, Autumn 1964, pp. 91-107.

Earl, M.J., and Hopwood, A.G., 'From Management Information to Information Management', in *The Information Systems Environment*, Lucas, Land, Lincoln, Sapper (eds), Amsterdam: North Holland, 1980, pp. 3-13.

Emmanuel, C., and Otley, D., '*Accounting for Management Control*', Wokingham: Van Nostrand Reinhold (UK), 1985.

French, J.R.P., Israel, J. and As, D., 'An Experiment on Participation in a Norwegian Factory', *Human Relations*, vol. 13, no. 1, February 1960, pp. 1-13.

Fleishman, E.A., 'Attitude Versus Skill Factors in Work Group Productivity', *Personnel Psychology*, vol. 18, no. 3, 1965, pp. 253-266.

Galbraith, J., *Designing Complex Organizations*, Reading, MA: Addison-Wesley, 1977.

Galbraith, J., *Organisation Design*, Reading, MA: Addison-Wesley, 1977.

Gambling, T., 'Magic Accounting and Morale', *Accounting, Organizations and Society*, 1977.

Gordon, L.A., and Miller, D., 'A Contingency Framework for the Design of Accounting Information Systems', *Accounting, Organizations and Society*, 1976.

Habermas, J., *Towards a Rational Society*, London: Heinemann Educational Books, 1971.

Hayes, D., 'The Contingency Theory of Management Accounting', *Accounting Review*, 1977.

Hofstede, G.H., *The Game of Budget Control*, Assen: Van Gorcum, 1968.

Hopwood, A.G., 'An Empirical Study of the Role of Accounting Data in Performance Evaluation', *Empirical Research in Accounting, Supplement to Journal of Accounting Research*, 1972, pp. 156-182.

Hopwood, A.G., Accounting and Human Behaviour, *Accountancy Age*, 1974.

Hopwood, A.G., 'Towards an Organizational Perspective for the Study of Accounting and Information Systems', *Accounting, Organizations and Society*, 1978.

House, R.J., 'A Path Goal Theory of Leader Effectiveness', *Administrative Science Quarterly*, Sept. 1971, pp. 321-328.

Irvine, V.B. and Brennan, G.P., 'The Components of Budget Pressure', *Cost and Management*, July-Aug. 1979, pp. 16-22.

Jensen, R.E., 'An Experimental Design for a Study of Effects of Accounting Variations in Decision-making', *Journal of Accounting Research*, Autumn 1966 pp. 224-238.

Khandwalla, P.N., 'The Effect of Different Types of Competition on the Use of Management Controls', *Journal of Accounting Research*, Autumn 1972, pp. 275-285.

Lawrence, P.R., and Lorsch, J., *Organization and Environment*, Division of Research, Cambridge, MA: Harvard Business School, 1967.

Libby, R., and Lewis, B.L., 'Human Information Processing Research in Accounting: The State of the Art', *Accounting, Organization and Society*, 1977, pp. 245-268.

Likert, R., *The Human Organization*, New York: McGraw-Hill, 1967.

Likert, R., and Bowers, D.G., 'Organizational Theory and Human Resource Accounting', *American Psychologist*, September, 1968, pp. 585-592.

Livingstone, J.L. (ed.), *Managerial Accounting: The Behavioural Foundations*, Columbus, OH: Grid, 1975.

Locke, E.A., 'Toward a Theory of Task Motivation and Incentives', *Organizational Behaviour and Human Performance*, vol. 3, no. 2, Oct. 1968, pp. 157-189.

Lowe, E.A., and Shaw, R.W., 'An Analysis of Managerial Biasing: Evidence from a Company's Budgeting Process', *Journal of Management Studies*, 1968.

Lowe, E.A., and Shaw, R.W., 'The Accuracy of Short Term Business Forecasting: An Analysis of a Firm's Sales Budgeting', *Journal of Industrial Economics*, 1970.

Lowe, E.A., and Tinker, A.M., 'The Architecture of Requisite Variety', Part 1 and 2, *Kybernetes*, 1976.

March, J.G., and Simon, H.A., *Organisations*, New York: Wiley, 1958.

McGregor, D., *The Human Side of Enterprise*, New York: McGraw-Hill, 1960.

Morse, N. and Reimer, E., 'The Experimental Change of a Major Organizational Variable', *Journal of Abnormal and Social Psychology*, vol. 52, 1956, pp. 120-129.

Otley, D.T., 'Budget Use and Managerial Performance', *Journal of Accounting Research*, Spring 1978.

Otley, D.T., 'The Contingency Theory of Management Accounting: Achievement and Prognosis', *Accounting Organizations and Society*, vol. 5, no. 4, 1980, pp. 413-28.

Otley, D.T. and Berry, A.J., 'Control, Organisation and Accounting', *Accounting Organizations and Society*, 1981.

Pendlebury, M.W., '*An Investigation into the Role and Nature of Management Accounting in Local Government in England and Wales*, unpublished PhD, Cardiff: UWIST, 1986.

Perrow, C., 'A Framework for the Comparative Analysis of Organisations', *American Sociological Review*, 1967, pp. 194-208.

Piper, J., 'Determinants of Financial Control Systems for Multiple Retailers – Some Case Study Evidence', unpublished paper, University of Loughborough, 1978.

Rosenberg, D., Tomkins, C., and Day, P., 'The Accountant in a Social Service Department: Values and Interpretations of Work Role', Working Paper, University of Bath, 1980.

Sathe, V., 'Contingency Theory of Organizational Structure', in Livingstone, J.L., (ed.), *op. cit.*, 1975.

Stedry, A.C., *Budget Control and Cost Behaviour*, Englewood Cliffs, N.J.: Prentice-Hall, 1960.

Stedry, A.C., 'Aspiration Levels, Attitudes and Performance in a Loal-Oriented Situation', *Industrial Management Review*, vol. 3, no. 2, 1962, pp. 60-76.

Stedry, A.C., and Kay, E., 'The Effects of Goal Difficulty on Performance', *Behavioural Science*, 1966.

Swieringa, R.J., and Moncur, R.H., *Some Effects of Participative Budgets on Managerial Behaviour*, New York: National Association of Accountants, 1975.

Taylor, F.W., *The Principles of Scientific Management*, New York: Harper & Row, 1947.

Thompson, J.D., and Tuden, A., 'Strategies, Structures and Processes of Organisational decision', in J.D. Thompson et al. (eds) *Comparative Studies in Administration*, Pittsburgh, PA: University of Pittsburgh Press, 1959.

Thompson, J.D., *Organizations in Action*, New York: McGraw-Hill, 1967.

Tosi, H., 'A Re-examination of Personality as a Determinant of the Effects of Participation', *Personnel Psychology*, vol. 23, 1978, pp. 91-99.

Tosi, H., and Carroll, S., 'Some Factors Affecting the Success of Management by Objectives', *Journal of Management Studies*, vol. 7, 1970, pp. 209-223.

Vroom, V., *Some Personality Determinants of the Effects of Participation*, Englewood Cliffs, N.J.: Prentice-Hall, 1960.

Waterhouse, J. and Tiessen, P., 'A Contingency Framework for Management Accounting Systems Research', *Accounting, Organizations and Society*, 1978.

Waterhouse, J. and Tiessen, P., 'The Contingency Theory of Management Accounting: A Comment', *Accounting Review*, April, 1978.

Watson, D., 'Contingency Formulations of Organizational Structure: Implications for Managerial Accounting' in Livingstone J.L. (ed.), *op. cit.*, 1975.

Watson, D., and Baumler, J., 'Transfer Pricing: A Behavioural Context', *Accounting Review*, October, 1975.

Wildavsky, A., *The Politics of the Budgetary Process*, Boston, MA: Little Brown, 1974.

Wood, S., 'A Reappraisal of the Contingency Approach to Organization', *Journal of Management Studies*, October 1979, pp. 334-354.

Woodward, J., *Industrial Organization: Theory and Practice*, Oxford: Oxford University Press, 1965.

17

Pricing

John Sizer

Management accounting information is used in pricing decisions in many companies, but it is not always used constructively or appropriately. In this chapter Professor Sizer shows how management accountants can play a major part in the pricing decision by providing relevant information about cost–volume–profit relationships.

Cost–volume–profit relationships are not the only aspect of pricing, but they are important, and an area where the management accountant can play an significant role. Nor should it be forgotten that pricing is only one aspect of the marketing mix, but as Professor Sizer shows, CVP analysis can help product managers juggle the various elements of the marketing mix.

The first part of this chapter shows how a profit–volume chart can be used to map a product contribution curve. Such a curve combines the impact of different price levels on total contribution with demand estimates for the product. The result is a contribution curve showing the product contribution at various price levels, which can be used to develop a marketing strategy. There are of course severe difficulties in estimating the demand/price relationships in most practical circumstances. But estimates can be made and useful conclusions drawn about possible trade-offs. As Professor Sizer observes, weighing odds is an intrinsic part of management, and analysis such as this merely formalises that process.

He goes on to show how this approach can be used in practice, even where a company has insufficient market power to be a price maker. A case study illustrates the potential of contribution graphs in identifying how different aspects of the marketing mix might be most usefully manipulated to maximise each product's profitability.

The final section of the chapter considers the impact of inflation. Pricing decisions are clearly more important in times of high inflation and management are faced with difficult decisions about how much increased cost can be passed on in higher prices. Cost–volume–profit analysis can therefore be an especially useful tool in such circumstances.

It will be recognised that in many multi-product, multi-market companies, pricing is not simply a process of setting figures at which a company's products are offered to customers, but rather it is part of a broad and complex field which also embraces problems of determining characteristics of products to be sold, segmenting markets, choosing sales promotion methods, determining channels of distribution and obtaining a satisfactory volume of business. This chapter concentrates on cost–volume–profit analysis aspects of selling price decisions. It starts with a simplified example and moves towards the complexities of the real world. Inevitably, in a single chapter all these complexities cannot be considered fully. The author has examined elsewhere (Sizer, 1972 and 1979) the relationship between price and non-price variables in the marketing mix, and (Sizer, 1981) the wider subject of pricing policy in inflationary conditions.

A SIMPLIFIED EXAMPLE

When considering a selling price decision or a decision concerning the non-price variables in the marketing mix, the product and marketing managers should have sufficient understanding of the relevant cost and revenue concepts to be able to ask the management accountant the right questions and evaluate the significance of his answers. Provided assumptions are clearly stated, product profit–volume charts can be employed effectively to explore both the relevant cost and revenue concepts and the cost–volume–profit relationships.

Let us consider a simple example. It is assumed that the company seeks to fix its prices so as to maximise the total contribution to fixed costs and profit. Unless the manufacturer's products compete directly with each other, this objective is achieved by the price maker considering each product in isolation and fixing its price in each market in which the product is offered at a level which is calculated to maximise the total contribution in that market.

The Bang Bang Manufacturing Company is reviewing the selling price of Product X, a consumer durable, and, after carrying out extensive market research, has estimated the probable annual demands for the product at varying prices shown in Table 17.1. It is es-

Table 17.1
Product X: price/demand schedule

Price per unit	Estimated annual demand
£17.00	8 000
£17.50	7 800
£18.00	7 600
£18.50	7 200
£19.00	6 600
£19.50	5 700
£20.00	4 200

timated that each of these demands can be manufactured and marketed with existing capacity. The forecast average variable cost per unit over the relevant output range is constant at £12 per unit, in other words marginal cost equals average variable cost. The separable fixed costs are £25 000, that is the fixed costs associated with the product (such as the product manager's salary) as opposed to the common fixed costs (such as the managing director's salary). The calculation of the price which will make the greatest contribution towards fixed costs and profit is shown in Table 17.2, and it will be noted that the greatest profit improvement would result from raising the selling price of Product X from its existing level of £18 to £18.50, giving a direct product profit of £21 800 as against £20 600 at present.
The information in Table 17.2 is presented in Figure 17.1 in the

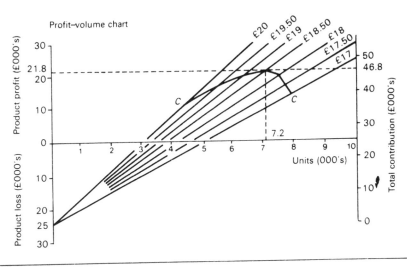

Figure 17.1   Product X: product profit – volume chart

Table 17.2
Product X: review of alternative selling prices

	£	£	£	£	£	£	£
Selling price	17.00	17.50	18.00	18.50	19.00	19.50	20.00
Marginal cost	12.00	12.00	12.00	12.00	12.00	12.00	12.00
Contribution	5.00	5.50	6.00	6.50	7.00	7.50	8.00
Estimated demand (units)	8 000	7 800	7 600	7 200	6 600	5 700	4 200
	£	£	£	£	£	£	£
Total contribution	40 000	42 900	45 600	46 800	46 200	42 750	33 600
Separate fixed costs	25 000	25 000	25 000	25 000	25 000	25 000	25 000
Direct product profit	15 000	17 900	20 600	21 800	21 200	17 750	8 600
Product break-even Sales (units)	5 000	4 545	4 167	3 846	3 572	3 333	3 125
Percentage of demand	62.5%	58.3%	54.8%	53.4%	54.1%	58.5%	74.4%

form of a profit–volume chart. 'CC' is the contribution curve for Product X, and shows the relationship between demand in units, direct product profit, total contribution, and breakeven units for each price. For example, a selling price of £18.50 would result in a demand for Product X of 7 200 units, a total contribution of £46 800, a direct product profit of £21 800, and a breakdown at 3 846 units. In establishing the contribution curve and determining the price which promises the highest contribution, the demand function has been taken into consideration and the cost function is based on a concept of cost (future marginal cost) that is relevant to the pricing decision at hand.

The product profit–volume chart can be related to marketing strategy at different stages of a product's life cycle. The introductory stage can be contrasted with the maturity stage. The product manager may adopt a skimming policy or a penetration policy towards selling price decisions at the introductory stage. Limited production capacity may rule out a penetration policy. A capacity limitation has been imposed in Figure 17.2 which restricts the choice of selling price. P_6 may be chosen with a view to successfully reducing price as (a) the price elasticity of demand increases, (b) additional capacity becomes available, and (c) competitors are attracted into the market.

If the new product introduction is successful, then as demand grows both the position and the shape of the contribution curve change. Alternatively, if there is no production capacity constraint, a penetration price such as P_3 or P_4 may be adopted which yields early high volume accompanied by slow competitive imitation, but lower

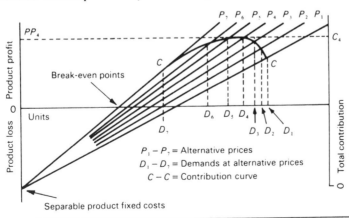

Figure 17.2   Product X: product profit – volume chart (with capacity constraint)

unit product profit. Again, with the growth in demand the position and shape of the contribution curves will change, but the company relies on the penetration price to maintain its share in a growing market without any need for successive price reductions.

At the maturity stage, the firm will have far less discretion over selling prices. Prices will probably have fallen during the growth stage as a result of economies of scale and competitive pressures. Prices decline further in the maturity stage, but may stabilise eventually. The profit–volume chart in Figure 17.3 shows that P_4 is the selling price promising the highest direct product profit. At this stage of the product's life cycle, the firm would probably be wise to maximise short run direct product profit. The management may, for what are usually described as 'long run policy reasons', decide upon some price other than P_4. If they do, they will deviate deliberately from the short run optimal price, and will be able to measure the short run cost of such a policy – which one suspects is considered only rarely in practice.

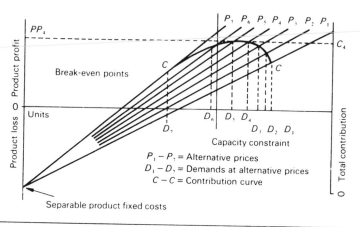

Figure 17.3   Product X: product profit – volume chart (maturity stage)

Accuracy of the demand forecast

It will be appreciated that the determination of the contribution curve 'CC' is dependent upon the accuracy of the demand forecast. When conducting seminars with marketing executives on marginal pricing using profit–volume charts, it is pointed out that the analysis is dependent upon their ability to provide a demand curve. Invariably they agree that they cannot provide estimates. However, after some discussion the following conclusions are reached frequently:

1   It is possible to answer sensitivity analysis type questions from the product profit–volume charts or from the contribution graphs. For example, if the price of Product X is increased to £18.50, how far can demand fall before the total contribution falls below that forecast for the current price of £18.00?

2   The contribution curve 'CC' can be drawn as a band and for each price there will be a range of possible units demanded, product profit and total contribution outcomes. Marketing has long been viewed as requiring mainly judgement, intuition, and experience, but marketing researchers are increasingly combining scientific techniques with judgement and intuition. While market researchers cannot predict accurately the shape of the demand curve, they should be able to attach subjective probabilities to a range of possible outcomes for each possible price. The accuracy of demand curve estimates generally outweighs the benefit derived from the improved accuracy.

3   Many assumptions underlie the product profit–volume chart and the analysis is only relevant to a limited range of output. It is more realistic to present to management a product profit–volume chart, such as that shown in Figure 17.4, which takes account of the uncertainty surrounding the pricing decision.

4   Normally, at the growth and maturity stages of the product life cycle, the product manager should be concerned with choosing between a limited number of alternative prices on the crown of the contribution curve. The lower and higher prices on the tail of the contribution curve are not normally relevant, except in a severe limited capacity situation or when considering a skimming policy or penetration policy at the introductory stage.

5   The subjective probabilities attached to demand curve estimates by market researchers can be incorporated into probability diagrams to determine alternative outcomes, and graphs or tabulations can be presented which array the probable price/contribution outcomes according to a rational combination of the possibilities involved. Risk profiles can be developed for each alternative price indicating the likelihood of achieving various total contributions.

The author has proposed a simple risk analysis procedure which uses a discrete probability density function (Sizer, 1970), while a more sophisticated approach has been developed by Flower (1971). Developments in software packages have led to a more widespread use of the approach advocated by Flower.

It may well be argued that, while the results of the types of analyses that employ subjective probabilities look impressively neat and

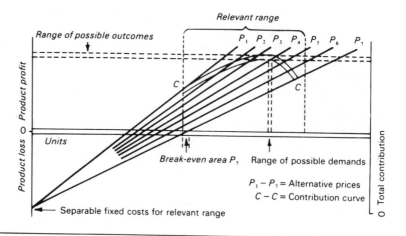

Figure 17.4 Product X: product profit – volume chart (under uncertainty)

infallible, they are, after all, based on purely subjective judgements. True, no one has yet developed a completely reliable method to measure precisely the price elasticity of demand of any brand or product, particularly where cross-elasticities of demand affect a number of brands. The product manager must estimate intuitively the effects of a proposed price change. He will rarely find precisely comparable circumstances in either his own or his firm's experiences. Subjective judgements of the range of likely outcomes, based on the cumulative experience of executives, are better than subjective most-likely estimates based on the same cumulative experience. As management becomes more accustomed to attaching subjective probabilities to demand forecasts and cost estimates, its ability to make such judgements improves markedly. Analysis formalises something that is always done in management decision processes: weighing the odds.

MOVING TOWARDS THE REAL WORLD

In the above simplified example, it has been assumed that the firm is either a price maker or, if it follows a price leader, has some choice around that leader's price. Situations in which the firm is a price taker or adopts a 'price-minus' approach to pricing can also be explored with profit–volume charts. With the price-minus approach, the company works backwards from a market price to alternative quality–cost–volume–profit relationships. Product managers must not view their responsibility as being merely that of determining the various demand elasticities of brands and products in different markets, but must also consider how they could alter those elasticities so as to improve a brand's or product's competitive position. This means that they must be prepared to shift the relative emphasis given to price, advertising, product improvement, product differentiation, etc., for each stage of the product life cycle in different markets. They may undertake simultaneous changes in price and non-price variables in the marketing mix. Profit–volume charts can be used to explore the financial aspects of such decisions with product and marketing managers.

In a multi-product, multi-market company, products will make different contributions at various stages of their life cycles in diverse markets. In this respect, it is important for the management accountant to recognise that marketing management requires a system for reporting current and forecast segment profitability, since marketing managers need such information when making pricing and other marketing mix decisions. An interesting and useful approach to examining volume-contribution relationships of products and markets, of products within a market, and customers within markets, which can prove effective in communications with marketing managers is the use of contribution graphs or pictures, as represented in Figure 17.5. By assuming constant marginal cost over the relevant output range, equi-contribution curves are derived by multiplying unit contribution on the vertical axis and units. For example, in Figure 17.5 a total contribution of £1 200 can be generated by any of the following combinations: 1 200 units at £1.00 per unit; 2 000 units at £0.60 per unit; 2 400 units at £0.50 per unit; 4 000 units at £0.30 per unit; and so on. The graphs can be segmented to show high and low unit and total contribution areas, and high and low volume areas. Products shown in the bottom lefthand corner (that is, numbers 1, 6, and 10) are candidates for withdrawal from the market. The most profitable products are shown in the top righthand segment (numbers 11, 2, and 8); they have high unit contributions and high volume and therefore generate a high total contribution. Against that background, the following case can be studied and analysed.

James Wilson & Son

This case is taken from Sizer (1979) and represents the second part of a longer case study of the same firm. Wilson was an old established company producing a wide range of knitted outerwear, leisurewear

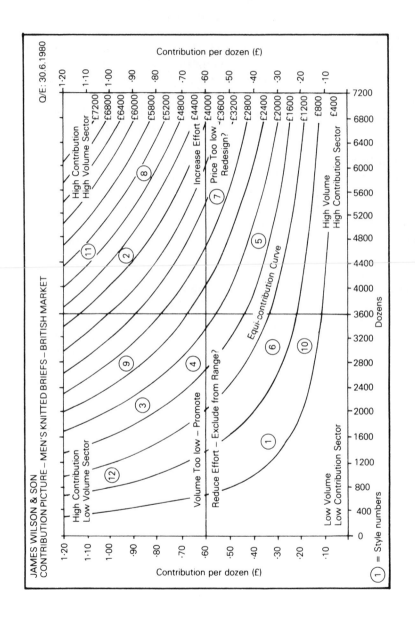

Figure 17.5 Contribution picture

and children's outerwear for a variety of outlets. They had premises in Bridge Street and South Street, Milchester, and recently had opened a new factory in North Ashfleet, ten miles south of Milchester. Underwear and leisurewear were produced at Bridge Street and knitwear at South Street and North Ashfleet. The company had an annual turnover of £1.3 million and some 500 employees.

Hawkeye, the management accountant at Wilson, calculated three possible costed selling prices for a garment and these are illustrated for three garments in Table 17.3; overheads were included by multiplying the total labour cost by the overhead recovery rate for the factory in which the garment was to be produced. The sum of the two columns represented total cost and variable cost; for example, the total cost of the boy's jersey was £16.08 and the variable cost £12.66. The three costed selling prices were determined by the following additions to total or variable cost:

1   Total cost plus 8.5 per cent gave a costed selling price of £17.45 for the boy's jersey.
2   Variable cost plus 43 per cent gave a costed selling price of £18.10 for the boy's jersey.
3   Variable cost plus 3-times making-up labour gave a costed selling price of £17.50 for the boy's jersey.

The mark-ups of 8.5 per cent and 43 per cent were calculated by Hawkeye by either relating required profit to total cost (which gave a mark-up of 8.5 per cent) or relating required total contribution to total variable cost (which gave a mark-up of 43 per cent), and the relevant calculations are shown in Table 17.4.

The factor that frequently limited the company's capacity to manufacture additional garments was making-up labour. The company had a making-up capacity equivalent to a standard cost for making-up labour of £50 000, and to achieve the budgeted contribution of £152 000 it had to obtain £3 contribution for each £1 standard making-up labour. Therefore, the third pricing rule was variable cost plus three times making-up labour.

Hawkeye used his costed selling prices in the following way. He recommended to Simpson, the sales manager, the highest costed selling price produced by the three methods. Everyone's criterion was then met. Simpson cannot always negotiate the highest selling price and sometimes has to come down below the lowest costed selling price. Hawkeye was very unhappy with any selling price below total cost. For example, maxi-cardigans were very popular at the time and were a recent introduction to the range. For the maxi-cardigan, as shown in Table 17.3, Hawkeye recommended a selling

Table 17.3
Wilson – costed selling prices for three garments

	Boy's jersey size 26 in.		Baby's cardigan size 18 in.		Maxi-cardigan size 36 in.	
	lb.	£	lb.	£	lb.	£
Yarn usage per dozen: Weight	8.88		2.26		16.44	
Waste	0.56		0.16		1.03	
	9.44		2.38		17.47	
Cost per dozen	£		£		£	
Yarn cost	7.08		1.93		14.15	
Draw thread and swatches	0.02	7.10	0.02	1.95	0.02	14.17
Needles	0.13		0.03		0.50	
Buttons		0.06		0.06		0.06
Sewing/tabs/tapes	0.26		0.25		0.30	
Plastic	0.90	1.29	–	0.28	–	0.80
Bags/boxes		0.15		0.13		0.30
Knitting labour	0.66		0.46		2.80	
Making-up labour	1.62		0.89		2.29	
Holiday pay/increase	2.28		1.35		5.09	
(24%) (24%) (11%)	0.55	2.83	0.25	1.60	0.56	5.65
Carriage packing		0.18		0.16		0.18
	11.61	11.61	4.18	4.18	21.16	21.16
Overheads (121%) (121%) (135%)	3.42		2.03		7.63	
Total cost/variable cost	15.03		6.21		28.79	
Commission discount (7%)	1.05	1.05	0.43	0.43	2.02	2.02
	16.08	12.66	6.64	4.61	30.81	23.18
+ 8.5%/43%	1.37	5.44	0.56	1.99	2.64	9.97
Costed selling price per dozen	£17.45	£18.10	£7.20	£6.60	£33.45	£33.15
Variable cost + 3 making-up labour	£17.50		£7.30		£30.05	

Table 17.4
Wilson – knitwear division budget 1970

Budgeted sales	£510 000
Estimated capital employed, with fixed assets valued on an assumed current cost basis	£270 000
Required return on capital employed	15%
Required profit	£40 000
Fixed overheads	£112 000

Mark-up on total cost

$$\frac{\text{Required profit}}{\text{Total cost}} \times 100 = \frac{£40\ 000}{(£510\ 000 - £40\ 000)} \times 100$$
$$= 8.5\%$$

Mark-up on variable cost

$$\frac{\text{Required total contribution}}{\text{Total variable cost}} \times 100 = \frac{£152\ 000}{£358\ 000} \times 100$$
$$= 43\%$$

price of £33.45 per dozen; in the event, Simpson sold twelve dozen at £40 per dozen. Business was hard to come by at the time and the North Ashfleet factory, which produced the maxi-cardigans, was working on short time. Hawkeye could not recommend the price of £30.05 based on making-up labour, because the total cost per dozen was £30.81 and overheads would not have been recovered.

Each quarter, Hawkeye produced an analysis of sales which distinguished between (a) sales below total cost, (b) sales between total cost and lowest desirable selling price, (c) sales between desirable selling price on labour and desirable selling price on variable cost, and (d) sales above highest desirable selling price.

An analysis

The case study is interesting in that Hawkeye appears to use a 'belt-and-braces' approach to pricing. He employs full cost plus, the rate of return on capital employed variant, and marginal cost methods to determine recommended 'costed' selling prices for garments.

It will be noted that Hawkeye calculates separate overhead rates for each of the factories, even though two of them appear to be capable of producing the same knitwear. The result is that, as shown in

Table 17.3, an overhead rate of 121 per cent is applied to the boy's jersey and the baby's cardigan, while a rate of 135 per cent is applied to the maxi-cardigan. Furthermore, a single overhead rate is applied for each factory. Hawkeye appears not to recognise that there are two distinct parts to a knitwear factory – the capital intensive knitting operation and the labour intensive making-up operation. In Table 17.3, it will be noted, the ratio of knitting labour to making-up labour varies significantly between the three garments. Should there be separate overhead rates for each operation? A machine-hour rate for the knitting operation and a labour-hour rate for the making-up operation? The point is that a number of equally qualified and competent accountants would produce different costed selling prices depending upon the methods of overhead absorption they favour. Further, the calculation of overhead absorption rates has the appearance to many managers of turning fixed overheads into variable overheads.

Hawkeye sees the costed selling price he recommends as the starting point for Simpson the sales manager, from which Simpson arrives at the final selling price.

The strength of Hawkeye's system is that it is directed towards achieving clearly defined objectives, the £40 000 profit and the 15 per cent return on capital employed, and also takes account of making-up labour – the factor that frequently limits the company's manufacturing capacity. When the company achieves or exceeds budgeted sales, provided Simpson gains the 'costed' selling prices, the profit and return on capital employed objectives should be met. Furthermore, Hawkeye directs management's attention to the relationship between his recommended pricing decisions and actual prices, highlighting those prices which appear to deviate from the profit and return on capital employed objectives. No doubt this leads management to consider price/demand relationships.

What Hawkeye's system fails to do is to take account formally of price–volume contributions for individual garments or the impact of pricing decisions on the company's cost–volume–profit relationships. In those circumstances, a budgeted profit–volume chart would assist. Individual pricing decisions will determine the weighted average profit–volume ratio and also the volume of sales. Variations in the profit–volume will increase or reduce the breakeven sales volume and also the profit or loss for a given sales volume. Therefore, should Hawkeye be placing greater emphasis on segmental volume-contribution analysis when presenting his analysis of actual pricing decision? (In fact, as shown in the first part of the case (Sizer, 1979), he had developed a comprehensive computer-based segmental reporting system.)

The weakness of the system as described in this case is that it does not provide Simpson with guidance on how to take account of and anticipate price–demand–contribution relationships when working out a final selling price, particularly when the company is operating below capacity. Thus, Hawkeye would have been unhappy to recommend the maxi-cardigans at a selling price of less than £33.45 and appears happy that Simpson had sold twelve dozen at £40.00 a dozen. He seems not to have taken into consideration that, at a lower price of, say, £30.00 a dozen, Simpson might have sold not twelve but, perhaps, fifty dozen when 'business is hard to come by'. Twelve dozen at £40.00 per dozen gives a total contribution of £201.84 (that is, 12 × (£40.00 – £23.18), whereas fifty dozen at £30.00 per dozen would have given a total contribution of £341.00 (that is, 50 × (£30.00 – £23.18). Simpson should take account of future as well as current market conditions. He could use contribution graphs, such as that shown in Figure 17.5, to provide price–demand–contribution relationships and indicate which garments to promote, which to redesign, which to exclude from the range, and which to give high priority. Alternatively, Haweye might develop a ready reckoner for Simpson so that he could quickly compare alternative selling prices – estimated sales volumes in terms of total contribution. Of course, Hawkeye and Simpson might have to develop a good working relationship which would encourage Simpson to request the information he needs and allow Hawkeye to provide informal advice on price–volume relationships.

THE IMPACT OF INFLATION

A full discussion of individual pricing decisions in inflation is beyond the scope of this chapter. However, the impact of high rates of inflation on cost–volume–profit analysis can be highlighted.

The high rates of inflation experienced in recent years have increased the importance of pricing decisions. The continuous pressure on profit margins has forced companies to review prices frequently, and in many cases continuously. An essential first stage in the pricing decision process is a comprehensive monitoring system that signals the need for a price review (Oxenfeldt, 1973). Such a system should be forward looking and aim to identify some of the shifts in demand that occur in the market place and the future trends in costs and product profitability. Furthermore, segment reporting has become more relevant, not only because the high rate of inflation and successive budget measures affect products and markets in different ways but also because the significant shift of net disposable income that has taken place makes current socio-economic groupings unreliable guides to disposable incomes.

The monitoring system should signal the need to review prices, and product profit–volume charts may be used for this purpose. Two situations may be analysed: a high rate of inflation and rising real disposable incomes; and a high rate of inflation and falling real disposable incomes.

High inflation and rising incomes

With a high rate of inflation and rising real disposable incomes, period costs, variable product costs and breakeven volume for existing prices are increasing continuously, but it is likely that the income elasticity of demand effects will allow the higher costs to be passed on in higher prices. The contribution curve is likely to move upwards and to the left and compensate for the increase in variable costs and period costs. The company is likely to generate a higher total contribution and direct product profit in money terms at the optimal price, assuming any prices legislation allows the company to charge its target price. These effects of inflation are shown in Figure 17.6. While increases in costs and breakeven volume for a given price can be forecast with reasonable accuracy, the move in the contribution curve cannot; an effective monitoring system should assist in that direction.

High inflation and falling incomes

Consider now the situation in a period of high inflation and falling real disposable incomes. Period and variable costs still rise continuously, but as real disposable incomes fall the income elasticity effects no longer compensate for the increase in costs. The contribution curve may move *downwards* and to the left as consumers move onto lower indifference curves. The shape of the contribution curve may change as demand switches to cheaper products or to substitutes, or as some consumers stop purchasing the product. As shown in Figure 17.3, many companies in 1975–77 found themselves in a position of rising costs, falling demand, and disappearing total contributions. The optimal price was no longer that allowed by prices legislation or

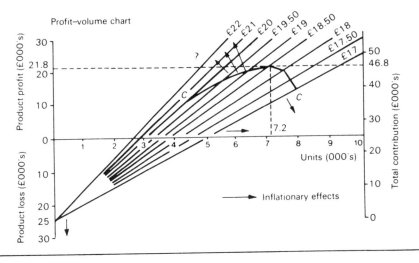

Profit–volume chart

Figure 17.6 Effect of inflation with rising real disposable incomes

some higher price, but a lower price difficult to determine. In that situation, companies were forced to take a long hard look at both variable product costs and period costs.

At the time of writing, companies in the United Kingdom are considering pricing decisions and examining cost–volume–profit relationships against a background of a deep domestic recession and relatively high interest rates, a stagnant world economy, and high rates of cost inflation. All these factors reinforce the inflationary effects in Figure 17.7 and force companies to review the profitability of products and markets, and reduce their capacities and related period costs.

A similar analysis can be hypothesised for producers of industrial goods. An important difference is that the customers in these markets are professional buyers. In a recession, companies marketing industrial products can soon find themselves in a buyers' market. A similar profit–volume chart can be developed, for example, for a firm producing industrial components, by substituting alternative percentage contribution margins or profit–volume ratios for alternative prices. The effect of a high rate of inflation in a period of recession is very similar. Period costs are rising, contribution margins are being eroded by increasing variable costs, and demand is falling at the same time. It is very difficult to raise prices in a buyers' market; if losses are to be avoided, it will be necessary to reduce period costs.

There is a clear need for segmental reporting and contribution pic-

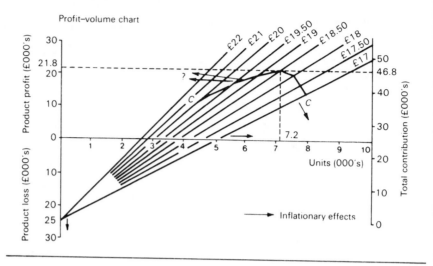

Figure 17.6 Effect of inflation with falling real disposable incomes

ture analysis of the impact of falling demand and rising costs on products and markets, for comprehensive forecasting and monitoring systems, and for effective cost control systems and cost reduction programmes.

It must be recognised that margins are more important than volume when a company has liquidity and profitability problems in a declining market. A company that attempts to maintain or increase volume by reducing prices and cutting margins in a period of rising costs and declining market size may suddenly find it has no margins!

To sum up, a high rate of inflation increases the importance of pricing decisions. An essential first stage in individual pricing decisions is a comprehensive monitoring system which signals the need for a price review. Managements have the difficult task of deciding to what extent higher costs can be passed on in higher prices. They have to examine price–volume–contribution relationships of different products in different markets. They have to estimate the position of contribution curves on product profit–volume charts. As such, cost–volume–profit analysis is an essential technique for the management accountant concerned to produce relevant information for managerial decision making.

REFERENCES AND FURTHER READING

Flower, J.F., 'A risk analysis approach to marginal cost pricing: a comment', *Accounting and Business Research*, Autumn 1971.

Oxenfeldt, A.R., 'A decision-making structure for price decisions', *Journal of Marketing*, January 1973.

Sizer, J., 'A risk analysis approach to marginal cost pricing', *Accounting and Business Research*, Winter 1970.

Sizer, J., 'Accountants, product managers, and selling price decisions in multi-consumer product firms', *Journal of Business Finance*, Spring 1972.

Sizer, J., 'Pricing policy in inflation: a management accountant's perspective', *Accounting and Business Research*, Spring 1976.

Sizer, J., *Case Studies in Management Accounting*, Harmondsworth: Penguin, 1979.

Sizer, J., *An Insight into Management Accounting*, 2nd edn, Harmondsworth: Penguin, 1979.

Sizer, J., *Perspectives in Management Accounting*, London: Heinemann/Institute of Cost and Management Accountants, 1981.

18

Transfer pricing

Jeffrey Davies

The mid-1980s merger boom has created another generation of conglomerates, larger than their predecessors and therefore with greater problems of co-ordination and potential conflict between units which trade with each other.

Divisionalisation remains a common approach to tackle the management problems of conglomerates, with a varying element of decentralisation so that units are treated as profit centres. But inevitably in large groups all units are not totally independent and this creates particular difficulties in measuring unit performance and in avoiding actions by unit managers which are detrimental to the group as a whole.

Any interference in unit management's affairs inevitably waters down a philosophy of decentralisation and can be seen as undermining managerial independence. On the other hand a divisionalised structure cannot imply total independence for units, since they remain part of the group. Compromise between unit independence and corporate co-ordination is inherent in any such structure. Indeed, interference is often essential to prevent sub-optimal behaviour by subsidiary managements, who have been shown in many research studies to play accounting games to produce better results for their own divisions at the expense of overall group performance. Such interference is particularly important over the thorny problem of transfer pricing.

In this chapter Jeffrey Davies shows, using an economic approach, that the group's performance will be optimised when total marginal revenue equals total marginal cost. But at that point divisions may be at different levels of profitability, with associated problems of performance assessment and motivation.

Some form of transfer pricing is essential if the trading units are treated as profit centres, but Davies shows a number of problem arise

*in determining a system for setting prices and in determining compara-
tive outside prices. He argues that transfer pricing must been seen as
part of the company-wide planning and control process, which should
lay down corporate procedures for determining prices and manage the
potential conflict between inter-trading divisions.*

*Davies proposes a general rule for calculating transfer prices and
shows with a case study how it can be applied in practice.*

*Finally he emphasises that the management accounting system must
be capable of producing the information required, and integrating the
procedures in the planning and control system.*

As merger activity continues and concentration increases, in-
dustrialised business systems are increasingly composed of multi-
product, multiprocess companies. It has been shown that to facilitate
greater efficiency, and hence profitability, a divisionalised organisation is advantageous for such firms, each such division being regarded as a profit centre.

There is a danger that, when each division is seen as a profit centre
and each manager knows that his performance is being appraised on
the basis of divisional profit, divisional managers will attempt to increase such profits by maximising transfer prices or other intracompany differentiations. The effect of such selfish behaviour will be
that the firm's contribution will fall, even though the individual division's profits may rise. All relationships between profits centres are,
therefore, compromises between the allowance of independence in
decision making and the facilitation of optimal corporate decision
making.

SUBOPTIMISATION

In economic theory, maximum profit will be earned where marginal
revenue is equal to marginal cost. In practice it is not always possible
to measure such costs and revenues precisely, but the logic is correct.
The example of a divisionalised company, Croeso Cycles, can be
used to illustrate the various points for discussion. Croeso Cycles has
three operating divisions; the Wheels and Gears Division supplies,
among others, the Frame and Assembly Division which, in turn,
supplies completed but unpainted cycles to the Marketing Division.

Subject to the constraint that the firm feels for strategic reasons
that it must produce the majority of its own components in order to
maximise profits, the following problems must be resolved:

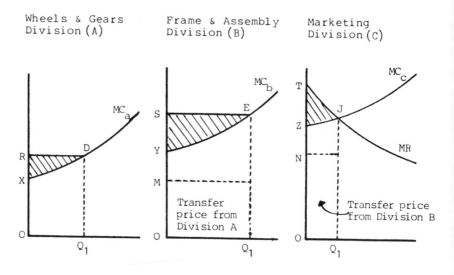

Figure 18.1   Divisional costs and revenues

1   the output to be achieved;
2   the method for determining transfer prices between divisions;
3   the level of profits to be earned by each division.

Pursuing the economic approach, the best joint level of output will be determined at that level of output where total marginal cost (TMC) is equal to marginal revenue (MR). To obtain that output, each divisional manager should prepare a schedule of respective processing costs for various levels of output. That will give the marginal cost (MC) of producing each additional unit. These marginal curves can be aggregated to produce a total marginal cost curve; by comparing that total marginal cost curve with the marginal revenue curve, the optimum production level can be determined.

Figure 18.1 shows the marginal cost and revenue curves for the three divisions, although only the Marketing Division has a marginal revenue curve. The costs OX, MY, and NZ are the fixed costs incurred by each division respectively. Figure 18.2 shows the total marginal cost curve for the company and indicates that its profit will be maximised where total marginal cost equals marginal revenue – at point J with output at a level of OQ_1.

By looking at each divisional marginal cost schedule, the cost of producing the output quantity can be determined and transfer prices between each division can be built up in the following manner.

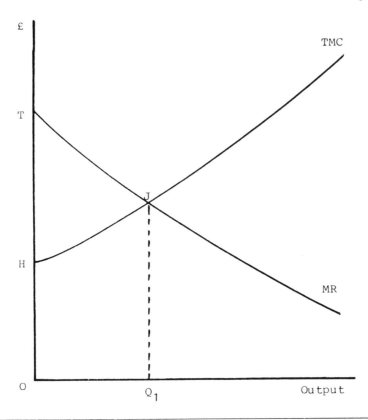

Figure 18.2   Company costs and revenues

For output OQ_1, the Wheels and Gears Division has incurred a total cost of $OXDQ_1$ (in Figure 18.1) and it will use as a transfer price the marginal cost of producing the $OQ1$th unit. Price charged will be, therefore, OR and total revenue obtained will be $ORDQ_1$; divisional profit will be represented by the triangular area XRD. The Frame and Assembly Division adds the transfer price to its own processing costs, and determines a transfer price at which to charge the units handed over to the Marketing Division. In this case, the transfer price will be 'OS' and the division will make a profit of 'YSE'. The Marketing Division sells the finished product on the open market, earning a profit of 'ZTJ'.

The overriding aim of the firm's endeavours should be to maximise its profits as a whole, or its aggregate contribution towards fixed costs and profits. As shown in Figure 18.1, different levels of profit are earned by each division. It is vital that managers responsible for

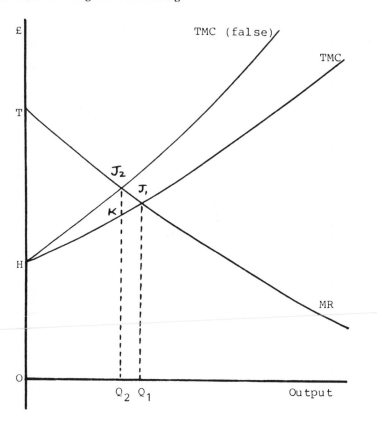

Figure 18.3   Company costs and revenues

decision taking should understand the importance of the firm's interests; it is not necessary for each division to earn the same profit. It is the maximisation of total company profits which is important, and any attempt by a divisional manager to increase his own division's profits at the expense of another division will lead to a shortfall in total company profits – suboptimisation, in other words.

Figure 18.3 shows the situation that would obtain if the manager of the Wheels and Gears Division overstated his costs deliberately so as to increase the transfer price he charged to the Frame and Assembly Division, and therefore boost his own divisional profit.

The result of this falsification is that central management will derive a different total marginal cost curve for the firm as a whole – labelled TMC (false) in the figure. The result of that false impression will be that the apparent total marginal cost curve intersects the marginal revenue curve at the point J_2 rather than the true point of intersection, J_1. The output is determined at Q_2, to the left of the optimal product point Q_1. As a direct result, total company profits fall from HTJ_1 to HTJ_2K, a loss of profit of KJ_2J_1.

The firm as a whole will be convinced that the profit maximising output is Q_2 and that could have serious repercussions on other aspects of the firm's business operations – the loss of sales to other manufacturers, for instance.

Research into transfer pricing practices proves that there is inevitably a tendency to act in divisional interests and pursue suboptimising policies – unless the calculation of transfer prices is integrated into the group planning and budgeting system and unless managers are fully aware of the effects of their activities on other divisions and on the attainment of the short and long term objectives of the firm.

For example, it is commonplace for the manager of a buying division not to be concerned about the fixed and variable cost elements of an intracompany transfer price; the whole transfer price is a variable cost in his opinion, since the actual price charged will vary with the quantity bought. However, as far as the selling division is concerned, the amount of fixed cost included is dependent on the number of units sold, so that a change in the number of units will have a significant effect on the profitability of the selling division. Full cost can never make a satisfactory foundation for the establishment of transfer prices, and full information must be transferred to the purchasing division on the costs of the product quantity transferred.

Second, a transfer pricing system which uses marginal cost to the supplying division, and therefore does not permit that division to earn a profit, will ignore the divisional performance measurement aspect. It cannot be employed, therefore, without damaging the decision-making autonomy of divisional management. As long as marginal cost transfer pricing is in operation, the fixed costs of the supplying division will not be absorbed in the transfer price. A loss will be shown and divisional managers will be reluctant to determine transfer prices at levels which will affect head office assessment of their effectiveness and may even prefer to eschew intracompany trade in favour of selling their products on the external market. In situations where marginal costs increase with volume, marginal cost will vary according to the total demand of the buying division plus the demands of the selling division's external customers. In those circumstances, neither division can make its decisions independently and divisional autonomy is endangered, if not impossible to maintain.

Third, because accounting systems seldom record the opportunity costs of the best alternative rejected, an important aspect of the transfer pricing problem is overlooked in practice. Where excess operating capacity can be eliminated by a small decrease in the selling price of the intermediate product to outside buyers, the opportunity cost of selling the intermediate product internally becomes significant, and the profits accruing from existing sales of the finished product must be reviewed. Each time the forecast of opportunity cost is changed, the optimal decision relating to the volume of interdivisional trading must be revised.

There is also the problem of determining the validity of the price at which the intermediate product is available from outside suppliers. Where this price can be interpreted as a 'distress' price (offered by the outside supplier in a desperate effort to retain business), it can hardly be a valid guide for establishing transfer price. Whether or not a price can be interpreted as a distress price depends on the circumstances obtaining at the time, of course. Where the question arises of a division ceasing to produce an intermediate – as a result of that product being available at a cheaper price on the external market – careful attention must be paid to the probable costs of seeking to re-enter the market at a later date if the external supplier raises his 'distress' price to a more acceptable level.

Finally, it has to be realised that the existence of a market price arrived at by arm's length bargaining between an independent buyer and an independent seller does not always guarantee the best price for the optimum benefit of the organisation as a whole. Transfer prices agreed in those circumstances can motivate divisional managers to take decisions which are not in the best interests of the firm as a whole.

If the determination of transfer prices causes so much difficulty and is so surrounded by snags, why are such prices necessary? It could be argued that they are not really necessary in a vertically integrated firm. Products could be passed from one division to the other, it might be said, and profit could be calculated for the firm as a whole. Such a practice cannot be recommended.

The abolition of transfer prices would prevent the meaningful measurement of the profits of individual operating units. It would also prevent the accurate estimation of likely earnings on proposed investment projects. Further, transfer prices give divisional managers an economic base and incentive for correct decision making. Finally, transfer pricing is a means of facilitating decentralisation.

There has been an unfortunate tendency among managers and practitioners to see transfer pricing as a problem in isolation and to ignore its role in the total planning and control system.

386

TRANSFER PRICES AND BUDGETARY PLANNING AND CONTROL

A comprehensive budgetary planning and control system should exist in all firms, and multidivisional firms have a particular need for such a system to draw together the disparate and diverse elements within the group and to ensure the appropriate pursuit of the firm's long run objectives.

Transfer pricing practices and techniques must form an integral part of that budgetary system and transfer pricing plays a vital role in interdivisional relations. That role can be examined under four headings: establishing transfer pricing policies and administrative procedures; selecting transfer prices; reconciling divisional and corporate interests; and measuring profit performance of divisional units.

Policies and procedures

Polices must be clearly stated and communicated to those concerned. However, a degree of flexibility must be present to accommodate the complexities and fluctuating nature of the transfer pricing problem. There is no single universal rule for establishing transfer prices; each company needs to devise transfer pricing policies and practices that are consonant with its own affairs and characteristics.

The task of communicating policies and procedures is crucial, and their incorporation in some form of company manual is probably the most efficient way of conveying their characteristics. As a minimum, such procedures should include the following:

1 formulae for setting transfer prices;
2 sources to be used when determining market prices;
3 price lists;
4 price ceilings;
5 lists of transfer pricing units and the price formula applicable to them;
6 statement of corporate policy regarding purchases from extra-company sources;
7 procedures to be followed in the case of a dispute.

Selecting transfer prices

The actual transfer price chosen will depend upon a number of factors:

387

1   the existence or not of an external market price for the product;
2   the market structure in which the company operates;
3   the degree of interdependence or independence existing between divisions.

Transfer prices have been established, therefore, by the following methods: some concept of cost; some appreciation of market cost; some assessment of negotiated or bargained market price.

Among the reasons given for using costs as the determinants of transfer prices have been the following considerations. First, the selling division is regarded as a cost centre and not a profit centre. Second, emphasis has been placed on the profitability of products rather than the profitability of operational units. There are advantages, of course, in using costs as determinants of transfer prices. Data are readily available and easily interpreted. Prices based on costs are usually more acceptable to buying divisional managers – and to certain government departments!

The use of costs as a base has disadvantages as well as advantages, of course, as has been recognised by many managers. It weakens the authority of a divisional manager, and it can interfere with the evaluation of divisional performance. It becomes more difficult to decide the profit contribution of each division when freedom to operate is limited to costs over which divisional managers have less than complete control.

More important perhaps, there are alternative criteria for determining cost – full cost; standard cost; marginal cost. Actual full cost is not a good base to use because it is seldom known until the end of a trading period, and is never available in sufficient detail at the time at which a decision has to be made. Standard cost is preferable to full cost but suffers from the problems associated with standard costs of any type. There is a danger of carrying forward the last period's inefficiencies. Direct or marginal cost is rarely used in practice.

A common practice is to base transfer prices on some assessment of cost augmented by a mark-up derived in one of a number of ways: a percentage on cost; a percentage of some notional return on capital employed; a percentage of some estimate of aggregate group profit; a fixed amount per item. The actual mark-up chosen will probably be determined by custom and practice, and its impact on divisional performance and managerial motivation will be hazardous and haphazard. Such a procedure will not provide valid guidelines for the efficient allocation of resources between divisions.

Transfers at market prices are generally recognised to be correct – if a market price exists and if the market is competitive. The use of a market price will create the actual market conditions facing divisions if they were operating as separate businesses rather than as divisions. Furthermore, to the extent that they can be established as dependent on outside forces of supply and demand, they form an excellent performance indicator because they cannot easily be manipulated by individual divisional managers with personal interests in the resultant profits.

Ascertaining market prices is not always as easy as might appear, and care has to be taken to ensure product comparability, to account for handling or distribution costs, to obtain up-to-date prices, and to make sure that there is ready access to the external market without damaging side effects. The appearance of a former internal buyer in an external market might drive market prices up or alter trading conditions.

Market prices used for transfer price determination must be adjusted for the above factors, and internal transfers are frequently negotiated at market price less a discount to compensate for cost savings – marketing or debt collecting expenses, for instance.

Dean (1955) suggested that provided each division of a firm is a profit centre and divisional managers have relative autonomy it would be preferable to determine transfer prices through a process of negotiation. Three simple procedures must then be followed:

1 Transfer prices into and from a profit centre should be determined by negotiation between buyers and sellers.
2 Negotiators should have full access to all data on alternative sources and markets.
3 Buyers and sellers should be free to deal in external markets.

Such a scheme has considerable advantages over calculating transfer prices on a market price formula, particularly where it is difficult to establish a market price. The process of negotiation takes account of such matters as reduced selling costs or handling costs. The drawbacks are that such a negotiation system is expensive of time and is subject to manipulation by stronger divisional managers.

There has been a move towards the establishment of a 'general rule' for transfer price setting, so that the chosen transfer price should:

1 be consistent with decentralised profit responsibility;
2 permit a valid comparison of divisional performance;
3 identify unprofitable or inefficient operations;
4 provide greater incentive for cost reduction.

The general rule is discussed further in a later section of this chapter.

Reconciling divisional and corporate interests

Management must prevent the interests of a particular division from interfering with the achievement of corporate goals. Corporate interest must always take precedence over divisional interests. The management processes for setting transfer prices must ensure that such prices are scrutinised and validated to remove the possibility of dysfunctional special interests affecting the optimum corporate behaviour.

Measuring profit performance

As discussed in the preceding chapter and elsewhere in this handbook, the evaluation of divisional performance depends on a number of factors, of which profit is the most important in many measurement models. Transfer pricing plays a critical role in the determination of divisional profits and management must ensure that a spirit of fairness and realism permeates the transfer price setting processes.

THE GENERAL RULE

Transfer pricing must assist in the process of allocating scarce resources, and it does this by breaking the tendency to suboptimise. A series of requirements must be satisfied if the firm is to achieve its maximum potential.

First, the intracompany pricing method must generate a competitive price; this concept is central to the whole notion of decentralisation. Profits are the more commonly used yardsticks for the measurement of managerial effectiveness and if intracompany transfer prices are not competitive, an important tool in management evaluation is lost.

Senior management must use divisional income statements to arrive at policy decisions concerning the profitability of divisional ventures. The decision on whether to make various components or to sub-contract their product will be greatly influenced by the apparent performance of a division. At one extreme, the continuance of a division might be influenced by operational results affected by intracompany transfer prices.

The intracompany pricing system must therefore be realistic and prices must be designed to foster a healthy interdepartmental spirit of competition, to provide an adequate profit yardstick against which departmental managers can be judged, and to provide reliable figures and information for central management decision making.

Benke (1980) argued for the establishment of the general rule to help create an efficient pricing system.

The general rule can be expressed as follows: The transfer price (TP or, more conventionally, p*) should equal the standard variable cost (SVC) plus the lost contribution margin (LCM). The lost contribution margin is the contribution margin per unit on an external sale which is forgone when that unit is sold or transferred internally.

There are, therefore, two separate costs to a firm when a product is transferred internally rather than sold on the outside market. The first is the cost of the product itself, the standard variable cost of manufacturing the product and selling it internally. The second is the opportunity cost of carrying out the transaction as an internal transfer rather than an external sale. The standard variable cost in this general rule will not always be the same as the standard variable cost of products manufactured and sold in external markets. Internal transfers or sales will allow cost savings on selling and distributing expenses, advertising and promotional expenses, financing and collecting charges, and so on. The standard variable cost in the general rule application will usually be lower than the standard variable cost of goods sold in external markets.

The lost contribution margin depends on the ability of the selling division to place the product in the external market, and the quantity released to the external market has a significant impact on that ability. Also, if a supplying division is operating at full capacity, any internal transfer will reduce external sales. The full contribution margin is forgone in respect of each unit transferred rather than sold externally. On the other hand, if the supplying division is operating at less than full capacity and cannot sell any further units in the external market without cutting the unit selling price, the full contribution margin is not forgone.

Most large firms organised on divisional lines produce a number of items that require many different components. The market supply and demand conditions for each of those components vary enormously and may range from widespread competition to near-monopoly. The relevant market conditions must be considered in each case, and products can be divided into four broad categories for that purpose.

Category 1 products

These are products transferred between divisions that are never likely to be produced outside the company. For reasons of quality control, secrecy, relative value or patent protection, management wishes to produce some products within the company – irrespective of any economic considerations. Competitive market prices are not available, therefore, for products of this type; the common practice is to set a 'phantom' market price, based on standard variable cost plus a contribution allowance. The contribution allowance will be a negotiated figure based on capital employed or some other measure, on similar products' contributions, and on the firm's general contribution experience.

Category 2 products

These are products which management may be willing to buy from outside sources, but only on a relatively long term basis. Their manufacture will generally require a considerable investment in manufacturing skills and facilities. Here, the lost contribution margin should be calculated on estimated long run competitive prices. Short term fluctuations should be ignored, since the source of such products would be changed infrequently owing to the special manufacturing technologies and expertise required.

Category 3 products

These are products that could be produced outside the company without any significant disruption to current operations. They will be relatively small in volume and capable of being produced with general purpose equipment and facilities. No problems arise in pricing because a ready market exists.

Category 4 products

These are products that can be bought and sold readily within and without the company. With the existence of an established outside market, there are no problems in arriving at a transfer price based on standard variable cost and lost contribution margin.

Practical application

The example of Croeso Cycles can be used again to illustrate the application of the general rule. Figure 18.4 represents the alternative situations facing the divisions of the company.

The Marketing Division not only sells and distributes cycles but

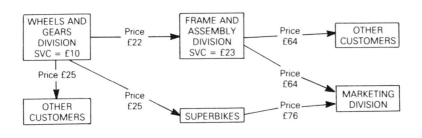

Figure 18.4 Croeso Cycles – alternative opportunities

also paints them and applies transfers, flashes, and so on. Until recently, it has obtained all its unpainted assembled frames from the Frame and Assembly Division. However, it has been offered a similar unfinished cycle by Superbikes. The Frame and Assembly Division makes the frame and the brakes, but purchases the wheels and gears from the Wheels and Gears Division before final assembly. The Frame and Assembly Division is currently operating at 90 per cent capacity.

The Wheels and Gears Division sells wheels and gears to a number of outside firms and is currently operating at full capacity. Superbikes plans to purchase wheels and gears from the Wheels and Gears Division. The net cost to the company of the unfinished cycles from Superbikes is therefore £61 – calculated on the basis of a sales price to the Marketing Division of £76 less the contribution earned by the Wheels and Gears Division of £15 (£25 selling price to Superbikes less the standard variable cost of £10). This is a significant alteration to the cost and revenue pattern shown in the figure, where the Frame and Assembly Division appears to have a price advantage of £12 (£64 as against £76).

Should the Marketing Division purchase its unfinished cycles from Superbikes? Only a calculation of the transfer prices based on the general rule can tell. The transfer price from the Wheels and Gears Division to the Frame and Assembly Division is £22, but the application of the general rule reveals that the transfer price should be £25: standard variable cost = £10; lost contribution margin = £15 (£25 selling price to external customers less £10 standard variable cost). The Wheels and Gears Division is operating at full capacity and the full opportunity cost is therefore applicable.

The transfer price from the Frame and Assembly Division to the Marketing Division should be £58: standard total variable cost = £48

(£25 plus £23); lost contribution margin = £10 (see below for an explanation of this estimate). The £58 transfer price is less than the net cost of £61 for cycles purchased from Superbikes, so the Marketing Division should purchase its cycles from the Frame and Assembly Division.

The apparent lost contribution margin derived from a selling price of £64 and a standard total variable cost of £48 is £16. However, the Frame and Assembly Division is operating at 90 per cent capacity (producing 9 000 assembled but unpainted cycles) and to increase production to 10 000 cycles, say, would call for a price reduction of £0.60 per cycle. Table 18.1 shows the contributions derived from outputs (and sales or transfers) of 9 000 cycles and 10 000 cycles. The additional or incremental contribution from each of the extra 1 000 cycles is £10. Because of the excess capacity, the current selling price and its contribution of £16 are not relevant to the calculation of the lost contribution margin; the appropriate lost contribution margin is the £10 derived in Table 18.1.

By calculating the transfer price using the general rule, the true economic cost of trading within and without the company is established. With a transfer price of £58, the Frame and Assembly Division is indifferent to selling the 1 000 extra cycles internally or externally. Sales of 10 000 cycles at £63.40 will generate a total contribution of £154 000; selling 9 000 cycles at £64 will generate a total contribution of £144 000 and selling 1 000 cycles at £58 would generate a further total contribution of £10 000, making an aggregate total contribution of £154 000.

Table 18.1
Lost contribution margin – Frame and Assembly Division

	£
9 000 cycles	
Revenue (9 000 @ £64)	576 000
less Standard variable cost (9 000 @ £48)	432 000
Contribution	144 000
10 000 cycles	
Revenue (10 000 @ £63.40	634 000
less Standard variable cost (10 000 @ £48)	480 000
Contribution	154 000
Net increase in contribution	10 000

CONCLUSION

Studies of transfer pricing systems indicate that there is often considerable disparity between the practical applications of transfer pricing mechanisms and what might be reasonably expected from a study of the theoretical analyses of the subject. In some instances, special circumstances account for this disparity. Where, for example, an organisation supplies a range of finished products to the outside market and the sales of each item are largely dependent on the availability of other products in the range, transfers of intermediate products or sub-assemblies will continue to take place internally, although external sales might be more profitable. Similarly, there may be some justification, in isolated cases, for sanctioning economically unviable transfer prices in the short term, where central management is anxious to support a division as a vital part of the firm's long run structure.

There are still many instances, however, in which the chosen transfer price cannot be justified on any logical grounds. There is considerable evidence that managements are influenced by a variety of factors other than economic considerations. Many managements are unaware that suboptimising behaviour is occurring in their companies or that a change in transfer pricing policies could markedly affect their group profitability.

For the general rule to be applied effectively, the management accounting system must be efficient and capable of producing the necessary relevant information. As always in any consideration of management planning and control, systems are crucial and rules and procedures have little value in the absence of timely, relevant and clear information. Transfer pricing is an integral part of the budgetary planning and controlling system for divisionalised companies and there are many problems still to be solved. The scope for empirical research is considerable.

REFERENCES AND FURTHER READING

Benke, R.L., *Transfer Pricing: Techniques and Uses*, New York: National Association of Accountants, 1980.

Davies, J.R., 'How to determine transfer prices', *Management Accounting*, October 1978.

Dean, J., 'Decentralization and inter-company pricing', *Harvard Business Review*, July–August 1955.

Emmanuel, C.R., 'Transfer pricing: a diagnosis and possible solution to dysfunctional decision-making in the divisionalized company', *Management International Review*, 1977.

Finnie, J., 'Transfer pricing practices', *Management Accounting*, December 1978.

Hirschleifer, J., 'On the economics of transfer pricing', *Journal of Business*, July 1965.

Institute of Cost and Management Accountants, *Management Accounting Guidelines No 1: Inter-unit Transfer Pricing*, London: ICMA, 1981.

Manes, R.P., 'Birch Paper Company revisited: an exercise in transfer pricing', *The Accounting Review*, July 1970.

Solomons, D., *Divisional Performance: Measurement and Control*, New York: Financial Executives Research Foundation, 1965.

Tomkins, C., *Financial Planning in Divisionalised Companies*, London: Haymarket, 1973.

Watson, D.J.H., and Baumler, J.V., 'Transfer pricing: a behavioural context', *The Accounting Review*, July 1975.

Young, A., *Pricing Decisions: A Practical Guide to Interdivisional Transfer Pricing Policy*, London: Business Books, 1979.

19

Cost reduction

Anthony Hollis

As increasing competition squeezes margins, managements pay more attention to cost containment as a way of preserving or improving profitability. Management accountants are naturally involved at the heart of any such exercises. This chapter therefore describes the scope for cost reduction, discusses why cost reduction exercises often fail, and concludes with suggestions for more positive approaches to this sensitive area.

Anthony Hollis stresses that for cost reduction to be effective it must be long-lasting, that it can be used over a wide range of activities, and that it inevitably involves qualitative judgements as well as hard figures. Throughout the chapter he emphasises that motivational factors are crucial, pointing out that cost reduction exercises often fail through lack of commitment from senior management, and that schemes usually require changes in managerial behaviour. The behaviour consequences of cost reduction proposals must therefore be considered, and efforts made to gain the commitment and enthusiasm of those who will have to make the schemes work.

The author examines the scope for cost reduction in a series of functions, ranging from design through production to finance. He explains how value analysis and value engineering techniques can help in many areas, but a common theme is the need to address physical issues such as plant layout, qualitative factors such as service levels, and motivational issues. He warns against three common approaches which virtually guarantee failure.

In the final section Hollis proposes that a positive approach is necessary to gain commitment, suggesting that the very term 'cost reduction' is a problem because it carries negative connotations. Finally, he argues for a coherent, structured approach to cost reduction.

The process of cost reduction has been defined by the Chartered Institute of Management Accountants (1959) as follows:

> The achievement of real and permanent reductions in the unit costs of goods manufactured or services rendered without impairing their suitability for the use intended.

The definition sets the parameters for any study of cost reduction techniques and underlines the importance of qualitative information. Particular emphasis is placed on the lasting nature of any cost reduction, it should be 'real and permanent', indicating that any technique employed should be judged on the following criteria:

1 It must be appropriate to the organisation or activity under consideration.
2 Its introduction and implementation must be planned soundly on a participative basis.
3 Its effects must be monitored regularly.
4 It must result in genuine, identifiable, reductions in unit costs.

The definition indicates also that the scope for the use of cost reduction techniques ranges across the entire spectrum of an enterprise's operations – from design to production, from distribution and marketing to financing and administration. Particular emphasis must be placed, however, on the importance of retaining the essential purpose of the good or service; its suitability for the purpose intended must be preserved. Clearly, any reduction in the unit cost of a product brought about by the elimination of wasteful and unnecessary resources employed in its design, manufacture, sale and distribution can properly be regarded as cost reduction. Equally clearly, reductions in the quality of a product or the range of its uses cannot be regarded as fitting cost reductions.

FACTORS FOR CONSIDERATION

For the purposes of this chapter, detailed study of specific cost reduction techniques will be illustrated by the selection of some of the more important methods within each area of management control. It should be recognised at an early stage, however, that cost reduction schemes can affect many aspects of a business, and that the use of categories to identify them is largely a matter of convenience.

It must be stressed also that the success of these techniques depends upon the cooperation of all those involved, whether directly or indirectly. The motivational implications of cost reduction schemes are discussed later in this chapter, but suffice it to say here that such schemes must be planned thoroughly and their effective implementation and results monitored closely. The mechanics and operations of such schemes must be communicated clearly and concisely to organisational members – preferably in a written form. Those required to operate a cost reduction scheme must be convinced of the personal benefits to them.

Monitoring and assessment systems must be understood by all participants in the scheme. Where any cost reduction scheme includes monetary or staff appraisal aspects, its introduction and working must be by agreement – both as to the nature of the scheme and its appraisements.

Finally, there is a continuing requirement for management to assess the schemes in the light of experience, ensuring that:

1   There is no overlap between schemes, or 'double counting' of reductions or savings.
2   Success in one area is not severely hindering or damaging other aspects of the business, or that success in one area is not being eroded by failure in another area.
3   The measures have no undesirable effects on external parties, for example suppliers or customers.
4   The schemes are within the letter and the spirit of national or local legislation and regulation, for example in the areas of health and safety standards.

A number of factors should be considered by senior management when designing or implementing a cost reduction scheme; some have been outlined above. First, the degree of skill or efficiency of operational management has a direct effect on costs. Inefficient management will invariably lead to extra costs being incurred or to projects being abandoned, with costly severance payments. When the enterprise is facing difficult trading conditions, the attention of managers will be forced to focus on costs; when conditions improve, there may be less inclination to control costs and their impacts.

Secondly, it has to be recognised that even the most efficient business incurs unnecessary costs. The skill of management is tested in identifying those unnecesary costs and acting to eliminate or reduce them. Thirdly, it is vital that costs are examined and restrained at source. The sources of costs and the areas within which reductions can be achieved are examined at length later in this chapter.

Fourthly, it is essential for the enterprise's wellbeing that cost reductions should be maintained. There is little long term benefit in a short term reduction which is not sustained. Executive attention to cost items – such as telephone charges or stationery costs – will typically last for a fixed period, during which such attention will occasion marked reductions in those costs. Once executive attention is directed elsewhere, those cost levels will increase again. There is, therefore, a need for continuous monitoring and control of costs.

Cost reduction schemes depend for their success on the participation of organisational members, at whatever level, and will nearly always call for changes in managerial behaviour. Thus, the fifth factor we must list is the recognition of the reluctance of managers and workers to change their patterns of behaviour. The need for consultation and participation is vital to the success of a cost reduction scheme.

Sixthly, it must be appreciated that a perfect scheme covering all eventualities will be both expensive and complicated to implement. This calls for realistic appreciation of the costs and benefits involved in any such scheme. Complex refinements to eliminate unnecessary costs may be more expensive than the underlying costs themselves. There is no point in spending £1 000 a year to eliminate stationery wastage running at £5 a week. Equally, the motivational expense of a scheme must be considered fully. For example, keeping all the stationery in a central locked cupboard, with access restricted to departmental secretaries, might not involve much additional cost and might generate significant savings. But if managers and executives have to ask every time they want an envelope or a scrap pad, the demotivating effects of such a procedure may be more expensive in the long run than having an open, easy access cupboard.

COST AREAS

The following areas have been selected for more detailed consideration in this chapter: design; purchasing; production; marketing; distribution; finance. That order does not necessarily reflect the degree of individual importance of cost reduction to the profitability of an organisation, but it does present a logical sequence of events in the life of a product and serves to illustrate the benefits which can accrue across the board.

Design

The design function offers management the greatest potential for cost reduction. Designers are concerned with the aesthetic values of their product and are usually determined to achieve their objectives of style, quality and serviceability. They wish to see their ideas translated into a finished product, without enduring too many constraints. Management must find a balance between the quest for reductions in unit design costs and the requirement to develop a marketable product. In areas of high technology, it will be necessary to plan to restrict design costs to a level commensurate with the expected life cycle of the product and its derivatives. A key factor in the control of design costs is the involvement of management accounting specialists at the very earliest stage. Costs must be estimated with great care. A number of relevant factors must be taken into account: alternative materials, production techniques, production sites, market size and proximity, and so on.

A programme of design cost reduction should not be restricted solely to new products, but should include critical analysis of all products within the enterprise's range. There should be awareness of the possibility of introducing cheaper materials, of changing production methods, and of responding to consumer preferences. This will inevitably include competition intelligence appraisal, involving a thorough analysis and understanding of competitors' products.

The technique of value analysis or 'value engineering' involves the systematic evaluation of materials, components, design features, and so on. The process involves asking the following questions (Institute of Cost and Management Accountants, 1959):

1 Does the use of the product contribute value?
2 Is the cost proportionate to its usefulness?
3 Does it need all its features?
4 Is there anything better for the intended use?
5 Can a usable part be made by a lower cost method?
6 Can a standard product be found which will be usable?
7 It is made on proper tooling, considering the quantities used?
8 Do material, reasonable labour, overhead and profit total its costs?
9 Will another dependable supplier provide it for less cost?
10 Is anyone buying it for less?

The British Productivity Council (1964) issued a valuable series of case studies in value analysis, incorporating most of the above features.

Directly linked to value analysis is the quest for standardisation and simplification of the materials, equipments and methods involved in design, production and distribution. Competition analysis involves examining and evaluating a competitor's product, and aims to assess the materials and other costs of production of that rival item.

Pre-production purchase analysis entails detailed analysis of all design work with a view to identifying areas for cost reduction before materials are purchased and machines set up. It involves the close cooperation of designers with other managers and production personnel. All departments should be conscious of the time factors influencing design and production. Product introduction programmes should be established to match the availability of materials and other resources to production plans, thereby reducing the possibility of 'missing the market'.

Purchasing

The purchasing function provides a most important link in an enterprise. This link, between the design function and the production process, is vital to profitability and is fundamental to any programme of cost reduction. The technique of value analysis, mentioned above in relation to design, can usefully be employed throughout the purchasing function.

Benefits from the efficient selection of materials have been mentioned, and its success will depend to a great extent on the skills of the purchasing department. The aim should be to provide a material of sufficient specificiation to meet requirements at the minimum cost.

Capital equipment analysis involves the evaluation of potential investment in equipment. The analysis is designed to determine the cost effectiveness of investing in new equipment compared with that of retaining existing equipment. The operating costs and enhanced benefits from technological improvements should be identified where possible, and a cash flow approach taken to the appraisal of the potentialities.

If full value is to be gained from the purchasing function, the following additional factors must be considered. Deliveries must correspond to production requirements, storage capacity, cash flow, and the level of short term capital investment in stocks. Ordering practices must follow the economic order quantity approach. There must be an efficient system of monitoring the receipt of goods from suppliers, checking both the quantity and the quality of goods accepted.

Production

The production function is a very large area for cost reduction scrutiny. Covering planning, plant layout, stock control, material handling and usage, and production, the function offers considerable scope for scope savings. The four principal elements of cost are: materials, labour, overheads, and capital. Hundreds of techniques exist for reducing production costs; for the purposes of this chapter, the more important methods are summarised below.

In terms of production planning, the Institute of Cost and Management Accountants (1959) defined the problem in a precise manner:

> Production planning and control are so established that they exert their influence upon the business from the receipt of orders to the final dispatch of the product to the customer. . . . There is no doubt that the high output per man and the apparent smooth flow of work from start to finish were in no small measure due to careful planning and effective control, [that is] having the right material at the right place at the right time.

The effective arrangement of plant and equipment is a major factor in production planning. A successful plant layout will have the following features: optimal use of space; efficient control of work flows; minimal materials handling; minimal waste; effective built-in flexibility; worker satisfaction and productivity enhancement.

A sound system of stock control is a fundamental requirement. Among the possible areas for cost reduction would be the following:

1 the storage location and its associated costs;
2 the indirect services involved in the system, for example, administration and its costs;
3 the incidence of stock losses and write-offs, whether due to pilfering, deterioration, obsolescence, or other causes;
4 the requirements for inspection and stocktaking.

Material handling, usage and yield offer further significant opportunities for cost reduction. One method of assessing the effectiveness or otherwise of material handling procedures is through the use of ratio, where the quantity of material handled is related to the quantitative output of finished product. Establishment of comparative standards for material usage and yield are important for cost reduction in terms of unit costs. Those standards must reflect acceptable levels of usage and waste. Adverse variances may reflect faults or inefficiencies in the materials themselves or in the machinery used or in the inspection processes. They may also point to the need for increased or improved training of labour.

The control of production overheads is an important factor in costs minimisation. A system of budgetary control and standard costing provides the most effective framework for monitoring and controlling such overheads. The quest for voluntary reductions through incentives, or enforced reductions through imposing cash spending limits, helps management to restrict the overhead cost content of unit costs. Individual investigations will delve into the effectiveness of factory and plant layout, of inspection and maintenance of plant and equipment, and of normal controls on utilities and services.

In most manufacturing enterprises, and in all service undertakings, the cost of labour is the largest single element in total prime cost. Thus, the cost reduction programme finds its best opportunities in the areas of direct and indirect labour. The factors affecting labour costs have been studied and debated for many years, and the following summaries of typical techniques and their applications indicate the possible areas for intervention. They are considered in no particular order, other than partially alphabetical which is no reflection of their respective importance.

Absenteeism is an increasing problem for industry, and one solution might be to make bonus payments for regular attendance. Labour turnover is one of the most expensive factors in labour cost behaviour, and the reduction of turnover rates is essential to the maintenance of cost effectiveness, particularly where recruitment, induction and training costs are comparatively high. Provision of suitable and amenable working conditions is extremely important to the maintenance of morale and motivation. Improvements will be possible in both factory environment (heating, lighting, ventilation, and so on) and in operating conditions (noise, heat, dust, and so on); they may also be possible in welfare and leisure facilities. The effects vary, as many contradictory studies have indicated, but as a corporate strategy such improvements will help to create an environment in which productivity and loyalty will be enhanced.

In addition, the application of such scientific techniques as ergonomics and operations research, will aim to establish a working environment which matches the needs of the workforce as closely as possible.

Any programme of cost reduction must take into account the legal and moral requirements of health and safety legislation and other occupational regulations. Proper attention to these factors will serve to create marked non-financial incentives.

A variety of monetary incentives can be considered. These range from direct wage schemes, productivity agreements, bonus payments and the like to 'perks' and ancillary benefits. Again, these factors can boost labour motivation.

Payroll costs can be reduced markedly, through the use of computerised payroll services or through the introduction of direct transfer pay schemes, whereby wages and salaries are transferred direct to bank or building society accounts. For most small companies, such a change in payment patterns offers a fruitful area for cost reduction.

Performance rating is an effective technique for comparing employees with a view to ranking, and a system of job evaluation (matching pay and skills on a comparative basis) may have significant cost saving implications.

Careful selection and training of employees are key factors in the creation of an harmonious and efficient working unit in which the cost-effective use of resources can be promoted. Non-productive or wasted labour time is a principal cause of high product costs and is a prime target for cost reduction strategies.

Workforce specialisation, by the use of the comparative advantage technique, will give the maximum advantage over other workers or enterprises and should result in beneficial cost reductions.

Marketing

The selling aspect of marketing covers salesmen and their sales office support and administration, market research and advertising, and after sales service. The marketing function does not lend itself so readily to cost reduction as other business functions. None the less, a number of techniques exist for reducing costs, and it is important to recognise the opportunities for making economies in marketing.

Clearly, the success of an enterprise hinges on how well its products or services sell, and management must have access to detailed analyses of sales and markets. Those analyses are valuable in themselves, of course, but they are even more useful when conducted in terms of trends and deviations. The establishment of sales targets is an important strategy in marketing a product, and analysis of individual performance – on either a personal or a departmental basis or both – will reveal areas for further examination. There may be a lack of, or inefficiencies in, training in sales techniques and product knowledge. An awareness of competitive products and their comparative advantages or weaknesses may be absent. There my be a marked lack of motivation and incentive. There may be poor or disabling 'support' from sales office personnel. More important there may be serious errors in market potential assessment and customer demand. Proper attention to such weaknesses will pay rich dividends.

Selling expenses – commissions, travelling expenses, and the like –

can be examined and a number of areas isolated for further scrutiny. A reorganisation of sales regions or territories, for example, might lead to a substantial reduction in travelling times and associated costs.

Market research and advertising are obvious areas for both the better expenditure of money and the closer examination of costs. The technique of value analysis can be most aptly applied to these considerations. Pricing strategies have been discussed earlier in this handbook and they offer effective ways of improving and maintaining profits. On this aspect of a business enterprise's activities, the management of value added tax receipts and payments offers a most useful mechanism for cost and cash flow control. The impact of VAT might be reduced, for example, by eliminating processes in which value is added or by reducing the value-adding steps through which a product goes before reaching its final consumer.

Distribution

Distribution management is discussed in Chapter 14 of this handbook, but a brief word may be in order here to maintain the sequence of this overview. The distribution function includes the method of disposition of the product (wholesale, retail or direct), the method and location of warehousing, the packing and transport of the finished product. There can be considerable scope for comprehensive reorganisation of existing methods and concomitant reductions in cost.

The chosen method of disposition will tend to be influenced by trade customs, by tradition, and by the nature of the business. There is scope for improvement, either by changing the method or changing the agency. Either solution is extreme, of course, and should only be chosen after careful consideration.

The general principles applying to the storage and safekeeping of stocks are no less relevant to the warehousing of finished goods. Physical layouts are obvious candidates for scrutiny. The access to and handling of stored goods can be improved by such techniques as palletisation, mechanical handling procedures, and so on.

Packaging requirements are integral to design function, but the method of storage and of distribution will impose further conditions – most of which will be susceptible to examination as part of a cost reduction programme.

There are many factors to consider when reviewing the transport arrangements in an enterprise. The means used can vary from road, rail, sea, canal or air; the method from own fleet, leased fleet, contract hire, casual hire, contracted carriage, *ad hoc* carriage, freight-liner or any number of variants thereon. In broad terms, there are three principal considerations:

1   Is the present method the most suitable, and can it be adapted for higher volumes if necessary?
2   Is the type of transport used the most appropriate in terms of customer satisfaction, damage incidence, cost effectiveness, distances covered, and so on?
3   Is the method chosen most efficient in terms of factory and warehouse locations, distributor and customer locations, and so on?

Finance

The effective employment of capital in a business is of paramount importance. The investment in the right machinery at the right time, for example, can yield significant cost advantages.

The capital equipment and investment programmes of a business can be appraised and analysed in a variety of ways (see Chapter 3, for example) and the control of projects and their expenditures is vital to the proper monitoring of costs (see Chapter 3, for example). The methods of funding capital expenditure should be examined from the point of view of cost effectiveness and the likely requirement for replacement or refurbishment.

APPROACHES

In general terms, most managerial approaches to cost reduction founder on one or more of three fundamental barriers.

The first failing is to issue a directive calling for an organisation-wide 'pulling up of socks' or some such emotive phrase. The general reaction to falling profits and rising costs is one of modified panic! If senior management orders that cost must be cut across the board by a given percentage or by an absolute amount, it ignores the fact that some costs cannot be cut or that costs in other areas must be cut drastically to protect further areas. The workforce, whether shop floor workers or middle managers, is not impressed with such a 'shotgun' approach to the task in hand and reacts apathetically – or even negatively.

Secondly, an isolationist approach is often taken to cost reduction. The managers of individual departments are singled out for reprimand. On their part, this prompts a demotivating awareness that other departments are not being asked to cut costs and that there is a lack of team spirit. Equally, of course, such a departmental approach may have serious effects on the level of service provided to other, non-reprimanded departments.

The third shortcoming of most cost reduction exercises is that they are conducted in a routine and almost nonchalant fashion. Instructions to reduce costs are issued in an unexceptional way, with no apparent enthusiasm or commitment on the part of senior management. In those circumstances, the bulletin or memorandum is filed and very little action is taken.

The burden of this section is that it is vital to motivate all those responsible for the incurrence of costs. Without the full and committed cooperation of all participants in the enterprise's operations, any cost reduction programme is doomed before it starts.

It can be argued that the use of terms such as 'cost reduction' or 'cost cutting' has significant negative motivational impacts, introducing notions of waste and extravagance and ineffective management. Nobody relishes being told that he is performing badly or less well than he might.

In those circumstances, it might be better to employ a more positive term – say, for example, 'profit maintenance' or 'profit improvement'. These have connotations of betterment and greater effectiveness, and would generate more positive reactions to a cost reduction programme.

As mentioned earlier, any programme of cost reduction must include marked changes in the behaviour of managers and workers. Given that most managers and workers are reluctant to change their behaviour significantly, incentives will be needed to engineer essential changes, and to involve responsible employees in the processes of determining and designing the cost reduction exercises. Communication is vital – good communication, that is. The introduction of a cost reduction or profit maintenance programme must be accompanied by clear and agreed explanations of every aspect involved, how it will be assessed, and – perhaps most important – how it will be rewarded. Unless the means of implementing and appraising such a programme are clearly understood by those responsible for the underlying activities, the programme will not be effective, and there may well be dysfunctional consequences as workers and managers act to frustrate what they perceive as 'unfair' or 'meaningless'.

Notwithstanding the organisational theorists who predicate the 'organisational loyalty' of workers and managers, the success of any organisational program designed to enhance or change employee behaviour will frequently be frustrated by the human nature of those employees. Current organisational theory is naive, it has been argued (Ramos, 1981), because it is predicated on 'rationality' and implies loyalty to the organisation. Cost reduction programmes will only succeed if supported by incentives and if introduced after a process of negotiation and consultation at all relevant levels in the business.

Ad hoc 'one off' approaches are less likely to succeed than structured and integrated programmes. To ensure effective cost reduction, the exercise must be implemented throughout the organisation. The cost behaviour of one functional department may be dictated by individual, selfish needs – speed of delivery or long production runs, for instance – which conflict with other departments' needs. While each functional departmental manager acts in the best interests of the enterprise in respect of his own function, the aggregate effect of such individual efforts may prove disharmonious rather than cohesive. There is, therefore, a clear need for an integrated and comprehensive plan for the entire enterprise.

REFERENCES AND FURTHER READING

British Productivity Council, *Sixteen Case Studies in Value Analysis*, London: BPC, 1964.
British Productivity Council, *Variety Reduction*, London: BPC, 1961.
Gage, W.L., *Value Analysis*, New York: McGraw-Hill, 1967.
Institute of Cost and Management Accountants, *Cost Reduction*, London: ICMA, 1959.
Kotler, P., *Marketing Management: Analysis, Planning and Control*, 3rd edn, Englewood Cliffs, N.J.: Prentice-Hall, 1976.
Lockyer, K.G., *Factory and Production Management*, 3rd edn, London: Pitman, 1974.
Ramos, A.G., *The New Science of Organizations*, Toronto: Toronto University Press, 1981.
Ross, J., *Productivity, People and Profits*, Englewood Cliffs, N.J.: Prentice-Hall, 1981.
Schmenner, R.W., *Making Business Location Decisions*, Englewood Cliffs, N.J.: Prentice-Hall, 1982.
Solomons, D. (ed.), *Studies in Cost Analysis*, London: Sweet & Maxwell, 1968.

20

Value added

Bernard Cox

Value added statements date back to the 1930s, but still only a minority of organisations make use of them in either external or internal reporting. The accounting profession's failure to build on the recommendations of the 1970s' Corporate Report are perhaps good enough reason for many companies not to include a value added statement in their published accounts. But such considerations are not relevant to management accounting, which could perhaps also make use of the value added concept.

In this chapter Bernard Cox shows how value added statements can be used both for external reporting and internally. He suggests that value added can be a more meaningful measure of corporate perform-ance than conventional measures based on traditional financial accounting, and can be particularly useful for employee relations pur-poses. The word 'profit' has emotive connotations which do not attach to 'value added'. The latter can therefore allow more fruitful dis-cussions with employees, and can be especially useful in productivity agreements.

Indeed the value added concept attempts to neutralise the distinction between capital and labour by focusing on the creation of wealth, i.e. the fund from which all payments to capital, labour and the govern-ment must come. It formally recognises this relationship by highlight-ing the two aspects of wealth creation and application. In this respect it is more akin to a funds flow statement than a conventional profit and loss account.

After exploring these aspects of value added Cox looks in turn at the use of this approach in external and internal reporting. Stock valu-ation is a problem in both cases, since conventional accounting refuses to recognises unrealised profits, but value has undeniably been added in progressing raw materials through various stages of manufacture.

Investment income and payroll costs are also difficult issues for exter-nal reporting purposes, while depreciation and inflation are thorny problems in developing performance ratios for management.

Value added can be particularly useful to management in compar-ing the performance of businesses within a group, or comparing a company's performance with its sector as a whole. But there are diffi-culties in comparing internally-generated figures with the national accounts statistics, and Cox discusses how these difficulties can be overcome.

Finally he examines value added incentive schemes—one of the most widely-used applications of the value added concept within or-ganisations. He emphasises the requirement for clear definitions of a scheme's key aspects, and for the calculation of the bonuses, and he stresses the need for clear communication of the scheme to employees covered by it.

Cox concludes by suggesting that managers using value added are enthusiastic about its potential, suggesting that it could introduce a wider and more meaningful perspective to planning and control.

When the discussion document on the future of corporate reports was published by the Accounting Standards Steering Committee (1975), one of the new accounting statements advocated was a 'state-ment of value added'. The committee said that such a statement was the simplest and most immediate way of putting profit into proper perspective *vis-à-vis* the whole enterprise as a collective effort of capital providers, managers and employees. Value added was the wealth the reporting entity had managed to create by its own, and its employees', efforts.

The rationale behind that thinking is not hard to discern. Anyone with cash or credit can buy products and use his own capital and skills to turn them into items of greater value. The greater his skill, the greater the wealth produced. If the person is not a single individual but a manufacturing and trading organisation, the same con-siderations apply. In addition, the identification of value added gives interested parties the chance to measure the efficiency of the organis-ation in various ways.

A simple calculation of value added will serve to illustrate the con-cept. A market trader sells women's dresses for £20 each, having purchased them direct from the manufacturer for £15. The dress manufacturer bought the cloth to make a dress for £5 from a cloth manufacturer. The cascade of transactions is shown in Table 20.1, and it can be seen that wealth has been created as follows: stage 1 (the cloth manufacturer) – £2; stage 2 (the dress manufacturer) – £8;

stage 3 (the market trader) – £3; total value added – £13. At each stage, the total value added is the fund from which the particular enterprise will pay wages, salaries and other employment costs, the costs of obtaining capital, the costs of consuming capital (depreciation), dividends to shareholders, and taxes. In the simple example presented here, all the conditions of the opening definition have been met. Further, the final market value has been realised. In real life, there will usually be work in progress and unsold stocks at the end of the accounting period. How these will be dealt with is discussed later in this chapter. Having set the scene, the company statement of value added can be considered.

Table 20.1
The value added picture (£)

	Purchases	Value Added	Sales
Stage			
1 *Cloth manufacturer*			
Sells cloth to the dress manufacturer			5
Incurs costs;			
Raw materials, dyes	2		
Rent, rates, and other bought-in expenses of factory	1		
	3	2	5
Stage			
2 *Dress manufacturer*			
Sells the dress to the market trader			15
Incurs costs:			
Length of cloth	5		
Rent, rates and other bought-in expenses of factory	2		
	7	8	15
Stage			
3 *Market trader*			
Sells the dress			20
Incurs costs:			
Price of dress from manufacturer	15		
Rent for the market stall	1		
Running cost of motor van	1		
	17	3	20

COMPANY STATEMENT OF VALUE ADDED

Suggested layouts for value added statements abound, and one such is shown in Table 20.2. That example emphasises the two aspects of value added – the means by which it has been created and the ways in which it has been used. In broad terms, the beneficiaries were employees (71 per cent), capital providers (5 per cent), government (11 per cent), and the company (13 per cent). In a survey of listed companies, Gray and Maunders (1980) found that around a fifth of large companies presented such a statement in their published reports. The larger the company, apparently, the more likely it was to publish a statement of value added.

Companies have experimented with different forms of value added statement and the manner of presentation has varied considerably. Fanning (1978) discussed alternative formats and their

Table 20.2
Typical value added statement

%			Year to 31 Dec. (£ million)		Previous year (£ million)
	Turnover		103.9		102.3
	Bought-in materials and services		67.6		72.1
	VALUE ADDED		36.3		30.2
	Applied in the following way				
	To pay employees				
71	• wages, pensions, fringe benefits		25.9		17.3
	To pay providers of capital				
	• interest on loans	0.8		0.6	
	• dividends to shareholders	0.9		0.9	
5		—	1.7	—	1.5
	To pay government				
11	• corporation tax payable		3.9		3.1
	To provide for maintenance and expansion of assets				
	• depreciation	2.0		1.8	
	• retained profits	2.8		6.5	
13			4.8		8.3
100	VALUE ADDED		36.3		£30.2

constituents, and other writers have conducted similar analyses. A number of problems arise in preparing a value added statement for publication:

1   the treatment of investment income;
2   the treatment of work in progress and stocks;
3   the treatment of payroll costs.

Investment income

Where a company has income from associated companies or royalties, should that income be added to turnover in the source section of the value added statement? The alternatives are to add it to turnover (identifying it separately, of course), or to obtain a value added calculation from sales less purchases and then to add the other income. If the non-sales income is not very large, the distinction may not matter too much, but the company should be consistent in its presentation.

Work in progress and stocks

In company financial accounts, work in progress and stocks are valued at the lower of cost or market value; only in the case of long term work in progress will that valuation include an element of profit. However, if true value added is the *increase in value* created by the company, changes in stocks and work in progress should be included at market value. This is, in fact, the case in the National Accounts discussed later. However, for published accounts, generally accepted accounting principles argue against the inclusion of unrealised profit. As long as that distinction is understood, users of such statements can draw their own conclusions.

Payroll costs

The other main difficulty with published statements concerns payroll costs. Should they be the actual costs incurred in the period, or the costs which are related to the sales achieved? Where companies reveal separately the aggregate amount of payments to employees, it seems illogical to include a different amount in the value added statement. At the same time, if there is a substantial change in finished stocks and work in progress, part of the period's actual costs will be included in the valuations carried forward. Most companies simply show the total payroll costs for the period.

Usefulness of statements

Despite many anomalies and possible inaccuracies, Cox (1979) reported that management has found such statements especially useful for explaining company results to employees. The very concept of 'profit' is often an emotive one and employees may well find the concept of 'creating wealth' or 'adding value' more acceptable. Whether value added statements are useful to outsiders is more questionable. The statements contain summarised information and rarely give any data of vital import. It is unlikely that the management accountant would find disaggregated area or sector data in competitors' value added statements. Value added figures are rarely sufficiently detailed for valid conclusions to be drawn. The management accountant's most useful source of information will be government statistics – especially the Census of Production reports used in calculating the National Accounts.

VALUE ADDED AND NATIONAL INCOME

As discussed above, value added at the company level can be considered in two ways – its creation and its distribution. The same standpoints are used in calculating national incomes. Indeed, at the macro level, there are three measures, which should produce the same answer, subject to errors in estimation. National income is calculated as follows: either by adding together the income of all residents (including income from employment, company trading profits, public bodies' trading surpluses, rents, and an imputed charge for the consumption of non-trading capital), or by adding together the expenditure of all residents (including consumers' expenditure, general government final consumption, fixed capital formation, increases in stocks, and net of the value of imported goods and services), or by adding together the wealth created by all activities of all residents.

In general terms, each of those methods produces an approximation to gross domestic product at factor cost. To that value are added the amounts of net property income from abroad, giving gross national product; deducting the value of capital consumed gives national income.

The most useful part of the UK National Accounts for the management accountant in manufacturing is the Census of Production. Each year the Business Statistics Office of the Department of Trade and

Industry conducts a census of manufacturing industry and publishes the results in around 112 separate reports in the Business Monitor PA series. Each report covers a separate Group of the 1980 Standard Industrial Classification. Because of the time needed for collection, checking, collation, analysis and printing, the published figures do not start to appear until 15 months after the end of the period to which they relate. Then it usually takes a further six months for all the reports to be published. Because of that delay, most companies will not use the report's analysis for short term comparisons but will use it for the study of long run trends in their own industries. As an example of the nature of the information presented in the report, Table 20.3 gives the reported figures for two contrasting industries:

Table 20.3
1983 Census of Production figures (UK)

			Shipbuilding etc (£ Million)	Pesticides (£ Million)
1	Sales of goods produced, receipts for work done and services rendered		1 718.3	382.0
2	Merchanted goods		43.6	307.2
3	Increase during year in work progress and goods on hands for sale		245.2	22.4
4	GROSS OUTPUT (1+2+3)		2 007.1	711.7
5	Cost of purchases		837.0	404.9
6	Cost of industrial services, increases during the year of materials, stores, and fuel		139.7	15.6
7	NET OUTPUT (4−(5+6))		1 028.0	314.3
8	Cost of non-industrial services, rates, motor vehicle licences		99.8	16.2
9	Gross value added at factor cost (7−8)		928.1	298.1
Employment				
10	*Operatives*	*(Thous)*	75.3	1.6
11	*Others*	*(Thous)*	24.7	1.9
12	*Total employment (including working proprietors)*	*(Thous)*	100.3	3.6
Wages and salaries				
13	Operatives	(£m)	544.4	13.2
14	Others	(£m)	219.6	18.5

Source: The Business Statistics Office, Newport, Gwent.

the shipbuilding and marine engineering industry, and the pesticide manufacturing industry. (The reasons for choosing these two industrial sectors will be discussed later in this chapter.) For the sake of brevity, the table only gives the figures for 1983.

As can be seen from the table, the various constituent items are sub-totalled as gross output (line 4), net output (line 7), and gross value added (line 9), and the distinctions between those values can be seen readily enough. Many companies which claim to use value added in planning or periodic management accounts are, in fact, using net output. That difference may not be important, as long as users and preparers are aware of the distinction, but comparisons must be made in terms of similar quantities or categories.

DERIVING VALUE ADDED FROM MANAGEMENT ACCOUNTS

If a company intends to use value added to compare its performance with that of other companies in the same industry, or simply to compare one part of its business with another, it will need a more accurate calculation than that obtained by the published corporate statement of value added described earlier. The procedure need not be complicated, but some items of expense will call for special treatment. Table 20.4 gives the results of a typical company, analysed in value added terms.

Column A shows the results before analysis, and each line is then examined and transferred to the appropriate category column, divided where appropriate into different heads of expenditure. In the example, £100 000 had been transferred to the fixed asset accounts, being the cost of homemade fixed assets; since it represents value created, however, it has been brought back into the accounts and treated as sales revenue, with the bought-in costs of £30 000 and employee costs of £70 000 being transferred to their appropriate category columns. Column H shows an adjustment to profit of £50 000 being the residual book value of fixed assets scrapped during the year; it is taken back to profit since it is neither wealth created not wealth distributed during the year. Similarly, adjustments are made for such movements as increases in bad debt provisions, depreciation charges, and the like.

This form of analysis provides a simple and systematic approach to the calculation of value added and ensures that less straight-forward items are considered properly and adjusted as necessary. It provides a suitable basis for interim employee reports and for the calculation

Table 20.4
Value added and management accounts

		A	B	C	D	E	F	G	H (£000)
		Management accounts	Sales and income	Bought-in costs	VALUE ADDED	Employee costs	Depreciation	Profit	Adjustment to profit
Sales	1	+12 000	+12 000						–50
Cost of Sales	2	– 8 000		–3 900		–3 650	–400		
Gross profit	3	+ 4 000							
Other income	4	+ 500	+ 600	– 30		– 70			+50
Admin. expenses	5	– 1 230	+ 100	– 100		– 920	– 50		
Selling expenses	6	– 500		– 300			– 10		
Financial expenses	7	– 320		– 400			– 25		–75
				– 300			– 20		
Profit before tax	8	+ 2 450						+2 450	
	9							+ 75	
	10		+12 700	–5 030	7 670	4 640	505	2 525	–75

Value added creation

Sales & income	12 700
Deduct bought-in	5 030
	£ 7 670

Value added distribution

Employee costs	4 640
Depreciation	505
Profit before tax etc.	2 525
	£ 7 670

of a range of management ratios for inter-group comparison. This approach can be called the 'cost of sales method' of calculating value added.

If it is intended to compare the results of such an analysis with Census of Production results, certain fundamental differences must be borne in mind. Census results include an element for increases in the value of work in progress and stocks. Census figures for wages and salaries do not include the employers' cost of social security and superannuation. Census wages and salaries are those incurred in the calendar year, whereas management accounts' figures will be those of the income period being reported. Few companies fit happily into one census industrial category; the company's results might have to be disaggregated to render comparisons valid.

Table 20.5
Value added ratios

	TRADITIONAL	VALUE ADDED
Gross Margin	*Gross profit* Sales	*Value added* Sales *Operating profit* Value added
Stock turnover	*Sales* Stocks	*Gross output* Stocks
Fixed assets turnover	*Sales* Operating assets	*Value added* Operating assets
Labour productivity	*Sales* No. of employees *Operating profit* No. of employees *Sales* Employment costs *Operating profit* Employment costs	*Value added* No. of employees *Value added* Direct hours worked *Value added* Employment costs
Capital productivity	*Net profit* Capital employed	*Value added* Capital employed
Rate of investment		*Capital expenditure* No. of employees

Value added ratios

Different authors have suggested a number of value added ratios, with some ratios proving more reliable than others. Table 20.5 shows those suggested value added ratios and their more traditional financial accounting counterparts. The list is not exhaustive, but for the most part it is self-explanatory.

There are three specific difficulties in using value added ratios: the treatment of depreciation; the valuation of work-in-progress and finished goods; the impact of inflation.

Depreciation has been considered, up to this point, as an application of value added. Some authorities, such as Morley (1978), insist that net value added should be used in preference to gross value added. The argument is that depreciation is as much a cost of the period as materials consumed and that it cannot be distributed without damaging the substance of the business.

National accounts report a notional profit in respect of value added to work in progress and finished goods, so should company accounts follow suit? There is no sound reason why a company should not follow that practice in its internal management accounts. Although many accountants will be reluctant to take credit for unrealised profits, the value added results will be markedly distorted in some cases if that element of profit is not included.

The effect of inflation on ratios cannot be ignored. Where the denominator is a non-financial ratio (such as number of employees or hours worked), comparisons between one period and another will be distorted by the impact of inflation on the numerator. The application of some index or of the techniques of current cost accounting will go some way to alleviating these difficulties.

An example or two

Using the information presented in Table 20.3, an elementary form of ratio analysis can be undertaken. The reasons for choosing two such divergent industries are simple: by illustrating extremes, it is easier to draw conclusions and provide pointers for the management accountant dealing with less disparate manufacturing units within a company group. Table 20.6 gives two ratios, extracted from the Census of Production, for the two industrial sectors chosen for study.

These ratios can be examined in turn. Each employee in the pesticide industry creates about nine times as much wealth as the employee in the shipbuilding sector. Some underlying explanations must be, for example, that the pesticide manufacturing industry is

Table 20.6
Comparative value added ratios

	Shipbuilding	Pesticides
Gross value added per head	£9 253	£82 778
Wages and salaries as a percentage of gross value added	82.3%	10.6%

more capital intensive, with machines doing most of the work, or that each employee in the pesticide industry is more productive. It might be safe to assume that productivity in shipbuilding is lower than in the pesticide industry.

The proportion of wages and salaries as percentages of gross value added offers the greatest degree of divergence between the two industries. In the shipbuilding industry, employment costs, excluding social security and pension payments, amounted to some 82 per cent of gross value added. Other inescapable costs of employing people, such as social security and pension payments, would easily add 20 per cent or so to those costs. Thus, the total costs of employment exceeded value added, leaving nothing whatsoever for other purposes. That is the picture of a bankrupt industry – borne out by everything else reported about the shipbuilding industry. By contrast, the pesticides industry appeared to be in a particularly healthy position.

VALUE ADDED BONUS SCHEMES

One of the significant uses of the concept of value added is its incorporation in company incentive schemes or bonus schemes. These schemes originated in the United States in the 1930s and have been in use in the United Kingdom since the 1950s, although it was not until the late 1970s that they came into vogue as typical self-financing productivity schemes.

The schemes work by establishing a base ratio of value added to payroll costs, thereby creating a base index. If the index moves favourably in later periods, a bonus is payable to scheme members. Research conducted by the author on some fifty such schemes revealed a number of different aspects worthy of further consideration and the remainder of this chapter describes some of the more important variations.

421

Calculation of bonuses

There are two principal methods of using the base index to calculate bonuses. Under the first method, the company calculates a productivity ratio by relating value added to payroll costs. For example, a value added total of £720 000 and a payroll cost of £480 000 would give a productivity ratio of 1.5:1. For each susbsequent bonus period, the company pays employees a part of any improvement in value added generated. If the next period resulted in a value added total of £72 000 and actual payroll costs of £40 000, the productivity improvement would be calculated by comparing the value added achieved against the actual payroll cost multiplied by the productivity ratio of 1.5. In this instance, the improvement would be calculated at £12 000 (£72 000 less £60 000). Most commonly, that improvement is shared between the company and the scheme members in pre-agreed proportions. This method uses a productivity ratio calculated on the basis of a standard value added expected for each £1 of payroll cost.

The second method uses a reciprocal of the productivity index and calculates an expected or standard payroll cost for each £1 of value added generated. Using the same figures as before, the productivity ratio is calculated at 0.667 (£480 000/£270 000), and the expected payroll cost for the ensuring period would be calculated at £48 000 (£72 000 × 0.667). The actual payroll cost was £40 000, giving a productivity improvement of £8 000.

Two quite different results are derived from the same set of figures. The first method cannot be recommended due to the danger of paying a level of bonus the company cannot afford. The two methods can be expressed in algebraic terms, and a number of schemes have failed to ensure that the actual cash implications of those algebraic formulations have been made clear to employees – thereby reducing the significant motivational impact of such incentive schemes. Clear communication of the 'nuts and bolts' of such productivity-encouraging schemes is essential if they are to work well.

Alternatives and problem areas

One of the first points to consider is the definition of value added which will be employed in the scheme – gross value added or net value added. Additionally, payroll costs must be more closely defined and should generally include social security and pension payments costs. Some schemes have made a sound case for excluding certain items of expenditure from their calculations, on the grounds that employees could neither control nor influence certain classes of expenditure such as rent and rates.

There are, in addition, considerations of who should be eligible for participation in such schemes and to what extent absentees should be allowed full participation in bonus payments for periods during which they were away sick or on holiday. The period of the best time for calculating productivity indices and ratios would need to be defined precisely and could be a subject for negotiation. The practice of using historical data is widespread, but there are instances of firms using current budget figures to complete a base ratio. Whether to include all classes of employee or to restrict membership to specific classes is a further possible source of contention.

The frequency with which the bonus payment is made will have a significant impact on the enhancement of productivity, and managements tend to pay such bonuses monthly – although the absolute amount of the bonus payment is another important consideration.

Results of schemes

Of the schemes examined by the author, ten failed to make a bonus payment at all and were either abandoned or held in abeyance. The others paid regular bonuses over a number of years. The bonuses actually paid ranged from 60 per cent on gross pay to 0.5 per cent. Generally, sponsoring companies saw the schemes as helping to generate employee interest in company affairs and enhancing productivity. Schemes are often regarded as complementing annual pay negotiations and, in some cases, as making up for otherwise unfavourable pay rises.

All the companies that paid bonuses would claim increased productivity and the expressed intention of their managements to continue with the schemes is a clear indication of perceived value.

CONCLUSION

This chapter has considered the use of value added in reporting company results, in the analysis of ratios within companies, and in the operation of incentive schemes. Time and time again, there is welcome evidence of the enthusiasm of practising managers for the wider use of value added concepts in planning and control. It brings a different and useful perspective to company affairs, and in the words of Wood (1978), it is the key to prosperity:

Creating added value is a fundamental objective of good management. By creating more added value we can all enjoy a higher standard of living.

REFERENCES AND FURTHER READING

Accounting Standards Steering Committee, *The Corporate Report: A Discussion Document*, London: ASSC, 1975.

Bentley, T., 'Added value and contribution', *Management Accounting*, March 1981.

Cox, B., *Value Added: An Appreciation for the Accountant Concerned with Industry*, London: Heinemann, 1979.

Cox, B., *A study of value added incentive schemes in the UK*, London: Institute of Cost and Management Accountants, 1983.

Fanning, D., 'Banishing confusion from the added value equation', *Financial Times*, 13 December 1978.

Gilchrist, R.R., *Managing for Profit*, London: Allen & Unwin, 1971.

Gray, S.J., and Maunders, K.T., *Value Added Reporting*, London: Association of Certified Accountants, 1980.

Morley, M.F., *The Value Added Statement*, London: Gee, 1978.

Rutherford, B.A., 'Five fallacies about value added', *Management Accounting*, September 1981.

Wood, E.G., *Added Value – the Key to Prosperity*, London: Business Books, 1978.

21

Mathematical techniques

Roger Groves

This chapter considers three approaches to modelling – inventory models, production and investment planning models, and forecasting models. As Professor Groves argues, quantitative models can be of considerable assistance to management and help both to control day to day activities and to plan future activities. The three models considered in this chapter are comparatively elementary, and more sophisticated models are in common use. Nevertheless, the author's treatment presents a comprehensive introduction to the use of mathematical models in control and planning. It is essential, of course, that the user of these models should appreciate their limitations and drawbacks. The usefulness of mathematical models depends very much on their key ingredients and the effects of measurement errors can be far-reaching, especially where fundamental decisions are being taken. Notwithstanding those reservations, accountants and managers are coming to rely more and more on mathematical models, particularly those susceptible to representation in a computer program. The increasing use of sophisticated data processing equipment has enabled managers to build, adapt and use mathematical models as effective aids to optimal managerial decision making.

Models are representations of reality – whether physical representations, such as model cars of aeroplanes, or conceptual representations, such as models of the economy. Accounting and financial reports are models also, because a model portrays the multi-faceted inter-relationships between factors in a real life situation.

Many models are expressed in mathematical form to help analyse the quantitative aspects of a problem. Building a model can help in the discovery and description of the patterns of order that underpin business operations. Through their formal structure, models can identify the relevant factors in a decision making process and, by supplementing the intuitive or heuristic judgements of managers, can lead to better decisions.

Frequently, models are criticised on the grounds that they over simplify reality, by being based on restrictive assumptions, or that they ignore important underlying factors, or that they are static representations of a dynamic environment. Without doubt, in their contexts all those criticisms could be maintained, but at the same time there are numerous examples of successful applications. The real test is that of costs versus benefits; comparing the benefits accruing from the alternative techniques for decision making (including modelling) with the costs of providing and processing information under each approach.

This chapter deals with three approaches to modelling, the first being inventory models which are representations of the buying and storing processes of stock and work-in-progress. The second approach is the use of mathematical programming algorithms in the planning and control of production and investment planning. The third section looks at models used for forecasting.

INVENTORY MODELS

Systems for the planning and control of corporate inventories have been in operation successfully for many years. The objective of these systems is to ensure that an organisation holds the smallest amount of inventory or stock, as economically as possible, to suit its internal or external needs. The quantity of inventory for each different item of stock or work-in-progress will be computed by using a model so as to minimise the total of related costs. The model discussed here can be applied to raw material stocks, work-in-progress, and finished good stocks, though the examples will concentrate on bought-in items, for example, raw materials.

Two main inventory policies can be modelled. The first, the re-order level policy, is based upon replenishment at certain inventory levels, while the second, the re-order cycle or periodic review policy, replenishes at regular times. Each policy has distinct and different advantages. The periodic review policy enables the regular raising of a single order for numerous items from a common supplier, thereby saving money, but probably requires higher stock levels to be carried, which costs money. Use of the re-order level policy, reduces the probability of 'stock-out', through the greater awareness of stock levels gained from frequent reviews.

Obviously all these points must be borne in mind in the choice of group policy for items held in stock. So must the investigation of costs associated with ordering and carrying inventory, or with being out of stock.

Using the re-order level policy as the example for modelling, the major objective of managing inventory is to discover and maintain the optimal level of investment in inventory. The optimum level will be that quantity which minimises the total costs associated with inventory. Costs of ordering stocks can include:

1   the preparation of the purchase or production order;
2   the costs of receiving the goods;
3   the documentation processing costs;
4   the intermittent costs of chasing orders, rejecting faulty or unacceptable goods, etc;
5   the additional costs of frequent or small-quantity orders.

Carrying costs – that is, storing and holding costs – will include the following:

6   storage space costs;
7   required rate of return on investment in current assets;
8   obsolescence and deterioration costs;
9   insurance and security costs.

Stock-out costs are the most difficult to assess and incorporate in a model, especially a simple one, because they are based on qualitative, subjective judgements such as loss of customer goodwill, workforce alienation, loss of market share, and so on. Normally such costs would be incorporated in the more sophisticated models, which are outside the scope of this chapter, but managements must not neglect to consider the quality of service provided and should undertake an implicit valuation of each level of service.

Before discussing the simple model in more detail, it will be of value to direct attention to the question of actually calculating stock-out cost. As Horngren (1977) emphasised:

> The most difficult cost to determine is stockout cost, consisting mainly of the forgone present and future contribution to profit from losing an order because the lack of inventory. . .

and he went on to argue that managers might choose to maintain a suitable level of safety or buffer stock according to the maximum probability of being out of stock or a minimum probability of not being able to meet all demands from customers. If there are no demands during the time an item is out of stock, there are not stock-out costs and no forgone contribution to profit. If there are demands but customers are prepared to accept substitutes, again there are no stock-out costs and no forgone profit. On the other hand, if there are unsatisfied demands and a consequence loss of present and future business due to dissatisfaction, the stock-out costs will prove substantial. Thus, most inventory control techniques concentrate on maintaining a minimum stock level, however derived, rather than on minimising stock-out costs.

Economic order quantity and order timing

The two main questions to be answered, then, by this model are: What is the optimal order quantity? When should orders be placed? The optimal size of the order for an item is known as the economic order quantity (EOQ) and is calculated so that total inventory costs are at a minimum for that particular stock item. Total inventory costs for an item of stock are computed for a given period – usually a trading year – by combining the costs of ordering and the costs of carrying that item. Using simple notations.

$$C_t = C_o + C_s$$

where C_t is the total inventory cost, C_o is the cost of ordering, and C_s is the cost of carrying. The pattern of supply and demand for the item is assumed to be known with certainty and the various costs are assumed constant over the period under review.

The cost of ordering is the cost of placing a separate order multiplied by the number of separate orders placed in the period. If D is the annual demand for the item, if q is the size of each other, and P is the cost of placing a single order, then

$$C_o = P \times (D/q)$$

Similarly, the storage costs can be calculated easily. Assuming that S is the annual cost of carrying one stock item, and that throughout the year, on average, half the stock is on hand all the time in addition to the safety or buffer stock, B, decided upon, then

$$C_s = S \times (B + q/2).$$

That gives

$$C_t = P \times (D/q) + S \times (B + q/2)$$

and, by using calculus to find the minimum value of C_t, an optimal value of q can be found, q^*, the economic order quantity. Figure 21.1 shows that the point of intersection of the two cost lines, C_o and C_s, gives the point of minimum total cost, because the costs of ordering and of carrying tend to offset one another. The fewer the orders, the lower the costs of ordering but the greater the size of each other and the greater the costs of carrying.

As a result of the differentiation of C_t, the value of q^* is derived from the following:

$$q^* = \sqrt{2DP/S}$$

If the cost of placing an order is £5.00, if the annual demand is 5 700 units, and if the annual unit carrying cost is £1.50, then

$$q^* = \sqrt{2 \times 5700 \times 5.00/1.50} = 195 \text{ items.}$$

The company would, therefore, make 29 orders during the year, each for 195 items, so as to minimise total inventory costs. Note that the safety or buffer stock has no bearing on the EOQ, only on the timing of orders.

The usual length of time between the placing of an order and its fulfilment has an important bearing on order timing. For instance, using the above example, it might be assumed that a supplier would take one week to satisfy each order fully. Average weekly demand is 114 items per week, say; on the basis that the company takes two weeks' holiday – 5 700 divided by 50 is 114. On that basis, the company should re-order when stock falls to 114, the minimum re-order quantity or level. However, the supplier may not always meet the order within a week, or there may be a greater than average call-off by production, so a buffer stock of, say, a further week's average demand might be required. That would give a re-order point of 228 items. Figure 21.2 presents a diagrammatic representation of the stock movements of the typical item discussed here.

In Figure 21.2, stock is called off until the level reaches the re-order level at time t_1 which triggers the order for an amount equal to the EOQ. Meanwhile, the held stock is still being called-off. The stock is replenished at time t_2 and call-off continues, with a further order for the EOQ being triggered at time t_3. Between order time, t_3, and replenishment time, t_4, the amount called-off exceeds anticipated demand and part of the buffer stock is used. The cycle continues in this manner.

The model just described is the most simple form of the inventory

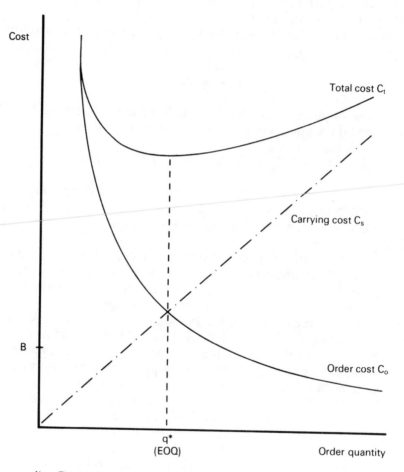

Note: The incorporation of safety or buffer stock would have the effect of moving the carrying cost line upwards, beginning, say, at point B, and having the same slope. The effect would be to reduce the quantity q*.

Figure 21.1   Evaluation of economic order quantity

models and can be made much more sophisticated by introducing additional variables to incorporate such factors as stock-out costs, supply and demand irregularities, quality control, and the like.

Accuracy and classification

Considerable amounts of time and effort can be expended in trying to ensure that the most appropriate, accurate and up-to-date cost information is used in the inventory modelling process. Simulation studies have demonstrated, however, that even very large deviations from the so-called 'correct' costs have neither greatly affected the EOQ nor produced large deviations from the optimal total cost per item. For instance, it has been shown that errors in individual costs of the order of 50 per cent have only affected total cost by some 2 per cent – that is to say that the total cost is not particularly sensitive to

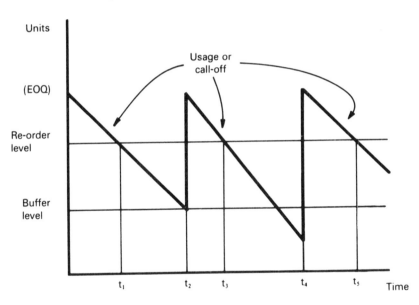

Note: Usage exceeds anticipated rate between time t_2 and t_4, so the re-order level is reached earlier, at time t_3. Supplies are received, however, on the regular date, at time t_4, occasioning utilization of part of the buffer stock.

Figure 21.2   Stock movements and the EOQ

large inaccuracies in carrying or ordering costs. This reduces the need to use a costly sophisticated inventory model; it also cuts down the time and effort involved in estimating costs for incorporation in any model, thereby reducing the cost of building and using the model.

Before applying the model, it would be helpful to classify the inventory, using characteristics such as value, usage rate, or other important criteria. Often, a small quantity of the inventory accounts for the majority of stock value – designated as, perhaps, Category A stock – and these items need a high degree of control and security. In that case, a re-order cycle model would probably be supplemented by a policy of periodic stock review. Category B items might be less valuable but would still be held in reasonable quantities, so a re-order level model of appropriate sophistication would be used. The low-value, high-quantity group of stock items, those in Category C, would be handled best through a simple reorder model using simple calculations of the EOQ and re-order levels.

In many cases, re-order models and their constituents may not be revised for considerable periods of time – if only because of the costs of alteration, which may well exceed the value of any savings accruing from the revision. Inventory models are used extensively by firms to help plan and control this fundamental part of their working capital, especially as the cost of funds needed to finance inventory is very considerable.

PROGRAMMING MODELS

A second group of models using some form of mathematical programming can assist management in the planning of production, investment, distribution, and so on. The mathematical approach allows the planner to allocate limited or scarce resources in an optimal manner and facilitates the achievement of corporate objectives, such as maximising share prices. The best known and easiest algorithm is the linear programming approach, discussed and explained in this section.

Most enterprises have more than one objective in view, but the financial management literature tends to emphasise the maximisation of shareholder wealth (or, more tangibly, maximisation of share price). The models which employ a mathematical programming approach can accommodate either a single objective or multiple objectives. Linear programming, however, assumes the optimisation of one objective function, subject to any number of limiting constraints. Some of those constraints, of course, could be the minimum hurdles necessary for the achievement of other objectives.

The level, size and sophistication of the model depend on the needs of the user, as well as the costs and benefits attached to building and using the model. They depend also on the faithfulness with which the model represents the situation it purports to portray. For instance, there is no point in building a sophisticated linear programming model, assuming all relationships between variables to be linear, when this is patently not the case.

The first step is to formulate and construct the linear programming model. The exact details of performing linear programming computations are not within the scope of this chapter and explanations and practical examples can be found in any standard treatment of quantitative methods in management or accounting. For the most part, in real life these computations are handled most effectively by preprogrammed software packages or specially written programs for advanced calculators or simple computers. The example used here is concerned with production planning, but could as easily have dealt with investment planning or distribution control.

The fundamental problem or concern of the linear programming model is to establish the specific combination of factors that will satisfy all constraints and, at the same time, maximise the objective sought. It is possible, where there are only two or three variables, to solve this type of problem by heuristic or intuitive methods or by graphical means; when there are more variables, however, such methods become impracticable. In most cases what is needed is an iterative, step-by-step procedure, from the first statement of the available resources and constraints to the final, optimal statement. Such a method is known as the simplex method, which proceeds by the solution of sets of simultaneous equations. The simplex method begins by presenting a feasible solution – typically one in which nothing is done – and proceeds to see if that solution can be improved by substitution. Substitutions continue until no improvement is possible, at which point the optimal solution is deemed to be identified. Descriptions of the simplex method can be found elsewhere, and the following example omits many steps in the procedure.

Production planning

A company makes fishing reels and is considering the quantities to be produced of its three models A, B, and C. By categorising the costs, it is possible to identify the variable and fixed costs involved in the

433

manufacture and selling of the reels. The linear programming approach assumes that sales and production volumes are equal; deviations from that assumption can be investigated by conducting sensitivity analysis after the derivation of the optimal solution. All fixed costs are ignored because they are not affected by changes in volume in the range around the optimal solution. The contribution of each product is calculated and, as in simple cost–volume–profit analysis, the aim is to maximise the short term contribution of the firm's product lines.

The firm will have to contend with numerous restrictions or potential restrictions on production levels or distribution rates. For instance, given the machine population in the factory and a one-shift operation, there is a limit to the number of hours that the machines can be worked; given the van population, there are limits to the quantity that the firm can ship. In both those instances, the restrictions are not completely binding, since they are susceptible to relaxation; the firm could work overtime or a second shift or it could buy or hire additional vans or use alternative distribution methods.

The three types of fishing reel can be re-designated 1, 2, and 3 and the quantities to be produced (and sold) labelled x_1, x_2, and x_3. If the models have respective contributions of £2.00, £3.00, and £4.00, then the total contribution from selling those quantities would be:

$$Z = 2x_1 + 3x_2 + 4x_3$$

where Z is total contribution. The problem then is to maximise Z.

Limits on production possibilities are present in four areas: machine time available; supervisors' time available; assembly time available; and floor space availability for storage of assembled products. Model 1 takes 5 hours of machining time, Model 2 takes 1 hour, and Model 3 takes 1 hour; the maximum availability of machine hours is 8 000 hours (the resource constraint). In equation form, this can be stated as follows:

$$5x_1 + x_2 + x_3 \leqslant 8\ 000$$

where a simple solution might be to make 1 600 units of Model 1 and none of either Model 2 or Model 3, or to make 8 000 units of either Model 2 or Model 3, and none of Model 1, or some feasible combination of the three models. Supervisors' time availability is 8 000 hours, with Model 1 requiring 2 hours, Model 2 requiring 4 hours, and Model 3 requiring 2 hours. Equally, assembly time availability is 8 000 hours, with Model 1 needing 1 hour, Model 2 needing 2 hours, and Model 3 needing 4 hours. There are 4 000 square feet of storage space available, and for ease of calculation, it is assumed that each reel will take up 1 sq ft of storage space.

434

The problem to be solved takes the following form:

$$\text{Maximise } Z = 2x_1 + 3x_2 + 4x_3$$
$$\text{subject to } 5x_1 + x_2 + x_3 \leqslant 8\ 000$$
$$2x_1 + 4x_2 + 2x_3 \leqslant 8\ 000$$
$$x_1 + 2x_2 + 4x_3 \leqslant 8\ 000$$
$$x_1 + x_2 + x_3 \leqslant 4\ 000$$

and that x_1, x_2, and x_3 must each be greater than or equal to zero, that is, none can be negative. Here each constraint allows the combined products of x's and their technical coefficients (the individual values ascribed to each x according to the individual time or space requirements for each model) to be less than or equal to the resource capacity.

The fishing reel production problem can be stated as the first solution or tableau in a simplex procedure. The problem is converted from inequalities to equations and set out in tableau form. Conversion takes place by adding 'slack' variables for each inequality associated with the resource constraint equations, so that, for example, the machine hours equation reads as follows:

$$5x_1 + x_2 + x_3 + x_4 = 8\ 000.$$

The first tableau for this problem is shown in Table 21.1, wherein the first row, the C_j row, states all the contribution coefficients of the variables in the objective function. None of the variables associated with resource constraints has any contribution, and therefore they have zero coefficients in the objective function. The technical coefficients are given in the third, fourth, fifth and sixth rows under the columns P_1 through to P_7. P_0 is the vertical vector of values for the variables in the solution vector at each stage of computing, listing the quantities to be produced and any unused resources. At the outset, with no production, all resources are unused and available and thus appear under P_0. Z, the value of the objective function, is zero at this point – as indicated by the number in the Z_j row of the P_0 column. When the optimum solution is reached, this element in the tableau provides the calculation of the total contribution from that optimal plan. The element in the Z_j row are the contributions per unit lost if that variable is to be used in excess of the quantity shown in the P_0 column. The final row, the C_j-Z_j row, lists the values for C_j less the values for Z_j in the row above and represents the net contribution for each variable after each iteration.

The final tableau for this problem is also shown in Table 21.1 and can be interpreted as follows. In order to achieve the optimal contribution of £9 925.19, the firm should produce 1 185.41 Model 1 reels, 740.51 Model 2 reels, and 1 333.21 Model 3 reels. There will be

Table 21.1
Fishing reel problem – simplex tableaux

First tableau

P_1	P_2	P_3	P_4	P_5	P_6	P_7	P_0		
2	3	4	0	0	0	0			C_j
5	1	1	1	0	0	0	8 000	P_4	0
2	4	2	0	1	0	0	8 000	P_5	0
1	2	4	0	0	1	0	8 000	P_6	0
1	1	1	0	0	0	1	4 000	P_7	0
0	0	0	0	0	0	0	0		Z_j
2	3	4	0	0	0	0			C_j-Z_j

Final tableau

P_1	P_2	P_3	P_4	P_5	P_6	P_7	P_0		
2	3	4	0	0	0	0			C_j
1	0	0	.222	-.037	-.037	0	1 185.41	P_1	2
0	1	0	-.111	.352	-.148	0	740.51	P_2	3
0	0	1	0	-.167	.333	0	1 333.21	P_3	4
0	0	0	-.111	-.148	-.148	1	740.88	P_7	0
2	3	4	.111	.314	.814	0	9 925.19		Z_j
0	0	0	-.111	-.314	-.814	0			C_j-Z_j

740.88 sq ft of storage space unused. From that total contribution should be deducted the fixed costs still to be recovered so that net trading profit could be calculated. It should be remembered that this is only the net profit for one trading period.

What this optimal solution provides is an indication of what future plans should be. If this linear programming solution is used as the basis of the next period's budget, then the approach could be used again at the end of that period to calculate a revised optimal solution. The difference between the original plan and the revised plan is the opportunity loss occasioned by changing circumstances, and the difference between the actual results and the revised optimal plan indicates the operating variances.

Turning to long term planning, by the use of an objective function which maximises the net present value of the possible investments and a set of constraints, some of which are related to cash restrictions over a coming period, the linear programming model can be used just as easily for that type of problem. Such approaches and their associated problems are discussed in Salkin and Kornbluth (1973), Carsberg (1969), and Bhaskar (1978, 1979). The constraint vector, P_0, in such a formulation would comprise the expected cash amounts available in each of the years in the period under review, as well as other restrictions within which the firm has to work, such as ensuring profit levels are maintained, keeping financial ratios acceptable, maintaining staffing levels, and so on.

Assumptions and limitations

Underlying the linear programming model are a number of assumptions and the practical application of the model may require relaxation of one or more of those assumptions – a practice which has led to the model being criticised. The assumptions implicit in the linear programming model are as follows:

1 Linearity of objectives. It is assumed that the constants of proportionality – for example, the rate of contribution per unit of product – do not vary with levels of production, or at least that in practice the linear relationship holds over the relevant range for which the model is designed.
2 Proportionality. It is assumed that the amount of input required by an activity is directly related to the level at which the activity is happening. Doubling the activity level would double the amount of input required.
3 Divisibility. It is assumed that activities and resources are divisible – for example, using 4.15 lbs of raw material to produce 1.75 units of output.
4 Non-negativity. It is assumed that activities can only occur at a positive level – for example, there can be no negative output.
5 Accountability. It is assumed that it is possible to account for the whole physical capacity of each resource, including the unused part – for instance, the 740.88 sq ft storage space in the earlier example.
6 Certainty. It is assumed that the values in the model are known with certainty and will remain unchanged over the range being planned – for example, cost estimates for the production process will be constant, despite any learning effect.
7 Independence. It is assumed that the variables in the objective function are strictly independent of each other.

In practice, the linearity assumptions need not be too constricting, provided that they approximate actual relationships. Divisibility of resources and activities can be accommodated by approximation or by the use of integer programming, which dispenses with this assumption and operates only with integer values. Non-negativity is not an obstacle, because in building the model this possibility can be overcome by introducing a specific variable for the item concerned. Thus, there could be variables for both lending and borrowing in an investment model, so that there were no negative lending outputs but positive borrowing ones.

Both accountability for resources and independence of output variables are easily handled, as mentioned above. However, when making any plans and forecasts it is accepted that the numbers used are only estimates and not known with certainty. Therefore, to answer the 'what if' type of questions that all decision makers pose before making their decisions, it is helpful to provide further information based on sensitivity analysis. Weingartner (1963) explored all the altnerative forms of mathematical programming that could be used in the investment decision context and covered those problems associated with certainty.

Sensitivity analysis

The optimal solutions revealed by the final tableau in a linear programming iteration are only valid over a given range. Formally entitled parametric linear programming, sensitivity analysis seeks to determine the range of variations in the coefficients over which the solution will remain optimal. The variations can be classified under five headings:

1 variations in the objective function coefficients;
2 variations in the technical coefficients;
3 variations in the constraint vector coefficients;
4 the addition or deletion of constraints;
5 the addition or deletion of variables.

Jensen (1968) has given a thorough description of the computational and interpretational aspects of sensitivity analysis and standard software packages can provide sensitivity analyses.

Using the fishing reel example and the final tableau shown in Table 21.1, it is possible, for instance, to calculate the relevant range of variations in the constraint vectors. Table 21.2 presents the reduction and increase limits for each resource – on the basis that those are the maximum changes from the original values which can be accommodated before the solution loses its optimality.

Interpreting those limits, it is possible to say, for example, that machine hours could be increased by 6 671 or reduced by 5 340 before

Table 21.2
Fishing reel problem – sensitivity analysis

Constraint vectors – relevant ranges	Reduction limit	Increase limit	Relevant range
Machine hours	5 340	6 671	2 660-14 671
Supervisor hours	2 104	5 006	5 896-13 006
Assembly hours	4 004	5 003	3 996-13 003
Storage space	741	infinity	3 259-infinity

the solution decayed; or that storage space could be reduced by 741 sq ft before the solution was impaired – there is no upper limit, since there is a surplus of storage space under the optimal solution.

It is also possible to argue that the values shown in the C_j-Z_j line in the final Tableau in Table 21.1 reveal the opportunity costs or shadow prices of one more or less unit of each limited resource. For instance, the loss of one hour of machine time would incur a loss in contribution of £0.111; the acquisition of an extra hour of machine time would add £0.111 to the total contribution. If an hour of machine time could be acquired for, say, £3.00 it would not be worthwhile; if it could be acquired for £0.10 it would be worthwhile. A relatively straightforward discussion of these matters can be found in many texts, for example Dev (1980) or Mepham (1980).

Goal programming

Another application of linear programming is in goal programming. This recognises that companies have more than one goal – and that these goals are often of a qualitative nature. It also allows objectives to be ranked. The approach is based on the objective of minimising the variance around each goal, incorporating the goals as constraints. Ranking of goals is identified and effected in the objective function.

Using the fishing reel problem illustrated earlier, it is possible to add two more objectives. For instance, assume that some governmental prices legislation dictates that profit contribution in the coming trading period must not exceed £9 000, and further assume a sales target of £23 000. Take selling prices for the three models as £5.00, £8.00, and £10.00 respectively. Underachievement of the profit target is designated by U_p, while overachievement is designated V_p; similarly, underachievement and overachievement of the sales target are designated U_s and V_s respectively. The profit goal is more important, and given a weighting of 100 in the objective function. The problem can be stated thus:

Minimise $V = 100U_p + 100V_p + U_s + V_s + 0x_1 + 0x_2 + 0x_3$
subject to $2x_1 + 3x_2 + 4x_3 + U_p - V_p = 9\ 000$
and $5x_1 + 8x_2 + 10x_3 + U_s - V_s = 23\ 000$

and additionally subject to the production constraints present in the problem stated before on pages 434-5. Without going through all the iterations and manipulations, the solution to this problem proposed that no Model 1 reels should be produced, that 1 000 Model 2 reels should be produced, and that 1 500 Model 3 reels should be produced. The optimal solution indicated that there would be no surplus assembly time, but that there would be unused 5 500 hours machine time and 1 000 hours supervisors' time. Additionally, there would be 1 500 sq ft of storage space unused. The mix of products has altered markedly and three of the production facilities are under-used. Fortunately, profit restrictions are not one of the problems faced by manufacturing industry – at least at the time of writing!

This section has shown how to choose from a selection of alternatives restricted by resource scarcity and how to satisfy a set of objective criteria.

DEMAND ANALYSIS AND FORECASTING

Prediction features as an important use of quantitative models and all plans are based on someone's estimates of future costs, sales, labour requirements, and so on. Forecasts can be based on intuition or models, of course, but there are obvious attractions in having a set of forecasts based on a quantified and verifiably objective (that is, non-subjective) set of assumptions.

The level and sophistication of the forecasting techniques depend very much on the task to be performed, the speed and accuracy required of the information generated, the costs of preparation and inaccuracy, and so on. This section looks at two relatively straightforward techniques for forecasting: the moving average model, and the exponential smoothing model.

The procedure for building a forecasting model has five stages:

1   Past data are analysed and the main sources of variation distinguished. There are three principal sources: the trend effect, the seasonal effect, and the random effect. The trend effect over time can be tested by regression analysis, though it shall be

Table 21.3
Sales experiences and forecasts (£000s)

Actual monthly sales	Running 6-month total	Running 6-month average	Original sales forecast	Trend	Running 4-month average trend	Trend adjusted forecast
30.0						
29.0						
31.0						
32.0						
34.0						
36.0	192.0	32.0				
39.0	201.0	33.5	32.0			
37.0	209.0	34.8	33.5	+1.5		
40.0	218.0	36.3	34.8	+1.3		
42.0	228.0	38.0	36.3	+1.5		
42.0	236.0	39.3	38.0	+1.7	+1.5	44.0
44.0	244.0	40.6	39.3	+1.3	+1.45	45.1
47.0			40.6	+1.3	+1.45	46.4

assumed here to be linear. Such an analysis may highlight also the cyclical pattern of any seasonal variation. Any other unexplained variation is assumed to be of random nature.

2 Forecasts are prepared.
3 Possible forecasting errors are calculated, indicating the accuracy of the forecasts and whether there is a trend in the accuracy level which would need attention.
4 Additional factor should be incorporated, such as changes in corporate policy or budgetary guidelines.
5 Forecasts are applied.

Moving average approach

The average of the past period is taken as the forecast for the next period, unless amended for trend and seasonal effects. The length of time over which the moving average is taken depends on the nature of the business, but the longer the period the less sensitive the forecast to more recent happenings. The accuracy of the forecast may be impaired unless it is adjusted for trends or recent developments. Table 21.3 gives details of the sales experiences of a company and forecast sales.

In that example, it is assumed that the company began trading in Month 1 of Year 1; by the end of the sixth month, its total sales have reached £192 000, giving an average for the first six months of £32 000 a month. That average is used as the base for the forecast for Month 7, because the company has decided that it operates on a six-monthly cycle. So, under column 4 for Month 7 this original forecast is shown. The actual sales for the month are £39 000, and the error in forecast is £7 000. The forecast for Month 8 is the average sales for the prior six months – £33 500. Since this forecast assumes that the underlying mean is constant and that fluctuations about the mean are due to random events, then the moving average will lag behind a persistent trend, being an average of past data.

To remedy that defect, the original forecast must be adjusted. Column 5, the trend, is calculated by finding the difference between successive forecasts. The trend for Month 8, therefore, is the difference between the forecasts for Month 7 and Month 8. To smooth the monthly differences, a running average of the trend is taken over a shorter period than the original six months; this is shown in column 6. The average for the previous six months is given in column 3 and reveals the average monthly sales for the middle of that six-month period. Thus, three more months have elapsed between then and the end of the period. To obtain a forecast of sales for the following month, the moving average is augmented by the addition of four times the running average trend for that month – three for the gap from the middle to the end of the period and one for the month to be estimated. For Month 12, for example, the revised trend-adjusted forecast is calculated by combining the original sales forecast (£38 000) and four times the running 4-month average trend (4 × £1 500), giving a revised forecast for Month 12 of £44 000.

The forecast error between the adjusted forecast and the actual month's sales is much smaller than that between the original sales forecast and the actual sales, because the underlying upward trend has been recognised and incorporated. A multiple regression analysis would give a more accurate and reliable representation of the trend than this simple approach. In that method, an algebraic relationship – a regression equation – is fitted to the past data and projected forward. The data treated could comprise more than one set of dependent variables – not just past sales, but, say, past sales, changes in gross national product, past sales of complementary products, advertising and promotion expenditure, and so on.

Exponential smoothing approach

A weighted form of moving average is used in the exponential smoothing approach and is calculated as follows. A smoothing con-

Table 21.4
**Sales experiences and forecasts (£000s) – exponentially
smoothed**

Actual monthly sales	Original sales forecast	Forecast error	Weighted error	Trend adjustment	Adjusted sales forecast
39.0	35.51	3.49	2.79	2.279	
37.0	38.30	-1.30	-1.04	1.947	41.15
40.0	37.26	2.74	2.19	1.971	39.69
42.0	39.45	2.55	2.04	1.978	41.91
42.0	41.49	0.51	0.41	1.821	43.96
44.0	41.90	2.10	1.68	1.807	44.18
47.0	43.58				45.84

stant, $\propto$, is found by trial and error and assigned a value between 0 and 1. The constant is derived from past data and is incorporated so that the new average equals the latest sales figure and the most recent average both adjusted by the smoothing constant. The equation can be written algebraically as follows:

$$E_t = \propto S_t + (1 - \propto) E_{t-1}$$

where E_t is the exponentially weighted moving average for period t, where S_t is the actual sales level for period t, where E_{t-1} is the previous period's exponentially weighted moving average, and where $\propto$ is the smoothing constant. Simplifying that equation gives:

$$E_t = \propto (S_t - E_{t-1}) + E_{t-1}.$$

Like the simple moving average, a trend factor can be built in to improve the the accuracy of the forecast, and this uses also a smoothing factor, ß, and a similar estimation equation:

$$M_t = M_{t-1} + ß (m_t - M_{t-1})$$

where M_t is the weighted trend average for period t to be added to the forecast to get the revised forecast, where M_{t-1} is the previous weighted trend average, where ß is the smoothing constant, which has to be calculated from past data, but from experience is best if $0.001 \leqslant ß \leqslant 0.1$, and where m_t is the weighted forecast error $\propto (S_t - E_{t-1})$.

Using part of the data presented in Table 21.3 gives the forecasts recorded in Table 21.4. The forecast sales figures and the trend adjustment for Month 7 (the second and fifth columns of the first line in this new table) made use of data from the earlier periods. Sales, which are growing monthly, are very dependent upon the most recent past period sales, so a high value of $\propto$ is appropriate, hence $\propto =$

0.8 in this example. The forecast for Month 8, which we will call F_8, is calculated as follows:

$$
\begin{aligned}
F_8 = E_7 &= \propto (S_7 - E_6) + E_6 \\
&= \propto (S_7 - F_7) + F_7 \\
&= 0.8 \,(£39\ 000 - £35\ 510) + £35\ 510 \\
&= 0.8 \,(3\ 490) + £35\ 510 \\
&= £38\ 300.
\end{aligned}
$$

The actual sales for Month 8 turned out to be £37 000. Column 1 shows the actual sales that occurred, while the original sales forecast, E_{t-1} or $F_t 1$, is shown in the second column, the error in forecasting being given in the third column. This error term is used to help adjust for trend. For Month 8, the adjustment term is

$$
M_8 = M_7 + ß \,(m_8 - M_7)
$$

where $ß = 0.1$ and where the weighted error term, m_8, is given in the fourth column, calculated as follows:

$$
m_8 = 0.8 \,(£37\ 000 - £38\ 300) = -£1\ 040.
$$

by substitution, the following is derived:

$$
M_8 = £2\ 279 + 0.1 \,(-£1\ 040 - £2\ 279) = £1\ 947.
$$

The current exponentially derived weighted moving average, E_{t-1}, lags behind the current sales level and it can be shown that the size of this lag is $(1 - \propto)/\propto$ time periods. The trend line projection must also be lagged, and thus the forecast for i periods from now, t, is F_{t+1} such that

$$
F_{t+1} = E_t + (1 - \propto)/\propto \times M_t + iM_t.
$$

The estimated trend is multiplied by $(1 - \propto)/\propto$ to bring it up to date and also by i to add the additional trend estimates for the extra i periods. Here $i = 1$ and hence

$$
\begin{aligned}
F_8 &= E_7 + (1 - \propto)/\propto \times M_7 + M_7 \\
&= £38\ 300 + (1 - 0.8)/0.8 \times £2\ 279 + £2\ 279 \\
&= £41\ 150.
\end{aligned}
$$

The adjusted sales forecasts are listed in the sixth column and are more accurate predictors and easier to compute, with less need for data, than the simple moving average technique.

CONCLUSION

The past three sections have endeavoured to introduce three areas in which quantitative models can help management to get better information upon which to base decisions. As mentioned earlier, far more sophisticated models can be built and there are many other areas in which combined mathematical models and accounting can be useful to management – regression analysis in the measurement of costs, decision theory, game theory, service cost allocation by matrix algebra techniques, and so on. The bibliography suggests further reading on the ideas discussed in this chapter and those for which room has not been found.

REFERENCES AND FURTHER READING

Bhaskar, K.N., *Building Financial Models: A Simulation Approach*, London: Associated Business Programmes, 1978.

Bhaskar, K.N., *Manual to Building Financial Models*, London: Associated Business Programmes, 1979.

Box, G.E.P., and Jenkins, R.M., *Times Series Forecasting and Control*, New York: Holden-Day, 1968.

Brown, R.G., *Statistical Forecasting for Inventory Control*, New York: McGraw-Hill, 1959.

Brown, R.G., *Smoothing, Forecasting and Prediction of Discrete Time Series*, Englewood Cliffs, N.J.: Prentice-Hall, 1962.

Carsberg, B., *Introduction to Mathematical Programming for Accountants*, London: Allen & Unwin, 1969.

Demski, J.S., *Information Analysis*, Reading, Mass.: Addison-Wesley, 1972.

Dev, S., 'Linear programming and production planning', *in* Arnold J., Carsberg, B., and Scapens, R. (eds), *Topics in Management Accounting*, Oxford: Allan, 1980.

Feltham, G.A., *Information Evaluation*, Sarasota: American Accounting Association, 1972.

Grinyer, P.H., and Wooller, J., *Corporate Models Today*, 2nd edn, London: Institute of Chartered Accountants in England and Wales, 1978.

Horngren, C.T., *Cost Accounting – A Managerial Emphasis*, 4th edn, Englewood Cliffs, N.J.: Prentice-Hall, 1977.

Jensen, R.E., 'Sensitivity analysis and integer linear programming', *The Accounting Review*, 1968.

Livingstone, J.L. (ed.), *Management Planning and Control: Mathematical Models*, New York: McGraw-Hill, 1970.

Mepham, M.J., *Accounting Models*, Stockport: Polytech, 1980.

Miller, D.W., and Starr, M.K., *Executive Decisions and Operations Research*, 2nd edn, Englewood Cliffs, N.J.: Prentice-Hall, 1969.

Salkin, G., and Kornbluth, J., *Linear Programming in Financial Planning*, Englewood Cliffs, N.J.: Prentice-Hall, 1973.

Wagner, H.M., *Principles of Operations Research with Applications to Managerial Decisions*, 2nd edn, Englewood Cliffs, N.J.: Prentice-Hall, 1975.

Weingartner, H.M., *Mathematical Programming and the Analysis of Capital Budgeting Problems*, Englewood Cliffs, N.J.: Prentice-Hall, 1963.

Appendix: Terminology

Management accounting is a highly practical subject which is aimed squarely at analysing, reporting and improving business performance. While it is admirable that this focus is maintained, one consequence is perhaps a lack of rigour in defining terms and in maintaining a common language.

The Chartered Institute of Management Accountants has sought to develop such a common language, to which end it has since 1937 maintained an 'official terminology' of management accounting (*Management Accounting: Official Terminology of the ICMA*, reprinted with amendments January 1984, London: ICMA). This appendix contains extracts for the current terminology, in an attempt both to explain individual terms and to clarify any confusions in the mind of the reader where there are different usages. While every attempt has been made throughout the book to use terms consistently with the terminology, the subject is evolving, and the lack of standardisation of language is so great that deviations may have occurred. Any confusion can therefore be avoided by reference to the relevant item in this appendix.

Note: in the examples A = adverse variance, F = favourable variance.

absorption costing
A principle whereby fixed as well as variable costs are allotted to cost units and total overheads are absorbed according to activity level.

The term may be applied where (a) production cost only, or (b) costs of all functions are so allotted.

447

administration cost variance

The difference between the budgeted cost of administration for a specified period and the actual expenditure incurred.

Formula: Budgeted administration costs – Actual administration costs

Example: £26 000–£27 100=£1 100 A

attainable standard

A standard which can be attained if a standard unit of work is carried out efficiently, a machine properly or material properly used.

Allowances are made for normal shrinkage, waste and machine breakdowns. The standard represents future performance and objectives which are reasonably attainable. Besides having a desirable motivational impact on employees, attainable standards serve other purposes, e.g. cash budgeting, inventory valuation and budgeting departmental performance.

avoidable costs

Those costs which can be identified with an activity or sector of a business and which would be avoided if that activity or sector did not exist.

basic standard

A standard established for use over a long period from which a current standard can be developed.

beta factor

The measure of a share's relative volatility in terms of market risk.

If a specific stock market share indicator moves up or down by 10 per cent and share X rises or falls by 20 per cent in the same direction, then share X is twice as volatile as the average share in that sector and is assigned a beta factor of two.

breakeven chart

A chart which indicates approximate profit or loss at different levels of sales volume within a limited range.

breakeven point

The level of activity at which there is neither a profit nor loss.

This can be ascertained by various methods, including the use of a breakeven chart. The breakeven point may also be calculated by formulas, as follows:

$$\frac{\text{Total fixed cost}}{\text{Contribution per unit}} = \text{Number of units to be sold to breakeven (a)}$$

$$\frac{\text{Total fixed cost} \times \text{sales value}}{\text{Total contribution}} = \text{Sales value at breakeven point}$$

Alternatively, the sales value at breakeven point can be calculated: (a) × selling price per unit.

budget

A plan quantified in monetary terms, prepared and approved prior to a defined period of time, usually showing planned income to be generated and/or expenditure to be incurred during that period and the capital to be employed to attain a given objective.

budget centre

A section of an organisation for which separate budgets can be prepared and control exercised.

budgetary control

The establishment of budgets relating the responsibilities of executives to the requirements of a policy, and the continuous comparison of actual with budgeted results, either to secure by individual action the objective of that policy or to provide a basis for its revision.

capital expenditure authorisation

Formal authority to incur capital expenditure which meets the criteria defined to achieve the results laid down under a system of capital appraisal.

Levels of authority must be clearly defined and the reporting structure of actual expenditure must be to the equivalent authority levels.

capital expenditure budget

A plan for capital expenditure in monetary terms.

capital expenditure control

Procedures for the control of capital expenditure through prior authorisation on a formal proposal basis, and monitoring as expenditure is incurred.

cash flow budget

A detailed budget of income and cash expenditure incorporating both revenue and capital items.

The cash flow budget should be prepared in the same format in which the actual position is to be presented. The year's budget is usually phased into shorter periods for control, e.g. monthly or quarterly.

contribution

The difference between sales value and the variable cost of those sales, expressed either in absolute terms or as a contribution per unit.

This is a central term in marginal costing, when the contribution per unit is expressed as the difference between its selling price and its marginal cost. In turn this is then often related to a key or limiting factor to give a sum required to cover fixed overhead and profit, such as contribution per machine hour, per direct labour hour or per kilo of scarce raw material.

contribution centre

A profit centre where expenditure is calculated on a marginal cost basis.

control and monitoring

The continuous comparison of actual results with those planned, both in total and for separate sub-divisions and taking management action to correct adverse variances or to exploit favourable variances.

controllable or managed cost

A cost, chargeable to a budget or cost centre, which can be influenced by the actions of the person in whom control of the centre is vested.

It is not always possible to predetermine responsibility, because the reason for deviation from expected performance may only become evident later. For example, excessive scrap may arise from inadequate supervision or from latent defect in purchased material.

cost accounting

That part of management accounting which establishes budgets and standard costs and actual costs of operations, processes, departments or products and the analysis of variances, profitability or social use of funds.

cost allocation

The charging of discrete identifiable items of cost to cost centres or cost units. Part of cost attribution.

cost apportionment

The division of costs amongst two or more cost centres in proportion to the estimated benefit received, using a proxy, e.g. square feet. Part of cost attribution.

cost attribution

The process of attributing cost to cost centre or cost units resulting from cost allocation and cost apportionment.

cost behaviour

The way in which costs per unit of output are affected by fluctuations in the level of activity.

Since these costs cannot always be precisely assessed they may be determined by the use of a scattergraph, or more precisely by regression techniques.

cost–benefit analysis

The measurement of resources used in an activity and their comparison with the value of the benefit to be derived from the activity.

cost centre
A location, function or items of equipment in respect of which costs may be ascertained and related to cost units for control purposes.

current standard
A standard established for use over a short period of time, related to current conditions.

direct labour efficiency variance
The difference between the standard hours for the actual production achieved and the hours actually worked, valued at the standard labour rate.
Formula: (Standard hours produced – actual hours worked) ×
Standard rate per hour
Example: (11 000–12 500) × £2.0 = £3 000 A

direct labour rate variance
The difference between the standard and the actual direct labour rate per hour for the total hours worked.
Formula: (Standard rate per hour – actual rate per hour) ×
Actual hours
Example: (£2.0–£1.8) × 12 500 = £2 500 F

direct labour total variance
The difference between the standard direct labour cost and the actual direct labour cost incurred for the production achieved.
Formula: (Standard direct labour hours produced × Standard rate per hour) – (Actual direct labour hours × actual rate per hour)
Example: (11 000 × £2) – (12 500 × £1.8) = £500 A

direct material mix variance
Explanatory note: If a process uses several different materials which could be combined in a standard proportion, a mix variance can be calculated which shows the effect on cost of variances from the standard proportion.

There are two recognised ways of calculating this mix variance. Some authorities regard the variance as a sub-set of the usage variance but others treat it as part of the price variance.

If the mix variance is treated as a sub-set of the usage variance, then the definition and formula are:
Definition: The difference between the total quality in standard proportion, priced at the standard price and the actual quantity of material used priced at the standard price.

Formula: (Quantity in standard mix proportions – Quantity in actual mix) × Standard price

direct material price variance

The difference between the standard price and actual purchase price for the actual quantity of material. It can be calculated either at the time of purchase or at the time of usage. Generally, the former is preferable.

Formula: Actual quantity × (Standard price – Actual price)

Example: 12 000 × (£3 – £2.8333) = £2 000 F

direct material total variance

The difference between the standard direct material cost of the actual production volume and the actual cost of direct material.

Formula: (Standard units × standard price) – (Actual units × actual price)

Example: (11 000 × £3) – (12 000 × £2.8333) = £1 000 A

direct material usage variance

The difference between the standard quantity specified for the actual production and the actual quantity used, at standard purchase price.

Formula: (Standard quality specified for actual production – actual quantity used) × Standard price

Example: (11 000 – 12 000) × £3 = £3 000 A

direct material yield variance

Explanatory note: Apart from operator or machine performance, output quantities produced are often different to those planned, e.g. this arises in chemical plants where plant should produce a given output over a period for a given input but the actual output differs for a variety of reasons.

Definition: The difference between the standard yield of the actual material input and the actual yield, both valued at the standard material cost of the product.

Formula: (Standard yield of actual input – Actual yield of input) × Standard material cost.

discount rate (capital investment appraisal)

A percentage used to discount future cash flows generated by a capital project.

Two rates commonly used are:

(a) internal rate of return,

(b) weighted average cost of capital.

discounted cash flow

An evaluation of the future net cash flows generated by a capital project, by discounting them to their present-day value.

The two methods most commonly used are:

(a) yield method, for which the calculation determines the internal rate of return (IRR) in the firm of a percentage,

(b) net present value (NPV) method, in which the discount rate is chosen and the answer is a sum of money.

economic order quantity

A quantity of materials to be ordered which takes into account the optimum combination of:

1. bulk discounts from high volume purchases,
2. usage rate,
3. stock holding costs,
4. storage capacity,
5. order delivery time,
6. cost of processing the order.

exceptions reporting

A system of reporting based on the exception principles which focuses attention on those items where performance differs significantly from standard or budget.

feedback

Modification or control of a process or system by its results or effects, by measuring differences between desired and actual results.

Feedback is an element in a feedback system and forms the link between planning and control. This can be illustrated by a simple central heating system, where differences between planned and actual temperatures are used as signals to effect automatic control.

fixed budget

A budget which is designed to remain unchanged irrespective of the volume of output or turnover attained.

flexible budget

A budget which, by recognising the difference in behaviour between fixed and variable costs in relation to fluctuations in output, turnover, or other variable factors such as number of employees, is designed to change appropriately with such fluctuations.

goal congruence

The state that exists in a control system when it leads individuals and/or groups to take actions which are both in their self-interest and also in the best interest of the entity.

ideal standard

A standard which can be attained under the most favourable conditions.

No provision is made, e.g. for shrinkage, spoilage or machine breakdowns. Users believe that the resulting unfavourable variances will remind management of the need for improvement in all phases of operations. Ideal standards are not widely used in practice because they may influence employee motivation adversely.

internal control system

The whole system of controls, financial and otherwise, established by the management in order to carry on the business of the enterprise in an orderly and efficient manner, ensure adherence to management policies, safeguard and assets and secure as far as possible the completeness and accuracy of the records.

The individual components of an internal control system are known as controls or internal controls.

internal rate of return (IRR)

A percentage discount rate used in capital investment appraisal which brings the cost of a project and its future cash inflows into equality.

investment centre

A profit centre in which inputs are measured in terms of expenses and outputs are measured in terms of revenues, and in which assets employed are also measured, and excess of revenue over expenditure then being related to assets employed.

limiting factor or key factor

A factor which at any time or over a period may limit the activity of an entity, often one where there is shortage or difficulty of supply.

The limiting factor may change from time to time for the same entity or product. Thus, when raw materials are in short supply, performance or profit may be expressed as per kilo of material, or, in a restricted skilled labour market, as per skilled labour hour. Alternatively, the limiting factor may be one critical process in a chain.

linear programming

The process of using a series of linear equations to construct a mathematical model, the objective of which is to obtain an optimal solution to a complex operational problem, given a number of alternative values of stated variables and quantitative constraints as to their use.

long term strategic planning

The formulation, evaluation and selection of strategies involving a review of the objectives of an organisation, the environment in which it is to operate, and an assessment of its strengths, weaknesses, opportunities and threats for the purpose of preparing a long term strategic plan of action which will attain the objective set.

management accounting

The provision of information required by management for such purposes as:
1. formulation of policies,
2. planning and controlling the activities of the enterprise,
3. decision taking on alternative course of action,
4. disclosure to those external to the entity (shareholders and others),
5. disclosure to employees,
6. safeguarding assets.

The above involves participation in management to ensure that there is effective:
(a) formulation of plans to meet objectives (long term planning),
(b) formulation of short term operation plans (budgeting/profit planning).

management audit

An objective and independent appraisal of the effectiveness of managers and the effectiveness of the corporate structure in the achievement of company objectives and policies.

Its aim is to identify existing and potential management weaknesses within an organisation and to recommend ways to rectify these weaknesses.

marginal cost

The variable cost of one unit of a product or a service, i.e. a cost which would be avoided if the unit was not produced or provided.

Note: In this context a unit is usually either a single article or a standard measure such as the litre or kilogram, but may in certain circumstances be an operation, process or part of an organisation.

marginal costing

A principle whereby variable costs are charged to cost units and the fixed cost attributable to the relevant period is written off in full against the contribution for that period.

market risk premium

The extra return required from a share to compensate for its risk compared with the average risk of the market.

market share

One entity's sales of a product or service in a specified market expressed as a percentage of total sales by all entities offering that product or service.

marketing cost variance

The difference between the budgeted costs of marketing (including selling and distribution costs) and the actual marketing costs incurred in a specified period.

Formula: Budgeted marketing costs – Actual marketing costs

Example: £25,000 – £25,900 = £900 A

master budget

A budget which is prepared from, and summarises, the functional budgets. The term *summary budget* is synonymous.

net present value (NPV)

The value obtained by discounting all cash outflows and inflows attributable to a capital investment project by a chosen percentage, e.g. the entity's weighted average cost of capital.

network analysis

A quantitative technique for the control of projects.

The events and activities making up the whole project are represented in the form of a graph.

non-controllable cost (indirectly controlled cost)

A cost chargeable to a budget or cost centre which can only be influenced indirectly by the actions of the person in whom control of the centre is vested (*see* note following definition of controllable cost).

Typically, these costs will be mainly an apportionment of overhead costs of the entity.

notional cost

A hypothetical cost taken into account in a particular situation to represent a benefit enjoyed by an entity in respect of which no actual expense is incurred.

opportunity cost

The value of a benefit sacrificed in favour of an alternative course of action.

overhead efficiency variance

The difference between the standard overhead cost of the production achieved and the standard overhead cost of the actual hours taken.

Formula: (Standard hours for production achieved – Actual hours taken) × Standard overhead rate

Example: (11 000 – 12 500) × £1.5 = £2 250 A

overhead expenditure variance

The difference between budgeted and actual overhead expenditure.

Budgeted overhead may be determined in different ways – it may be classed as totally fixed, or partly fixed and partly variable.

In the formula which follows, budgeted overhead has been determined as fixed overhead plus variable overhead for actual hours worked.

Formula: [Fixed overhead + (Actual hours × Standard variable overhead rate)] − Actual production overhead incurred

Example: £10 000 + (12 500 × £0.5) − £16 700 = £450 A

overhead total variance

The difference between the standard overhead cost specified for the production achieved, and the actual overhead cost incurred.

Formula: (Standard variable overhead + Standard fixed overhead) − (Actual variable overhead + Actual fixed overhead)

Example: (£6 500 + £10 000) − (£6 100 + £10 600) = £200 A

Where overhead costs tend to vary with the amount of an input, e.g. actual labour hours, the overhead total variance may be subdivided into expenditure, efficiency and volume variances.

overhead volume variance

The difference between the standard overhead cost of the actual hours taken and the flexed budget allowance for the actual hours taken.

Formula: (Actual hours × Standard overhead rate) − (Fixed overhead cost + [Actual hours × variable overhead rate])

Example: (12 500 × £1.5) − (£10 000 + [12 500 × £0.5]) = £2 500 F

payback

The period, usually expressed in years, which it takes the cash inflows from a capital investment project to equal the cash outflows.

When deciding between two or more competing projects the usual decision is to accept the one with the shortest payback. Payback is commonly used as a first screening method. It is a rough measure of liquidity and not of profitability.

planning

The establishment of objectives, and the formulation, evaluation and selection of the policies, strategies, tactics and action required to achieve these objectives.

Planning comprises long term/strategic planning, and short term operational planning. The latter usually refers to a period of one year.

planning horizon

The furthest time ahead for which plans can be usefully quantified with no more than a minimum acceptable degree of error.

It need not necessarily be the planning period.

planning period

The appropriate period of time which meets planning requirements and enables the decision making and/or control processes to be most effectively exercised.

For example, forestry may require a period of many years whereas fashion garments may require only a few months.

present value

The cash equivalent now of a sum of money receivable or payable at a stated future date at a specified rate.

product cost

The cost of a finished product built up from its cost elements.

product life cycle

The pattern of demand for a product or service over time.

production cost variance

The difference between the standard production cost of actual production volume and the actual production cost over the specified period.

Formula: (Actual number of units producted × Standard production cost per unit = Standard production cost) – (Actual total cost of materials, wages and production overhead)

Example: (£71 500) – (£73 200) = £1 700 A

profit centre

A segment of the business entity by which both revenues are received and expenditures are caused or controlled, such revenues and expenditure being used to evaluate segmental performance.

This may also be called a *business centre, business unit,* or *strategic business unit,* depending upon the concept of management responsibility prevailing in the entity concerned.

profit variance

The difference between the standard profit on the actual sales volume and the actual profit for a specific period.

Formula: (Standard profit) – (Actual profit)

Example: £31 500 – £38 800 = £7 300 F

quality cost variance

The difference (arising from failure to conform to quality specification) between the amount included in standard costs and the actual cost or loss incurred in scrapping, rectifying, or selling at sub-standard prices.

Formula: (Number of units produced × Standard allowance per unit) – (Number of units rejected or returned × Cost per unit + Rectification cost – Disposal value)

If considered significant the variance can be further analysed into variance such as returns, customer allowances and production rejects.

relevant costs

Costs appropriate to aiding the making of specific management decisions.

replacement price

The price at which material identical to that which is to be replaced could be purchased at the date of valuation (as distinct from actual cost price at actual date of purchase).

responsibility accounting

A system of accounting that segregates revenues and costs into areas of personal responsibility in order to assess the performance attained by persons to whom authority has been assigned. *See also* budgetary control.

responsibility centre

A unit or function of an organisation headed by a manager having direct responsibility for its performance.

revenue centre

A centre devoted to raising revenue with no responsibility for production, e.g. a sales centre, often used in a not-for-profit organisation.

revision variance

The difference between an original and a revised standard cost.

It arises when an interim adjustment of a standard cost is made without adjusting the budget, and is required to allow full analysis of the difference between budgeted and actual profit. The variance can be further analysed to reflect revisions to prices of materials, labour and overhead rates, and changes of method.

rolling budget

The continuous updating of a short term budget by adding, say, a further month or quarter and deducting the earliest month or quarter so that the budget can reflect current conditions.

Such procedures are beneficial where future costs and/or activities cannot be forecast with any degree of accuracy.

sales mix profit variance

The difference between total profit, calculated at individual product standard profit and at average standard profit, based on total actual units sold.

Formula: (Actual units sold at standard profit) – (Total units sold at average standard profit)

Example: For three products A, B and C, based on budgeted sales units, standard profits and actual sales units are as follows:

		Standard			Actual
Product	Units	Profit per unit £	Total profit £	Average profit per unit £	Sales units
A	3 000	2.0	6 000		3 000
B	4 000	2.5	10 000		3 000
C	3 000	3.0	9 000		6 000
	10 000		25 000	2.5	12 000

$(3\ 000 \times £2) + (£3\ 000 \times £2.5) + (6\ 000 \times £3) - (12\ 000 \times £2.5) = £1\ 500\ F$

(Actual units at standard profit) – (Total units at average standard profit).

Where sales are analysed by individual products or lines, a profit due to sales mix may be calculated: this may be more important than the selling price variance or the sales volume profit variance.

sales volume profit variance

The difference between the actual units sold and the standard quantity, priced at the standard profit per unit.

Formula: (Actual units – Standard units) × Standard profit

selling price variance

The difference between the actual selling price per unit and the standard selling price per unit multiplied by the actual quantity sold.

Formula: Actual units × (Actual selling price per unit – Standard selling price per unit)

Example: 11 000 units × (£15 – £14) = £11 000 F

sensitivity analysis

A modelling procedure used in forecasting whereby changes are made in the estimates of the variables to establish whether any will critically affect the outcome of the forecast.

standard

A predetermined measurable quantity set in defined conditions against which actual performance can be compared, usually for an element of work, operation or activity.

While standards may be based on unquestioned and immutable natural law or facts, they are finally set by human judgement and consequently are subject to the same fallibility which attends all human activity. Thus a standard for 100 per cent machine output can be fixed by its geared input/output speeds, but the effective realisable output standard is one of judgement.

standard cost

A predetermined calculation of how much costs should be under specified working conditions.

It is built up from an assessment of the value of cost elements and correlates technical specifications and the qualification of materials, labour and other costs to the prices and/or wage rates expected to apply during the period in which the standard cost is intended to be used. Its main purposes are to provide bases for control through variance accounting, for the valuation of stock and work in progress and, in some cases, for fixing selling prices.

standard costing

A technique which uses standards for costs and revenues for the purpose of control through variance analysis.

standard direct labour cost

The planned average cost of direct labour for a specified amount of direct labour effort to be used at standard performance over a specified period. *See* standard performance.

Usually expressed as a cost per unit of time, i.e. standard hour or standard minute.

standard direct material cost

The predetermined cost price for a specified quantity of material to be used at a standard material usage rate over a specified period.

standard hour/minute

The quantity of work achievable at standard performance, expressed in terms of a standard unit of work in a standard period of time.

standard material usage

The quantity of material or rate of use required as an average, under specified conditions, to produce a specified quantity of output.

standard operating profit – unit

The predetermined profit from the sale of a specified unit of a product or service at the standard selling price.

standard overhead cost

The predetermined cost of overhead of a cost/revenue/profit centre over a specified period, using an agreed overhead absorption method: in marginal costing, this will be in respect of variable overhead only.

standard performance – labour

The rate of output which qualified workers can achieve as an average over the working day or shift, without over-exertion, provided they adhere to the specified method and are motivated to apply themselves to their work.

This is represented by 100 per cent on the BS scale (BS 3138).

standard performance – machine

The rate of output achievable by a machine as an average, under specified conditions over a given period of time.

It may include the standard performance of the operator.

standard price

A predetermined price fixed on the basis of a specification of a product or service and of all factors affecting that price.

standard production cost – total

The predetermined cost of producing or providing specified quantities of products or service at standard performance over a specified period.

standard production cost – unit

The predetermined cost of producing or providing a specified quantity of a product or service at standard performance.

standard profit – total

The predetermined profit arising from the sale of actual quantities of products or services at standard selling prices, over a specified period.

Formula: Actual number of units sold × (Standard selling price per unit – Standard cost per unit) = Standard profit

Example: 11 000 × (14 – £11.1364)* = £31 500

Standard profit may be at the level of net profit, gross profit, or contribution. Profit which relates only to trading activities is often referred to as operating profit.

* In practice this would probably be rounded to £11.14.

standard selling price – unit

A predetermined price for a product or service for a specified unit to be sold.

A unit may consist of a single item or a batch of processed output.

standard time

The total time (hours and minutes) in which a task should be completed at standard performance, i.e. basic time plus contingency allowance plus relaxation allowance.

standard unit of work

A unit of work consisting of basic time plus relaxation allowance and contingency allowance where applicable.

The unit of work may be for labour output only, a combination of machine and labour output, or for a machine only.

strategic management accounting

The provision and analysis of management accounting data relating to a business strategy: particularly the relative levels and trends in real costs and prices, volumes, market share, cash flow and the demands on a firm's total resources.

strategy

A course of action, including the specification of the resources required, to achieve a specific objective.

transfer price

A price related to goods or other services transferred from one process or department to another or from one member of a group to another.

The extent to which costs and profit are covered by the price is a matter of policy. A transfer price may, for example, be based upon:

> Marginal cost
> Full cost
> Market price
> Negotiated price

For further information see CIMA Management Accounting Guideline No. 1.

variance

The difference between planned, budgeted, or standard cost and actual costs (and similarly in respect of revenues).

Note: This is not to be confused with the statistical variance which measures the dispersion of a statistical population.

variance accounting

A technique whereby the planned activities of an undertaking are quantified in budgets, standard costs, standard selling prices and standard profit margins, and the differences between these and the actual results are compared.

The procedure is to collect, compare, comment and correct.

variance analysis

The analysis of variances arising in a standard costing system into their constituent parts.

It is the analysis and comparison of the factors which have caused the differences between predetermined standards and actual results, with a view to eliminating inefficiencies.

weighted average cost of capital

A percentage discount rate used in capital investment appraisal to calculate the net present value of the costs and future revenues of the project.

It is the average cost of the combined sources of finance (equity, debentures, bank loans) weighted according to the proportion each elements bears to the total pool of capital available. Weighting is usually based on the current market valuations and current yields or costs. Example:

Capital	Market value		Rate		Cost
Equity	£800 000	×	10%	=	£80 000
Debt	£400 000	×	15%	=	£60 000
Total	£1 200 000				£140 000

Weighted average 11.67%

zero base budgeting

A method of budgeting whereby all activities are re-evaluated each time a budget is formulated.

Each functional budget starts with the assumption that the function does not exist and is at zero cost. Increments of cost are compared with increments of benefit, culminating in the planned maximum benefit for a given budgeted cost.

Index